Interfaces for Information Retrieval and Online Systems

Interfaces for Information Retrieval and Online Systems THE STATE OF THE ART

Edited by
Martin Dillon

Prepared Under the Auspices of the American Society for
Information Science

GREENWOOD PRESS
New York • Westport, Connecticut • London

Library of Congress Cataloging-in-Publication Data

Interfaces for information retrieval and online systems : the state of
the art / edited by Martin Dillon.
      p.   cm.
    ''Prepared under the auspices of the American Society for
Information Science.''
   Includes bibliographical references and index.
   ISBN 0–313–27494–0 (alk. paper)
   1. Information retrieval.   2. User interfaces (Computer systems).
3. On-line data processing—Library applications.   4. Library
catalogs and readers.   5. Catalogs, On-line.   I. Dillon, Martin,
1938– . II. American Society for Information Science.
Z699.35.U74I57   1991
025.3'132—dc20   91–8240

British Library Cataloguing in Publication Data is available.

Library of Congress Catalog Card Number: 91–8240
ISBN: 0–313–27494–0

First published in 1991

Greenwood Press, 88 Post Road West, Westport, CT 06881
An imprint of Greenwood Publishing Group, Inc.

Printed in the United States of America

The paper used in this book complies with the
Permanent Paper Standard issued by the National
Information Standards Organization (Z39.48–1984).

10 9 8 7 6 5 4 3 2 1

Contents

Illustrations

FIGURES

TABLES

Acknowledgments

Many individuals contribute to a successful conference. First and foremost, the conferees are responsible for its quality; the conference stands or falls through their energies and excellence.

Much is required to transform the raw materials of a conference into a memorable and valuable experience. Among the many who are owed our thanks are: Irene Gilbride, who handled on-site arrangements flawlessly; Dick Hill and Linda Resnick from ASIS, who advised capably and willingly on all matters large and small; Linda Smith, who supplied structure and detail from her own experience as chair last year; Deborah Shaw, who helped organize the SIG program; and SIG/HCI, which offered support and expertise at every stage of the evolution of this conference. Finally, special thanks to Becky Hawk, who managed the flow of paper, and to Mary Taylor, who assumed many of the responsibilities of technical program director.

The 1989 midyear meeting was fortunate in the number and enthusiasm of its attendees. The plenary speakers contributed by their distinction and by the substance of their presentations. The subject matter of the papers was rich and varied, as this volume attests.

Introduction

Martin Dillon

This volume arises from the 1989 Mid-year Conference of the American Society for Information Science (ASIS), the theme of which provides the topic of this book: the user interface. Moreover, the conference and the chapters collected here focus on interfaces to information retrieval systems. Such systems are relatively new and quite complex; it should not be surprising that their designers have not yet succeeded in solving all problems associated with their use.

Dr. Donald Norman, a plenary speaker at the Conference, argued that poor design bedeviled the interface between man and machine long before the computer revolution. Dr. Norman, professor and chair of the Department of Cognitive Science at the University of California, San Diego, and also director of the Institute of Cognitive Science, has devoted a lifetime of research to making systems and devices understandable and usable by a wide range of people. His comments reflected his authorship of *The Psychology of Everyday Things* (1988), a book highly recommended for its practical discussions of design issues. As an example of poor design, Dr. Norman described the electronic drinking fountain, which is activated by a sensor that recognizes when an individual bends over it for a drink. With no visible mechanism for turning on the water, there is no obvious action to take; people stand before it unable to figure out how it operates, frustrated in addition to being thirsty. "The lack of cues is one of the major culprits of modern automation. A sure sign of difficulty is posted signs; signs hung here and there, urging the user on to ever greater efforts."

Dr. Norman addressed the primary question posed by the Conference and the papers reproduced in this volume, "How can we give users the benefit of usability while also giving them the power and versatility of the new, modern systems?" He stated that the answers lie in "task analysis, studies, interaction—from the very beginning of the design process." Not surprisingly, the key is in understanding those for whom the system is being designed: "If you expect to design systems for people, you have to understand those people.'' Alas, he warned, the promise of the information revolution is in danger of being wasted through failure of design.

To understand the difficulties faced by designers of software systems, it is helpful to divide them into two types, those that engage the look and feel of an interface and those that involve the functionality provided by a system to accomplish the task at hand. The first type involves issues such as whether prompts are easily understood or whether menus are logically defined and easy to navigate; with the second, functional deficiencies are less clear, but have to do with such questions as whether a system has a certain capability or will perform a certain task with only a small effort by the user.

The following dialogue exemplifies an interface problem of the first type:

C:format
PRESS ANY KEY TO BEGIN FORMATTING DRIVE C:
ARE YOU SURE?[Y/N]

It derives from early MS-DOS systems, which required that disks, hard or floppy, be formatted before use. From the user's point of view, the required functionality could not be simpler: two procedures, one to format hard disks, the other to format floppy disks. The system dialogue in the example represents a truly first-class case of poor design. The FORMAT command was supplied by the system to carry out both of these procedures. In the first line of the example, a user has invoked this command without stating which of the possible drives contains the disk to be formatted. In the second line, the system has responded with the suggestion that C be the disk to be formatted. It turns out that for a system with both a hard disk and one or more floppy disks, C designates the system's hard disk. As with today's systems, the hard disk usually contains all working files and a copy of all software in use. Typically, it also contains the active version of MS-DOS itself; to suggest that it be formatted is therefore a form of software suicide. Perhaps as a sign of concern, in the next line—Are you sure?—the system seeks assurance from the user that no error has been made. Pressing Y at this point formats the hard disk, erasing all the existing files on C, often a catastrophic, unrecoverable error. When working with my first hard-disk system, I erased the C disk twice in the first week's use.

It is surprising how many design principles have been violated in this example. First, two commands should be provided: (1) format a floppy disk, and (2) format the hard disk. The perversity that led to treating these as variants of one another would make an interesting object of study. The conflation of these two commands yields a small efficiency for system developers and a large inefficiency for users, a common enough trade-off. Second, a dangerous obscurity lurks in the ostensibly straightforward request to ''Press any key'' to begin formatting. What key do you press to prevent formatting: Pressing *Control-C* will get you out of this for most MS-DOS utilities, but that is not indicated in the prompt. Third, a basic principle of design is to place obstacles between a user and a catastrophic mistake. The prompt, "Are you sure?" does not qualify. It is almost a reflex to press the Y key in such circumstances. Finally, and most important, the system does not display the consequences of the user's actions. A simple provision would avoid virtually all catastrophes of the sort occurring here: always show the user which files will be destroyed. If there are too many to be listed conveniently, an abbreviated list could be given, with a comment stating how many more there are.

GRAPHICAL USER INTERFACES

The kinds of mistakes evident in the example above are typical of systems developed for character-based screens. They have very little to do with the basic functionality provided by a system and very much to do with the care with which this functionality is presented. Interfaces designed for high-resolution, bit-mapped screens have been far superior. Although high-resolution screens are a recent phenomenon in the mass market—the Macintosh was the first personal computer with a high-resolution screen to achieve success there—research in their use, especially for interface design, dates to the sixties. Curtis (1989) provides a good general introduction and overview.

Graphical User Interfaces (GUI), the genre of interfaces that has arisen from this research, provide many advantages over Character-based User Interfaces (CUIs). Another acronym captures their essence: Window, Icons, Menu (or Mouse), Printer—or WIMP. Visibility is the keynote. High-resolution screens can display much more information than character-based screens. Thus, through an appropriate use of windows, text, and icons, both the actions and the objects available to a user at a given point can be presented.

Figure I.1, a screen image taken from the Sun File Manager, is a good example. The command bar at the top lists available actions: File, View, Edit, and so on. The two windows below the command bar show the directory structure belonging to the user. File card icons represent directories, and the directory structure is indicated by the hierarchical arrangement of the icons. The bottom window shows the files present in the "mail" directory. The icon is highlighted on the screen because it has been "selected"—the mouse cursor has been moved to the icon, and the button on the mouse has been pressed. Selecting the icon displays the directory's tree.

Screen visibility through graphics and icons and the ability to perform actions with the mouse—to point, to drag icons around the screen—enable a second major feature of GUIs: direct manipulation or interaction (Hutchins, Hollan, and Norman, 1986). To relocate a file or directory, one moves the mouse cursor to the icon, depresses the mouse button (holds down rather than clicks, the difference between holding the shift key down in a typewriter and pressing a character key), and drags the icon to its new position by moving the mouse on its pad. To delete a file or directory, one performs the same series of actions, but moves

Figure I.1
Sun File Manager

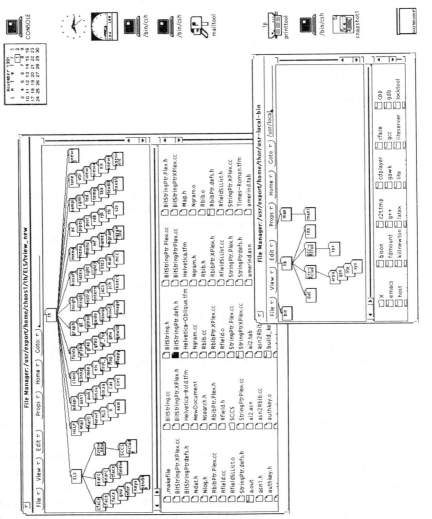

Source: Sun Microsystems.

the icon to the wastebasket in the lower right-hand corner. One actually can see what one has wrought. Contrast this with the FORMAT command in MS-DOS. An added bonus: most GUIs allow a great deal of "undoing"—the ability to undo a command with which one is unhappy.

The general consensus of users is that GUIs are far superior to their predecessors. The well-established Macintosh family of interfaces and now the success of Microsoft Windows 3.0 certify their worth as a valuable contribution to our mastery of the computer. Advances in technology, particularly the high-resolution screen, have created the opportunity for an evolutionary step in interface design. It is of interest to discuss briefly technology that is exotic today, but which one day may become commonplace in interface design. Two aspects of that technology stand out: multimodal interfaces and natural language interfaces.

MULTIMODAL INTERFACES

In his plenary talk given at the 1989 ASIS Mid-Year Conference, Nicholas Negroponte, director of the Massachusetts Institute of Technology Media Lab, argued that the next major step in interface design will occur when multimodal input is commonplace in personal computers. He posed many arguments, but one of the stronger ones dwelt on the physical limitations of the keyboard as computers become more compact and portable. As he put it, finger size is not a design variable, and our fingers are not likely to be reduced in size to be able to take advantage of the smaller computers. As long as the keyboard is the primary input device, miniaturization will be sorely restricted. With voice input, for example, computers can become much smaller.

Dr. Negroponte went further, however, in describing the coming interface revolution. Human communication is multimodal, with gesture, tone of voice, posture, and other body-language signals each playing a part. Indeed, when given a choice between hearing the actual words of a remark or the tone in which it is given, many people choose to hear the tone. Similarly, different modalities might ease the problems in communicating with computers. In the July 1990 issue of *Byte* magazine, a series of reviews presents the state of the art in multimodal input/output for microcomputers and touches on the various options: voice input/audio output; stylus, pen, or touch-screen input, and eye movement for indicating data elements on the screen or menu selection; the data glove for gesturing or "touching" data in three dimensions; and the ultimate, the virtual world, which allows one to simulate the experience of a three-dimensional world through a head-mounted stereoscopic display system.

Each of these has special application areas where they are especially valuable. Sound, for example, can be used effectively to reduce interaction errors with GUIs. This has been demonstrated with the SonicFinder developed at Apple's Computer Interface Group, which produces a dragging sound when an icon is moved. It also emits a "bump" sound when a dragged object collides with a container, such as the Trashcan or a file folder. This aural feedback is very helpful in signaling when a significant event has occurred during an interaction, and it reduces inadvertent actions such as dropping a file into the Trashcan by mistake.

The possibility of voice input is a more serious matter, as Negroponte pointed out in his talk. Most of us easily speak at a rate of 200 words a minute; few of us type better than 60. Many applications require or would be enhanced by effective voice input, whenever the hands are busy—when handling packages or controls, when sight is not possible, over telecommunication devices, and many, many more instances (Lee, Hauptmann, and Rudnicky, 1990). Most voice input applications require accurate translation into machine-readable alphabetic characters (two that don't are annotating a document and sending voice mail), a crucial step that prevents any use other than the most restricted ones. Speech recognition using computers is still not very effective, as indicated by the 10% error rate for an experimental system developed by researchers at IBM (quoted in Lee, Hauptmann, and Rudnicky, 1990). For commercial systems, when accuracy is a must, voice input is restricted to vocabularies of a very few words, with *yes* and *no* and the digits zero through nine a likely set of acceptable input symbols.

Speech recognition, nonrestricted recognition of the sort humans experience, which is continuous (without pauses between words) and freely employs unrestricted vocabulary and grammar, is a complex process and one not yet solved for computers. Similarly, the process of accurately converting handwritten notes into machine-readable alphabetic characters is only partially solved (Martin et al., 1990). As a consequence, the electronic notepad using an electronic pen is not yet available except for the most constrained of applications—uppercase, printed characters placed in boxes.

NATURAL LANGUAGE INTERFACES

It has been argued that natural language understanding by computers must precede effective speech recognition. The reasons, dealt with recently by White (1990), involve the ambiguity of the acoustics of speech, which humans resolve through a knowledge of the language and the world in which it is used. Natural language understanding by computers, a research area in its own right for more than 30 years, is progressing slowly and does not yet anticipate the substantial breakthroughs that would be required to make it useful for such applications as speech recognition. Although Napier presents evidence that even very restricted natural language interfaces would help reduce errors in computer use (Napier et al., 1989), no one can say when such interfaces will generally be available; nor can we say when interfaces will make use of unrestricted natural language. Some insight into the difficulties that must be overcome is provided by Barnett (1990) and Lenat (1990); natural language understanding seems to require a broad knowledge of the world. Lenat's CYC System, 5 years into a 10-year project to build a system with "common" sense, is expected to contain somewhere near 100 million axioms.

It is pertinent at this point to mention the comments of Charles Hildreth, who completed the plenary program of the ASIS Conference with his presentation, "Interface Intentionality: Real Dialogue or Just Another Pretty Face?" Hildreth, formerly a senior research scientist at OCLC and now chief consulting scientist with READ (Research, Education, Analysis, and Design), a firm that provides consulting and planning services for library operations and information systems, is an authority on online catalogs, the application of new information technologies to library functions, and standards for information retrieval systems.

Hildreth began his talk by criticizing the WIMP interface as a simple-minded and incomplete representation of reality, although WIMP interfaces are the state of the art in graphical user interfaces. While acknowledging that graphics can be fun and helpful, Hildreth argued that a special kind of creative imagination is necessary to produce something useful. He was particularly opposed to the "desktop" metaphor as the organizing idea for information seeking behavior, which he found inappropriate for his own environment and habits.

To focus on what he considered a more promising direction, Hildreth discussed the meaning of human-computer interactions, with an emphasis on interaction and "interactive systems." He preferred to pursue the ideal of a language-based, dialogue-centered user interface, the aim of many designers prior to the popularity of graphics interfaces. An attractive ideal is a system possessing an artificial personality that "will behave the way we want it to." Hildreth contrasted the aims of a system that simulates human conversation to one that emulates. The latter is probably beyond our reach for some time, while the former is realizable. In the information retrieval process, systems should "advise us, persuade us, warn us, clarify their interpretations of our language, or explain their decisions or intentions."

These recommendations go beyond the "feel" of interaction and touch on the functionality provided through an interface. In our area of interest, retrieval systems, there is a great need to reexamine both the context in which retrievals take place and the tools provided to their users. In the chapters that follow, two different systems are dealt with, systems like DIALOG, where users retrieve references to journal articles, and systems that enable library patrons to retrieve references to library collections. These two system types have much in common. They share the bibliographic record as the primary item to be retrieved, and they use similar means, usually keyword searching with Boolean queries, to retrieve them. Moreover, the two systems converge in what is being referred to as a distributed library made available through national networks. The emergence of this network—now referred to as the internet, and one day presumably NREN, the National Research and Educational Network—will transform the information system landscape. As this transformation takes place, users will increasingly be expected to use both system types more or less interchangeably. The following considers issues of interface functionality by discussing them within the framework of this network viewed as a distributed library.

A distributed library is the sum of all the information sources made available to a user over a network. Information distributed on the Internet includes bulletin board collections, electronic journals, news services, OPACs, other collections or bibliographic records—those of individual scholars or special collections—and eventually full-text files of every variety and size (Lynch, 1989). What is of concern in this context is the functionality required to enable the individual library patron to get access to information in such a broad and diverse collection. Among the problems that are raised, the most immediate is coping with the variety of database designs, retrieval system types, and interfaces that could potentially be scattered across the network. How is a potential user supposed to cope with all of this variety? Certainly a requirement that we master each of the systems available across the network is hopeless.

A helpful step in the right direction is to detach the interface problem from the retrieval problem, enabling users or institutions to design interfaces suitable for their own environment. Developing systems that conform to the Z39.50 standard (discussed in McGill, 1989) for information retrieval systems would make a crucial contribution. This standard defines a protocol for system-to-system communication for carrying out most of the retrieval functionality available in today's systems. With file servers on the network responding to this protocol, clients on the network could then develop interfaces suitable for their own applications. Indeed, interface toolkits become a possibility, providing the wherewithal to build easily and quickly a wide range of interfaces to suit preferences of individuals. Or, systems like HyperCard may be used, given the necessary Z39.50 capability. Distributing the design function for interfaces encourages a more rapid evolution of interfaces.

Will a Z39.50-based network architecture solve all of our problems? Of course not. What it will do is allow us to focus on the true substance of the problem. The deficiency most evident in today's retrieval systems is not a more friendly front end, but sufficiently powerful functionality. The next generation of interfaces must have far more capability than we are yet providing. When we eliminate the surface difficulties that inhibit users of our current systems, functional deficiencies will stand out more clearly.

In order to clarify what functionality is most required, I would like to take the notion of the distributed library as a serious metaphor of the information environment on the Internet and compare its problems with those dealt with in traditional librarianship. Two of the more important ingredients of the library are the catalog and reference services. How would these appear in our NREN?

The Catalog

Library catalogs traditionally provide an inventory of what the library contains. Each item owned by the library is described sufficiently to differentiate it from all other items both descriptively (details about its physical being and manner of production: what, who, where, and when) and by content (what the item is about or how it is to be used). A second piece of information is how to gain access to the item. In the distributed library, one of the basic needs will be a catalog. Of course, there are differences between a network catalog and a traditional library catalog. Most of these differences arise from differences in the kinds of things available on a network—collections of items, services—from those things available in a library, usually books and serials. A second difference is the need for detailed information on how to use something on the network, instructions usually not needed for books taken from the library.

The Reference Service

A second important facility available in a library is the reference service. While the reference service provides many functions, the crucial one here is as a guide to the library's materials. The reference librarian takes the rough expression of an information need provided by a patron and either guides the patron to the right service in the library or helps the patron identify (and sometimes use) the items most likely to serve the patron's need. A reference service on a national network will have a similar function with the following roles:

1. *Serve as system interface*: We take it for granted that a library will have people nearby to answer questions such as how to use the catalog. The systems and services connected to the network will vary greatly and require substantial resources merely to link users to them effectively.

2. *Act as guide to the right databases*: Given a patron's specific information need, that same variety among systems, in form as well as content and functions, will require expert help in guiding a patron to the database most appropriate for the need. A high-school student looking for a book or two on Martin Luther King, Jr., for example, would likely not be best served by the OCLC Online Union Catalog of 22 million records, where books on King number in the hundreds. A scholar, on the other hand, would be best served by such a database.

3. *Aid in query formation*: We are back to Boolean queries. Most systems available on the network, whether full-text or bibliographic, are likely to require some form of Boolean query. The form differs; the results are largely the same. Help is badly needed in this quarter.

4. *Aid in information delivery*: A new and large-scale need is hidden here. No one wants to look at the results of searches carried out over many databases, one database at a time. Some form of merging will be required, a task that is far more difficult than it would at first appear. Identifying duplicates is one aspect of the problem; producing well-ordered and sensibly formatted output from databases with divergent structures is another.

The national network will be a resource of enormous usefulness, likely to transform the scholarly landscape. The list above barely scratches the surface of the difficulties designers and users can expect to encounter. Many of them are, strictly speaking, problems of interface design. Others require the creation of new functionality.

CONCLUSIONS

In this volume, we explore some of the changes to be expected in interfaces and the need for development and implementation of standards. Much more is at stake. Tools and systems developed over centuries—the book, libraries, class-rooms—all will be redefined. New tools, new theories of information and library science, new systems for organizing, retrieving, navigating, and displaying information will take their place. The chapters presented here are an appropriate starting point for the long road ahead.

Selected papers in six topic areas, first presented at the conference, appear here as expanded chapters with introductions by invited guest editors. The six parts of this book, which reflect major areas of research and endeavor associated with user interfaces, and the guest editors are the following:

- Interface Styles, Martha J. Lindeman, research scientist, Office of Research, OCLC Online Computer Library Center
- Artificial Intelligence, Amy J. Warner, assistant professor, School of Information and Library Studies, The University of Michigan
- Hyperdocuments, Gary Marchionini, assistant professor, College of Library and Information Services, The University of Maryland at College Park
- Case Studies in Human-Computer Interaction, Thomas H. Martin, associate professor, School of Information Studies, Syracuse University
- Evaluation, Martin Dillon, director, Office of Research, OCLC Online Computer Library Center
- Trends in Technological Standards, M.E.L. Jacob, chair, National Information Standards Organization Z39 Board and chair of the ASIS Standards Committee from 1984 to 1987

The chapters presented in part I, Interface Styles, discuss the fundamentals of human-computer interaction and the various models behind system designs. Through direct examination and comparison with other interface methods, the strengths of the much ballyhooed graphical user interface are made plain, and methods for overcoming their weaknesses are offered.

Part II focuses on the role of artificial intelligence in interface design and function. The user interface can be viewed as the meeting ground between the users and the system, both of which bring certain information and capabilities to the interaction. Research in the area quite logically investigates how both user and system can better apply knowledge to meet the user's information need more effectively.

A recent entrant in the field of computerized document systems, hypertext is the subject of part III. Chapters focus on the use of hypertext in information retrieval systems and the new-found demands this technology places on the user interface and information display.

In part IV, Case Studies in Human-Computer Interaction, the authors present information gained either through the design or evaluation of an information system. The value of case study methodology is reconfirmed by the chapters in this part, each of which reports the importance of capturing data from both the system and the user.

Closely related, but with a narrower focus, is part V, which discusses the evaluation of systems and interfaces. While the scientific evaluation of user interfaces is relatively new, the need for improved methods of assessing system effectiveness is as old as information retrieval itself. The chapters in this part reveal methods and findings obtained from users of operating systems and through prototyping and simulation.

The final part presents a balanced look at standards and current trends among various standards organizations. Standards can affect system design profoundly and often to the good. But standards have limits and even drawbacks, and should not, indeed cannot, be expected to provide an answer to every design problem.

Taken as a whole, this volume couples breadth and depth in an attempt to distill and to synthesize the forces and trends that bear on user interface design. This scope ensures its usefulness as a guide for current interface designers and as a well-rounded introduction for those entering this quickly evolving field of human inquiry.

Special thanks are due the authors for expanding their papers for this volume and to the guest editors for bringing their subject expertise to bear.

REFERENCES

Bailey, Robert W. 1990. "Designing Quality User Interfaces." In *Annual Review of OCLC Research: July 1989-June 1990*, 67–69. Dublin, Ohio: OCLC.

Barnett, Jim, Kevin Knight, Inderjeet Mani, and Elaine Rich. 1990. "Knowledge and Natural Language Processing." *Communications of the ACM* 33(8): 50–71.

Curtis, Bill. 1989. "Engineering Computer 'Look and Feel': User Interface Technology and Human Factors Engineering." *Jurimetrics Journal* 30: 51–78.

Hutchins, Edwin L., James D. Hollan, and Donald A. Norman. 1986. "Direct Manipulation Interfaces." In *User Centered Systems Design: New Perspectives on Human-Computer Interaction*, Donald A. Norman and Stephen W. Draper, eds., 87–124. Hillsdale, N.J.: Lawrence Erlbaum Associates.

Lee, Kai-Fu, Alexander G. Hauptmann, and Alexander I. Rudnicky. 1990. "The Spoken Word." *Byte* 15(7): 225–32.

Lenat, Douglas B., Ramanathan V. Guha, Karen Pittman, Dexter Pratt, and Mary Shepherd. 1990. "CYC: Toward Programs with Common Sense." *Communications of the ACM* 33(8): 30–49.

Lynch, Clifford A. 1989. "Library Automation and the National Research Network." *Educom Review* 24(3): 21–26.

McGill, Michael J. 1989. "Z39.50 Benefits for Designers and Users." *Educom Review*
    24(3): 27–30.
Martin, Gale, James Pittman, Kent Wittenburg, Richard Cohen, and Tom Parish. 1990.
    "Sign Here, Please." *Byte* 15(7): 243–51.
Napier, H. Albert, David M. Lane, Richard R. Batsell, and Norman S. Guadang. 1989.
    "Impact of a Restricted Natural Language Interface on Ease of Learning and
    Productivity." *Communications of the ACM* 32(10): 1190–98.
Norman, D. A. 1988. *The Psychology of Everyday Things.* New York: Basic Books.
White, George M. 1990. "Natural Language Understanding and Speech Recognition."
    Communications of the ACM 33(8): 72–82.

Interfaces for Information Retrieval and Online Systems

PART I

INTERFACE STYLES

Martha J. Lindeman

The chapters in this part on interface styles focus on the direct manipulation style of human-computer interaction. In essence, a direct manipulation style exists when the user can perform task-related operations on a visible model of reality. For example, the user may resize an object by placing a cursor (controlled by movement of a mouse) on a corner of the object and then moving the cursor to the new position for that corner. In contrast, in other interface styles in which the computer is perceived as an intermediary agent, the user might input the numeric values of the x, y coordinates of the new position. The computer would then change the appearance of the object without any analogical movement by the user.

Although the distinctions among various types of interfaces are often blurred (Lindeman, 1989), two papers succinctly summarize the essence of users' experiences with direct manipulation interfaces. Rutkowski (1982) states that the computer system and its user interface become "transparent." In other words, the computer system disappears as an intermediary agent, and the user is directly involved with the objects and operations involved in the task (Hutchins, Hollan, and Norman, 1986). The representation of reality used to model the task in the interface is critical to users experiencing a direct involvement in the task.

DEFINITIONS OF REALITY AND HYPERTEXT

The problems associated with sequential organization of information, as in the medium of paper documents, have been given as the primary reason for the use of hypertext (linked, stand-alone chunks of text). However, a good direct manipulation interface can combine the advantages of both the computer and printed documents without many of the disadvantages that have been associated with either. While it is true that paper documents have an inherent linear format such as that imposed by page numbers, it is inappropriate to confound format and access. Users of nonfiction paper documents do not usually access the contents of those documents linearly and, in fact, typically read only portions of a document (e.g., Sabine and Sabine, 1986; Prabha and Rice, 1988; Lindeman, Bonneau, and Pocius, 1989). Thus, they typically use nonlinear methods of access such as opening a book to a random page, opening to a page identified for a specific term in the index, or opening to the beginning of a section listed in the table of contents. Thus an inherent linear format does *not* limit nonlinear access. Quite the opposite—the identifiers comprising the structure of a linear format can make it much easier to find the desired information by either browsing or searching.

At issue is the definition of "reality" for any particular computer system. Reality may be multilayered; for example in a text retrieval system, the user's direct manipulation may be (1) on the text itself, (2) on separately stored information that "points to" locations within the text, or (3) on both within the same system. In the first instance, a user does not manipulate a separate representation of the structure of the text. Instead, in some hypertext systems the user might choose which section of text to display next by selecting a highlighted word or phrase (e.g., "Treaty of Paris") in the currently displayed text. The computer would then display the section of text associated with (linked to) the phrase "Treaty of Paris." This cycle of choice and display would then continue throughout the user's reading session. Thus, the user is always manipulating the reality of the text. This is a very bottom-up approach that emphasizes the units of text and de-emphasizes any structure of the text larger than two units. This lack of identified structure is a major contributor to users' sense of not knowing where they are in documents and not knowing how to get to another specific location.

When the user is directly manipulating a separate representation of the structure of the text (rather than the text itself), a user might choose which sections of text to display by selecting entries on intermediary objects that control which sections of text are displayed. Thus, a user might access a section of text by selecting its subheading from the document's table of contents. The user could then select another portion of text from the table of contents, or the index, or by selecting a position on a scrollbar that represents the length of the document. Visible cues showing a user's current location in one or more documents aid users in moving around among various sections of texts. This is a very top-down-oriented approach that emphasizes textual structure similar to those of paper documents.

It is preferable to use a mixed approach that provides both bottom-up and top-down access. For example, adding a map of the links connecting the sections of text converts the bottom-up interface into a "multilayered reality" that is easier to use. Similarly, adding the ability to page forward or backward within a document by a single keypress converts the top-down interface into a multi-layered reality. The user can manipulate the text directly by keypress or indirectly by means of intermediary objects such as tables of contents. This type of simple, multilayered interface was described in Prasse et al. (1988).

As the reality that can be manipulated by the user gets more complex, it becomes even more important that interface designers communicate a cogent model of that reality to the user. This is often done by basing the reality on a metaphor. For example, the Macintosh uses a desktop metaphor for organizing files and utility programs such as a clock and a calendar. The use of a relatively easy-to-understand metaphor is one major advantage of direct manipulation interfaces. A good metaphor typically increases

- transfer of knowledge from other environments
- ease of learning
- ease of use
- retention of knowledge about the system by infrequent users
- user satisfaction with the system

and decreases

- the number of necessary error messages
- user anxiety

A fundamental problem for information retrieval systems has been the lack of a cogent metaphor. Most search systems have command-language interfaces that are not based on any metaphor. Browsing systems such as bottom-up hypertext systems also do not have a cogent metaphor, other than linked chunks of text. Solving the problem of developing a good metaphor to model the task reality would probably increase the acceptance of text retrieval systems more than any other single characteristic (assuming a database that is relevant to the users' tasks).

The first step in developing a metaphor is to identify the objects, their attributes, the possible operations on objects and attributes, and relationships among objects, attributes, and operations that are necessary to carry out users' tasks. These objects, attributes, operations, and relationships are then incorporated into a coherent metaphor.

For information retrieval systems, current library environments are a source of metaphors. In her chapter in this section, Chiang reviews problems users have with current online public catalogs (OPACs) that have command-language or menu interfaces. Then she describes how a direct manipulation interface could be designed for an OPAC based on the classic model of information retrieval.

(See chapter 4 for a detailed discussion of the classic model of information retrieval.)

However, appropriate and perhaps better metaphors may be drawn from seemingly irrelevant aspects of "real-life" events. These metaphors may be recognized when analyzing what people do in the current environments. An excellent example of this type of modeling reality is presented by Bates in her chapter, "The Berry-Picking Search: User Interface Design." More work of this type needs to be done to build a foundation for truly successful information retrieval systems.

Other very different metaphors may also be appropriate because of the distinction between task semantics and task syntax that Rose and Belew point out in their chapter in this section. A metaphor can conserve the basic concepts of a task (the semantics) without being limited by the traditional methods of performing the task (the syntax). Thus, as Rose and Belew illustrate in their descriptions of the AIR and SCALIR information retrieval systems, a graphical display of a network of connections can serve as a good model of relationships among documents, authors, and keywords (AIR), and of relationships among statute sections, court decisions about cases, and terms (SCALIR). The network model is expanded in the SCALIR system to include citation relationships between cases, taxonomic relationships between terms, and structural relationships between statute sections. Thus, a fairly simple model (based on the metaphor of connections in the brain) can be used to present a complex, multilayered reality to the user. There are two major differences between the network model as used by Rose and Belew and the basic network model used for hypertext: (1) there are various types of nodes, and (2) the model is presented as an inherent, visible part of the graphical interface. This last difference makes it much easier for users to understand and interact with the model than when it is simply an underlying implicit structure linking various parts of the database.

Although the emphasis in this section is on the advantages of direct manipulation interfaces, they do have major disadvantages as well. Because direct manipulation interfaces often involve graphics, they may have slower response times than other types of interfaces. However, this disadvantage is becoming less important as hardware continues to improve. Second, because of the emphasis on visual representation, direct manipulation interfaces may require an excessive amount of screen space. Finally, as interfaces become easier to learn and use, they also typically become much more difficult to program. Larson addresses this issue in his chapter, which examines design tools for rapid prototyping and code generation for graphical user interfaces using direct manipulation interfaces.

REFERENCES

Hutchins, E. L., J. D. Hollan, and D. A. Norman. 1986. Direct manipulation interfaces. In *User Centered System Design: New Perspectives on Human-Computer Inter-*

action, ed. D. A. Norman and S. W. Draper, 87–124. Hillsdale, N.J.: Lawrence Erlbaum Associates.

Lindeman, M. J. 1989. Interface styles from an interface designer's perspective. *Bulletin of the American Society for Information Science* 15(4): 16–17.

Lindeman, M. J., J. R. Bonneau, and K. E. Pocius. A task analysis for a hyperlibrary system. In Part III of this volume.

Prabha, C., and D. Rice. 1988. *Assumptions about information-seeking behavior in nonfiction books: Their importance to full-text systems.* In *ASIS '88: Proceedings of the 51st ASIS Annual Meeting, Atlanta, Georgia, October 23–27, 1988,* ed. C. L. Borgman and E.Y.H. Pai, 147–51. Medford, N.J.: Learned Information.

Prasse, M., M. Dillon, M. Gordon, B. Mortland, and A. Repka. 1988. F-TAS: A full-text access system. In *National Online Meeting: Proceedings of the Ninth National Online Meeting, New York, May 12–14, 1988,* comp. M. E. Williams and T. H. Hogan, 327–32. Medford, N.J.: Learned Information.

Rutkowski, C. 1982. An introduction to the Human Applications Standard Computer Interface, Part 1: Theory and principles. *Byte* 7(10): 291–310.

Sabine, G. A., and P. L. Sabine. 1986. How people use books and journals. *Library Quarterly* 56(4): 399–408.

1

Comparison of Direct Manipulation, Menu Selection, and Command Language as Interaction Styles for Online Public Access Catalogs

Dudee Chiang

Online Public Access Catalogs (OPACs) were introduced to libraries over the past decade. Initial responses from librarians and library patrons were positive in general. However, user data indicated that most systems were far from perfect (Borgman, 1986). Thus, improving the existing OPACs is a challenge for designers. To do this, designers need to focus on the strengths and weaknesses of the current systems.

User interfaces have become a major focus of research in recent years. The user interface is the domain where users formulate their requests and transmit them to the system, and where the system conveys its responses and messages back to the users. User interface design includes, but is not limited to, how users interact with the system, how the system expresses its responses, and how the responses are shown on the terminal. There are three basic types of interaction between humans and computers (Shneiderman, 1987), namely, command language, menu selection, and direct manipulation. The interaction style found in most existing OPACs is either command language or menu selection, or sometimes a combination of the two. This chapter explores the possibility of a direct-manipulation interface for OPACs. Can such an interface help decrease user problems when searching OPACs?

The chapter begins by examining the common user errors and problems described in previous studies. The advantages and limitations of command language and menu selections are summarized. The major focus of the chapter is on direct manipulation. Its basic philosophy, advantages, and limitations are discussed in detail. The final section of the chapter describes an imaginary OPAC with a direct-manipulation user interface. The purpose is to illustrate how a direct-manipulation interface may help reduce user problems.

USER PROBLEMS WITH OPACs

The Council on Library Resources (CLR) sponsored an extensive study of OPAC usage between 1979 and 1983. OPACs were relatively new at that time. Many people thought they were fun and felt that OPACs saved time; but they also had many suggestions for improvements (Markey, 1984).

Borgman (1986) reviewed literature on user studies of information retrieval systems and OPACs. She stated that in order to perform a successful search, a user must know two different aspects of searching: mechanical and conceptual. Mechanical knowledge includes the syntax and semantics of entering search terms, structuring a search, and negotiating through the system. Conceptual knowledge includes when to use which access point, how to narrow or broaden search results, and why the result of a search is zero.

Users encounter problems when either aspect is not fully understood. Mechanical errors include typographical errors or misspellings, unrecognizable commands, incorrectly formatted commands, and invalid item numbers. Errors do not happen as isolated incidents: they tend to occur in clusters. Users tend to quit after getting error messages rather than seeking online help. Conceptual problems include a misunderstanding of database scope and system features, and misuse of Boolean operators and truncation symbols. Boolean logic is not common sense that comes naturally to everyone, and many people have difficulties with it. Users often have problems in broadening search results when the retrieval set is too small, and they usually are not quite sure what to do when they have a huge retrieval set. Furthermore, studies have shown that most searches do not venture beyond a minimum set of commands. Even the most experienced searchers do not fully utilize all possible commands and features (Borgman, 1986).

Transaction logs are records of the information exchange between a system and its users. By studying the transaction log, researchers can ascertain information that is not obtainable through questionnaires, interviews, or other types of study (Penniman and Dominick, 1980). Several transaction log studies have shown strikingly similar results. The percentages of zero hits were relatively high in most known-item searches (Tolle, 1983; Dickson, 1984; Peters, 1989). The zero-hit rates of author searches from the different studies are: 32.7% (Tolle, 1983), 23% (Dickson, 1984), and 30.2% (Peters); while the percentages of zero matches from title searches are 40.5% (Tolle, 1983), 37% (Dickson, 1984), and 43.8% (Peters).

The OPAC that Dickson studies has a command-language interface. She examined the commands users had entered and identified some reasons for zero hits. Only a small percentage of the zero-hit requests were for items not in the database. The more common reasons for zero hits were

- typographical errors or misspellings
- inclusion of initial article for title searches
- reversed name order for author searches

- incorrect first name or middle initial included
- misuse of abbreviations in either formatting the command or as part of the search request
- attempted Boolean search when there was no such function
- searching the wrong file
- multiple errors

The OPAC system studied by Peters was a menu-driven system. He also studied the terms entered by users in order to find out user problems. The types of errors he found were not much different from those identified by Dickson. Typographical errors and misspellings accounted for most errors. Other reasons for zero hits were: wrong name order or inclusion of a middle initial, wrong type of searches (e.g., an author search that should have been a subject search), violation of system-specific rules and procedures for entering data, and basic misunderstanding of controlled vocabulary (e.g., input the entire phrase "books about dogs" or "information for people considering opening a health club" in a subject search).

Mischo and Lee reviewed studies on end-user bibliographic database searching. They summarized the reasons for the overall poor performance as (1) inconvenience of searching, (2) infrequency of searching, (3) convenience of using intermediaries such as librarians, (4) problems with command languages, (5) difficulties with microcomputer searching protocols, (6) other pressing demands on users' time, and (7) the high cost of searching (Mischo and Lee, 1987, 237).

According to the CLR study, people who did not use OPACs believed that it took time to learn the system, and they did not have the time. When asked how long it would take them to learn, many answered less than 30 minutes (Borgman, 1986; Markey, 1983). It may sound amazing that many people would not spend 30 minutes to learn to use the library catalog. However, it is not hard to understand considering the reasons for the overall poor performance rate of end-user searching. End users search OPACs infrequently, and there are other demands on their time. Library research is usually an interim step in their work. People come to the library to gather information and materials. They do not expect to spend time in learning how to use the library's catalog. The library's catalog, be it online or manual, should be a tool that helps users to locate materials and should not be an obstacle to their final goal.

COMMAND LANGUAGE AND MENU SELECTIONS

Command languages originate from operating system commands. The user issues a command and watches what happens. If the result is correct, the next command is issued; if not, some other strategy is adopted. Each command is chosen to carry out a single task. The number of commands in a system matches the number of functions the system can perform (Shneiderman, 1987).

Most commands are in the form of verbs, followed by one or more arguments

that indicate objects to be manipulated. Commands and arguments may also
have options to indicate special cases. As the number of commands, arguments,
and options grows, rules must be established to show the relationships between
the command and its arguments and options. These rules become the syntax of
the command language. Many times, those rules also become the source of user
problems. Incorrectly formatted commands or unrecognizable commands may
be due to users' misunderstanding or uncertainty about the rules.

Many command languages use abbreviations or mnemonics for their command
names. Command names, abbreviations, and symbols are other sources of user
errors. For example, type, print, display, and list mean similar but different
functions among different systems. They can denote "show me the results on
my terminal" or "show me my previous steps." Many OPACs have different
commands for showing the results on a screen or displaying them on a printer.
But to users, one more command name means one more item to learn, which
makes the system a bit more complicated.

Menu-selection systems are attractive because they can eliminate training and
memorization of complex command sequences. However, a good menu-selection
interface needs to take the following factors into considerations (Shneiderman,
1987):

- organization of menu structure
- item presentation sequence
- selection mechanism
- response time and display rate
- movement among menus
- menu screen design

Menu items should fit logically into categories. The number of menus and the
number of items in each menu can affect the efficiency and effectiveness of the
system. It is inefficient if the user has to go through five or six menus before
getting an answer. On the other hand, if too many items are crowded into one
menu, the clarity of the menus may be sacrificed. The meaning of each selection
should be clear, and wording of the items should be concise. If the items in one
menu follow some logical order, then they should be presented accordingly (e.g.,
in chronological order). However, most menu-selection items do not have such
a logical relationship. Author, title, subject, and call number are common choices
found in an OPAC menu. There is no definite way to arrange these choices.
Some systems may arrange them in alphabetical order; other systems may list
them by number.

A critical consideration that affects the attractiveness of a menu-selection
interface is the speed at which the user can move through the system. The speed
is measured in terms of response time and display rate. Response time is the
time between when the user enters a choice/command and the system's first

response. Display rate is the time required for the system to display the entire response. Multiple menu traversing may become annoying if the response time is long. A menu with many choices becomes annoying if the display rate is slow. In other words, if the response time is slow, menus with more items should be created to reduce the number of menus; if the display rate is slow, then more menus with fewer items in each should be created to reduce the time for displaying a full menu. If both are slow, menu selection is not a good choice of interaction style.

Frequent users may become impatient with the menus, even with good response time and display rate. There should be some mechanism to allow users to type ahead for a known choice or to chain selections together. Finally, the design of screen displays for a menu-selection interface is more complicated than for a command-language interface. Selecting a proper title for each menu, phrasing the menu items, and displaying the layout of each menu are all critical to menu-selection interfaces.

In general, menu-driven systems have the advantage of being easier to use for nonexperts. All options are presented on the screen. The user is led through the system step-by-step. There are fewer keystrokes, which reduces the chance of mistakes. In comparison, the greatest advantage of command language is the power for handling complex queries. Interactions with commands can be much faster than with menus (Monahan, 1984). Users feel much more in control with command languages. At the same time, they must remember the syntax rules and initiative actions.

Larson compared five different OPACs. He observed that "the most striking aspect of the comparison among the systems . . . is the enormous variety represented in these systems: variety in command structure, features, and command-language" (Larson, 1983). Only one of the five systems used menu selections as its interaction style; others used command language as their interaction style. However, the menu-driven system had a much lower error rate than the other four systems. In spite of this, Peters's study shows that even with menu selections, errors still occur when users have to input their requests. Since the frequency of errors correlates with the amount of typing, one may conclude that the fewer characters a user has to type, the less chance for mistakes.

DIRECT MANIPULATION

As an interaction style, direct manipulation means that the user manipulates objects on the display directly in order to accomplish certain goals. The best way to explain direct manipulation is by examples. Video games are good examples. Players control the systems as if they were manipulating the objects in the game. They move their hands from left to right when they want their characters to move from left to right. They push buttons when they want to fire missiles, and so on. The WYSIWYG (what you see is what you get) word processors demonstrate other important characteristics of direct manipulation.

The screen represents the page. The user creates a document by typing onto the screen. Inserting characters is accomplished by placing the cursor at the desired position, then simply typing in the characters. Any change of document style (single or double spacing, and centering or justifying of text) and character styles (fonts and sizes) is shown immediately on the screen. Whatever is shown on the screen can be printed out as is. Video games and WYSIWYG word processors share one common characteristic: their users can concentrate on their actions, and the medium is almost transparent. "Transparency" of the medium, or the tool, should be the ultimate goal of a direct manipulative interface (Shneiderman, 1982, 1987).

The Xerox's 8010 Star workstation user interface is one of the earliest direct-manipulation interfaces. The Apple Macintosh interface is one of its variations. The Xerox 8010 Star designers had discussed and listed elements of what is easy and what is difficult for users. The table is repeated here (Smith, Irby, Kimball, and Verplank, 1982a):

Easy	Hard
concrete	abstract
visible	invisible
recognize	generate
choose	fill in
copy	create
edit	program
interactive	batch

Concrete objects are easier to understand than abstract concepts. Physical metaphors can simplify and clarify systems that are difficult to comprehend. For example, electronic documents are not just file names in disks; they can be represented as papers on the display screen. Transferring documents then becomes the electronic equivalent of picking up a piece of paper and walking with it somewhere.

A well-designed system should make everything relevant to a task visible on the screen. When everything is visible, the display becomes the "reality." Objects can be understood in terms of their visible characteristics. Actions can be understood in terms of their effects on the screen. Visibility also relieves the user of the burden to memorize all options. When all applicable options are shown on the screen, the user needs only to recognize and choose one. This is easier than generating a command and issuing it according to the syntax rules. The common expression, "I can't describe it, but I'll know it when I see it," explains why "to recognize" is easier than "to generate."

It is easier to copy and make modifications of existing files than to create one from scratch. For example, offices have form letters for routine business correspondence. The secretary makes minor changes for each situation instead of composing a new letter each time. Similarly, computer graphics can be made by copying existing ones and then editing and modifying them to suit new needs.

The elements that are easy for users are the basis of the design principles for the Xerox Star interface (Smith, Irby, Kimball, and Verplank, 1982a). These principles are (1) use familiar mental models, (2) use seeing and pointing rather than remembering and typing, (3) employ "what you see is what you get," (4) have fewer but more general commands, and (5) keep the interface consistent and simple. These principles can be considered as the foundation of a direct manipulation interface.

Hutchins and others explained direct manipulation is another way. There are basically two metaphors for the nature of human-computer interaction, namely, the conversation metaphor and the model-world metaphor. In a conversation metaphor, the interface is the language medium in which the user and computer have dialogue about an assumed, but not explicitly represented, "world." Command-language and menu-selection interfaces are based on this conversation metaphor. On the other hand, direct manipulation is based on the model-world metaphor. In the model-world metaphor, the interface is the environment on which users can act. Users do not "tell" the system what to do; instead, they perform actions on the interface directly (Hutchins, Hollan, and Norman, 1986).

The model-world metaphor requires a special type of relationship between the input and output expressions in order to be truly direct manipulation. This is called the "inter-referential I/O." For example, when a user asks for a display of items in a file, he or she can then open, move, or delete the representation of the items on the screen, and the system will react by performing the specified function. Thus, the representation becomes the "reality" to the user. This is not the case in the conversation metaphor, where the user issues a command for displaying items in a file, then issues another command and specifies what to do with which item. The user cannot "act" on the selection directly. A new type of menu selection has emerged with menu items represented by "buttons" or icons. Those buttons or icons can then be selected with a mouse or by touching the screen directly. When menu items can be chosen directly to serve as the input of the next action, the interface can be considered as direct manipulation. The goal of inter-referential I/O is to permit the user to act as if the representation were the thing itself. When an interface presents a world of behaving objects rather than a language of description, manipulating a representation can have the same effects and the same feel as manipulating the thing being represented.

The inter-referential I/O requirement is applicable with icons and pictures, as well as with words and descriptions. Icons, or small images, are usually associated with direct manipulative interfaces. "A good icon will awake the same reaction in most people, irrespective of their background, education, and nationality" (Jervell and Olsen, 1985). Icons can help simplify and clarify the model-world metaphor. The pictures of concrete objects can exemplify abstract ideas. They also facilitate the visibility of actions. For example, a piece of paper can represent a document. Bringing the paper to a printer icon means "print the

document through the printer''; moving the paper to a wastebasket icon means
''discard the document.'' A study by Arend, Muthig, and Wandmacher (1987)
has shown that user response time is quicker and the error rate is lower with
icons than verbal description.

However, the use of icons does not guarantee a superior interface. In a recent
study, Lansdale (1988) has shown that iconic methods do not automatically result
in a high level of performance. The meaningfulness of the icon, or the association
between the icon and the idea it represents, has an impact on the effectiveness
of the icon. Abstract shapes do not perform as well as shapes that have some
representative meanings (Lansdale, 1988). As a design guideline, Arend suggested that within a selection set, icons should not be visually similar to each
other; instead they should possess features distinct from each other. Those features can be the shape, color, size, or closure of the figures. Variation of lines
or structures within figures are not as effective as variations in shape, color,
size, and so on (Arend, Muthig, and Wandmacher, 1987).

Icons facilitate the implementation of direct-manipulation interfaces. At the
same time, they have to be carefully constructed and chosen. Direct manipulation
is not a panacea. Task domain problems cannot be solved by the interface alone.
Bates, Hildreth, and Hjerppe in separate papers have described design principles,
features, and ideas for better OPACs (Bates, 1986a, 1986b; Hildreth, 1987;
Hjerppe, 1986). Although none of them used the term *direct manipulation* to
describe their interfaces, a direct-manipulation interface would definitely facilitate the use of their systems.

A HYPOTHETICAL TOUR OF A DIRECT
MANIPULATION OPAC

In this section, the author presents a hypothetical OPAC with a direct-manipulation interface. The focus is on the interactions between the user and the system.
It is assumed that the structure of the database is able to support all the described
functions. This imaginary OPAC system can be installed either in a corporate
environment or an academic institution.

The library's OPAC is accessible from any terminal or workstation within the
institution. Each workstation is equipped with a high-resolution display screen
and a pointing device. With a click on the icon for the catalog, the user is
presented with three windows. Each window lists the authors, titles, and subjects
present in the database. To search the OPAC, the user scrolls through the listings
and scans the headings. When a relevant heading shows up, the user simply
points at it and clicks to see the corresponding record(s). The user can speed up
the scrolling process or leap back and forth within the listings. These functions
can lead the user to the general area of interest quicker than regular scrolling.
However, the action for speed-up scrolling is basically the same as regular
scrolling, only it is a continuous action.

An alternative way to search the OPAC is by typing the keywords in a blank space provided on the screen. The catalog then matches the keywords in all author, title, and subject fields. The matches or near matches are displayed and highlighted in each window. The user does not need to specify which file to search. If the user wants to find information about a person, works by the person and about the person will be shown in the author and subject windows, respectively. The title window may display titles having the person's name in it, as well. If a user inputs "textbook on anatomy," the catalog will show a list of works containing the keywords in the subject window. The purpose of this keyword matching is to establish starting points between the user and the OPAC; from there, the user can then browse and navigate through the catalog.

The user chooses the heading of interest by clicking on the item. He or she can choose more than one item from each of the windows, or from more than one window. In such cases, the OPAC will initiate a dialogue to find out whether the user wants all of the chosen terms to be present in one item, or if materials with any one of the terms presented can suffice. The user does not need to understand the concept of Boolean logic. The OPAC will determine whether to use Boolean AND or Boolean OR according to the answers given by the user.

A temporary "library work area" is provided to the user whenever he or she logs on to the OPAC. Whenever a user chooses a heading, it is automatically stored in the work area. When the user has reviewed all records corresponding to one heading, the OPAC signals that other terms remain in the area. When additional subject headings or authors' names are found within descriptions, the user can add them to the list by moving the image of the heading to the icon of the work area. The user may also jump to other records having the same heading by clicking on the term. The system will remember which terms the user has reviewed. In addition to seeing a detailed description of each reference, the user may move the record to the icon the desk (or office), which signals the catalog to check out this item and send it to the desk. The user can move a group of records at one time or move individual records separately. If the item is already checked out, a hold option will show up. The user can activate it, and have his or her name added to the waiting list.

When the user cannot find what he or she wants, a message can be sent to the librarian for help. All terms, names, and keywords stored in the "library work area" can be sent together with the message. The user may edit the list and describe what is wanted in more detail before sending it to the librarian. Thus, the librarian could know how the user had searched in the OPAC, which can help the librarian in the reference work.

There is an icon of the workstation within the OPAC. The user can move specific records of lists of materials to the workstation. Such action downloads the bibliographic records to the user's workstation without checking out the materials. These bibliographic records can then be manipulated by the file management system or text editor residing in the workstation. There is also an icon for the printer. Moving the records to the printer will generate a hard copy of the records. Anytime during the search session, the user can leave the online catalog simply by clicking on the icons of other functions.

This online catalog not only helps the library users but also the librarians and library staff. The requests for materials are received in a file separated from the requests for help. Therefore, the professional librarian can concentrate on reference questions and let support staff handle circulation functions. All incoming requests are automatically recorded by the catalog's administrative function, thus monthly and annual statistics can be accurately calculated.

This imaginary direct-manipulation OPAC has several advantages. Typing has been reduced to a minimum, thereby reducing the chance of user errors. Most of the time, the user can scan through lists of items or headings, recognize and choose them without the need to generate descriptions. Users do not need to issue Boolean logic operators; the OPAC asks questions and assigns the appropriate operators according to the answers. The many commands for checking out materials, downloading records, and printing records have been eliminated. All of these commands have become one action of choosing an item and moving its representation on the screen to the appropriate icons. It is very easy to learn and to search the OPAC, and the system is still very powerful, nonetheless.

CONCLUSIONS

Previous studies have identified user problems with existing OPACs. Some of the problems are related to the interaction styles of the system. Because most OPAC users are infrequent users, and they do not want to spend a lot of time learning the system, the user interface should help its end users in locating information with the least amount of effort.

Designers have identified some practical guidelines for interface design. Familiar physical metaphors can help nonexpert users to comprehend the electronic system. Visible objects and visible actions clarify the system's actions and responses. It is easier for users to recognize and choose rather than to generate and fill in; to copy and edit rather than to create and program. These guidelines have become the fundamental principles of direct-manipulation interface design.

An interface that demands less mental effort from its users is easier to learn and easier to use. Instead of concentrating on the learning and remembering of computer syntax, the user can focus efforts on finding and choosing the needed material. With all options shown on the screen, all effects of all user actions immediately visible, and fewer commands and simpler rules, a direct-manipulation interface is less demanding on users. At the same time, a direct-manipulation interface can accommodate as many functions as a command-language interface can. Functionalities are not sacrificed for ease of use. A direct-manipulation interface can also give its users a full sense of control. Therefore, it is an alternative interaction style worthy of further study and experimentation.

REFERENCES

Arend, U., Muthig, K. P., and Wandmacher, J. 1987. "Evidence for Global Feature Superiority in Menu Selection by Icon." *Behaviour and Information Technology* 6: 411–26.

Bates, Marcia J. 1986a. "An Exploratory Paradigm for Online Information Retrieval." In B. C. Brookes, ed., *Intelligent Information Systems for the Information Society: Proceedings of the Sixth International Research Forum in Information Science (IRFIS 6), Frascati, Italy, September 16–18, 1985.* New York: Elsevier.

―――. 1986b. "Subject Access in Online Catalogs: A Design Model." *Journal of the American Society for Information Science* 37 (November): 357–76.

Bewley, William L., Roberts, Teresa L., Schroit, David S., and Verplank, William L. 1983. "Human Factors Testing in the Design of Xerox's 8010 'Star' Office Workstation." In Ann Janda, ed., *Human Factors in Computing Systems: Proceedings of the CHI'83 Conference, Boston, MA, 12–15 December 1983*, 72–77. Amsterdam: North-Holland.

Bishop, David F. 1983. "The CLR OPAC Study: Analysis of ARL User Responses." *Information Technology and Libraries* 2 (September): 315–21.

Borgman, Christine L. 1986. "Why Are Online Catalogs Hard to Use? Lessons Learned from Information Retrieval Studies." *Journal of the American Society for Information Science* 37: 387–400.

Cheng, Chin-Chuan. 1985. "Microcomputer-Based User Interface." *Information Technology and Libraries* 4 (December): 346–51.

Crawford, Walt. 1988. "Common Sense and User Interfaces: Issues Beyond the Keyboard." *Library Hi Tech* 6(2): 7–16.

Dickson, Jean. 1984. "An Analysis of User Errors in Searching an Online Catalog." *Cataloging & Classification Quarterly* 4(3): 19–38.

Gittins, D. T., Winder, R. L., and Bez, H. E. 1984. "An Icon-Driven End-User Interface to UNIX." *International Journal of Man-Machine Studies* 21: 451–61.

Goodwin, Nancy C. 1987. "Functionality and Usability." *Communications of the ACM* 30 (March): 229–33.

Hildreth, Charles R. 1982. *Online Public Access Catalogs: The User Interface.* Dublin, Ohio: OCLC.

―――. 1984. "Pursuing the Ideal: Generations of Online Catalogs." In Britan Aveney and Brett Butler, eds., *Online Catalogs, Online Reference: Converging Trends*, 31–56. Chicago, Ill.: American Library Association.

―――. 1987. "Beyond Boolean: Designing the Next Generation of Online Catalogs." *Library Trends* 35: 647–67.

Hjerppe, R. 1986. "Project HYPERCATalog: Visions and Preliminary Conceptions of an Extended and Enhanced Catalog." In B. C. Brookes, ed., *Intelligent Information Systems for the Information Society: Proceedings of the Sixth International Research Forum in Information Science (IRFIS 6), Frascati, Italy, September 16–18, 1985*, 211–32. New York: Elsevier.

Hollands, J. G., and Merikle, P. M., 1987. "Menu Organization and User Expertise in Information Search Tasks." *Human Factors* 29: 577–86.

Hutchins, Edwin, Hollan, James D., and Norman, Donald A. 1985. "Direct Manipulation Interfaces." *Human-Computer Interaction* 1: 311–38.

Jervell, H. R., and Olsen, K. A. 1985. "Icons in Man-Machine Communication." *Behaviour and Information Technology* 4: 249–54.

Lansdale, M. W. 1988. "On the Memorability of Icons in an Information Retrieval Task." *Behaviour and Information Technology* 7: 131–51.

Larson, Ray R. 1983. *Users Look at Online Catalogs, Part 2: Interacting with Online Catalogs*. Final Report to the Council on Library Resources. ERIC document no. ED231401.

Larson, Ray R., and Graham, Vicki. 1983. "Monitoring and Evaluating MELVYL." *Information Technology and Libraries* 2: 93–104.

Lipkie, Daniel E. 1982. "Star Graphics: An Object-Oriented Implementation." *Computer Graphics* (ACM-SIGGRAPH) 16: 115–24.

McCracken, Donald L., and Akscyn, Robert M. 1984. "Experience with the ZOG Human-Computer Interface System." *International Journal of Man-Machine Studies* 21 (October): 293–310.

Markey, Karen. 1984. "Barriers to Effective Use of Online Catalogs." In Brian Aveney and Brett Butler, eds., *Online Catalogs, Online Reference: Converging Trends*, 57–72. Chicago, Ill.: American Library Association.

———. 1983. "Thus Spake the OPAC User." *Information Technology and Libraries* 2 (December): 381–87.

Mischo, William H., and Lee, Jounghyoun. 1987. "End-User Searching of Bibliographic Databases." In Martha E. Williams ed., *Annual Review of Information Science and Technology*, vol.22, 227–63. Amsterdam: Elsevier.

Monahan, Michael. 1984. "Command Language and Codes." In Paul E. Peters, ed., *Command Language and Screen Displays for Public Online Systems*, 15–24. Report of a meeting sponsored by the Council on Library Resources, Dublin, Ohio, March 29–30, 1984. Washington, D.C.: Council on Library Resources.

Nielsen, Brian. 1986. "What They Say They Do and What They Do: Assessing Online Catalog Use Instruction Through Transaction Monitoring." *Information Technology and Libraries* 5 (March): 28–34.

Owen, David. 1987. *Direct Manipulation and Procedural Reasoning*. Office of Naval Research, Arlington, Va. #BBB05183. ERIC document no. ED287454.

Pejtersen, A. M. 1986. "Design of Intelligent Retrieval Systems for Libraries Based on Models of Users' Search Strategies." In *Proceedings of the 1986 IEEE International Conference on Systems, Man, and Cybernetics*, 1082–87. New York: Institute of Electrical and Electronics Engineers.

Penniman, W. D., and Dominick, W. D. 1980. "Monitoring and Evaluation of On-Line Information System Usage." *Information Processing and Management* 16: 17–35.

Permenter, Kathryn E. 1986. "Human Factors Design for Library User System Interface." In *Proceedings of the 1986 IEEE International Conference on Systems, Man, and Cybernetics*, 1088–91. New York: Institute of Electrical and Electronics Engineers.

Peters, Thomas A. 1989. "When Smart People Fail: An Analysis of the Transaction Log of an Online Public Access Catalog." *Journal of Academic Librarianship* 15(5): 267–73.

Shneiderman, Ben. 1982. "The Future of Interactive Systems and the Emergence of Direct Manipulation." *Behaviour and Information Technology* 1(3): 237–56.

————. 1987. *Designing the User Interface: Strategies for Effective Human-Computer Interaction*. Reading, Mass.: Addison-Wesley.

Siegel, Elliot R., Kameen, Karen, Sinn, Sally K., and Weiss, Frieda O. 1984. "A Comparative Evaluation of the Technical Performance and User Acceptance of Two Prototype Online Catalog Systems." *Information Technology and Libraries* 3 (March): 35–46.

Smith, David Canfield, Irby, Charles, Kimball, Ralph, and Verplank, Bill. 1982a. "Designing the Star User Interface." *Byte* 7 (April): 242–82.

Smith, David Canfield, Irby, Charles, and Kimball, Ralph. 1982b. 'The Star User Interface: An Overview." In Howard L. Morgan, ed., *AFIPS Conference Proceedings: 1982 National Computer Conference*, vol. 51, 515–28. Arlington, Va.: AFIPS Press.

Tolle, John E. 1983. "Understanding Patron's Use of Online Catalogs: Transaction Log Analysis of the Search Method." In Raymond F. Vondran, Anne Caputo, Carol Wasserman, and Richard A. V. Diener, eds., *Productivity in the Information Age: Proceedings of the 46th ASIS Annual Meeting*, vol. 20, 167–71. White Plains, N.Y.: Knowledge Industry.

————. 1984. "Monitoring and Evaluation of Information Systems via Transaction Log Analysis." In C. J. van Rijsbergen, ed., *Research and Development in Information Retrieval: Proceedings of the Third Joint BCS and ACM Symposium*, 247–58. Cambridge: Cambridge University Press.

2

Rapid Prototyping and Code Generation for Direct-Manipulation Interfaces

Ray R. Larson

This chapter examines design tools for rapid prototyping and code generation of graphical user interfaces using direct-manipulation techniques. It concentrates on tools that utilize direct manipulation of interface elements (e.g., windows, icons, scrollbars) in the development process. Direct-manipulation interfaces are rapidly replacing the text-based conversational interaction methods supported by most existing user interface management systems (UIMS) and operating systems.

The tools to be examined include HyperCard for the Macintosh, Application Builder of the NeXT computer, and UICAD for the Amiga (a prototype user interface management system developed by the author). The notion of separating the user interface from application (the advantages and disadvantages), strategies for inter-process communication, and the advantages of reusable user interface components will also be examined.

INTRODUCTION

In the past, research in online information systems has concentrated on the theory, implementation, and evaluation of algorithms, data, and file structures for effective and efficient retrieval of documents or bibliographic citations. Many tools have been designed to aid the programmer or designer of these systems in the task of development. Most notably, database management systems have been used to handle low-level file access and index control. Until recently, there has been less concern for development of principles and tools to aid in designing the best or most effective user interfaces for online information systems. I would suggest that the characteristics of the user interface for a computer-based system have significant effects on the use and perceived utility of the system, and that these may outweigh the benefits of any particular retrieval mechanism in determining user satisfaction with the system.

This is not a new observation; it was stated succinctly by C. N. Mooers as "Mooers Law of Information Retrieval" nearly 30 years ago: "An information retrieval system will tend not to be used when it is more painful and troublesome for a customer to have information than for him not to have it" (Mooers, 1960, ii). Concern with the user interface for computer systems may be seen in the increase of research into user interaction and in the development of User Interface Management Systems (UIMS) and other software tools to aid the developer of online systems (see Shneiderman, 1987: ACM SIGGRAPH, 1987). The trend toward graphical, direct-manipulation interfaces and away from the line-by-line teletype model of computer interaction, as seen in the Apple Macintosh Presentation Manager for OS/2 and visual shells for UNIX systems, has increased the ease of using computer systems at the expense of increasing complexity in the supporting programs.

In developing the user interface for online systems, it is usually recommended that the end users of the system be involved in an iterative process of design, prototyping, testing, and redesign. Without software tools to support prototyping of the user interface, the increasing complexity of programs with graphical interfaces threatens to make this iteration impractically expensive and much too time consuming.

In this chapter some tools are examined for user interface design, prototyping of applications, and code generation that are based on graphical representation and interactive direct-manipulation techniques (Shneiderman, 1982). The basic hardware and software components of graphical interfaces and the principles and characteristics of direct-manipulation techniques for such systems are briefly examined. Three tools for construction of direct-manipulation interfaces that employ direct-manipulation techniques in the design process (HyperCard for the Macintosh, Application Builder for the NeXT computer, and UICAD for the Amiga) are then discussed.

GRAPHICAL INTERFACE CONCEPTS

As the name suggests, graphical interfaces utilize the graphics capabilities of a workstation or personal computer to provide enhanced display and interactive features for systems and application software. A graphical user interface requires fairly substantial hardware and software support to provide effective interaction with the user. Most systems that offer a graphical interface rely on bit-mapped display devices for output. Bit-mapped display devices use one or more bits of memory to represent the status of each pixel on the display screen. The displays may be monochrome (usually black on white) with a single bit per pixel, or color (commonly with 2 to 8 bits used to select a color from a table of color values).

Some form of pointing device (such as a mouse, touchscreen, or lightpen) is used in addition to conventional keyboards for input. Pointing devices permit the user to select information displayed on the screen easily. Since a system may incur considerable computational and memory overheads in dealing with these devices, local processing power, tightly coupled to the display and input devices, is generally necessary for adequate performance of a graphical interface. Some workstations and personal computers that provide a graphical interface use specialized graphics coprocessors to offload display generation and manipulation from the main processor. These often use high bandwidth bit block transfer (or "blitter") hardware to support fast operations on display memory. Bit-mapped displays and pointing devices are rapidly becoming as common for personal computers (e.g., the Apple Macintosh, IBM PC, and PS/2 under Microsoft Windows or OS/2 Presentation Manager, Amiga, and Atari/ST) as they have been for advanced workstations (such as those produced by Sun, Apollo, IBM, and Symbolics).

DIRECT MANIPULATION FEATURES AND CONTROLS

Windows

Systems that provide graphical interface features usually make use of system-level software for support of windows and graphic element creation and control (such as the Macintosh Toolbox [Apple, 1986], the Andrew system developed at Carnegie Mellon University [Morris, et al. 1986], the X Window system developed at MIT [Scheifler and Gettys, 1986], the Intuition system for the Amiga [Mical and Deyl, 1987], MicroSoft Windows and the NEWS windowing system developed by Sun Microsystems [Stern, 1987]). Myers (1988) provides an interesting examination and classification of a number of windowing systems and the interfaces they present to the user.

Windowing software permits independent display and interactive regions to be defined on the user's screen. Each of these windows may contain text, graphics, and interactive control elements, such as menus or icons. In these systems, text is usually treated as a special form of graphic under software control. Text may be displayed using a variety of different fonts in a variety of point sizes and colors (on systems supporting color).

Buttons and Icons

Control elements of graphical interface systems usually consist of a set of selectable buttons and menus in addition to (or in place of) commands entered from the keyboard. For the sake of consistency we will define a button as an area of the display screen that may be selected by the user with a pointing device to indicate that certain actions are to be performed.

Buttons usually have an associated image to define the selection area on the screen, although "invisible" buttons are used in some systems. Button images range from simple menulike text or boxes to representative or symbolic depictions of an object (e.g., a file or document) or an action to be performed. Buttons that represent windows, application programs, files, and similar objects are usually called icons. Buttons may change their imagery or position on the screen in response to user manipulation. A common example of the latter is found in scrollbars, where manipulation of the button by "sliding" it up or down will scroll through windows of text.

Principles and Characteristics of Direct-Manipulation Interfaces

Many graphical interface systems are based on a metaphor or analogical representation of a task domain. For example, the Apple Macintosh system uses stylized images of pieces of paper and file folders spread over a "desktop" to represent disk files and directories. To perform an action such as moving a file, the mouse is used to pick up the "piece of paper" icon in one "folder" and move it to another, causing the computer to move the underlying file from its current directory to the directory represented by the second folder. The use of a metaphor based on a noncomputer environment is intended to ease the learning process for the user and to allow transfer of knowledge from familiar work environments to the computer environment.

Metaphors may be extended to be as realistic and helpful as possible. For example, utility programs on the Macintosh such as a clock, calendar, or calculator are treated as "desk accessories" that can be placed and manipulated on the desktop. For instance, the mouse can be used to "press" buttons on the calculator, and the calculator display will show the numbers, operations, and results for each button pressed.

Shneiderman (1982; 1987) has called user interfaces that make use of visual representations of objects and actions, and that replace command syntax with direct interaction with those objects, direct-manipulation interfaces. He interprets direct manipulation quite broadly and includes programs such as electronic spreadsheets, "What You See Is What You Get" (WYSIWYG) text editors, and video games (in addition to the window- and icon-based interfaces discussed above). Shneiderman suggests that there are the following three basic principles of direct manipulation:

1. continuous representation of the objects and actions of interest to the user,
2. physical actions or labeled button presses instead of complex syntax or textual description of actions, and
3. rapid incremental, reversible operations whose impact on the object(s) of interest is immediately visible. (Shneiderman, 1987, 201)

In examining the research on direct-manipulation interfaces, Shneiderman suggests that a number of characteristic benefits may be derived from well-designed direct-manipulation interfaces based on these principles. These are the following:

1. The basic functions of the system can be learned easily by novice users through demonstration

2. Expert users can usually work rapidly to carry out a wide range of tasks

3. Infrequent users usually find it easier to retain their knowledge of how to operate a direct-manipulation interface when compared to a command-language-based system

4. Error messages are needed less frequently (forbidden actions are simply not possible to perform in many cases)

5. Users can immediately see the results of their actions, and whether those actions are furthering their goals. If not, they can undo or change the direction they are pursuing

6. Users experience less anxiety because the system is comprehensible and because actions are easily reversible

7. Users gain confidence and mastery because they are the initiators of action; they feel in control and the system's responses are predictable

Naturally, it is possible to construct direct-manipulation interfaces that lack some (or even all) of these benefits. For naive users, or users familiar with more conventional (command or menu) user interfaces, there may be considerable cognitive difficulties in learning how to use a graphical interface. Carroll and Mazur (1986) suggest that many of the difficulties in learning a direct-manipulation interface can be traced to differences in the user's metaphor and the system metaphor, when common terms are used to denote actions or system functions that behave differently from their real-world counterparts. For example, on the Apple Lisa system some novices had difficulties in dealing with the system "clipboard" because, to them, a clipboard holds paper to write on and is not usually considered as a temporary storage space for text and graphics (the system function).

Difficulties in Designing and Maintaining Graphical Interfaces

The ease-of-use and apparent simplicity of graphical direct-manipulation interfaces are achieved only through vastly increased complexity in the underlying programs. One recent article (Rosenthal, 1988) showed how the famous "Hello, World" program (usually one executable statement in four or five lines of C source code) required 40 executable statements and 25 calls to shared library routines in over 150 lines of C source code under Version 11 of X Windows.

In developing graphical direct-manipulation interfaces, programmers must deal with multiple forms of input (mouse movements, button clicks, and keyboard input, for example). They must also maintain the consistency and readability of displays when windows are rearranged and resized by the user, and must handle the setup, opening, positioning, scaling, and closing of those windows. In addition, they must deal with the use of different fonts, graphics routines, color maps, and other elements peculiar to a graphical interface. The graphic elements of a particular window or screen must have their positions (x and y coordinates), size, colors, and interactive properties specified.

Some of the details of the specification may be handled for the programmer by the particular windowing system (or window manager) and predefined libraries of routines for displaying and positioning graphical elements and windows. Even with these aids the programmer must usually maintain large lists of data structures and parameters to be passed to the window manager and library routines. Depending on the complexity of the task, it is not unusual for the interface routines to become the largest portion of a program. Tools that can help the programmer in managing this complexity are extremely valuable in saving time and effort and in debugging the construction of graphical user interfaces. Such tools help the programmer (and possibly nonprogramming designers or end users) to construct and modify the user interface portions of programs rapidly, permitting new ideas and display elements to be tested without the laborious coding and debugging that would be needed using a programming language alone.

The methodology for such development is called *rapid prototyping*. A prototype is a partially functional version of a system. Luqi defines a prototype as "a concrete executable model of selected aspects of a proposed system," and rapid prototyping as "the process of quickly building and evaluating a series of prototypes" (Luqi, 1989, 13). Using rapid prototyping, the conventional software development cycle is supplemented by a series of prototype design and evaluation stages that precede development and coding of the full system.

GRAPHICAL INTERFACE DESIGN TOOLS

This section examines some tools for rapid prototyping and code generation of direct-manipulation interfaces. Myers (1989) provides a good survey of a number of user interface design tools, their features, philosophy, and components. Myers defines a user interface development system (UIDS) as "an integrated set of tools that help programmers create and manage many aspects of interfaces" (Myers, 1989, 16).

User interface design tools range from window manager "toolkits" accessible only to the programmer as a set of subroutines, through formal specification languages, to tools offering graphical specification and layout of the interface. The tools discussed here, HyperCard for the Macintosh, Interface Builder for the NeXT computer, and UICAD for the Amiga, all use direct-manipulation techniques to give the programmer or designer immediate visual feedback during the process of designing and laying out the interactive elements of a graphical interface. Creating an interface using these tools is more like using a "paint" program than programming in the conventional sense of providing a textual specification of algorithms and data structures. The programmer (or interface designer) usually selects from a set of predefined interface objects (such as windows, icons, or scrollbars) and directly positions them on the screen, mod-

Figure 2.1
HyperCard Button Ideas Stack

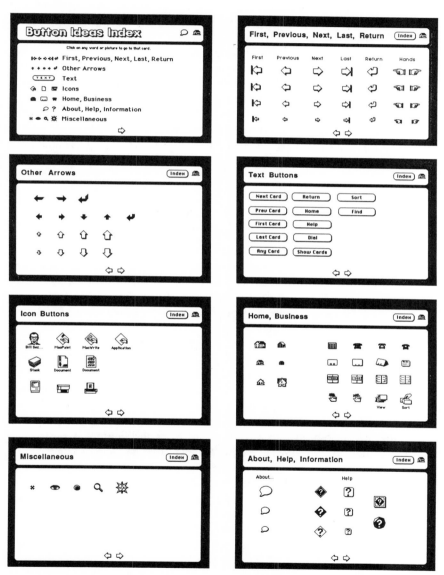

Source: Various HyperCard graphics and icons ©Apple Computer, Inc. Used with permission.

ifying size, position, and graphical elements (text and images) with simple movements of a mouse.

Once the graphic elements of a screen or window have been drawn by the interface designer, the operations invoked by the interface components may be specified through a combination of direct manipulation and more conventional specification or programming languages. The interface design may be saved for later modifications, and (in Interface Builder and UICAD) compilable source code for the interface may be generated automatically. These systems differ considerably in their internal structure, philosophy of system integration, and end results. Each has adopted (to greater or lesser extents) the notion of object-oriented programming, where the data structures constituting the internal representation of interactive elements and the procedures that operate on those elements are bound together into various classes of "objects" that may be treated as a unit. Communications and parameter passing between objects take the form of "messages" sent from one object to another specifying actions to perform.

HyperCard

The HyperCard system (Goodman, 1987), designed by Bill Atkinson of Apple Computers, is perhaps best known as a system supporting hypertext features. HyperCard was, however, intended to be a complete application development system for the Macintosh and has been called by its author a "software erector set." It is based on the conceptual model, or metaphor, of stacks of 3"x5" file cards. HyperCard permits only a single "card" to be displayed on the screen at one time. Each card is the full size of a standard Macintosh screen and may contain text fields (including scrollable text windows), bit-mapped graphics, and buttons that can invoke routines written in the underlying "HyperTalk" script language. Hypercard cards are collected into "stacks," each of which is stored as a separate disk file. Figure 2.1 shows a set of "cards" from a HyperCard stack containing button icon examples.

The user of HyperCard creates an application using direct manipulation to design the displayable and interactive elements of the individual cards. The system provides full WYSIWYG editing for text fields and a complete "paint" package for designing graphics. Text, graphics, and buttons may be "cut" or copied from other stacks and "pasted" into the application, permitting the user to build new stacks rapidly using standard elements. Custom buttons may also be designed, and invisible buttons may be defined to overlay graphic elements of a card. Figure 2.2 gives an indication of the variety of interface styles that can be developed in HyperCard (the examples are drawn from stacks developed by students in the author's user interface design seminar).

Actions to be taken by the application are specified using the HyperTalk language to attach "message handlers" to the card elements. For example, a simple HyperTalk script attached to a button might be on mouseUp

go to next card

end mouseUp

This action, going to the next card in the stack, would be invoked when the user clicked and released the mouse button while the pointer was over the button graphic on the screen. The HyperTalk language includes most of the features of conventional high-level programming languages and may be extended to include new primitives by writing ''XCMDs'' in conventional programming languages. This latter feature has led to some interesting capabilities, such as controls for

Figure 2.2
HyperCard Interface Styles

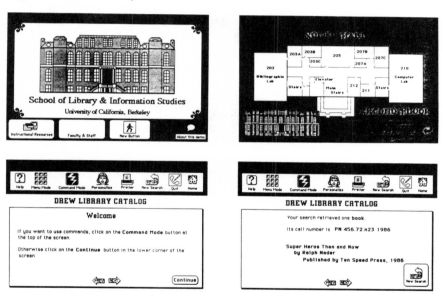

Source: Various HyperCard graphics and icons ©Apple Computer, Inc. Used with permission.

videodisc and CD-ROM players, and HyperCard-based, customizable interfaces for database management systems.

HyperCard applications are interpreted by the system during execution, requiring that the Hypercard program be resident on the machine where the application is running. HyperCard is, therefore, an application development and presentation environment rather than a tool for development of stand-alone systems.

Interface Builder

The Interface Builder is provided as system software on the NeXT computer system. While the entire system is still in the final beta-testing stage before release in 1989, Interface Builder has been available in its prerelease form to various universities and commercial sites. The NeXTStep environment, running under the Mach version of UNIX, consists of a window manager (Window Server), file and application manager (Workspace Manager), a system toolkit of display elements and routines to manipulate them (Application Kit), and the Interface Builder, which provides a graphical, direct-manipulation interface to the Application Kit. Thompson (1989) provides a good description of the architecture of the NeXTStep environment and elements of the Application Kit.

The Interface Builder, as its name implies, is primarily a tool for specification and layout of the user interface elements of a NeXTStep application program. It provides graphical menus of standard interactive elements and window components, shown in the windows labeled "Grab a View" and "Grab a Window" in figure 2.3. The programmer can also define the appearance of custom display objects. These standard objects are selected with the mouse "dragged" into position in the application window. They can then be "customized" by changing the size, text labels, and graphics of the object.

Once the programmer has laid out the elements of an application window, the message passing links between display objects and underlying application code may be specified using the "connect" tool. In figure 2.3 the connect tool window shows a connection being built between the "gravity" slider of the "Ideal" window, the Chamber object, and the oscilloscope graph object. The "Actions" and "Outlets" menu windows represent the message to be received and emitted by the "Target" Chamber object. (Note that figure 2.3 shows the beta test 0.8 version of Interface Builder. In the 0.9 version, this portion of the system has been completely redesigned.)

Once these connections have been specified, the Interface Builder generates a file that is used when the application is executed to define both the specific instances of the objects and the PostScript code that renders the graphical and text elements of the application on the screen. This project file can be retrieved and modified by the Interface Builder.

The Interface Builder does not generate complete applications. Definition of the underlying executable code for user-defined objects (as opposed to standard

Figure 2.3
NeXT Interface Builder Screen

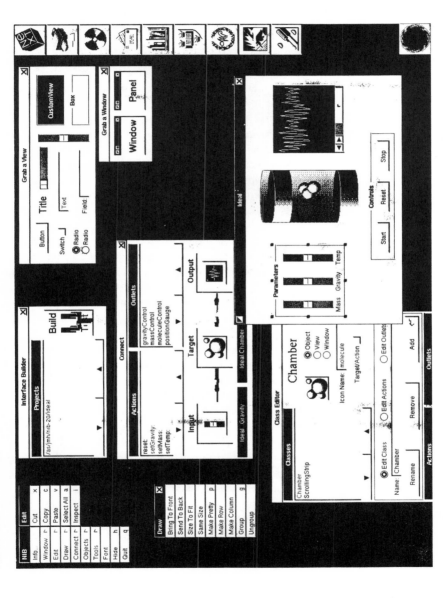

Source: NeXT, Inc.

interface elements) in the application must be programmed in Objective C, making use of the Application Kit objects for communication with the interface and system functions. However, once such an object has been programmed, it can be used in other applications.

UICAD

The UICAD (User Interface Computer Aided Design) system was designed by this author to automate many aspects of user interface design and code generation for applications written in C on the Amiga personal computer. While the system is still under active development, it has already proved useful in creating some of its own interface features. UICAD runs under the multitasking AmigaDOS operating system using the Intuition user interface toolkit (Mical and Deyl, 1987) for window management and graphics primitives.

UICAD uses direct manipulation to lay out the windows and interactive elements of a user interface and define or modify their appearance. The interactive elements include ''gadgets'' (the Intuition term for buttons), and pull-down or pop-up menus. Three main classes of gadgets are available: Boolean gadgets, which function as simple buttons; proportional gadgets, which function as sliders to provide variable potentiometer-style input; and string gadgets, which function as an editable, single-line keyboard input window (see figure 2.4). Pull-down menus (shown in figure 2.4) and pop-up menus (that appear at the current position of the mouse pointer) may be defined using a menu editor.

Gadgets may have associated text (in a variety of fonts and colors), bit-mapped graphics with up to 4,096 colors, or simple line or vector graphics (usually used as borders). The UICAD system provides tools for creating and editing these elements and for importing graphics from paint programs and digitizers (using the Amiga standard Interchange File Format, IFF).

A set of standard prototype gadgets may be selected from a menu and customized using the editing tools and gadget definition menus (figure 2.5). Custom gadgets may also be defined and edited using the same tools, including importing images from paint programs (see figure 2.6). Graphics may also be drawn in the image editor or imported as ''backdrops'' for windows in any of the Amiga's display resolutions including the Hold and Modify mode that permits 4,096 colors to be displayed simultaneously on a screen (figures 2.7 and 2.8).

The user or interface designer may attach executable scripts to any gadget, written in the REXX programming language. REXX was originally developed as a high-level macro language for IBM mainframes (Cowlishaw, 1985). The Amiga version, AREXX (Hawes, 1987), permits communication and data sharing between concurrent programs as well as providing all of the features of the mainframe version.

AREXX interfaces exist in many Amiga programs, including text editors, database management systems, telecommunications packages, and an expert system shell. UICAD can utilize the services of any of these other programs or

Figure 2.4
UICAD Standard Gadgets and Menus

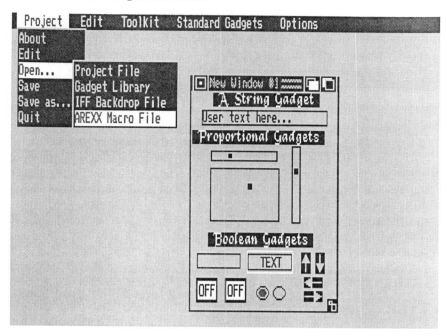

provide alternative user interfaces for them via the AREXX interpreter. However, the main purpose of UICAD is to generate C program code for compilation into stand-alone programs. UICAD user interface designs may be saved and retrieved for later modifications. Sets of gadgets and menus may also be stored as "palettes" of items for later retrieval and use, aiding the designer in standardizing these elements across applications.

SEPARATING THE USER INTERFACE AND APPLICATION

Research in user interface management systems (ACM SIGGRAPH, 1987) has suggested that separation between the user interface and the parts of an application that carry out the manipulation of files and data may be a desirable goal. However, complete logical and physical separation may not always be possible or desirable when it results in performance penalties. For example, in an application requiring immediate graphical feedback of the results of user actions, such as a paint program, the input received should be reflected immediately on the user's display, and additional layers of interpretation may result in lags in this feedback (Hill, 1987).

Effective communication between the user interface and other parts of an

Figure 2.5
UICAD Gadget Definition Request

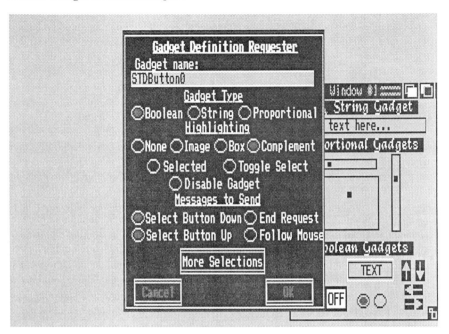

application depends largely on the facilities provided by the operating system or window manager supporting the application. The design tools discussed above approach this communication in a variety of ways.

In HyperCard, the application may be defined entirely within the HyperCard system using the HyperTalk language. Alternatively, XCMs may be used to communicate with external procedures that carry out the application functions. For example, the Macintosh version of the Oracle DBMS uses XCMDs to transmit SQL queries to the DBMS and to retrieve and store the results in HyperCard fields.

In Interface Builder on the NeXT computer, interface designs may use the Mach Inter-Process Communications protocol to send messages (including data) between applications, supported by the ''speaker'' and ''listener'' objects in the Applications Kit. In theory, this permits any message that may be handled internally by an application to be issued by another application. Since all communication within NeXTStep consists of messages passed between objects, this provides a uniform method of separating the interface and application functions.

In UICAD, communication between concurrent processes, and between interactive elements of an interface and the application, are handled as messages transmitted using the Intuition Direct Communication Message Ports (IDCMP)

Figure 2.6
UICAD Image Editor

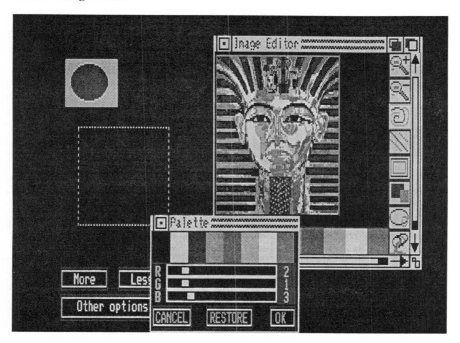

system. In the source code generated by UICAD, a message handler routes IDCMP messages from gadgets and menus to user-designated C routines that implement the application functions. IDCMP messages are also used to communicate with AREXX, and through it to other concurrent processes.

In each of these systems, the goal of separating the application and interface may be achieved to varying extents. The degree of separation obtained depends on the demands of the particular application and the variety of input and display methods supported. (For example, UICAD does not yet directly support scrolling text windows such as those available in HyperCard.) So far, no single tool (other than conventional programming languages) can anticipate and manage the universe of potential applications in a form that maintains complete independence of the interface and functional portions of the system.

One of primary benefits of these interface design tools is their ability to store and reuse elements of an interface. The interface designer is able to pick from a set of ''standard'' elements (either provided by the system, previously designed and saved, or borrowed from other applications) and thus present a consistent appearance and interactive syntax (sometimes called ''look and feel'') for applications. Elements of an interface may also be selected from the standard set and customized for a particular application. Given the ability of these tools to

Figure 2.7
UICAD 4,096-Color Backdrop Display

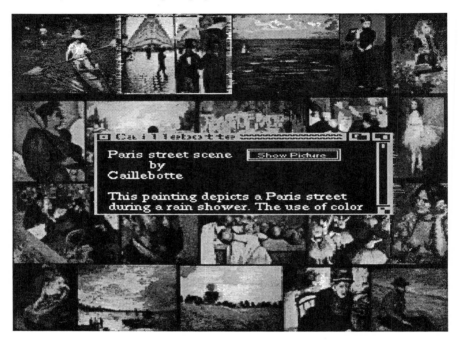

provide some degree of separation from the underlying functional portions of
an application and to modify and store interface elements, it is just a small step
to envision the end user employing them to ''tailor'' an interface to suit individual
preferences in screen layout, graphics, labeling of interactive objects, and so
on, without affecting the underlying application.

CONCLUSIONS

Frederic P. Brooks (1987) has suggested that there are no single solutions, or
''silver bullets,'' offering even an order of magnitude increase in the speed and
effectiveness of developing complex software systems. The tools discussed in
this chapter are but a few of the many partial solutions, which also include
Computer Aided Software Engineering (CASE) systems, application generators
(for restricted sets of problems), Structured Analysis tools, and Fourth-Generation Languages (4GL) for database systems. While these tools and techniques
may permit large portions of a system to be designed and implemented without
conventional programming, there comes a point where the tools' efficacy ends
and the programmer must take over.

What the tools examined here do offer is a vastly simplified approach to the

Figure 2.8
UICAD High Resolution Windows with Backdrop Images

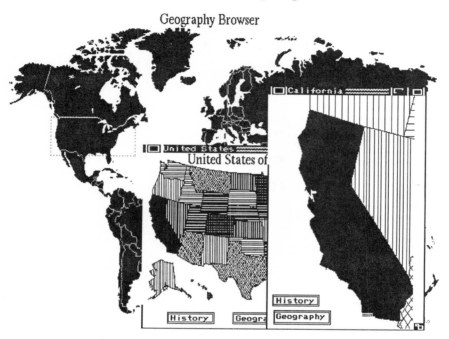

development and programming of direct-manipulation graphical interfaces. Any-one who has been through the process of programming a graphical interface can testify to the frustration of recompiling a program dozens of times to get the placement or colors of a button "just right." With the aid of these tools, the programmer can leave the layout and graphics of the interface to the analysts, graphic designers, and even end users most concerned with them, and concentrate on the functional aspects of the system. From the interface designer's point of view, these tools provide a method for rapidly defining the graphical elements of an interface, permitting the cycle of design, user-acceptance testing, and redesign to be carried out without having to deal with the many complexities of graphical interface programming.

REFERENCES

ACM SIGGRAPH. 1987. Workshop on Software Tools for User Interface Management. *Computer Graphics* 21: 71–147.

Apple Computer, Inc. 1985. *Inside Macintosh*. Reading, Mass.: Addison-Wesley.

Asente, Paul. 1988. Simplicity and Productivity. *UNIX Review* 6(9): 57–63.

Brooks, Frederick P. 1987. No Silver Bullet. *Computer* 20(4): 10–19.

Buxton, W., M. R. Lamb, D. Sherman, and K. C. Smith, 1983. Towards a Comprehensive User Interface Management System. *Computer Graphics* 17(3): 35–42.

Carroll, John M., and Sandra A. Mazur. 1986. LisaLearning. *IEEE Computer* 19(11): 35–49.

Cowlishaw, M. F. 1985. *The REXX Language: A Practical Approach to Programming*. Englewood Cliffs, N.J.: Prentice-Hall.

Fischer, Gerard. 1989. Human-Computer Interaction Software: Lessons Learned, Challenges Ahead. *IEEE Software* 6(1): 44–52.

Foley, James, W. C. Kim, S. Kovacevic, and K. Murray. 1989. Defining Interfaces at a High Level of Abstraction. *IEEE Software* 6(1): 25–32.

Goodman, Danny. 1987. *The Complete HyperCard Handbook*. New York: Bantam.

Hartson, Rex. 1989. User-Interface Management Control and Communication. *IEEE Software* 6(1): 62–70.

Hawes, William S. 1987. *AREXX User's Reference Manual Version 1.0: The REXX Language for the Amiga*. Maynard, Mass.: William S. Hawes.

Hill, Ralph D. 1987. Some Important Features and Issues in User Interface Management Systems. *Computer Graphics* 21(2): 116–20.

Hudson, Scott E. 1987. UIMS Support for Direct Manipulation Interfaces. *Computer Graphics* 21(2): 120–24.

Lewis, T. G., Fred Handloser III, Sharada Bove, and Sherry Yang. 1989. Prototypes from Standard User Interface Management Systems. *Computer* 22(5): 51–60.

Luqi. 1989. Software Evolution Through Rapid Prototyping. *Computer* 22(5): 13–25.

Mical, Robert J., and Susan Deyl. 1986. *Amiga Intuition Reference Manual*. Reading, Mass.: Addison-Wesley.

Mooers, C. N. 1960. Mooers Law or, Why Some Retrieval Systems Are Used and Others Are Not. *American Documentation* 11(3): ii.

Morris, J. H., M. Satyanarayanan, M. H. Conner, J. H. Howard, D.S.H. Rosenthal, and F. D. Smith. 1986. Andrew: A Distributed Personal Computing Environment. *Communications of the ACM* 29:184–201.

Myers, Brad A. 1988. A Taxonomy of Window Manager User Interfaces. *IEEE Computer Graphics and Applications* 8(5): 65–84.

———. 1989. User-Interface Tools: Introduction and Survey. *IEEE Software* 6(1): 15–23.

Nye, Adrian. 1988. *Xlib Programming Manual for Version 11 of the X Window System*. Newton, Mass.: O'Reilly and Associates.

Rosenthal, David S. 1988. Going for Baroque. *UNIX Review* 6(6): 70–79.

Rosson, Mary Beth, Susanne Maass, and Wendy A. Kellogg. 1988. The Designer as User: Building Requirements for Design Tools from Design Practice. *Communications of the ACM* 31:1288–98.

Scheifler, Robert W., and Jim Gettys. 1986. The X Window System. *ACM Transactions on Graphics* 5(2): 79–109.

Shneiderman, Ben. 1982. The Future of Interactive Systems and the Emergence of Direct Manipulation. *Behaviour and Information Technology* 1(3): 237–56.

———. 1987. *Designing the User Interface: Strategies for Effective Human-Computer Interaction*. Reading, Mass.: Addison-Wesley.

Stern, Hal L. 1987. Comparison of Window Systems. *Byte* 12(13): 265–72.

Tanik, Murat M., and Raymond T. Yeh. 1989. Rapid Prototyping in Software Development. (Guest Editors' Introduction). *Computer* 22(5): 9–10.

Thompson, Tom. 1989. The Next Step. *Byte* 14(3): 265–69.

3

Toward a Direct-Manipulation Interface for Conceptual Information Retrieval Systems

Daniel E. Rose and Richard K. Belew

A direct-manipulation interface for information retrieval (IR) systems allows users to treat the IR domain as a model world that they can examine and modify. We describe two IR systems, AIR and SCALIR, which share the property that the user has greater perception of and control over both the queries and the items retrieved. AIR, a conceptual information retrieval system based on a connectionist network, accomplishes this in two ways. First, it graphically displays all retrieval items, allowing the user to provide feedback simply by pointing at those to be pruned or explored further. Second, it retrieves related terms and authors as well as documents, so that the system's response to one query includes suggestions for other queries. SCALIR, an IR system for legal documents, incorporates many of AIR's features and adds symbolic inference mechanisms required by the legal domain. Legal researchers are interested in logical relationships between documents (e.g., one court decision reversing another) that are difficult to express in traditional IR systems. SCALIR allows users to ask about these relationships directly, by "drawing" their queries in the same window displaying the retrieval set. Together, these systems offer concrete steps toward a direct-manipulation interface, closing the gap between the user's intentions and the system's actions.

INTRODUCTION

In his book on user interface design, Shneiderman (1987) discusses several ideas for using a direct-manipulation approach for several tasks that traditionally had been performed with command or menu interfaces, or had not been feasible at all. One of his examples was bibliographic retrieval:

A basic system could be built by first showing the user a wall of labeled catalog index drawers. A cursor in the shape of a human hand might be moved over to the section labeled "Author Index" and to the drawer labeled "F–L." Depressing the button on the joystick or mouse would cause the drawer to open, revealing an array of index cards with tabs offerings a finer index. . . . Depressing the button while holding a card would cause a copy of the card to be made in the user's notebook, also represented on the screen. Entries in the notebook might be edited to create a printed bibliography or combined with other entries to perform set intersections or unions. (Shneiderman, 1987, 206)

At first glance, these ideas have some immediate appeal. The user is presented with visual representations of familiar objects—drawers and cards from a card catalog—that can be directly moved about on the screen in a manner analogous to using their real-world referents. The user does not have to learn the syntax of a new system and translate this to the task at hand.

What is wrong with this approach? One way to understand the problem is by examining Shneiderman's model of user knowledge. He divides user knowledge into two categories, semantic and syntactic. Semantic knowledge is further divided into task knowledge and computer knowledge. The problem with the card catalog model is that there are actually two kinds of syntax,[1] just like the two kinds of semantics, and we have simply replaced a focus on computer syntax with a focus on task syntax. In other words, rather than using ideas about the task *semantics* (the concept of retrieving information stored in documents by finding relevant points to them), we are using ideas about *the way the task has been traditionally performed*—its syntax. Just as the use of a typewriter as an analogy for word processing is as often harmful as helpful (Card, Moran, and Newell, 1983), restricting our notion of IR browsing to those dimensions currently supported by the library's (physical) card catalog limits our design of electronic systems unnecessarily.[2] In short, the task, not features of our current tools for accomplishing it, should drive the design of the system.

In this chapter we describe two information retrieval systems, AIR and SCA-LIR, whose designs are consistent with the approach. In each case, the system attempts to accomplish the user's goals. How easily this can be done depends on both the system's representation of the problem and its interface.

Shneiderman gives several examples of what he considers direct-manipulation interfaces and then attempts to define the term:

Each example has features that can be criticized, but it seems more productive to construct an integrated portrait of direct manipulation:

- Continuous representation of the objects and actions of interest

- Physical actions or labeled button presses instead of complex syntax

- Rapid incremental, reversible operations whose impact on the object of interest is immediately visible (Shneiderman, 1987, 201)

While every system is different, these features seem to form the core of what most researchers mean by direct manipulation. Nevertheless, these characterizations are subject to individual interpretation, and it is not surprising that several authors introduce the concept by giving examples of it.

In the following sections we describe the AIR and SCALIR systems, focusing on their interfaces, and then examine whether our systems exhibit the three features of direct manipulation—and whether they should.

AIR

The AIR[3] system represents a connectionist approach to the IR problem, demonstrating that this is a reasonable representation for the task and showing that this representation allows AIR to learn. Our current implementation operates on a collection of approximately 1,500 bibliographic citations to documents on the subject of artificial intelligence (AI). A simple heuristic is used to assign initial keywords to each of these citations, and then the documents' citations, their authors, and the keywords are represented in a connectionist network. Initially, the only knowledge AIR has about a document is its title and authors. AIR uses feedback from its users (i.e., whether the documents retrieved were relevant or not) to change its representation of authors, index terms, and documents so that, over time, AIR improves at its task. AIR's goal is to build a representation that will retrieve documents that are more likely to be relevant to particular queries. Details of the system's representation and learning algorithm and our experiments with human subjects are reported elsewhere (Belew, 1986; 1987).

Users begin a session with AIR by describing their information need using a very simple query language. A query is composed of one or more clauses. Each clause can refer to one of the three types of "features" represented in AIR's network: keywords, documents, or authors; and all but the first clause in the query can be negated. This query causes "activity" to be placed on nodes in AIR's network corresponding to the features named in the query. This activity is allowed to propagate throughout the network, and the system's response is the set of nodes that become most active during this propagation. Figure 3.1 shows AIR's response to a typical query: (((:TERM "ASSOCIATIVE") (:AUTH "ANDERSON, J.A."))).

This is the network of keywords, documents, and authors considered relevant to this query. The nodes are drawn as a tripartite graph, with keywords on the top level, documents in the middle, and authors on the bottom. Associative links that helped to cause a node to become retrieved (and only those links) are also displayed. Heavier lines imply stronger weights. AIR uses directed links, and this directionality is represented by the concavity of the arcs; a clockwise convention is used. For example, a link from a document node (in the middle level) to a keyword node (in the top level) goes clockwise, around to the left.

Actually, this is only a picture of the *final state* of the system's retrieval. The network is actually drawn *incrementally*; the first nodes to become significantly active are drawn first and in the middle of the pane. As additional nodes become

Figure 3.1
AIR Interface

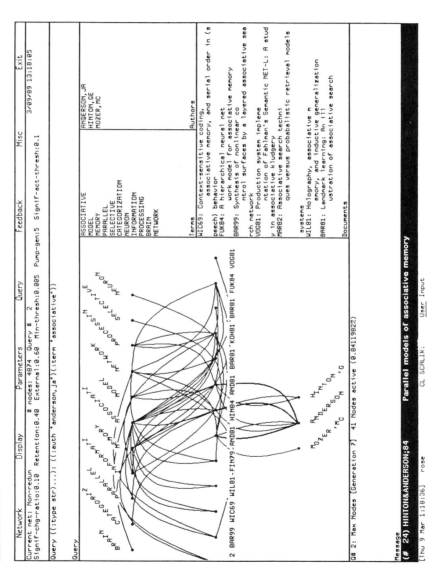

Source: Symbolics, Inc.

active at significant levels, they are drawn farther out along the three horizontal axes, and links through which they became active are drawn as well. We believe this dynamic display has at least two real advantages. First, the fact that AIR provides the first part of its retrieval almost immediately means that the user is not impatiently waiting for the retrieval to complete (typically 5–10 seconds in this implementation). Second, displaying the query's dynamics helps to give the user a tangible feeling of direct engagement; the user "prods" the network in a certain place and then watches as waves of activity flow outward from that place. Not only does this make AIR's results easily comprehensible, but it is also an excellent example of making the "impact" of user queries "immediately visible," as Shneiderman suggests.

Also, the regions immediately around each node are made "mouse sensitive" so that when the user puts the mouse near a node, more information about that node becomes visible in the "Who" line at the bottom of the screen. The additional information is most useful for document nodes. These nodes are labeled with only a brief "citation" string: the first three letters of the first author's name are concatenated with the last two digits of the year of publication. The "Who" line shows both a complete citation (i.e., full names of all authors) and the title of the document. For keywords and authors, this information is simply the full keyword or author's name, which may have been truncated on the node's label.

Relevance Feedback

Queries subsequent to the first are performed much differently. After AIR is done retrieving the network of features, the user responds with *relevance feedback*, indicating which features are considered (by that user) relevant to the query and which are not. Using a mouse, the user marks features with the symbols + +, +, − and − −, indicating that the feature was Very Relevant, Relevant, Irrelevant, or Very Irrelevant, respectively. Not all features need to be commented upon.

The system constructs a new query directly from this feedback. First, terms from the previous query are retained. Positively marked features are added to this query, as are the negated versions of features marked negatively. Equal weight is placed on each of these features, except that features marked Very Relevant or Very Irrelevant are doubly weighted.

From the perspective of retrieval, this relevance feedback becomes a form of browsing: positively marked features are directions that the user wants to pursue, and negatively marked features are directions that should be pruned from the search. This is perhaps AIR's strongest claim to having a direct-manipulation interface. For all but their first query, users are allowed to operate directly on features (keywords, authors, documents) of the "model world" of the IR task.

Although not central to our discussion here (but see Belew, 1987), it is also worth mentioning that from the perspective of learning, this relevance feedback will be exactly the *training signal* AIR needs to modify its representations through learning. This unification of learning (i.e., changing representations) and doing (i.e., browsing) was a central component of AIR's design. It means that the collection of feedback is not an onerous, additional task for the user, but a natural part of the retrieval process.

Comparison with Conventional IR Methods

AIR's feature query language is somewhat unusual because it is not strictly Boolean. No provision is made for the traditional Boolean connectives AND and OR. Salton calls this a "simple" query (Salton and McGill, 1983). It can be shown that these Boolean connectives are not missed (Belew, 1986, sec. 5.2). Briefly, the difference between AND and OR is a matter of degree,[4] and AIR's weighted, connectionist representation includes these two Boolean operators as special cases of a much richer class of potential interactions among features. Hence, a user searching for relevant documents can do the best he or she can describing *features* of the set in which they are interested, without needing to use Boolean constructs that may require more precision (or training) than is appropriate. AIR's feature language asks for less rigor, but generates retrievals that turn out to be a natural generalization of Boolean-like languages.

It can be shown that the "distance metric" imposed over documents, keywords, and authors by AIR's connectionist representation provides a total ordering over these features (Belew, 1989). As a consequence, AIR is able to make the size of its retrieval almost constant, independent of the query. This stands in marked contrast to the "feast or famine" retrievals of most IR systems.

Another difference is that the "input-output channel" from and to users has been widened by the AIR system. Typically, queries to IR systems are composed of keywords; it is also common to be able to specify authors of interest. But AIR also follows specification of documents in a query. The provision of this sort of "query by example" seems a very useful extension to the query language.[5]

The result of AIR's retrieval is even more uncommon. The traditional result of an IR query is only documents (or more typically, citations to or proxies of documents). While this is AIR's major output as well, the system also provides keywords and authors. Keywords retrieved in this manner are considered "related terms" that users may use to expand on their searches. Retrieved authors are considered to be closely linked to the subject of interest. It could be argued that these keywords and authors have no intrinsic value but are useful only to the extent that they ultimately lead to relevant documents. However, there are many ways in which a user might find related terms and centrally involved authors a valuable information product in their own right. For example, if a user wants to pursue a search in other information systems (such as a traditional library), these additional cues can be very useful. The fact that users had no more difficulty judging the relevance of keywords and authors than they did judging documents supports this view (Belew, 1986, sec. 7.3.2).

SCALIR

SCALIR[6] is an IR system for retrieving cases about copyright law. Internally, SCALIR contains a network of nodes representing terms, court decisions, and statute sections. A query consists of the activation of a few selected nodes. This activation spreads through the network; sufficiently activated nodes form the retrieval set. The user can then display the text associated with any of the retrieved cases or statutes.

Figure 3.2 shows the display screen of the prototype SCALIR interface. Below the title is a command menu. This menu need never be invoked by the user during normal searching; it primarily contains housekeeping operations (such as saving results to a file). The large window at the left, similar to AIR's, is the heart of the interface. Active nodes and their relationships are shown here. At right is a text window, which shows the text of the currently selected document.

SCALIR's design was largely influenced by AIR. Like AIR, SCALIR's underlying mechanism is spreading activation through a network of nodes. Both systems include some nodes for terms and some for documents; both systems allow all types of nodes to appear both as query items and retrieved items. SCALIR shares AIR's display of the network and the connections between its nodes. In both systems, users directly manipulate the representations on the screen to give the system relevance feedback used both for forming future queries and for learning. In short, SCALIR has adopted the basic AIR paradigm for information retrieval. Nevertheless, there are significant differences between the systems at both the conceptual and the implementational levels, and some of these will be described in the remainder of this section.

Symbolic Relationships in Legal Research

A major issue motivating the SCALIR design was the nature of browsing behavior in manual (noncomputerized) information retrieval. In the legal domain, there is at least anecdotal evidence that the users—law professionals in general, and attorneys in particular—are extremely dissatisfied with existing online retrieval systems. They seem to prefer using the various bound resources, such as the court reporters, the topically organized digests of West Publishing Co., and the citation-listing Shepard's indexes.[7] Some of the manual searching takes the form of seeing ''subsymbolic'' relationships, such as noticing that the case next to the one being studied is relevant. More often, however, the chain of research (or ''spread of activation'') is more directed. For example, the user might look up a case because it overruled the decision of another case. Three specific types of these symbolic relationships have been incorporated into SCALIR:

Figure 3.2
The SCALIR Display

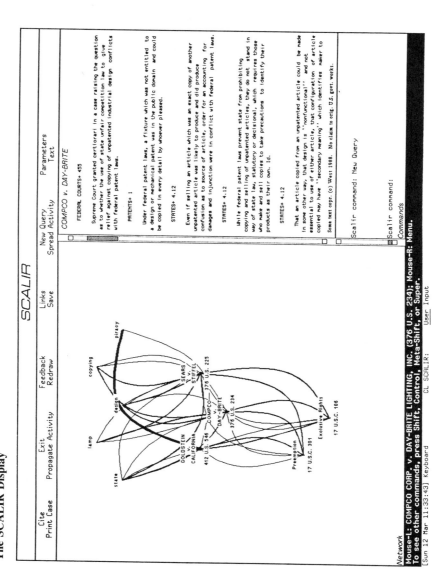

Source: Symbolics, Inc.

Citation relationships, which exist only between cases. There are many ways to classify a citation; the best known is the system used by Shepard's Index. Shepard's describes citations with "treatment phrases" such as harmonized, distinguished, criticized, and so on.[8] These might be used, for example, if an opposing lawyer in litigation is known to base his or her reasoning on a certain court decision, in which case one might wish to examine other decisions which criticized it. Case nodes in SCALIR are connected by labeled citation links.

Taxonomic relationships. These exist between terms and correspond to the taxonomy of the law provided by the West Publishing's well-known Key Numbering scheme. In SCALIR, term nodes, which represent Key numbers, are related by these taxonomic links. In copyright law, an example would be the breakdown of "subjects of copyright" into "Literary works; writings," "Pictorial, graphic, and sculptural works," and so on.

Structural relationships, which occur between statute sections, form the final type. These simply describe the hierarchical structure of a complex document; Title 17 of the United States Code contains Sections 100 through 914, Section 106 is subject to Sections 107 through 118, and so on. These are very similar to taxonomic relationships; in SCALIR they connect statute nodes.

The SCALIR network is formed by the superposition of these three types of symbolic relationships onto an AIR-like associative network.

Supporting Symbolic Relationships

Viewed from an IR perspective, several problems emerge that must be confronted if the system is to include symbolic relationships. We shall examine three of these and describe how they are handled in SCALIR.

The first problem is representation. How does the system represent these logical relationships internally? A homogeneous connectionist network works for the associative retrieval task, but it is not well suited for representing explicit symbolic relationships. The issue of representation is complex, and we have discussed it in some detail elsewhere (Rose and Belew, 1989). For the purposes of this chapter it suffices to say that SCALIR actually uses two interleaved networks to store and retrieve information: a connectionist network for simple associative relationships and a symbolic network for "logical" relationships.

The second problem is presentation. How does the system present the relationships to the user in a clear and understandable fashion? In the associative task, nodes are either related or they are not. This is easy to show in a graphic display of the network; more complex relationships are more difficult to present clearly. For presentation, SCALIR displays the network of nodes with user-controllable levels of internode relationships. Each type of relationship—for example, the different types of citations described above—is displayed as a different type of line (e.g., dotted, dashed). Color may be used for this purpose in future versions of the program.

The third problem is access. How can the user access the relationships in order to form more powerful queries? Users should be able to retrieve documents on the basis of specific relationships, without having to use a cumbersome query language. Most end users are uncomfortable with even Boolean connectives, and commercial IR systems often go to extremes to keep their query languages simple, even at the expense of reduced system functionality.

The access problem is perhaps the most difficult. SCALIR solves it by eliminating the notion of a query language entirely. Even the initial query step used in AIR is omitted. When a user begins a SCALIR research session, the system presents a set of dummy nodes for terms, cases, and statute sections. Selecting a node (moving the mouse pointer over until the node is highlighted with a box, then clicking) normally brings the text associated with that node to the text window. When the node is a dummy node, it will instead allow the user to fill in the appropriate values for Plaintiff, Defendant, and so on (see figure 3.3). This is reminiscent of the query-by-example model used in some database management systems.

So far, we have shown how users can do spreading-activation queries without a query language. Recall that the user must also be able to query about the special symbolic relationships. To solve this, SCALIR takes another step in the direction of the direct-manipulation interface: the user "draws" the relationships to be examined. "Dragging" the mouse from one node to another causes a link to be displayed between them; the different link types (presented as different line types) can be selected from a palette that also serves as the key.

The Role of the Text

As mentioned earlier, SCALIR's display of retrieved items as a network of nodes follows the similar technique used in AIR. But SCALIR differs in its simultaneous use of text. Legal researchers require full-text retrieval. Traditional legal IR systems provide this, but they do not allow users to view simultaneously the set of documents retrieved and the text of one of those documents. SCALIR overcomes this limitation. At any time during a session, a user can simply select a node (with the mouse) from among those visible in the network window. The text of the case immediately appears in the text window. The window is scrollable, so the user can move through it at leisure, returning to earlier portions of the document as desired. Figure 3.2 shows the SCALIR screen with the text of the selected document in the right-hand window.

In fact, SCALIR's text window is not a single window at all, but rather a series of overlapping windows. Each time the user wants to examine a new document, a window for that document's text is created and brought to the foreground of the text window region. As figure 3.2 shows, the window is labeled with the name of the case so that the user will not be disoriented if the top part of the text (containing the names of the litigants) has been scrolled off the screen. When a user selects a node whose text has been displayed previously, the system simply brings its next window to the foreground. This makes response

Figure 3.3
Dummy Nodes Used to Initiate Search

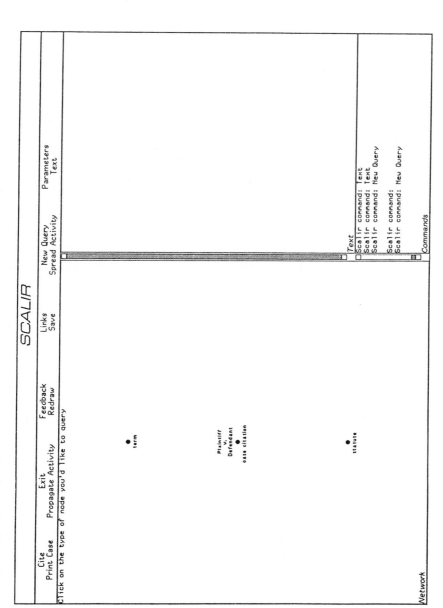

Source: Symbolics, Inc.

time almost instantaneous. As an additional feature, the user can select from a temporary menu of all text windows viewed so far.

DISCUSSION: THE ROLE OF THE DMI

Assessing Directions

We have discussed three features commonly used to characterize direct-manipulation interfaces. It is now useful to compare the results of the AIR and SCALIR interface design decisions with Shneiderman's criteria for the direct manipulation paradigm.

Continuous representation of the objects and actions of interest. The first question one must consider is, What are the objects of interest? In our systems, we believe that the objects of interest are not the retrieval tools (file drawers and index cards), but rather the documents being retrieved, features which they have in common (e.g., authors and terms), and the relationships between them. All of these are graphically displayed as long as they are active.

What about the representation of objects not currently active? In our systems, these are not visible. There is no analogue to a closed file drawer or other indication that there are more items available than those currently being examined. On the other hand, one might argue that only those active enough to be displayed are "objects of interest."

Physical actions or labeled button presses instead of complex syntax. AIR, designed to explore the associative retrieval approach to IR, contains what might be described as a "complex syntax" for initial query formulation. As discussed earlier, SCALIR replaces this with a technique similar to query-by-example. In both systems, however, much of the user's interaction—the browsing behavior—takes the form of moving a mouse pointer to selected nodes and clicking to indicate a desire to expand or prune the search further in those directions. SCALIR allows users to "open" a document by clicking on its node. While some unwieldy aspects may need improvement (such as model mouse-clicks), our systems are basically consistent with this criterion.

Rapid incremental, reversible operations whose impact on the object of interest is immediately visible. These are really distinct features; we will consider each separately. All operations in SCALIR and nearly all[9] operations in AIR produce immediate visible feedback. Those operations that concern user specification of the task (query formulation, relevance feedback) are reversible. In general, however, the primary IR task operation—retrieval—is neither incremental nor reversible. There are three reasons for this. First, since the system learns from experience, the user cannot "undo" a search the way one might undo a deletion in a text editor or an update in a spreadsheet. Second, since the IR task is viewed as the continual refinement of an ongoing exploration of the space of documents, there isn't really anything to undo. Third (in SCALIR), relevance in new searches depends on activity accumulated from previous searches. For these reasons, our systems are incompatible with the reversibility feature of a direct-manipulation interface.

It is worth pointing out that one of the most often cited examples—video games—also lacks the incremental/reversible feature. Time progresses forward, beyond the user's control, and spaceships destroyed cannot be undestroyed and moved to a safer location. As we will explain in the next section, if the model world is fundamentally dynamic, reversibility is not always an attainable (or desirable) goal.

The Model Worlds of AIR and SCALIR

Consider the general task of information retrieval. The user's goals are simple: to locate and/or retrieve documents relevant to (about) a particular topic of interest. Only one component is fixed: the existence and structure of the documents themselves. The other aspects of the problem—the form of the retrieval, how relevance will be defined, how the topics of interest will be expressed, and so on—are variables that are determined by the particular system and the particular user. A reasonable strategy for an IR system is to "instantiate" those variables (that is, make decisions about each of them) in order to provide a model world of the domain that the user can examine and modify.

Since the user's goal is to find documents about a topic, it is this "aboutness" that the system must model, and this model that the user must manipulate. In AIR, an article is originally classified as being "about" its author(s) and the terms mentioned in its title. Eventually, it learns a richer representation of what a document is about (as well as the "meanings" of terms and authors) by incorporating feedback from (and thus knowledge of) its users. Similarly, SCA-LIR's cases are originally about the terms, the other cases they cite, and the cases that cite them. This representation is also improved upon automatically by users.

This method for constructing the critical "aboutness" relation leads to a specific notion of semantics that underlines both our systems (we have expanded this argument elsewhere [Belew and Rose, 1989]). We will claim that the conventional IR model assumes an *omniscient* notion of relevance; that is, with respect to any query there is assumed to exist a single, well-defined set of "relevant" documents against which the retrieval of the IR system is compared, using measures such as recall, precision, and fallout for evaluation. When these evaluations are actually made, the relevant set is typically identified by some prima facie expert. Not only are such evaluations expensive and problematic for IR systems of realistic scale, but more to our point they are in fact *only the opinion of one person*. While this one person is, by definition, particularly well qualified to make these determinations in terms of knowledge of the domain, it can also be argued that they are also anomalous users when compared with the typically novice users of most IR systems. In short, one expert's opinion is not enough on which to base a notion of relevance.

We seek instead to build a *consensual* notion of relevance. While it is possible to envision versions of our systems that learn the idiosyncratic vocabulary of any one user, we prefer to consider situations in which our systems develop representations of the shared semantics of some group. Our learning mechanisms make only the smallest changes in response to any one user's opinions (or relevance). Only when many users manifest similar semantic interpretations of keywords and documents do these commonalities become encoded in our representations.

Obviously, then, our methods are sensitive to the group selected to train the system; we see this as an advantage. Different groups can each develop their own repositories of shared knowledge. Perhaps the clearest example of this is when SCALIR's group of users comes from within a single law firm. There is a strong tradition for a firm to build a collective expertise that becomes a shared resource for all lawyers in that firm. SCALIR's adaptive mechanisms will help extend this sharing activity to indices into the legal literature that the firm has found useful.

As we have discussed earlier, there are several ways in which users of our systems directly manipulate their model worlds. Users can point to representations of documents or terms and express their interest in them with relevant feedback. They can view the propagation of activity from one document to another, and they can observe the path that linked two nodes. They can use the responses from one retrieval as the query of another. In SCALIR, they can also "open" a document, examine its text, and "draw" the desired relationships to be pursued.

Yet the system does more than model the domain in the traditional sense. In AIR and SCALIR, users participate in the continual refinement of the model. Like any characteristic of a computer system, there are trade-offs involved with the use of this dynamic model. One of the costs is that user actions aren't reversible, for the system must learn from false starts and wrong turns just as it does from positive results. In the long run, however, we believe that the benefits are stronger: the system learns to meet the needs of the user.

CONCLUSIONS

Near the end of their assessment of direct-manipulation interfaces, Hutchins, Hollan, and Norman point out some of the dangers of limited design strategies: "If we restrict ourselves to only building interfaces that allow us to do things we can already do and to think in ways we already think, we will miss the most exciting potential of new technology: to provide new ways to think of and to interact with a domain" (Hutchins, Hollan, and Norman, 1986, 118). This sentiment parallels our views in the design of AIR and SCALIR. We agree with many of the virtues of the direct-manipulation interface, and we have attempted to incorporate them into our systems. There is room for improvement, hence the "toward" of our title. Yet the primary risk is to help the user achieve his or her goals the best way possible, not to follow an interface formula. Our systems may not have all the features of direct-manipulation interfaces, but we believe this is a small price to pay for the use of new and more powerful techniques for information retrieval.

NOTES

We would like to thank West Publishing Co. for making their data available to us for use in the section on SCALIR.

1. This model was designed to describe how people program computers; in that case, perhaps the unified notion of syntax is appropriate.

2. Or, in the legal domain, a set of court reporters, digests, citation index, volume, and the West key-numbering system.

3. Adaptive Information Retrieval.

4. This insight goes back to von Neumann.

5. Mike Mozer first made this important observation with respect to his connectionist IR system (Mozer, 1984).

6. Symbolic and Connectionist Approach to Legal Information Retrieval.

7. Shepard's is a registered trademark of Shepard's division of McGraw-Hill.

8. There are also citations that deal simply with the history of the case; for example, whether a decision was overturned on appeal.

9. The exceptions are the mode-changing operations.

REFERENCES

Belew, R. K. 1986. *Adaptive Information Retrieval: Machine Learning in Associative Networks*. Ph.D. diss., University of Michigan.

———. 1987. "Designing Appropriate Learning Rules for Connectionist Systems." In *Proceedings of the IEEE First International Conference on Neural Networks, San Diego, Calif., June 21–24, 1984*, ed. M. Candill and C. Butler, vol.2, 479–86. San Diego, Calif.: SOS Printing.

———. 1989. "Adaptive Information Retrieval: Using a Connectionist Representation to Retrieve and Learn About Documents." In *SIGIR '89: Proceedings of the Twelfth Annual International Conference on Research and Development in Information Retrieval, Cambridge, MA, June 25–28, 1989*, ed. N. J. Belkin and C. J. van Rijsbergen. New York: Association for Computing Machinery.

Belew, R. K. and Rose, D. E. 1989. "Learning Semantics from Word Use." Unpublished paper.

Card, S. K., Moran, T. P., and Newell, A. 1983. *The Psychology of Human-Computer Interaction*. Hillsdale, N.J.: Lawrence Erlbaum Associates.

Hutchins, E. L., Hollan, J. D., and Norman, D. A. 1986. "Direct-Manipulation Interfaces." In *User Centered System Design: New Perspectives on Human-Computer Interaction*, ed. D. A. Norman and S. W. Draper. Hillsdale, N.J.: Lawrence Erlbaum Associates.

Mozer, M. C. 1984. "Inductive Information Retrieval Using Parallel Distributed Computation." *Technical Report 8406*. La Jolla, Calif.: Institute for Cognitive Science, UCSD.

Rose, Daniel E. and Belew, Richard K. 1989. ''Legal Information Retrieval: A Hybrid Approach.'' In *The Second International Conference on Artificial Intelligence and Law*, 138–46. New York: Association for Computing Machinery.

Salton, G. and McGill, M. 1983. *Introduction to Modern Information Retrieval*. New York: McGraw-Hill.

Shneiderman, B. 1987. *Designing the User Interface: Strategies for Effective Human-Computer Interaction*. Reading, Mass.: Addison-Wesley.

4

The Berry-Picking Search: User Interface Design

Marcia J. Bates

A "berry-picking" model of searching is presented and contrasted with the classic information retrieval model. This model is said to represent real human searches of information stores more accurately than the traditional model does. Implications of the new model are briefly considered for online information system interface design, browsing capabilities, the relationships between human and machine effort in conducting information searches, and testing.

INTRODUCTION

The classic model of information retrieval (IR) used in information science research for over 25 years is characterized in figure 4.1. This model has been very productive and has promoted our understanding of information retrieval in many ways. However, it has come under increasing criticism in recent years, as further research has revealed its inadequacies (see Oddy, 1977; Belkin, Oddy, and Brooks, 1982; Bates, 1986a; Ellis, 1984).

This chapter presents another model of information retrieval, which, it is argued, is a more realistic representation of human information searching. Now that we can develop information retrieval systems with extraordinarily ingenious and powerful capabilities, we have the opportunity to design such systems so that they really allow people to search as they naturally do. It is consequently very important to develop an IR model that is as realistic a representation of human searching as possible.

In the next section of this chapter, the berry-picking model of IR is presented. In the third section, some implications of this model are drawn for interface design, browsing, the relationship between human and machine effort, and testing. Some conclusions follow.

Figure 4.1
The Classic Information Retrieval Model

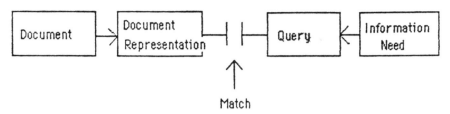

Match

THE BERRY-PICKING MODEL

Let us first take a closer look at the classic model. Fundamental to it is the idea of a single query presented by the user, matched to the database contents, yielding a single output set. Gerard Salton (1968) contributed to research in this area by developing the idea of iterative feedback to improve output. He developed a system that would modify the set of terms used in the query formulation based on user feedback to the preliminary output set. The formulation would be improved successively through the use of feedback on user document preferences until recall and precision were optimized.

But Salton's iterative feedback is still well within the original classic model as presented in figure 4.1, because the presumption is that the information need leading to the query is the same—unchanged throughout—no matter what the user might learn from the documents in the preliminary retrieved set. In fact, to change the query after seeing some documents would be "unfair," a violation of the basic design of the experiment. The point of the feedback is to improve the representation of a static need, not to change the need itself. So throughout the process of information retrieval evaluation under the classic model, the query is treated as a single, one-time conception of the problem. Although this assumption is useful for simplifying IR system research, real-life searches frequently do not work this way.

In real-life searches in manual sources, end users may begin with just one feature of a broader topic, or just one relevant reference, and move through a variety of sources. New information encountered during the search may yield new ideas and directions to follow and, consequently, a new conception of the query. At each stage, users are not just modifying the search terms used in order to get a better match for a single query. Rather, the query itself (as well as the search terms used) is continually shifting, in part or in whole. This type of search is here called an *evolving search*.

Furthermore, at each stage, with each different conception of the query, the user may identify useful information and references. In other words, the query is satisfied not by a single, final retrieved set, but by a series of selections of individual references and bits of information at each stage of the ever-modifying

Figure 4.2
A Berry-Picking, Evolving Search

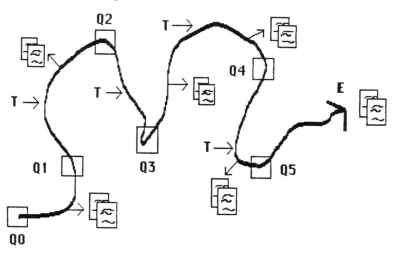

Q = query variation
T = thought
E = exit
= documents, information

search. A bit-at-a-time retrieval of this sort is here called *berry picking*. This term is used by analogy to picking huckleberries or blueberries in the forest. The berries are scattered on the bushes; they do not come in bunches. One must pick them out one at a time. One could do berry-picking of information without the search need itself changing (evolving), but in this chapter attention is given to searches that combine both of these features. Figure 4.2 represents a berry-picking, evolving search. In figure 4.3 the size of the picture is reduced to show the context within which the search takes place.

The focus of the classic model in figure 4.1 is the match between the document and query representations. The focus of the model in figures 4.2 and 4.3 is the sequence of searcher behaviors. The continuity represented by the line of the arrow is the continuity of a single human being moving through many actions toward a general goal of the satisfactory completion of research related to an information need. The changes in direction of the arrow illustrate the changes of an evolving search as the individual follows up various leads and shifts in

Figure 4.3
Context of Berry-Picking Search

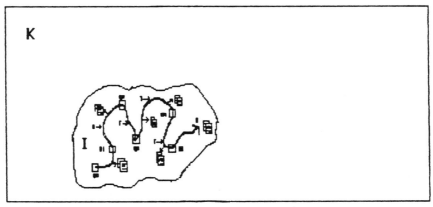

K = uniuerse of knowledge
I = uniuerse of interest

thinking. The diagram also shows documents and information being produced from the search at many points along the way, that is, through berry-picking. In the case of a straightforward, single-match search of the classic sort, we can think of the arrow as being short and straight, with a single query and a single information output set.

There is ample evidence of the popularity of searches of the evolving/berry-picking sort. Reviews of research by Line (1974), Hogeweg-de Haart (1984), Stone (1982), and Stoan (1984) attest to the popularity of this approach in a variety of environments, particularly in the social sciences and humanities. Recent empirical research by Ellis (1989) on social scientists continues to support and amplify the results of earlier studies. While the research reviewed here refers largely to academics. I would suggest that many searches by people in many contexts other than the academic one can be better characterized by the berry-picking/evolving model than by the classic IR model. The sources consulted may differ, but the process is similar.

IMPLICATIONS FOR INTERFACE DESIGN

How might these approaches be incorporated into modern information retrieval systems? In this section several suggestions are made regarding various aspects of system and interface design to allow berry picking.

Interface Design

Some suggestions for interface design follow:

- hypertext approaches appear tailor-made for berry-picking searching (Conklin, 1987);
- berry picking frequently requires the capability of seeing substantial quantities of information on the screen at once. Screens used should be high-definition for easy reading and scanning; and
- the interface design should make it easy to highlight or otherwise flag information and references to be sent to a temporary store. Said store can then be printed out when the searcher is ready to leave off searching. The necessity otherwise to write information down by hand before moving on would drastically lengthen and stall the search.

Browsing

The berry-picking model should change our ideas about browsing. Much of what is transpiring in a berry-picking search can be characterized as exploratory. At some points while searching, the user wants simply to be exposed to information that may possibly be of benefit. Interface design should make it easy for searchers to follow trails when they do not know where they will lead; that is, the searcher should not always have to state what information or topic is wanted, but instead may scan classification trees, follow ''see also'' references on an infinite regress through the subject thesaurus, or scan journal contents from a fairly arbitrary starting point. Some suggested designs for exploratory searching appear in Bates (1986a, 1986b).

Relationship Between Human and Machine Effort

The berry-picking model also carries implications about the relationship between human and machine effort in IR system design. A widespread assumption to date appears to be that our goal is to automate as much as possible of the IR process—that we want to be able to say to the system (forget typing!): ''Get me everything on the effects of nifedipine on heart function,'' or ''Get me everything on the causes of the Vietnamese invasion of Cambodia,'' and the system thereupon produces a perfect yield.

Many times users will want just that, namely, that the system do it all for them. But many other times they will not. Compare automobile transmissions: some people like automatic shifts; others insist on stick shifts. There are advantages to both. A similar situation exists with cameras: some people want the camera to do everything for them; others want to set the parameters by hand. Some people even own both types of cameras and use them at different times for different needs.

Particularly in the case of the evolving search, people generally want to follow their own noses, to go up side trails as the whim strikes them. Many researchers, particularly in the social sciences and humanities, would be horrified at the idea of any system making the judgments about information that they feel only they can and should make. That group can include the weekend history buff using a CD-ROM product at the local public library, too.

We may even conclude that some aspects of IR should not be automated at all, or at least not in some systems, even if we know how. After all, we do not have automatic hairbrushes, even though the technology is surely adequate to design such things. Some things people like to do for themselves. In the design of IR systems we should work to find the best mix between human capabilities and preferences on the one hand, and system capabilities on the other hand. We may find that for some types of searches at least, we want to keep some choices in the searcher's hands, even when the system can be designed to do that work for him or her (see also Bates, 1986c).

Testing

In various forums where early fragments of these ideas on berry picking have been discussed, Gerard Salton, with whom this discussion began, has criticized the approach on grounds that it is not testable—that it is much too fluid to test properly, and that variables cannot be controlled and varied systematically. But this model is not untestable; it just requires different research methods from those used to date with the more familiar model. Behavioral science methods using observation and verbal input from human beings are needed. The model is built around human behavior, and well-established methods for studying that behavior need to be brought to bear on the problem.

CONCLUSIONS

There are dozens of IR systems under development or being implemented that contain features that make berry-picking/evolving searches possible to at least some degree. I will not attempt to review them here. I suggest, however, that modern information retrieval system design should be motivated by a more realistic and representative model than the classic IR model. Such a model will promote a better understanding of the process being designed for, foster creativity in design, and make possible a more systematic testing of all the real variables that are operating in human search behavior in automated IR systems. The ideas presented here represent an attempt, if still inadequate, to provide such a realistic model.

REFERENCES

Bates, Marcia J. 1986a. "An Exploratory Paradigm for Online Information Retrieval." In *Intelligent Information Systems for the Information Society: Proceedings of the Sixth International Research Forum in Information Science (IRFIS 6), Frascati, Italy, September 16–18, 1985*, ed. B. C. Brookes, 91–99. New York: Elsevier.
———. 1986b. "Subject Access in Online Catalogs: A Design Model." *Journal of the American Society for Information Science* 37 (November): 357–76.
———. 1986c. "Terminological Assistance for the Online Subject Searcher." In *Pro-*

ceedings of the Second Conference on Computer Interfaces and Intermediaries for Information Retrieval, Boston, MA, May 28–31, 1986, 285–93. Defense Technical Information Center and M.I.T. Alexandria, Va.: Defense Technical Information Center, Office of Information Systems and Technology. Report no. NTIS/TR–86/5.

Belkin, N. J., Oddy, R. N., and Brooks, H. M. 1982. "ASK for Information Retrieval: Part I: Background and Theory." *Journal of Documentation* 38 (June): 61–71.

Conklin, Jeff. 1987. *A Survey of Hypertext.* Austin, Tex.: Microelectronics and Computer Technology Corporation, MCC Technical Report no. STP–356–86, Rev. 2, December 3, 1987.

Ellis, David. 1984. "Theory and Explanation in Information Retrieval Research." *Journal of Information Science* 8 (February): 25–38.

———. 1989. "A Behavioural Approach to Information Retrieval System Design." *Journal of Documentation* 45(3): 171–212.

Hogeweg-de Haart, H. P. 1984. "Characteristics of Social Science Information: A Selective Review of the Literature. Part II." *Social Science Information Studies* 4: 15–30.

Line, Maurice B. 1974. "Information Requirements in Social Sciences." In *Access to the Literature of the Social Sciences and Humanities.* Proceedings of the Conference on Access to Knowledge and Information in the Social Sciences and Humanities, 146–58. Library Science Dept., Queens College, CUNY. New York: Queens College Press.

Oddy, R. N. 1977. "Information Retrieval Through Man-Machine Dialogue." *Journal of Documentation* 33 (March): 1–14.

Salton, Gerard. 1968. *Automatic Information Organization and Retrieval.* New York: McGraw-Hill.

Stoan, Stephen K. 1984. "Research and Library Skills: An Analysis and Interpretation." *College & Research Libraries* 45 (March): 99–109.

Stone, Sue. 1982. "Humanities Scholars: Information Needs and Uses." *Journal of Documentation* 38 (December): 292–312.

PART II _____

ARTIFICIAL INTELLIGENCE AND THE USER INTERFACE

Amy J. Warner

Formerly, bibliographic retrieval systems placed the responsibility for learning and adapting on the searcher instead of the computer system. This seemed appropriate given the available technology at the time, the relatively small number of systems to learn, and the intended market, which assumed an expert human intermediary. Online catalogs, on the other hand, were never intended to be used by anyone other than an end user.

Experiences with end-user searching of online catalogs and increasing numbers of bibliographic retrieval systems revealed a need for tools that would enable end users to interact with a system without requiring them to learn the specific protocols and designs of these diverse systems. Making the system "transparent," in which more functions would be delegated to the machine, became a primary goal of the effort to design powerful interfaces.

The ultimate transparent system would enable a user to interact with all retrieval systems as if they were a single system and to engage in a cooperative dialogue with the system in unrestricted natural language. One of the hardest aspects of this problem is endowing systems with search strategy formulation and database selection capabilities that simulate those employed by a human. In order to achieve this, research and development efforts have been undertaken to endow user interfaces with capabilities from artificial intelligence, specifically from the fields of expert systems and natural-language processing.

According to the British Computer Society's definition, expert systems research focuses on the design and construction of systems that embody within the computer a knowledge-based component from an expert skill in such a form that the system can offer intelligent advice or make an intelligent decision about a processing function. Natural-language processing research focuses on the design of computer systems that take apart and manipulate linguistic structures (morphological, syntactic, semantic, or pragmatic). Furthermore, when a natural-language processing system contains a large component of world knowledge, it is often referred to as a natural-language understanding system.

Both expert systems and natural language-processing systems manipulate large amounts of "knowledge," much of it specific to a particular subject domain. Expert systems contain knowledge about the entities and events in a particular domain of specialized expertise, as well as knowledge about how, when, and with what degree of certainty to apply that knowledge. Natural-language processing systems contain knowledge about linguistic structures and also often contain knowledge about contexts, situations, and expectations about the language in the domain. In both expert and natural-language processing systems, the procedural and declarative knowledge is embodied in various artificial intelligence (AI) data structures, including scripts, frames, semantic networks, and production rules.

The human-computer interface is a logical place for expert systems and natural-language processing research and applications. Much of a human intermediary's interaction with a retrieval system, particularly in database selection, search strategy formulation, evaluation of results, and search reformulation, is a process where decisions are made based on knowledge of many factors. This knowledge is mainly heuristic—it is mostly informed guesses and good practice, rather than a standard set of rules that is followed with a known outcome. Furthermore, intermediaries bring knowledge of the language of documents, queries, and indexing languages to the retrieval system interaction, and linguistic problems exist in translating information needs phrased in natural language to a linguistic structure that can be mapped to full-text documents and document surrogates in one or more databases.

Initially, explorations of artificial intelligence within information retrieval, including the user interface, were mainly assessments of the feasibility and utility of the AI approach. As more systems have been developed, an awareness of specific implementation issues has been a major element in the reporting literature. There are several themes that can be identified, including the preoccupation with implementation time and expense, portability issues, and the need to constrain either the subject or task domain.

An expert system or natural-language processing system that is built from scratch can take a long time to develop. Furthermore, without adequate attention to the isolation of domain-dependent and domain-independent knowledge in the design and implementation process, there is the danger that the system will not be transportable to any other domain. Within expert systems development, a number of expert system shells may be used to aid in the implementation process by providing at least some of the domain-independent information in an off-the-shelf product. Similarly, natural-language front ends are often modularized in design in order to transport portions of them to new subject domains.

A way of further constraining the intelligent interface implementation problem is to narrow the subject or task domain. There is a trade-off here between depth and breadth; that is, as the subject domain narrows, the ability to incorporate more tasks and features and to make the system more flexible is increased, whereas as the subject domain widens, the analysis becomes shallower, more rigid, and more prone to failure, depending on the diversity of input.

Expert system search intermediaries constrain the domain in two fundamental ways. The more usual way is to constrain the class of questions that will be answered; for example, looking at cancer therapy questions rather than allowing questions on all of medicine. The other way of constraining the domain involves focusing on one type of decision in the interaction process; for example, looking at database selection rather than the entire interaction.

Within natural-language processing, the domain has been constrained by tending to focus on the purely linguistic aspects of queries, rather than bringing in large amounts of world knowledge. Traditionally, the focus has been on morphology and syntax, although semantics has recently been gaining favor. Pragmatics, including systems that take into account the structure of cooperative discourse, has barely begun to be explored.

The state of the art within intelligent interfaces to bibliographic databases and online catalogs seems to be either an expert system or some type of natural-language interface. Many expert systems currently employ menu/pointing devices or a set of closed questions as an interface, while many of the natural-language interfaces focus exclusively on the analysis of the linguistic structures involved. This argues for development in the direction of endowing the largely menu-driven expert systems with natural-language query and response capabilities. Expert search intermediaries will ultimately need to clarify their terminology, paraphrase input, correct the user's misconceptions about the domain, and cope with ill-formed input.

The debate continues regarding how far artificial intelligence can take us in information retrieval. Expert systems are more easily constructed in domains where there is a reasonable consensus among the experts on how to solve the field's problems and on what constitutes an acceptable solution, and where the subject domain is quite narrow with a relatively small number of objects and relations to be represented. The subject and task domains of potential fully robust interfaces to current commercial retrieval systems and online catalogs is much too wide and heterogeneous, encompassing entire fields of knowledge, as well as users and their information needs, documents and their descriptions, databases and their contents, and retrieval heuristics. Furthermore, whereas human expert intermediaries exist for online bibliographic retrieval systems, the heuristics they employ have not been widely studied, and no consensus regarding those heuristics has emerged; moreover, it is not at all clear whose input should be solicited in designing an intelligent interface to an online catalog. As far as linguistic issues are concerned, it is still unclear what degree of linguistic analysis is necessary or appropriate in retrieval system interaction, and the issues of meaning and aboutness of documents and queries are still largely unresolved at both the conceptual and operational levels.

Even more fundamental, three major issues should be considered, and they include: how many of the basically cognitive processes with which we are trying to endow machines are amenable to a computational process; what degree of robustness interfaces can attain; and how much of the eventual success in AI applications depends on good engineering, and how much on the investigation of the human cognitive processes involved.

5

Designing a Domain Knowledge Base for an Intelligent Interface

Doris Florian

Over the past 20 years online databases have been used by thousands of searchers throughout the world. Systems and techniques have grown and matured but, in general, have not changed very much. Information professionals are still faced with a bewildering array of vendors, databases, languages, and structures, which now also confront the end user. However, research in artificial intelligence, particularly in expert systems, natural-language interfaces, knowledge representation, and learning systems, has added a new perspective in handling heterogeneous database systems. Recent investigations have shown the importance of including the user's profile and domain knowledge in the user interface. Individual characteristics vary greatly and are based on various factors. Therefore, the conceptual framework has to be adaptable to different levels of users and subjects.

This chapter presents the current situation in the online field and reports on a project to develop an intelligent assistant for information retrieval. It details results gained from interviewing and observing researchers and intermediary searchers in Austria and in the United States and shows the preliminary design of the interface and the domain knowledge base.

INTRODUCTION

It has been more than 40 years since Vannevar Bush proclaimed his vision of the "memex . . . a device in which an individual stores his books, records, and communications, and which is mechanized so that it may be consulted with exceeding speed and flexibility" (Bush, 1945, 32). About 30 years have passed since H. P. Luhn (1960) suggested the usage of statistics for content analysis, and about 20 years ago the first online systems were commercially introduced. Although these systems are used worldwide on a daily basis, online searchers in the 1990s are still struggling with a bewildering array of vendors, databases, languages, and data structures. It is not clear how to represent the user's infor-

mation needs (Belkin, Oddy, and Brooks, 1982) nor how to build a profile of
the user (Daniels, 1986). Consensus on a method to represent document content
is lacking (Croft, 1987), and there are unresolved questions concerning the
meaning and use of information, judgment, and relevance in information retrieval
(Saracevic, 1975).

Current Situation in Online Retrieval

Figures taken from the *Directory of Online Databases*, published by Cuadra/
Elsevier (1988, vol. 9, no. 3), show that there are 3,893 databases available,
offered by 1,723 producers, on 576 host systems. These numbers are still increasing. Each of these host systems has its own command language as well as
a plethora of different database contents and structures.

"Intermediaries" or "information specialists" help to bridge the gap between
the information seeker and the various systems. In order to explore the information need, the intermediary works with the user through interviews, gathering
relevant information. The intermediary formulates the appropriate search strategy
and executes it on one or more databases, retrieving a number of documents for
the user. If possible, the inquirer supplies search terms and gives relevance
feedback. In most cases, document surrogates are used as the basis for judgments.

Intermediaries draw on knowledge related to users, such as their backgrounds,
experiences, and domains of expertise. Furthermore, intermediaries apply their
knowledge about online searching, indexing techniques and languages, and the
subjects of the queries. This requires, besides training and experience, an enormous amount of communicative and cognitive skills. Various techniques are
used including, for example, short, clarifying dialogues, and construction of
associations among similar events or facts. Obstacles occur while handling online
systems. Even with a thorough knowledge of online searching techniques and
performance of searches on a regular basis, intermediaries struggle with problems, especially as these heterogeneous systems change constantly.

For a variety of economic and social reasons, an ever-growing number of end
users have been observed recently (Florian, 1987b). Due to a lack of experience
and only occasional usage, users are confronted with severe problems in trying
to handle the various systems, languages, and databases. Current commercial
systems are based on an "exact-match" method. But the ultimate goal of online
systems should be to retrieve documents relevant to an information need, and
this cannot be achieved by simple matches between documents and queries.
Other developments that apply statistical methods have certain advantages but
are still too restrictive, especially when one considers their performance in terms
of precision and recall.

These and related problems have been addressed by several authors (Belkin,
Oddy, and Brooks, 1987; Borgman, 1985; Brajnik, Guida, and Tasso, 1987;
Brooks, 1987; Croft and Thompson, 1987; Marcus, 1983; Shoval, 1983; Smith,
1987). The lack of inclusion of various sources and associations of knowledge

in current online systems was in most cases found to be the major drawback. Test results showed that, in order to improve the current situation, systems should contain knowledge, including knowledge about users, subjects, domains, and online retrieval per se (Vickery, 1984). These sources of knowledge have to be carefully studied and analyzed. Their representation with current techniques is too restrictive and not sufficient for actual application.

Motivation

Over the past ten years, intermediary searchers at the Forschungsgesellschaft Joanneum Ges.m.b.H. Graz, Austria, have performed retrospective and current-awareness searches for information seekers from the academic world and various industries in Austria. Major areas searched included physics, chemistry, medicine, engineering, education, business administration, law, and Austrian history. The host systems accessed were DIALOG, DIMDI, DATASTAR, ESA, FIZ, and RDB. The intermediaries were confronted with a variety of users, subjects, and systems on a daily basis.

The major obstacles observed and their possible origins can be categorized in four ways:

1. Problems with mechanical techniques can be related to experience
2. Communication barriers occurring at the human-human interface are due to lack of subject familiarity and human information processing
3. Deep knowledge of many subjects cannot be achieved even after many years of experience
4. Unfamiliarity with a foreign language (English) leads to an additional bottleneck in the handling of these systems (Florian, 1987a)

Currently, it is the intelligence of the human intermediary that is applied to circumvent these problems.

In order to enhance the online searching facilities, the Pro-Search software package was introduced; it brought about, after only a short time, considerable improvements, mainly in automating nonintellectual tasks (also mentioned in Hawkins, 1988). Intellectual problems still existed in building the search strategy and coping with a variety of subjects and users. Differences in terminology and structure between the information seeker, the intermediary, and thesauri or dictionaries considerably influenced the outcome of a search. In some cases the discrepancies led to major false drops, that is, retrieval results matched the search criteria but nevertheless failed to meet the expectations of the information seeker. Generally, current user interfaces depend too much on the underlying database structure, which might not be comprehensible to the user, and intellectual support is still missing, which forces the user to encompass the constraints.

These problems provided the motivation for our project, which was built around the user and was concerned with information requests and personal characteristics. The intention was not to change the online systems themselves, but to build an intelligent assistant as a front end that would be in charge of some part of an intermediary's task. It would give advice where needed, remind the user of already available knowledge and old findings, and assist in building the strategy. The present chapter summarizes the design of the intelligent interface. The second part covers some general ideas of artificial intelligence (AI) and how they relate to online retrieval. The third part discusses the general outline of the interface design, and the fourth describes the design of the knowledge base. Finally, some general remarks and outlines for future activities are presented.

ARTIFICIAL INTELLIGENCE

Activities that require human intelligence include understanding language, engaging in reasoning, and solving difficult problems. These activities are based on the ability to store and retrieve large amounts of knowledge in a variety of ways over different time periods. The question of what knowledge is has been raised by various disciplines. In general, knowledge consists of certain concepts acquired from many sources. Knowledge can either be taught, or is based on examples or cases, and new knowledge can be derived from old knowledge. Humans can link concepts and facts in a variety of ways. Associations among different concepts may easily be varied depending on the context, leading to new ideas and possible solutions. Inferential capabilities are, in this respect, the basis for intelligent processes (Chiaramella and Defude, 1987).

Although there is still little agreement about the definition of *artificial intelligence*, particularly because of the connotations of the word *artificial*, it seems that artificial intelligence and information retrieval have some general ideas and aspects in common, since both are based on knowledge and information. Recent developments in artificial intelligence suggest solutions to some of the interface problems mentioned earlier. These include the representation, storage, and usage of knowledge.

Heavy criticisms and warnings have been issued concerning the methods and amount of knowledge needed to build intelligent systems. The issues involved include the need to restrict knowledge to a reasonable amount and the need to select the most appropriate form (or forms) of representation, given their respective advantages and disadvantages. Nevertheless, artificial intelligence may prove invaluable in providing researchers with techniques for enhancing information retrieval systems with some intelligence. According to Sparck Jones, an intelligent information retrieval system is a computer system with inferential capabilities. It can make use of prior knowledge to establish by plausible reasoning a connection between an ill-specified request and a set of relevant documents (Sparck Jones, 1983).

Related Work

Various approaches have been taken to integrate artificial intelligence techniques and information retrieval in more or less sophisticated ways. Some of the most important approaches follow:

1. The CONIT architecture allows detailed analysis of a query and provides the user with additional help for search modification and evaluation (Marcus, 1983)

2. IR-NLII focuses on casual users. The system allows user modeling using declarative and procedural knowledge to build stereotypes (Brajnik, Guida, and Tasso, 1987)

3. The I³R system developed by Croft provides assistance at all stages of the retrieval process. Its architecture is derived from the HEARSAY II system. Domain knowledge acquired from the user is stored in a framelike structure. A knowledge base contains the documents and their semantic representation (Croft and Thompson, 1987)

4. Chiaramella and Defude in their IOTA system use natural language for the analysis of query to obtain new concepts. Its architecture includes user models and a domain knowledge base. The system also allows management of full-text documents (Chiaramella and Defude, 1987)

5. GRANT is an expert system for finding sources of funding. Domain knowledge is represented as a semantic network where the search is performed by spreading activation (Cohen and Kjeldsen, 1987)

6. The RUBRIC system provides tools for users to develop comprehensive queries that then form a tree-structured knowledge base (Tong, 1985)

In contrast to these systems, which are all experiments, the project discussed here seeks to improve directly interaction with commercial online services and takes into account the special needs of a non-English-speaking environment.

INTERFACE DESIGN

User interfaces have become a key aspect in software design. They are particularly important if a range of users is accessing a variety of systems where it is necessary to produce an environment that promotes efficiency and satisfaction. For our project, the overall goal was to shield users from the various online systems.

To achieve this, the intelligent system interacts with users, providing them with additional knowledge while conducting the search in different databases. The dialogue with the user is based on a simplified natural language, as robust language capabilities were felt not to be the major emphasis for the project in a first stage. Future developments may include a fully developed natural-language interface.

The architecture of the system contains four major subsystems:

1. a user interface, including the user modeling component;

2. information about hosts and databases;

3. a language processor that automatically translates the search strategy into the various host languages; and

4. a domain knowledge base including information about computer science as the first application area.

The user interface accesses the systems and interprets the results for the user. Among other themes, it acquires information about users such as their background, interests, and preferences, to form user models. This information is then included while building search strategies. For example, a user looking only for journal articles in German and English can express that preference, which may be included for all future searches. Frames are the form of representation chosen.

Since databases vary greatly in topic and structure, information is provided about their availability, type and content, indexing policies, and special features. For example, when building a search strategy, the system will warn the user not to use a field that is not available in the selected database. The information is provided offline in order to be consulted before establishing host connections.

Information needs are expressed by using nouns and noun phrases. The system decides whether the query is sufficient for conversion into a search strategy. If it is not, it asks the user to provide further information or suggests use of the domain knowledge base. A first search version is then converted by the system into a Boolean expression. The language processor then uses templates to translate from this statement into any of the other retrieval languages. Thus, the user does not need to know the various structures of these languages. The output can be used to refine the query further.

Although the first three components are also important, this chapter concentrates on the domain knowledge base. As mentioned earlier, the intelligent assistant provides the user with knowledge where its availability is restricted. This led to the construction and provision of domain related knowledge.

DOMAIN KNOWLEDGE

Domain knowledge is defined as information about important topics and concepts in a specific domain and how the topics and concepts relate to each other (Croft, 1986). By using appropriate structures, such knowledge can be made available and accessible to many persons and at any time.

Intermediaries who have to deal with a variety of subjects when performing online searches are confronted with many problems. They have to cope with various subjects and their specialities, and these often do not conform with their background knowledge. Information seekers are more or less familiar with their fields, but often they use different terminology, which in some cases does not conform to any classification scheme or thesaurus. Furthermore, they often do not know the equivalent foreign language expressions (in English, for some Austrians). Our observations have also shown that the same query often leads to different formulations submitted by different users or intermediaries. This is especially true for search concepts in the form of single terms or phrases.

Therefore, a knowledge base was constructed to complement the knowledge of users, intermediaries, classification schemes, and thesauri in a certain domain. This domain knowledge base represents and stores knowledge that can then be used by intermediaries and inexperienced users. The intermediary may choose the appropriate knowledge base (e.g., computer science) before or while building the strategy. For users who lack searching expertise or knowledge of the subject domain, it may provide help and give assistance for further improvement of the strategies. For the first design, the field of computer science was chosen.

Knowledge is represented as a semantic network, since this structure resembles that of a thesaurus. The single concepts or phrases are represented as frames. This method has been chosen for several systems recently (Croft, 1987). It facilitates the construction of hierarchies of terms and concepts, and associates them with various properties. Various slots represent links to other nodes. Some of the slots are mandatory, others optional. The relations defined among the nodes are bidirectional, defining relations from one to another node. Inverse links are added automatically. Slots include general thesaurus links such as broader/narrower/related terms, used/used for, synonyms, and instantiations. A logical relation representing the Boolean AND expression might act as a complement of a phrase; e.g., "information AND retrieval" supplements "information retrieval." What was discovered to be important for non-English speakers was the availability of the English term for a German expression. A translation slot was therefore included. If both expressions are the same, only one has to be present. This may be extended for more languages if necessary. To provide for idiomatic expressions, up to three different formulations can be added for each term.

It did not appear to be reasonable to start with no knowledge at all. A coarse classification scheme, according to that of INSPEC, provides a basis from which to start. This general framework can then be extended by users if they want to add their own concepts. An example follows:

Name:	Künstliche Intelligenz
Translation:	Artificial Intelligence
Broader Term:	Computer Science
Narrower Term:	Wissensdarstellung
Personal 1:	KI
Personal 2:	AI
Name:	Wissensdarstellung
Translation:	Knowledge Representation

Broader Term:	Künstliche Intelligenz
Narrower Term:	Frame
Logic:	Knowledge AND Representation

Name:	Frame
Broader Term:	Wissensdarstellung
Related Term:	Semantisches Netz
Instantiation:	Slot

Name:	Semantisches Netz
Translation:	Semantic Net
Broader Term:	Wissensdarstellung
Related Term:	Frame
Instantiation:	Node

Knowledge is derived from the user through the interface while formulating the query. Rules of different types recognize stems and full concepts and match them with those in the knowledge base. Logical AND expressions or phrases point to each other. The same is true for translations. Terms may also be added on an individual basis, or can be taken from a thesaurus, or from relevant documents. This acquisition process leads to the growth of the knowledge base. To limit the size, the intermediary will eliminate from time to time those terms that represent synonyms or outdated expressions that are no longer of any use.

Users of current systems browse a thesaurus to look for terms. The same general idea is pursued for the domain knowledge base where browsing is based on the spreading activation method (Cohen and Kjeldsen, 1987). Query terms are used as starting points for exploration. A user browsing for a specific concept navigates through the knowledge base and is presented with all directly connected nodes of the initial concept. It is possible to select any frame of which the value is an instance and to proceed from this frame to its neighbors. Those that are selected for the search strategy are put in a separate list. If further refinement is needed, the user can continue at any selected node and extend the knowledge incorporated in using additional terms. In order to keep control over the spreading activities, thresholds from the activation point are included. Deriving data from the user model, preferences can be set up such that only English terms are used.

This architecture allows the designers to build knowledge bases for different domains, which can easily be chosen when establishing the concepts for online retrieval. With the availability of larger storage spaces (rewritable WORM), it will be possible in the future to link knowledge bases of different subjects to provide interdisciplinary access.

CONCLUSIONS

In this chapter some major concepts associated with using online systems have been discussed. Based on the needs of real-world situations, a project was developed to facilitate the search process. Conclusions were drawn from our observations and experiences that led to the design of an intelligent interface for bibliographic retrieval, more specifically, a domain knowledge base. The inclusion of user terminology and controlled vocabulary seems to be promising for enhancing current online systems.

Although some work has been undertaken, there is still a long way to go, and future work will include a more detailed analysis of the user model. Besides a better understanding of what intelligent retrieval can achieve, researchers from both artificial intelligence and information retrieval will have to share their experiences and developments.

Current online retrieval, electronic mail, and hypertext systems are becoming more widely available and allow access to numeric, bibliographic, full-text, and image databases. Users from any part of the world are increasingly able to access such systems in each other's countries. Friendly, intelligent systems should provide sufficient help to assist the various users in many ways. These systems should widen the availability of information, relieving the search burden and giving advice and support to the user.

NOTE

A preliminary study was performed under a grant from the Fonds zur Forderung der Wissenschaftlichen Forschung, Austria. Current research is supported by a scholarship from the Max Kade Foundation. The author is grateful for the assistance of the Graduate School of Library and Information Science, The University of Texas at Austin.

REFERENCES

Belkin, N. J., R. N. Oddy, and H. M. Brooks. 1982. ASK for Information Retrieval. *Journal of Documentation* 38 (2): 61–71.

Belkin, N. J., C. L. Borgman, H. M. Brooks, T. Bylander, W. B. Croft, P. Daniels, S. Deerwester, E. A. Fox, P. Ingwersen, R. Rada, K. S. Jones, R. Thompson, D. Walker. 1987. Distributed Expert-Based Information Systems: An Interdisciplinary Approach. *Information Processing & Management* 23 (5): 395–409.

Borgman, C. L. 1985. Designing an Information Retrieval Interface. In Research and Development in Information Retrieval: *Eighth Annual International ACM SIGIR Conference, Montreal, Quebec, Canada, June 5–7, 1985*, 139–46. New York: Association for Computing Machinery.

Brajnik, G., G. Guida, and C. Tasso. 1987. User Modeling in Intelligent Information Retrieval. *Information Processing & Management* 23 (4): 305–20.

Brooks, H. M. 1987. Expert Systems and Intelligent Information Retrieval. *Information Processing & Management* 23 (4): 367–82.

Bush, V. 1945. As We May Think. *Atlantic Monthly* 176 (1): 101–8.

Chiaramella, Y., and B. Defude. 1987. A Prototype of an Intelligent System for Information Retrieval: IOTA. *Information Processing & Management* 23 (4): 285–303.

Cohen, P. R., and R. Kjeldsen. 1987. Information Retrieval by Constrained Spreading Activation in Semantic Networks. *Information Processing & Management* 23 (4): 255–68.

Croft, W. B. 1986. User Specified Domain Knowledge for Document Retrieval. In *Ninth Annual International ACM SIGIR Conference: Proceedings of the Conference in Pisa, Italy, September, 1986*, 201–6.

————. 1987. Approaches to Intelligent Information Retrieval. *Information Processing & Management* 23 (4): 249–54.

Croft, W. B., and R. H. Thompson. 1987. I³R: A New Approach to the Design of Document Retrieval Systems. *Journal of the American Society for Information Science* 38 (6): 389–404.

Daniels, P. J. 1986. Cognitive Models in Information Retrieval—An Evaluative Review. *Journal of Documentation* 42 (4): 272–304.

Florian, D. 1987a. SAFIR—An Artificial Intelligence Impact on Information Retrieval. In *11th International Online Meeting: Proceedings of the Meeting in London, Great Britain*, 423–29. Medford, Mass.: Learned Information.

————. 1987b. SAFIR (Smart Assistant for Information Retrieval). In *International Congress on Terminology and Knowledge Engineering: Proceedings of the Congress in Trier, Bundesrepubik Deutschland, October 1987*, ed. H. Czap and C. Galinski, 148–53. Frankfurt: Index Verlag.

Hawkins, D. T. 1988. Applications of Artificial Intelligence (AI) and Expert Systems for Online Searching. *Online* 12 (1): 31–43.

Marcus, R. S. 1983. An Experimental Comparison of the Effectiveness of Computers and Humans as Search Intermediaries. *Journal of the American Society for Information Science* 34 (6): 381–404.

Saracevic, T. 1975. RELEVANCE: A Review of and a Framework for the Thinking on the Notion in Information Science. *Journal of the American Society for Information Science* 26 (November-December): 321–43.

Shoval, P. 1983. Knowledge Representation in Consultation Systems for Users of Retrieval Systems. In *Application of Mini- and Micro-Computers in Information, Documentation and Libraries: Proceedings of the International Conference*, ed. C. Keren and L. Perlmutter, 631–43. Amsterdam: North-Holland.

Smith, L. C. 1987. Artificial Intelligence and Information Retrieval. In *Annual Review of Information Science and Technology*, ed. M. E. Williams, 22: 41–77. Amsterdam: Elsevier.

Sparck Jones, K. 1983. Intelligent Retrieval. In *Intelligent Information Retrieval: Informatics 7*, ed. K. P. Jones, 136–42. London: Aslib.

Tong, R. M. 1985. RUBRIC: An Environment for Full Text Information Retrieval. In *Research and Development in Information Retrieval: Eighth Annual International ACM SIGIR Conference, Montreal, Quebec, Canada, June 5–7, 1985*, 243–51. New York: Association for Computing Machinery.

Vickery, A. 1984. An Intelligent Interface for Online Interaction. *Journal of Information Science* 9: 7–18.

6

Modality, Extensionality, and Computability

Diana D. Woodward

Despite the rapid progress made recently in language processing, we are far from being able to produce computers that converse with us as easily as did the fictional HAL in *2001* or the computerized car on "Knight Rider." For one thing, the logic of computers is, in most cases, first-order predicate calculus. The most sophisticated languages claim only second-order predicate calculus capability. As long as this remains true, we must either develop classical logic algorithms for modal, epistemic, deontic, and counterfactual reasoning; or we must abandon the idea of holding normal conversations with computers.

Advances in artificial intelligence will require computers that can process modalities. We already have classical logic algorithms for determining the validity of modal arguments and the consistency of modal claims, namely the cancellation system of Binkley and Clark as applied to modal logic.[1]

There are researchers in artificial intelligence who are interested in programming machines to imitate human thought processes. In the area of logic, this type of artificial intelligence (AI) research would involve programming derivation systems for logical proofs, because derivation rules (e.g., modus ponens, modus tollens, de Morgans) capture valid forms of human reasoning. However, constructing derivation proofs is a heuristic matter. One may apply derivation rules correctly, yet never construct a proof of conclusion from premises, even though the argument is valid and such a proof is constructible. Whether or not a person or a machine can construct a derivation proof of a valid argument depends on the strategies used in applying rules to construct such a proof. Knowing derivation rules and not always being able to construct a proof is analogous to knowing the rules of tic-tac-toe, yet not always being able to win.

Others engaged in artificial intelligence (and still others who simply want to improve the information-processing capabilities of machines) do not care whether the machines can determine, for any given argument, if that argument is valid.

Of course, when such effective procedures are devised for a machine, they also are available for humans to use.

In the area of logic, Smullyan trees are an effective procedure.[2] Following the rules for the tree procedure will show any consistent first-order set of sentences to be consistent, and they can be used to show any first-order argument to be valid. While people may have tree strategies that help them construct shorter or more efficient trees by avoiding excessive branching, a computer (which can keep track of a great many branches) can apply the tree rules in a set order and always obtain the correct result. The computer has, in effect, one strategy that may be inefficient in particular cases, but which always works.[3]

The cancellation system, devised by Binkley and Clark, is another such effective procedure for determining the validity of first-order arguments. This system is closely related to tree structures, but employs Polish notation. Cancellation is particularly relevant to this chapter because it has been expanded to provide effective procedures for each of the modal systems. Thus there are computable first-order algorithms for manipulation of modal symbols that allow one to determine the validity of modal arguments. This does not, however, solve the whole problem of making modal arguments machine computable.

MODALITIES

Modal contexts are often cited as examples of contexts that are not extensional. The test of extensionality is substitution *salve veritate*, and it is pointed out that one can take a true modal claim such as

(a)   necessarily 9>7,

substitute for 9 another term referring to that number (e.g., "the number of symphonies Beethoven wrote"), and thereby produce a false modal claim:

(b)   necessarily the number of symphonies Beethoven write >7

Thus, even though one may have classical logic algorithms for modal logic symbol manipulation, this does not provide an extensional algorithm for determining whether or not it is valid to infer (b) from (a).

What gets overlooked is how closely analogous this is to problems of reference that do not involve modalities. One argues that

(c)   9>7
      ∴ the number of Beethoven symphonies >7

not on the basis of logical rules for manipulating first-order predicate calculus symbols, but because one knows that "the number of Beethoven symphonies" and 9 refer to the same number. It is true of this world that 9 = the number of

Beethoven symphonies. In short, one has a suppressed premise and the full argument is:

> (*d*) 9>7
> 9 = the number of Beethoven symphonies
> ∴ the number of Beethoven symphonies >7

To make the modal inference from (*a*) to (*b*) one would need to know that 9 and "the number of Beethoven symphonies" denote the same number and that "9 = the number of Beethoven symphonies" is true in all possible worlds. One does not know this, of course, because it is not true. Hence the argument from (*a*) to (*b*) is not valid as it stands. When the missing premise is supplied, the resulting valid argument has a false premise:

> (*e*) necessarily 9>7
> necessarily 9 = the number of Beethoven symphonies
> ∴ necessarily the number of Beethoven symphonies >7

One can substitute *salve veritate* in modal contexts as long as one is substituting a term that has the same referent in all possible worlds, not merely in this one.

It is hard enough to say when two terms have the same referent in this world; now we want to know how to determine if two terms have the same referent in all possible worlds. Those who believe in "essence properties" may maintain that essence properties provide alternative ways of referring to an individual that will hold in all possible worlds. Indeed, essence properties may be used to determine what alternative worlds are possible. If the property of being equal to 3×3 is essential to 9, then 9 and 3×3 have the same referent in all possible worlds, and any work in which these terms do not have the same referent is not a possible world. The argument:

> (*f*) necessarily 9>7
> ∴ necessarily $3 \times 3 > 7$

may be maintained on the basis that being equal to 3×3 is an essential property of 9, hence 9 and 3×3 have the same referent in all possible worlds. In short, we have a suppressed premise and the full, sound, argument is:

> (*g*) necessarily 9>7
> necessarily $9 = 3 \times 3$
> ∴ necessarily $3 \times 3 > 7$

Outside of mathematics, however, it is exceedingly difficult to say what counts as an essence property of an individual. An essence property would be a necessary property, one the individual has in all possible worlds.

If each individual had an essence property (probably a compound property), then the task of a machine devised to carry on a normal modal conversation with humans would be difficult, but clear-cut. Just as the machine would have to know a great deal about the facts of the real world in order to substitute in nonmodal contexts, so also the machine would have to know the essence properties of each individual in order to substitute in modal contexts. The problem is that there do not appear to be such essence properties of individuals.

Try to name even one property that President Bush would need in all possible worlds. Being president of the United States? Being dark haired? Living in the twentieth century? According to Kripke's suggestion regarding rigid designators for people, any individual in another possible world whom we wish to identify with President Bush would have to have the same origin. If this means that, to be identified with Bush, an individual in another possible world would have to begin to exist at the same time and be of the same (sort of) genetic material, then it would seem that living in the twentieth century and being male are necessary, essence properties of Bush. However, we are perfectly capable of making sense of counterfactuals that begin "If President Bush were female..." or "If President Bush had been alive in 1789 and helped to write the constitution..."[4]

Indeed, within a single conversation we often shift what we wish to hold constant in counterfactual talk. The premises of the following argument are typical of counterfactual discourse.[5] We do not typically make the mistake of drawing the given conclusion:

> If Aunt Brachia had a baby, she would be an unwed mother.
> If Aunt Brachia were married, she would have a baby.
> Therefore:
> If Aunt Brachia were married, she would be an unwed mother.

Using the concept of a counterpart, we can block the inference by reading each premise as claiming that there is an Aunt Brachia counterpart set such that... It is only when both premises are understood to be about the same counterpart set that the inference is valid.

Whatever property is proposed as a necessary, essence property of an individual, we can construct counterfactuals that discuss the possibility of the individual in question not having that property. There is no essence property for each individual that we can give to a machine as a guide for substitution in modal contexts. The fact is that in some of our counterfactual and modal talk we treat certain properties as necessary for an individual, while in our next modal/counterfactual discussion of the same individual we are treating some other property as necessary instead. You do not have to be a machine to have trouble understanding counterfactual conversations. If Hitler were U.S. president now, then what? We would all be Germans, Hitler would be a naval officer, American Jews would be in danger, the American electorate would have preferred

Hitler to Carter? We don't know what properties of Hitler and/or the U.S. presidency to keep constant across the worlds this partial counterfactual invites us to consider.

To supply missing premises in modal arguments and to process counterfactuals, a machine would need the same sort of information that people need. There is no one set of essence properties for each individual that all people hold constant across possible worlds in modal and counterfactual talk. Instead, for any given modal or counterfactual claim, one must know what properties of the individual the speaker intends to hold constant and which are allowed to vary. In some contexts there is not much doubt about the speaker's intentions in this regard. It may be clear that mathematical properties or individuals' physical properties in a story or previous conversation may be held constant. On the basis of the discussion's context and purpose we guess about what is being held constant. When we don't know what properties of an individual the speaker is willing to vary and which to keep constant, we ask.

To enable a machine to process modalities, we must supply it with three capabilities: (1) we must give it a method of constructing hypotheticals, of assigning to individuals properties that will be kept constant in the discussion; and (2) we must program it to ask the speaker how these assignments are to be made. Once assignments have been made, the machine may (3a) use first-order predicate logic to deduce necessity (what can be proven from the assignments held constant) and possibility (what is consistent with the assignments held constant). Alternatively, the machine may (3b) be supplied with the cancellation algorithm and directed which modal system to use (which alternative relations among possible worlds) in checking modal arguments for validity and groups of modal claims of consistency.

If we can follow the directions above and program a machine to process modal claims, we will have constructed an extensional modal of what many philosophers have contended is an intensional context. For over 2,000 years, philosophers have assumed that there are essence properties of individuals and that essence properties determine what is necessary and possible for individuals. If machines can process modalities without using essence properties of individuals, then modality does not presuppose individual essences.

NOTES

1. R. W. Binkley and R. L. Clark, "A Cancellation Algorithm for Elementary Logic," *Theoria* 33 (1967):79–97. Applied to modal logics in D. Paul Snyder, *Modal Logic and Its Applications* (New York: Van Nostrand Reinhold, 1971).

2. Smullyan trees are adapted from the "semantic tableaux" of Evert W. Beth and from Hintikka "model sets." Raymond M. Smullyan, *First Order Logic* (Berlin, N.Y.: Springer Verlag, 1968).

3. Hugues Leblanc and William A. Wisdom, *Deductive Logic* (Boston: Allyn and Bacon, 1972), sec. 2.3.

4. There is an extensive literature on what is to be held constant in conditional dis-

course. The point made here is that while one may formulate theories that match what people often hold constant, there is no property (at least, no nonlogical property) of a named individual that must be held constant.

5. Ken Warmbrod, "Counterfactuals and Substitution of Equivalent Antecedents," *Journal of Philosophical Logic* 10 (1981):267–89.

7

A Domain Knowledge-based, Natural-Language Interface for Bibliographic Information Retrieval

Zbigniew Mikolajuk and Robert Chafetz

Users of information retrieval systems benefit from a user interface that uses built-in domain knowledge to allow communication on the user language level. This chapter describes how inferencing with a domain knowledge base (represented in a KL-One-like formalism) and natural-language processing are used to provide enhanced human-computer communication for personal bibliographic information retrieval. Bibliography Manager supports the user in acquiring concepts from title text by conducting a dialogue in which (*a*) phrase attachment and (*b*) word sense ambiguity are resolved, and (*c*) user concept placement is decided. The result is that references are linked to concepts in the knowledge base.

For retrieval, the user can formulate a query in restricted natural language. The system helps the user to reformulate the query in a dialogue, in which the user may further specialize or generalize the concepts he or she is interested in. In the dialogue the user can also change the focus of a query, if more relevant concepts related to the problem are presented by the system. A main benefit of the system is to understand or to conduct a dialogue to try to understand a text phrase even if the user (*a*) does not know exactly how to express it, or (*b*) the user's language is not as precise as the system needs. Elements of the bibliographic system have been implemented on a Sun–3 workstation using Quintus Prolog and Prowindows.

Issues in the user interface of information retrieval systems that concern us are the user's view of domain knowledge; user-guided, natural-language query understanding; communication of conceptual information to the user; syntactic and semantic disambiguation dialogues; the use of forms and menus; and the use of a "strict," KL-One-like knowledge representation.

INTRODUCTION

We describe a number of issues concerning the user interface for bibliographic retrieval using domain knowledge and natural-language processing. We are in-

Figure 7.1
Overview of Reference Title Processing

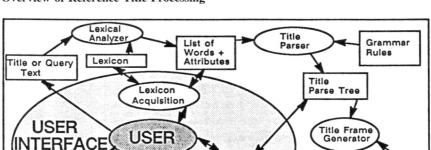

terested in the user interface issues for the situation where a user can formulate phrases (concepts) in natural language to express a conceptual focus for bibliographic retrieval. Then the user and system may conduct a dialogue to negotiate a natural-language query statement that is understood by the system. (For us, ''understanding'' by the system means text can be translated into internal system concepts, similar to Regoczei and Hirst, 1988, 21.)

We believe the user should not need to remember the details of system terminology in order for a query to be understood—the system should assist the user in rephrasing queries. In addition, even if the system fully understands the user's conceptual focus, it may not be able to provide a satisfactory result; for example, too few or too many references may be found. The system should provide assistance in reformulating to other concepts in the neighborhood of the initial query focus, guiding the user to a satisfactory number of retrieved references. We see a benefit in using a strict KL-One-like representation language (Brachman and Shmolze, 1985) to aid in the communication of conceptual knowledge (Mark, 1986).

OVERVIEW

Figure 7.1 shows an overview of reference title processing. Ellipses are processors, rectangles are data or knowledge, and arrows show data flow. In brief, the system lexically analyzes title text, produces a parse tree, translates the tree into concepts/frames, classifies the new concept into the existing concept network, and then processes user queries using the domain knowledge. Figure 7.1

Figure 7.2
Enter References

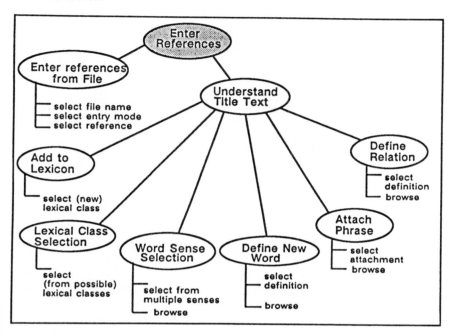

emphasizes data flow among the system modules. A user state view of the system and state transitions are discussed in the following sections.

After initialization of the system, the user can enter one of the following three states:

- Enter References—Understand new titles, engaging the user for lexicon, syntax, and semantics resolution as needed

- Browse—Browse the knowledge base by viewing an alphabetical index of concepts, a structured list representing the is-a hierarchy, or by viewing the relations of a single concept (its ''neighborhood'')

- Query—Understand a query (as was done for a title), then engage the user to reformulate the query based on the number of references

Figure 7.2 shows the *Enter References* state. Key actions available in states are shown under the ellipses. In *Enter References from File*, desired reference texts are selected and processed to extract the component parts, including the title text. *Understand Title Text* coordinates the dialogue for lexicon acquisition and syntactic and semantic disambiguation. Our approach to title text understanding is similar to Rich, Barnett, Wittenburg, and Wroblewski (1987) in that we delay decisions until relevant evidence is gathered. From a user interface

Figure 7.3
Browse

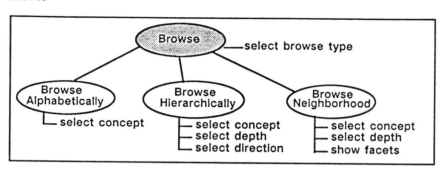

point of view, we do not wish to engage the user in unnecessary dialogue. If the system can solve a problem, dialogue is avoided; otherwise, it tries to suggest solutions.

The system begins understanding the title text (creating concepts) by constructing parse trees, which requires knowing the lexical classes of words in the title. *Add to Lexicon* asks the user to assign lexical classes to any new words. The remaining substates are entered opportunistically, depending on how much disambiguation the system can do automatically, using the domain knowledge. *Lexical Class Selection* is entered if a word could be assigned more than one lexical class and yield different title interpretations; the user is asked to make the class assignment. In *Word Sense Selection*, the user chooses between multiple senses/definitions of words. *Define New Word* allows the user to give a simple definition to a new word, by specifying its superconcept(s) in the existing knowledge base. In *Attach Phrase*, the user decides on the binding of words or phrases to other words or phrases in the title, for example by deciding on preposition attachment. In *Define Relation*, the user decides on the correspondence between slots/relations in a title concept and the knowledge base. As a general rule for the above states, the system suggests disambiguation choices based on conceptual context whenever possible.

Browsers can be used to learn about domain terminology, to check for the existence of concepts, and to see a detailed view of a concept's structure. Figure 7.3 shows that the *Browse* state has three substates: *Browse Alphabetically*, *Browse Hierarchically*, and *Browse Neighborhood*. Once one of these browsing types is chosen, a user can select a concept from which to start browsing. A browsing depth can be specified for neighborhood and hierarchy browsing. A hierarchy can be viewed in either the up direction (superconcepts) or down direction (subconcepts) from any concept. A neighborhood view may show only related concepts (value-type of relation) or the full details (all facets) of the neighborhood relations.

In the *Query* state, shown in figure 7.4, the user can disambiguate and re-

Figure 7.4
Query

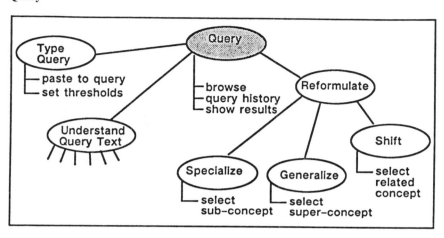

formulate a query. In the *Type Query* state, the user types a natural-language description of a subject area of interest. The *Understand Query Text* procedure is identical to *Understand Title Text*, and its result is called a query concept. Once the semantics of a query have been agreed upon, the user is interested in the pragmatic issue of results. The query is executed by retrieving subsumed references. The result may not be acceptable, because there may be too many or too few references retrieved. The system can automatically explore the neighborhood of the query concept (immediately related concepts) in order to suggest query reformulations. For example, generalizing a query may allow retrieval of 12 as opposed to 0 references, and specializing a query may allow retrieval of 12 as opposed to 200 references. A reformulated query is reexecuted and the reformulation process continues. When the query retrieval result is acceptable, it is displayed. In the next section we describe the three major user states, *Enter References*, *Browse*, and *Query* in more detail.

ENTER REFERENCES

Entering a reference involves extracting the reference components, building a knowledge representation for the title, and integrating the title knowledge into the knowledge base. New references may be entered by the user from the keyboard, or they may be read from an existing file. The user initiates the reference entry activity by selecting the appropriate command item in the menu of the initial state, as shown in figure 7.5.

Further specification of the command is done by selecting an entry type ("from file" or "from keyboard") from a submenu. Selection of the "from file" submenu item causes display of a dialogue box in which the user provides the name

Figure 7.5
Initial Bibliography Manager

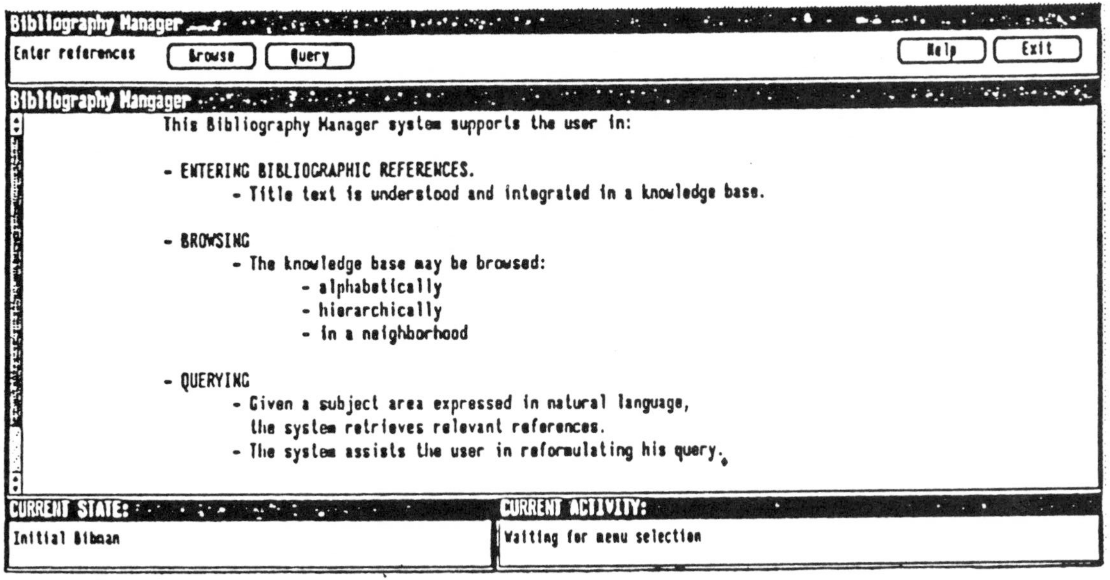

Bibliography Manager

Enter references   [Browse] [Query]

Bibliography Manager

This Bibliography Manager system supports the user in:

- ENTERING BIBLIOGRAPHIC REFERENCES.
  - Title text is understood and integrated in a knowledge base.

- BROWSING
  - The knowledge base may be browsed:
    - alphabetically
    - hierarchically
    - in a neighborhood

- QUERYING
  - Given a subject area expressed in natural language,
    the system retrieves relevant references.
  - The system assists the user in reformulating his query.

[Help] [Exit]

CURRENT STATE:
Initial Bibman

CURRENT ACTIVITY:
Waiting for menu selection

88

Figure 7.6
Enter Reference from File

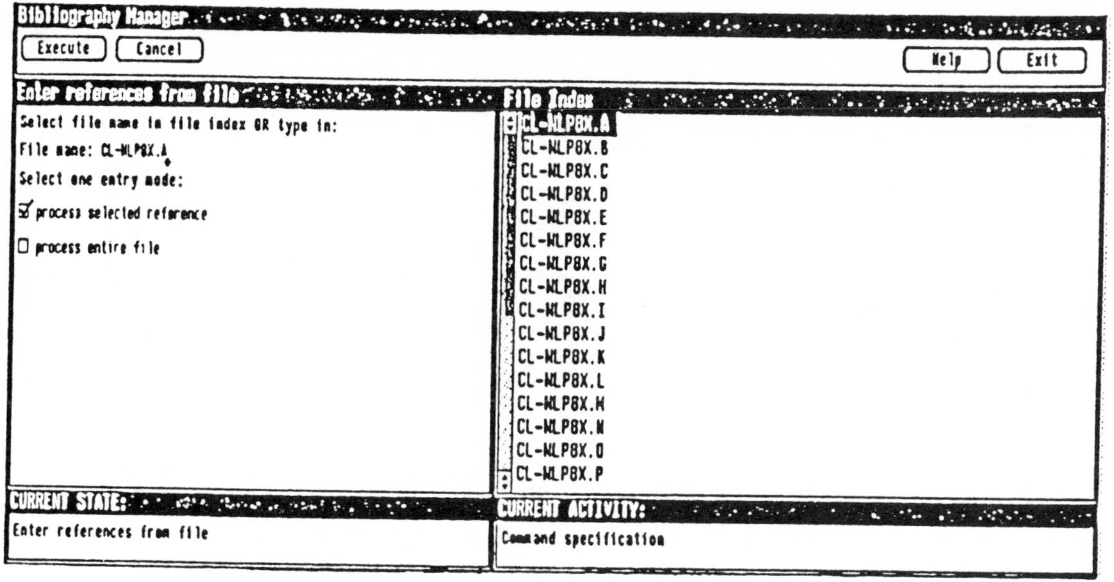

of a file and the entry mode, as shown in figure 7.6. The file name can be typed in or selected from the file index. The entry mode attribute (either "process selected reference" or "process entire file") is selected by clicking on the corresponding box. Command specification completion is signaled by selecting the "Execute" menu item. Selecting the "Cancel" item cancels the command specification and returns to the previous state.

Figure 7.7 shows the interface before choosing "Process." The file content is displayed so the user can pick a reference text to be processed. Figures 7.7 and 7.15 show sections of the file obtained from the University of Sussex (Gazdar, Franz, Osborne, and Evans, 1987). By selecting the menu item "Process," the user initiates reference processing. Following successful execution, the selected reference text will be marked as entered. If the system can automatically resolve the understanding of the title, then a message is displayed that the reference was processed and the user can select another reference to process. Alternatively, the user can terminate the entering of references from the current file by choosing "Select another file" or "Done entering." In the former case the dialogue box for file name specification is redisplayed (figure 7.6); in the latter case the system returns to the *Initial Bibliography Manager* state (figure 7.5).

The user can abort processing of selected references at any time using the "Abort" item in the menu. The system returns to the state existing before selection of the "Process" function, that is, all new objects created during processing (e.g., new words in lexicon) are retracted.

During the text understanding process, the system builds concept graphs representing the meaning of a title. At any point in this process there may be ambiguities that the system cannot resolve. Given that one or more of the following ambiguities occur at the same point of text understanding,

ambiguity 1: lexical class selection
ambiguity 2: word sense choice
ambiguity 3: define new word
ambiguity 4: attach phrase
ambiguity 5: define relation

the system prefers to ask the user to resolve ambiguity i over ambiguity j, where $i < j$. Automatic text analysis systems are not error-free (Salton, 1988); we propose a semiautomatic system that delegates to the user if needed. We now describe these states of ambiguity resolution, any one of which may be entered by the system after the user selects "Process" in figure 7.7.

Add to Lexicon

Figure 7.8 shows an example of a new title with three words, *recovery*, *communicative*, and *acts*, which are not in the lexicon. The user assigns a lexical

Figure 7.7
Reference Selection Screen Layout

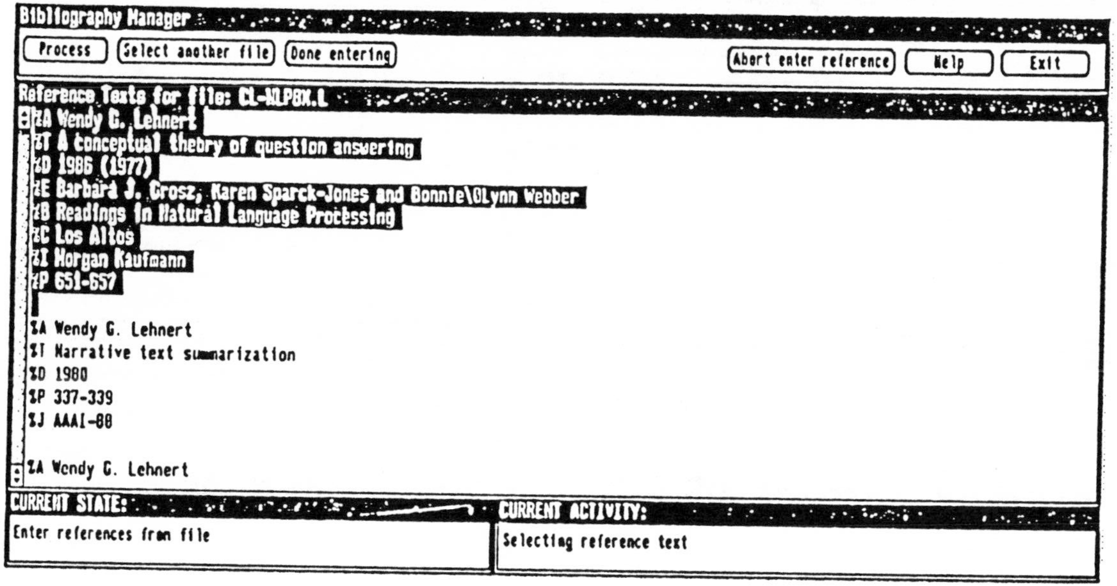

Bibliography Manager

[Process] [Select another file] [Done entering]　　　　　　[Abort enter reference] [Help] [Exit]

Reference Texts for file: CL-AD.PBDX.1

%A Wendy G. Lehnert
%T A conceptual theory of question answering
%D 1986 (1977)
%E Barbara J. Grosz, Karen Sparck-Jones and Bonnie\Olynn Webber
%B Readings in Natural Language Processing
%C Los Altos
%I Morgan Kaufmann
%P 651-657

%A Wendy G. Lehnert
%T Narrative text summarization
%D 1980
%P 337-339
%J AAAI-80

%A Wendy G. Lehnert

CURRENT STATE:　　　　　　　　**CURRENT ACTIVITY:**

Enter references from file　　　　　Selecting reference text

Figure 7.8
Add to Lexicon

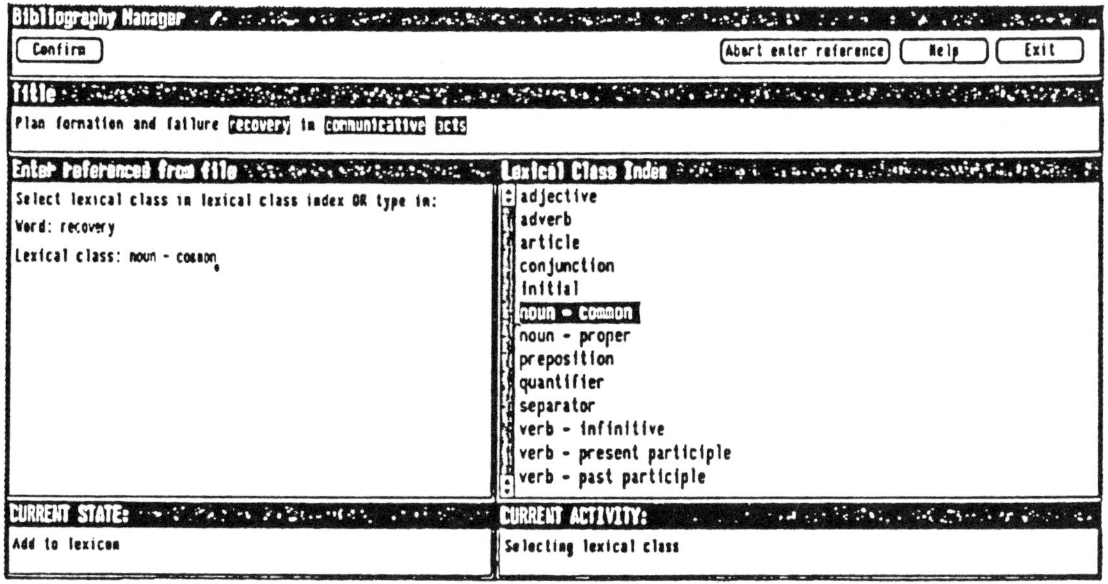

Bibliography Manager

Confirm

Abort enter reference   Help   Exit

Title

Plan formation and failure RECOVERY in COMMUNICATIVE acts

Enter References from file

Select lexical class in lexical class index OR type in:

Word: recovery

Lexical class: noun - common,

Lexical Class Index

adjective
adverb
article
conjunction
initial
noun - common
noun - proper
preposition
quantifier
separator
verb - infinitive
verb - present participle
verb - past participle

CURRENT STATE:

Add to lexicon

CURRENT ACTIVITY:

Selecting lexical class

class to each word by selecting from a lexical class browser or by typing in the class name. Once an assignment is confirmed (with the "Confirm" menu selection), the system builds the lexicon entry, unhighlights the newly entered word, and displays the next word for lexical class assignment in the dialogue area. After all assignments are made, the system continues parsing the title. In this implementation we provide a limited morphological module for verbs and nouns. The module builds verb lexicon entries consisting of three verb forms: basic form, past participle, and present participle; and noun entries consisting of singular and plural forms.

Lexical Class Selection

Once all the title words are in the lexicon, the system parses the title. Multiple parses could be found because of multiple lexical class assignments. Figure 7.9 shows a title in which the word *Retrieving* could be either in the "noun–common" or "verb–present participle" lexical class. The user selects the verb class as the appropriate class. Note that another *-ing* word, *skimming*, was not found to be ambiguous. This is because the grammar does not allow a pattern of the form: noun, verb–present participle, noun.

Word Sense Choice

When the user is asked to distinguish between multiple word senses, the system presents a browser that shows the immediate superconcepts of each sense as well as (currently uninterpreted) text definitions, if available. The user may open browsers to obtain further (browser-based) explanation of a sense. Figure 7.10 shows multiple senses of the word *dictionary*, as derived from the Collins dictionary (1988).

Define New Word

A new word that has just been entered in the lexicon must be defined (classified) in the knowledge base. The system can suggest definitions, by presenting more general concepts likely from the context in which the word was used in the title. The user may select from the suggested set of superconcepts or type in or select another list of superconcepts existing in the knowledge base.

In figure 7.11, the system is trying to understand the phrase "Collins English dictionary," and *Collins* and *English* are new lexical entries. The system makes use of the definition of the word *dictionary* as having a language and a publisher and suggests those concepts as likely superconcepts of the new word, *Collins*.

Attach Phrase

When there is insoluble, ambiguous attachment of a word or phrase, the user is prompted to make the decision. For example, figure 7.12 shows a title in

Figure 7.9
Lexical Class Selection

Bibliography Manager

Confirm

Abort enter reference   Help   Exit

Title

Retrieving information with a text skimming parser

Lexical class selection

Select lexical class in lexical class index OR type in:

Word: Retriev**ing**

Lexical class: verb - present participle

Lexical Class Index

⊟ noun - common

verb - present participle

⊟

CURRENT ACTIVITY:

Selecting lexical class

CURRENT STATE:

lexical class selection

94

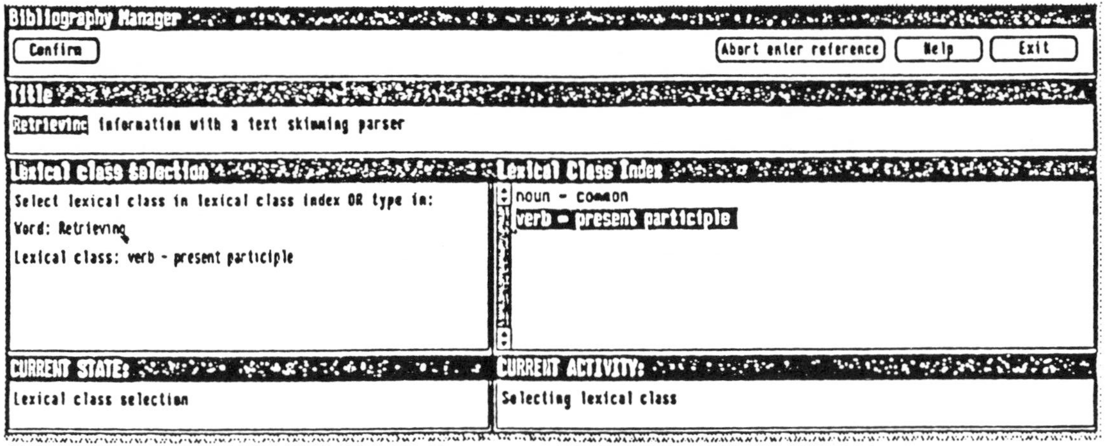

Figure 7.10
Word Sense Choice

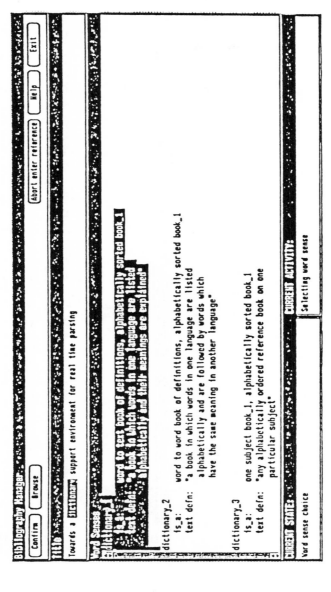

95

Figure 7.11
System-Guided New Word Definition

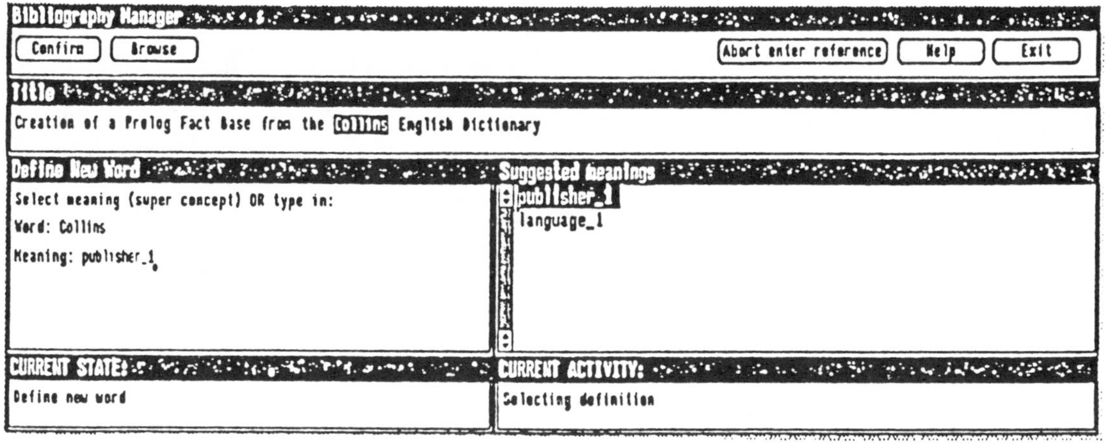

Bibliography Manager

Confirm | Browse

Abort enter reference | Help | Exit

Title

Creation of a Prolog Fact Base from the [Collins] English Dictionary

Define New Word

Suggested Meanings

Select meaning (super concept) OR type in:

publisher_1
language_1

Word: Collins

Meaning: publisher_1

CURRENT STATE:

Define new word

CURRENT ACTIVITY:

Selecting definition

Figure 7.12
Attach Phrase

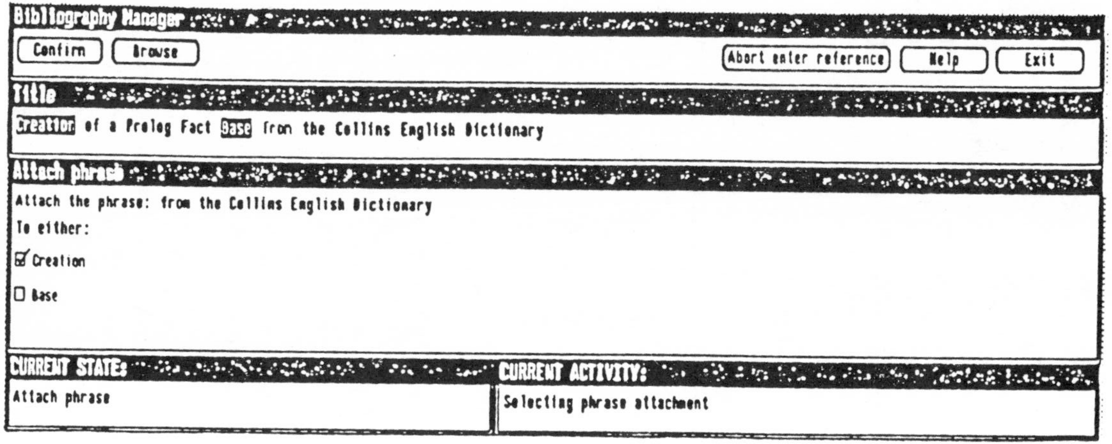

Bibliography Manager

Confirm Browse

Abort enter reference Help Exit

Title

Creation of a Prolog Fact BASE from the Collins English Dictionary

Attach phrase

Attach the phrase: from the Collins English Dictionary

To either:

☑ Creation

☐ Base

CURRENT STATE

Attach phrase

CURRENT ACTIVITY:

Selecting phrase attachment

which the user is asked to attach "from" ("from the Collins English dictionary") to either "Base" or "Creation."

Define Relation

To classify a new concept in the existing knowledge base, the new slots/relations must first be defined with respect to the slots of existing concepts. The system performs automatic relation definition when there are unambiguous slot-name and value-type matches. The system can automatically modify a slot in the new concept, if there is a superslot whose value type subsumes the value type of that slot. If contextual information does not help in unambiguous slot assignment, the system presents alternative superslot definitions for selection, as shown in figure 7.13.

BROWSE

A user is in one browse state at a time, but has available three main types of browsers (three windows), as shown in figure 7.14. Typically, the three browsers are used together. First, one may browse alphabetically for an existing concept with a similar spelling. Then, one may browse its super- or subhierarchy to see how the concept is defined in the knowledge base. If more detail is needed, the immediate relations of a concept can be viewed in the neighborhood browser.

QUERY

In a query (figure 7.15) the user specifies a single concept name (noun phrase) for which the system will find related publications by typing a phrase or using browsers to copy a concept name into the query specification. Once the query concept is understood and integrated with the knowledge base (the same process as for a title), the system starts a query dialogue by showing how many references are subsumed by the query concept, and, depending on the value of this number, the system suggests query reformulation. At any point in a reformulation dialogue the user may accept the result or continue reformulation. The final result of a query can be displayed in a window or be printed out.

Figure 7.15 shows how an initial query, "Dialog with computers in Dutch," is reformulated through a series of generalization, shift, and specialization steps. In this example, the user ended the query reformulation with the concept "answering systems." The subsumed reference texts are displayed in the query result window.

When a user browses concepts for reformulation in a query dialog, the system displays statistics indicating the number of related references. For example, the vector $(1, 1, 2)$ in the query history window of figure 7.15 indicates that there is one reference subsumed by the concept, one reference directly linked, and two references are subsumed by concepts in the neighborhood of the focus concept/

Figure 7.13
Define Relation

Bibliography Manager

[Confirm] [Browse]   (Abort enter reference) (Help) (Exit)

Title

ACCESSING knowledge through natural language

Define the word

Define the relation: through

To be either:

☑ means/method of Accessing

☐ by/agent of Accessing

☐ A NEW RELATION

CURRENT STATE: **CURRENT ACTIVITY:**

Define relation   Selecting relation definition

Figure 7.14
Browsers

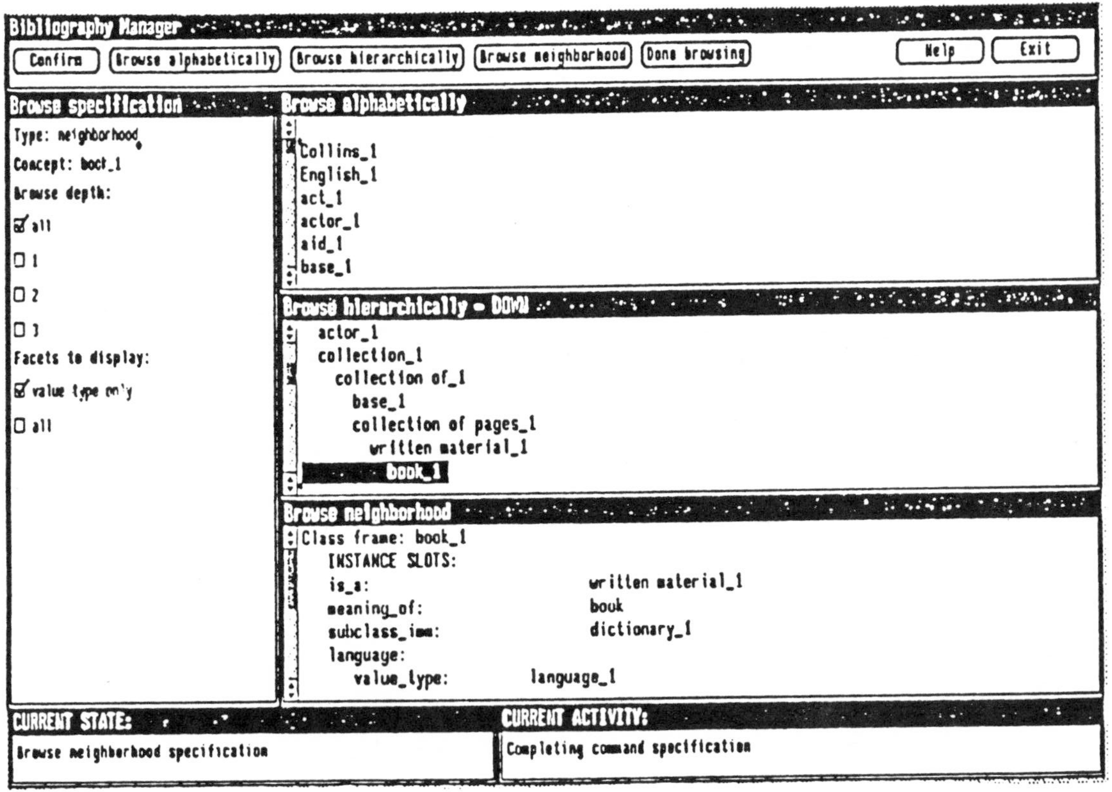

Bibliography Manager

Confirm | Browse alphabetically | Browse hierarchically | Browse neighborhood | Done browsing | Help | Exit

Browse specification

Type: neighborhood
Concept: book_1
Browse depth:
☑ all
☐ 1
☐ 2
☐ 3
Facets to display:
☑ value type only
☐ all

Browse alphabetically

Collins_1
English_1
act_1
actor_1
aid_1
base_1

Browse hierarchically - DOWN

actor_1
collection_1
collection of_1
base_1
collection of pages_1
written material_1
book_1

Browse neighborhood

Class frame: book_1
INSTANCE SLOTS:
is_a: written material_1
meaning_of: book
subclass_im: dictionary_1
language: language_1
value_type:

CURRENT STATE:
Browse neighborhood specification

CURRENT ACTIVITY:
Completing command specification

100

Figure 7.15
Query Dialog and Result Display

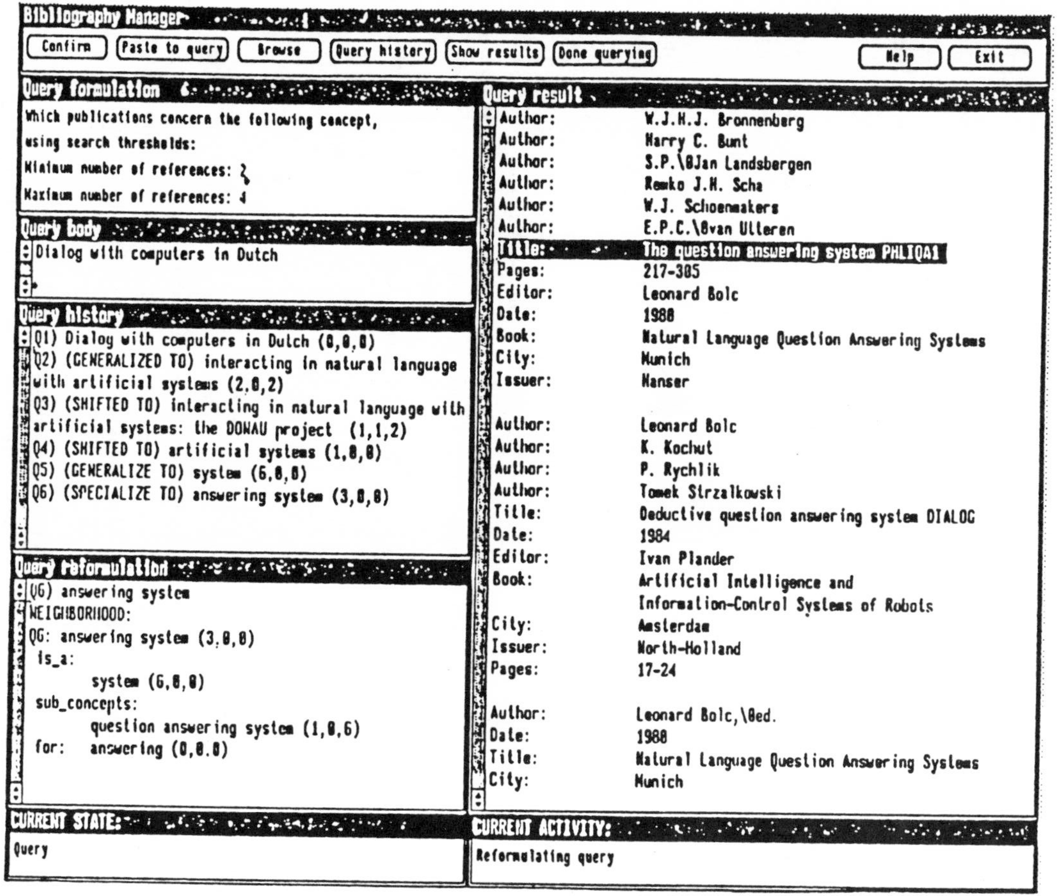

Bibliography Manager
[Confirm] [Paste to query] [Browse] [Query history] [Show results] [Done querying]   [Help] [Exit]

Query Formulation
Which publications concern the following concept,
using search thresholds:
Minimum number of references: }
Maximum number of references: 4

Query Body
Dialog with computers in Dutch

Query history
(Q1) Dialog with computers in Dutch (0,0,0)
(Q2) (GENERALIZED TO) interacting in natural language
     with artificial systems (2,0,2)
(Q3) (SHIFTED TO) interacting in natural language with
     artificial systems: the DONAU project (1,1,2)
(Q4) (SHIFTED TO) artificial systems (1,0,0)
(Q5) (GENERALIZE TO) system (6,0,0)
(Q6) (SPECIALIZE TO) answering system (3,0,0)

Query Reformulation
(Q6) answering system
NEIGHBORHOOD:
Q6: answering system (3,0,0)
is_a: system (6,0,0)
sub_concepts:
     question answering system (1,0,6)
for: answering (0,0,0)

CURRENT STATE:
Query

Query result

Author:	W.J.H.J. Bronnenberg
Author:	Harry C. Bunt
Author:	S.P.\@Jan Landsbergen
Author:	Remko J.H. Scha
Author:	W.J. Schoenmakers
Author:	E.P.C.\@van Utteren

Title: The question answering system PHLIQA1
Pages: 217-305
Editor: Leonard Bolc
Date: 1988
Book: Natural Language Question Answering Systems
City: Munich
Issuer: Hanser

Author:	Leonard Bolc
Author:	K. Kochut
Author:	P. Rychlik
Author:	Tomek Strzalkowski

Title: Deductive question answering system DIALOG
Date: 1984
Editor: Ivan Plander
Book: Artificial Intelligence and
      Information-Control Systems of Robots
City: Amsterdam
Issuer: North-Holland
Pages: 17-24

Author:	Leonard Bolc,\@ed.

Date: 1988
Title: Natural Language Question Answering Systems
City: Munich

CURRENT ACTIVITY:
Reformulating query

101

query. Pollitt's MenUSE system (Pollitt, 1988) also gives a number showing the total number of subsumed references.

In this chapter we present an initial implementation of Bibliography Manager designed for demonstration purposes. For the simplified version of the query algorithm we assume the following knowledge base structure:

- a reference instance is directly linked to only one concept representing the title;

- the knowledge base consists of title knowledge built from title texts and dictionary knowledge built from dictionary/user definitions of words; and

- all words with the same stem but from different lexical classes and/or inflection point to a single concept representing the meaning of the noun.

From the user's viewpoint each concept in the knowledge base is indexed by its name(s) and described by its set of superconcepts, subconcepts, definiens concepts (the concepts that define the given one), and definiendum concepts (the concepts that are defined by the given one).

In a query dialogue, the user is presented with a list of concepts. The user may select one to switch the query focus. This might happen, if too many or too few references are subsumed, but there are specializations or generalizations of the query concept. The user may also shift the query focus to a related concept in the immediate neighborhood (neighborhood 1) of the current query focus. It is possible to execute changing of query focus automatically according to built-in rules, for example, generalizing the original concept until the number of subsumed references is within given limits specified by the user (minimum and maximum number of references expected to be found).

We now describe the query reformulation process, using the following notation:

C - concept name

$C(T,S,P,R)$ - neighborhood (1) of concept C, where
$T = [T1, T2, \ldots, Ti]$ denotes the set of superconcepts
$S = [S1, S2, \ldots, Sj]$ denotes the set of subconcepts
$P = [P1, P2, \ldots, Pk]$ denotes the set of definiens concepts
$R = [R1, R2, \ldots, Rl]$ denotes the set of definiendum concepts

$C(s,d,p,r)$ - represents concept C, where
s is the number of references subsumed by C
d is a number of references directly linked (subsumed) to C
p is a number of references subsumed by concepts in P
r is a number of references subsumed by concepts in R

(Three numbers are used in the example of figure 7.15: $C(s,d,p)$.)

L - minimum number of references expected by the user
M - maximum number of references expected by the user
Q - query concept formulated by the user (initial focus)

Query reformulation dialog

Step 1:

$Q1(s,d,p,r)$

1. $Q1(s,d,p,r)$ is a concept in the knowledge base specified by the user.

1.1 If $s < L$ then

the system displays the hierarchy of superconcepts of $Q1$: $A1, A2, \ldots$, Ak, where $A1 = Q1$ and Am, for $m = 2, \ldots, k$, is a superconcept of $A1$ and $s' \leq M$ for each $Am(s',d',p',r')$

The user either accepts the query result or generalizes the query focus by selecting one of the superconcepts (Am)

1.2 If $s > M$ then

the system displays the hierarchy of subconcepts of $Q1$: $B1, B2, \ldots$, Bk, where $B1 = Q1$ and Bm, for $m = 2, \ldots, k$, is a subconcept of $B1$ and $s' \geq L$ for each $Bm(s',d',p',r')$

The user either accepts the query result or specializes the query focus by selecting one of the subconcepts (Bm)

In steps 1.1 and 1.2, in addition to generalization or specialization hierarchy, the system displays the neighborhood (1) of the current query focus. The user may select a concept in the neighborhood (1) of $Q1$ instead of one in a hierarchy.

1.3 If $L \leq s \geq M$ then

the system displays neighborhood (1) of $Q1$: $Q1(T,S,P,R)$

The user either accepts the query result or changes the query focus by selecting a concept in the neighborhood (1)

Step 2:

$Q2(s,d,p,r)$, where $Q2$ is a concept selected in Step 1. the system displays neighborhood (1) of $Q2$: $Q2(T,S,P,R)$

The user either accepts the query result or changes the query focus by selecting a concept in the neighborhood (1); the system performs the analysis of reformulated query as in step 1 and expects further reformulation or query result acceptance.

Step 2 can be repeated until the user terminates the query by selecting "Display result" or "Print result" or "Quit query" in the menu.

CONCLUSIONS

• The system presented in this chapter has been implemented using Quintus Prolog and Prowindows on a Sun–3. The current system allows entering references from a file, as shown in figures 7.5 through 7.7, allows "Add to Lexicon" and "Lexical Class Selection" (figures 7.8 and 7.9) of the text understanding process, as well as browsing, as shown in figure 7.14. The screen describing the query state, shown in figure 7.15, reflects results we have found from a knowledge base manually constructed from about 35 titles.

- The user interface to textual information retrieval systems can benefit from natural-language processing and knowledge-based technology.

- A system that maintains domain knowledge allows communication at the conceptual level and allows expansion of the knowledge base as needed.

- The quality of the presented system depends on the power of the natural language processing module, the power of the knowledge representation language, and the amount of relevant knowledge in the system.

- We compensate for limitations in the above areas by building a user interface to conduct a dialogue to disambiguate natural language and to maintain knowledge.

- The use of multiple windows allows the user to interact with a number of objects. A common window configuration for the interfaces consists of presentation of title text, presentation of knowledge, and a dialogue box for decision making. We prefer to use a fixed configuration of windows in order to reduce the user's burden in window manipulation.

- Conceptual knowledge presentation (explanation and browsing) is a factor in user acceptance of a practical, usable system.

- Use of a strict KL-One-like knowledge representation language puts a useful constraint on the complexity of knowledge structures.

REFERENCES

Brachman, R. J., and J. G. Shmolze. 1985. An Overview of the KL-ONE Knowledge Representation System. *Cognitive Science* 9:171–216.

Chafetz, B., and Z. Mikolajuk. 1988. Bibliography Retrieval Based on Title Understanding. Philips Electronics, Advanced Development Group report.

Collins COBUILD English Language Dictionary. 1987. London: Collins Publishers.

Gazdar, G., A. Franz, K. Osborne, and R. Evans. 1987. *Natural Language Processing in the 1980s—A Bibliography.* Stanford, Calif.: Center for the Study of Language and Information.

Mark, W. 1986. Knowledge-Based Interface Design. In *User Centered System Design*, ed. D. Norman and S. Draper, 219–38. Hillsdale, N.J.: Lawrence Erlbaum Associates.

Pollitt, A. S. 1988. MenUSE for Medicine: End-User Browsing and Searching of MEDLINE via the MeSH Thesaurus. Bethesda, Md.: National Library of Medicine. *RIA088*:547–73.

Regoczei, S., and G. Hirst. 1988. *Knowledge Acquisition as Knowledge Explication by Conceptual Analysis.* Technical Report CSRI–205. Computer Systems Research Institute, University of Toronto.

Rich, E., J. Barnett, K. Wittenburg, and D. Wroblewski. 1987. Ambiguity Procrastination. *IJCAI–87*:571–76.

Salton, G. 1988. Automatic Text Indexing Using Complex Identifiers. *ACM Conference on Document Processing Systems*, Santa Fe, N.M., December 5–9, 1988:135–43.

Structured Representation of Theoretical Abstracts: Implications for User Interface Design

Hannah Francis and Elizabeth D. Liddy

Information retrieval is concerned with finding those few documents in a system that best fit the users' current information needs. As such, the retrieval process is concerned with two types of representations: statement of the users' information needs, problems, or queries; and the documents or their surrogates stored in the retrieval system. Performance of the system could be upgraded by improving either of these representations.

There is much in the literature on users' problem statements (Taylor, 1968; MacMullin and Taylor, 1984; Belkin, Oddy, and Brooks, 1982) to suggest that expecting more of users' statements is not realistic. As Taylor pointed out in his seminal paper (1968), having users describe what it is they need, when they themselves are hardly articulate about what it is they don't yet know, is putting quite a strain on the communication aspect of the retrieval process.

At the same time, document representation techniques have advanced very little since the last major innovation of making the natural language portion of documents, usually abstracts, available for free text searching. This is not to say that more could not be done to improve the document representations, but until fairly recently, the reliance within information retrieval on statistical techniques of content representation showed few opportunities for substantive improvement. In current retrieval systems, a variety of term frequency measures are used in an attempt to determine which documents might be more *about* a user's topic of interest. Use of linguistic techniques, intuitively the most appropriate approach, has been limited to lower levels of linguistic analysis, namely morphology (stemming) and syntax (noun phrase identification). Recently, the feasibility of applying higher levels of linguistic processing, such as discourse analysis, for the improvement of document representation has been recognized. It may be possible for this new document representation to be of assistance to the user in increasing the understanding and statement of the information need.

In this chapter, we report on efforts to delineate a structured representation of one abstract type and suggest how this improved representation may affect the user-system interface of retrieval systems. The impetus for this investigation was the highly encouraging results found by Liddy (1988) in describing the discourse-level structure of empirical abstracts. In the hope of extending this general approach to a quite distinct type of abstract, we sought to discover whether abstracts reporting on theoretical work have a predictable set of information components and whether these occur in any predictable order within abstracts.

DISCOURSE ANALYSIS

Since documents and abstracts are texts, they are amenable to discourse analysis, the level of linguistics that is concerned with how units of language larger than a sentence function. Discourse linguistics is concerned with how these texts communicate, both through their structural organization and through the meaning imparted by sentences interpreted as a text, rather than singly. One major aspect of discourse linguistics is the investigation of the nature of the implicit structural organization of information in texts of different types. This is referred to as either text-level or discourse-level structure. It can be thought of as a superstructural organization of semantic content. However, it is not devoid of meaning, for the structure itself implicitly communicates semantically. For example, the simple fact that a sentence is the last line of a story communicates that what it contains is to be interpreted as the end of the story.

The theory of discourse linguistics suggests that texts that serve a common purpose among a community of users eventually take on a rather predictable structure and organization. Readers of office memos, city ordinances, academic course descriptions, and even obituaries could all attest to this fact.

STRUCTURE AND FORM

The overriding concern here is a search for the structure and form of the rhetorical reasoning process that can assist in the understanding of the nature of argumentation as it appears in theoretical abstracts found in information retrieval systems. Conventional argumentation theorists have been influenced by, and have rooted their work in, classical Aristotelian rhetorical proof (Anderson and Dovre, 1968, 235). The essence of this form differentiates between the treatment of probabilities (*enthymeme*) and that of certainties (syllogism).

A modern incarnation of this classical form is found in the work of McBurney and Mills (1968), who consider argumentation to be primarily concerned with levels of certainty. This orientation led the authors to develop a structure for analysis based on the inductive-deductive frame of reference. According to this model, argument is seen as a range of probabilities, that is, "possible, probable, plausible, or certainly true" (McBurney and Mills, 1968, 240). The authors also make the case for the inductive process as a means of getting at deductive argument. Here, induction is used as a linkage in the reasoning sequence to get at deductive arguments. Utilizing this philosophical base as a point of departure, McBurney and Mills developed a classification of arguments based on the logical relationship between the premise and conclusion. The forms of argument they identify are: cause, sign, example, and analogy.

Yet another approach to argument understanding has been posited by Brockriede and Ehninger (1968). Employing the conceptual principles developed by Toulmin (1964), these authors have devised a schema for classifying forms of argument. In addition to emphasizing the logical relationships between parts of an argument, the schema adds a new dynamic to argument understanding theory by incorporating logical (substantive) and nonlogical (authoritative, motivational) dimensions to the classificatory design. The Brockriede and Ehninger interpretation of the Toulmin model is useful for two main reasons in that it (*a*) provides a structure for analysis and criticism of rhetorical arguments, and (*b*) suggests a typology for classifying arguments based on rhetorical proofs.

Toulmin's Construct

It is useful to elaborate the structure for argument analysis developed by Toulmin (1964). This model provides a two-tiered analysis of argument described as "movement from accepted data through a warrant to a claim." The first tier consists of data, warrant, and claim.

Data consist of facts that reflect events, statistical data, citations from authority, and so on. If data do not exist, an essential component of argument is missing, because there is no factual base and the argument fails to inform. Claim is the substance of the idea conveyed in an argument. It has been referred to as the main proof line by Brockriede and Ehninger (1968). The claim can occur either as the final statement in an argument or at some midway position in an argument. The usual order is data first then claim. In this order, claim connotes *therefore*. The reverse order infers *because*. Warrant is the description of that component of the argument that moves the argument from data to claim. It certifies the proposition in the claim statement so that it becomes acceptable.

In addition to this first triad—data, warrant, and claim—Toulmin's construct contains a second set of components, of which all or some may exist in an argument. These are termed *backing*, *rebuttal*, and *qualifier*.

A backing is made up of measures of credentials designed to certify the beliefs of the warrant. This can be a single item or an entire argument within itself, complete with the first level triad of data, warrant, and claim. The rebuttal acts as a safety mechanism and is often attached to the claim statement. The rebuttal recognizes the cases in which the claim will be constrained, is invalid, or is in some way in need of a qualifier. The rebuttal places limitations on the scope of the validity of a claim by foreseeing possible objections. The role of the qualifier is to determine the strength of an argument. It does this by quantifying terms (e.g., *probably*), or by pointing out possible fallacies. When an argument is thought to be axiomatic and cannot be disputed, no qualifier is attached.

Classification Approaches

Brockriede and Ehninger devised their classification system based on the attributes of rhetorical proof. The first type of argument, substantive, is pictured as data that progress through to claim based on beliefs about things in the external world. The second, authoritative, is grounded in structures about the quality of the source from which the data are derived. The third, motivational, is based upon assumptions related to the emotive state such as the ambitions or inner drives of those who hear the argument. The assumptions of each class and its relationship to the two-level triad of elements for argument analysis are examined in turn.

Substantive Arguments. The substantive argument permits the discourse to move from data to claim and is rooted in assumptions about the logical relationships that exist in the external world. There are six possible orderings of this type of argument, as follows:

1. Cause. In this type of argument, data comprise facts about an event, person, object, or situation. The warrant provides the source of power for these facts and tells what effects they will have; claim relates these effects to the data

2. Sign. The data are made up of a set of symptoms. The warrant assigns appropriate meaning to these symptoms, and claim explains the objects, people, or situations that have these symptoms

3. Generalization. The data are made up of information about objects, persons, events, or conditions representative of given items in a class of things. The warrant posits that this representative sample will extend to the whole population. The claim clarifies the underlying assumptions of the warrant

4. Parallel Case. The data are made up of one or more statements about a single object, event, or condition. The warrant states that the case reported in the data resembles a second instance of the same category. The claim assumes that the new case can be likened to the first. A rebuttal in a parallel case argument obtains when (*a*) another parallel case has a strong similarity to the existing case or (*b*) some strong dissimilarity disaffirms the warrant

5. Analogy. The data report that a relationship of a certain nature exists between a pair of items. The claim amplifies the relationship implied in the warrant. The distinction between argument from parallel case and argument from analogy is that the former assumes resemblance between two cases while the latter assumes a similarity of relationship. Frequently, the relationship expressed in this type of argument requires the qualifier *possibly*

6. Classification. In this type of argument, the data reflect a generalized conclusion about known members of a class. The warrant assumes that the properties of the items under consideration can be extended to those items of the class that have yet to be examined. The claim gives to specific items the characteristics of the general statement. The provisos to argument from classification are (*a*) a class member may not share the special characteristics of the class specified in the data but may have enough other

characteristics to justify membership in that class, and (*b*) there may be instances when a given class member may not share the attributes of a class

Authoritative Arguments. In this type of argument, data are composed of either factual reports or stated opinions. The warrant attests to the reliability of these reports or opinions. The claim reinforces the data statements whose credentials are supplied by the warrant.

Motivational Arguments. The data in this type of argument are composed of statements grounded in the claims of previous arguments. The warrant provides the rationale for accepting the claim by appealing to some emotive quality, e.g., desire, in the hearer.

METHODOLOGY

In order to validate this classification scheme and the specific ordering of the different components of information in the various types of arguments defined above, a descriptive study was conducted on a sample of abstracts. Fifty-five argumentative-type abstracts were selected from different issues of *International Political Science Abstracts* under the headings *Political Thinkers and Ideas* and *Methods and Theories*.

Each abstract was classified by the first author (Francis) into one of three major groupings: substantive, authoritative, or motivational, based on the Brock-riede and Ehninger (1968) classification. The choice was made by locating different kinds of propositions, that is, those of value, fact, or policy. The abstracts reflecting each type of argument were subdivided into one of the six subcategories. Each abstract was examined for presence of both the first triad of elements (data, warrant, and claim) and second triad (backing, rebuttal, and qualifier).

Linguistic Clues

The second stage of the investigation was an examination of lexical clues and verb tenses. In this context, clue words are those words and phrases writers use to indicate explicitly how parts of the discourse should be interpreted. For our purposes, it was decided to concentrate on whether some of the clues to cohesion specified by Halliday and Hasan (1976) could be relied on to reveal which function of an argument was being performed by the different passages in each abstract.

Halliday and Hasan have outlined a taxonomy of types of cohesive relationships that conjoin one portion of text to another. One familiar type of explicitly marked cohesive relationship in texts is indicated by markers that relate what follows to what has been said before, for example, *and*, *but*, *so*, *then*. Halliday and Hasan (1976) provide an extended discussion of the relationships indicated

Table 8.1
Frequency of Second-Level Triad of Elements

	First Triad			Second Triad		
Substantive (n=38)	Data	Warrant	Claim	Backing	Rebuttal	Qualifier
Cause	11	11	11	7	—	5
Sign	20	20	20	9	11	11
Generalization	3	3	3	2	—	2
Parallel Case	3	3	3	3	1	2
Analogy	—	—	—	—	—	—
Classification	1	1	1	—	—	—
Authoritative (n=11)	11	11	11	6	3	7
Motivational (n=6)	6	6	6	1	1	3
Total	55	55	55	28	16	30

by such markers. For example, the classes of explicit markers for conjunctive relations are

- additive—and, or, furthermore, similarly, in addition;
- adversative—but, however, on the other hand, nevertheless;
- causal—so, consequently, for this reason, it follows from this; and
- temporal—then, after that, an hour later, finally, at last.

A frequency analysis was performed on all words occurring in the 55 abstracts in an attempt to determine whether there was a skewed usage of conjunctive clues within different components of the argumentative abstracts.

RESULTS

Of the 55 abstracts, 38 (68%) were found to belong to the substantive class, and 11 (20%) to the authoritative, while 6 (11%) were classed as motivational. The substantive class was subdivided into the six categories detailed above. Substantive/sign arguments occurred most frequently (20/38 times) followed by substantive/cause (11/38 times). There were no abstracts classed as substantive/ analogy.

Table 8.1 shows the number of occurrences of the two-level triad of elements with the three main classification groups as well as the subgroups of the substantive class. The first triad of elements (data, warrant, claim) was found in all 55 abstracts. In the case of second triad, rebuttal was found in 16 of the abstracts, while qualifier was found in approximately half of the abstracts (30). Backing occurred 28 times.

Table 8.2
Ordering of Argument Components

	Authoritative
Data	According to Tocqueville, the most important determinant of the character of any society
Claim	A political culture is shaped not only by sociological conditions and Laws, but also, in
Warrant	In Tocqueville's day, two dominant schools of thought were contending for influence
Backing	Neither one of these schools, Tocqueville argued, promoted a political culture that could
Qualifier	Unlike the opposing schools, the new political science could not be propagated directly
Backing	It's implementation relied on an indexed strategy - using institutions to inculcate certain

The results showed a reasonably predictable ordering of the structural components. Data preceded warrant (40/50) times; warrant preceded backing (33/55) times. An analysis was made of the observed orderings of the six components to detect what the most frequent order might be. As can be seen in table 8.2, there is no invariant ordering, although the most likely structure would be [DATA - WARRANT - BACKING - CLAIM]. There were no distinctive orderings for the three major classes of arguments established by Brockriede and Ehninger (1968); that is, substantive arguments, authoritative arguments, and motivational arguments do not differ significantly from each other in terms of the ordering of argument components. The conjunctive relations suggested by Halliday and Hasan's work on cohesion were not found to be predictive of the particular function in an argument being played by the pieces of text.

CONCLUSIONS

The above presentation of the different types of argument definitely suggests that patterns of form and structure can be found in argumentation texts. These results strongly support the premise that inspired this investigation, namely, that the rhetorical structure of argument is a useful framework in which to describe the structure of theoretical abstracts. In addition, since there were no significant differences between abstracts reflecting different types of arguments in terms of the ordering of components, it would appear that a single model will be suitable for describing the typical ordering of all such abstracts. However, the final goal of the researchers on the project, of which this study was a part, was to determine whether these orderings can be detected automatically by use of lexical clues. In this sense, the investigation was only partially successful. In order to present document representations that usefully identify the role that each portion of text performs in the argument, an automatic means of detecting these roles needs to be identified. Although this research did not successfully establish the set of lexical clues that could be relied on to structure theoretical abstracts automatically, it did delineate the culturally validated discourse structure of argumentative discourse as being the structure underlying theoretical abstracts.

The importance of this discourse-level structure to information retrieval systems is that it offers the potential of a predictable structured representation in which the specific content of individual theoretical abstracts might more easily be evaluated by users. If an interface could take advantage of a structure like that in table 8.2, those users who are not very familiar with the topic on which they are seeking information would be aided in improving their comprehension of the retrieved documents. Perhaps even more important, these structured representations of abstracts might be helpful to users as a means of refining their queries in the next iteration of the search.

REFERENCES

Anderson, J. and Dovre, P. 1968. "The nature of rhetorical reasoning." In *Readings in Argumentation*, ed. J. M. Anderson and P. J. Dovre, 235–41. Boston: Allyn and Bacon.

Belkin, N. J., Oddy, R. N., and H. Brooks. 1982. "ASK for information retrieval: Part I. Background and theory. Part II. Results of a design study." *Journal of Documentation* 38: 61–71, 145–64.

Brockriede, W. and Ehninger, D. 1968. "Toulmin on argument: An interpretation and application." In *Readings in Argumentation*, 263–78. Boston: Allyn and Bacon.

Halliday, M.A.K. and Hasan, R. 1976. *Cohesion in English*. London: Longman.

Liddy, Elizabeth. 1988. "The discourse-level structure of natural language texts: An exploratory study of empirical abstracts." Ph.D., Syracuse University.

McBurney, J. and Mills, G. 1968. "Probabilities." In *Readings in Argumentation*, 240–42. Boston: Allyn and Bacon.

MacMullin, S. and Taylor, R. S. 1984. "Problem dimensions and information traits." *The Information Society* 3: 91–111.

Taylor, R. S. 1968. "Question-negotiation and information seeking in libraries." *College and Research Libraries* 29: 178–94.

Toulmin, S. 1964. *The Uses of Argument*. Cambridge: Cambridge University Press.

PART III

HYPERDOCUMENTS

Gary Marchionini

Hypertext is text in electronic form that takes advantage of the random access capabilities of computers to overcome the strictly linear medium of print on paper. Hypertext consists of fragments of text called nodes that are related to one another through links that are traversable by simple keystrokes or mouse clicks. The effect of hypertext is to broaden the communication channel between author and reader. In addition to expressing their ideas as continuous sequences of words, authors are able to provide explicit links among their ideas that may be physically disparate in printed form, and provide implicit links to the ideas and tools of others. Readers are empowered to traverse documents according to their own needs and abilities and, in some systems, to change and edit the text. Thus, communication channel capacity is broadened both conceptually and physically for both authors and readers.

Hypertext is intuitively appealing because it seems to parallel human associative memory, which is able to link disparate memory traces purposefully and meaningfully. Systems that support such processing invite browsing and serendipity. The essence of hypertext is the freedom to present and use text in personal and interactive ways. However, freedom also demands responsibility, and therein lie many of the problems with hypertext systems. Authors must accept responsibility for providing logical links, readers must conduct sensible traversals, and designers must create systems that support the needs of both.

A variety of hypertext systems are commercially available and are being tested for a broad range of texts. Obvious applications include text meant to be used in discrete rather than comprehensive ''chunks'' such as technical documentation and user manuals; dictionaries, encyclopedias, and other reference works; and indexes and other secondary information sources. Since the very purpose of such texts is to provide well-defined collections of fragments of text that are organized for easy location and that include explicit pointers to related fragments, they are natural applications for hypertext systems. Another area of considerable interest is education and training, where text can be used by learners according to their own abilities and interests. Educational applications range from highly interactive texts completely under learner control and aimed at self-directed learning (the discovery learning approach) to hypertext editions of classic linear texts, where links are limited to augmentations such as teacher notes, published commentary, and dictionaries or encyclopedias. Comprehensive texts such as technical reports, journal articles, and monographs are also being tested in hypertext form since both links within the documents and out to other documents can be easily facilitated. Some authors are even experimenting with hypertext novels that allow readers great flexibility in reading the work.

As hypertext systems continue to improve, and as experience with hypertexts grows, it will become clearer exactly which types of texts are appropriate for hypertext and which are not. In the interim, it is likely that applications will continue to emerge that range from simple electronic representations of linear texts with flashy footnotes to random collections of words (perhaps produced by a monkey at a keyboard?), each of which is connected to every other word by a keystroke or mouse click sequence (hyperchaos). To avoid such useless extremes, systematic examination of the emerging applications is critical.

As with any emerging technology, advantages of application are accompanied by costs and disadvantages. The advantages of user control, browsability, parallels to human associative memory, and easy linking of disparate fragments of texts make demands on both authors and readers of hypertexts. New literacy for writing and reading is needed, publishing standards must be developed, and hardware and software engineering progress must be made. One important problem that hypertext presents to users is how to navigate text. In print, navigation is mostly top-down, with occasional interruptions for footnotes and citations. Hypertexts typically provide numerous explicit links to other text fragments at any given moment and often support implicit links to supplementary texts at any time (e.g., background readings, critiques, dictionaries, encyclopedias). Users, therefore, are continuously making choices about which fragment to read next. What effects this additional decision-making load will have on overall comprehension of information is an important research problem. In addition to the possible cognitive interference created by navigational decision making, undisciplined users may be easily distracted from their original information-seeking goals. Navigation in an electronic medium can also lead to disorientation as users jump from fragment to fragment. Similar questions related to node granularity, link types and methods, and interface standards must be addressed.

Hypertext offers users both challenges and opportunities for communication. Developments in hardware, software, and applications will surely continue, and the marketplace will eventually determine the viability of particular hypertext applications. Research and evaluation of systems and their applications should guide and shape these developments, however, so that valuable time and resources are not wasted on reinventions of old products and simple enthusiasm about a new technology. This part of the book represents the efforts of several groups that are grappling with the issues and problems of hypertext applications.

Marchionini, Liebscher, and Lin describe their experiences with group authoring of hypertexts from two perspectives: creating original hypertexts and importing and linking existing documents into hypertext form. They suggest that groups of authors must carefully plan both content and format before writing text and that editing must go beyond style and grammar to address continuity of links. Groups who retrofit existing text for hypertext systems must grapple with breaking the text into nodes, identifying and adding links, and importing text into the system.

Moline's work also combines two genres of software. She presents an example that combines hypertext with an expert system for identifying and managing coins as art objects. Her system has been implemented and illustrates how the best features of two powerful technologies can be combined to manage both textual and graphic information.

Girill considers the important issue of node granularity—how large text fragments should be. He argues from both the user's and system's points of view in favor of large-sized chunks of text rather than small chunks. Based upon his considerable experience with a large-scale online documentation effort, he suggests that large chunks of text help users conduct searches and minimize the system overhead needed to support searching and maintain the databases.

Shepherd and Watters address the problem of paths defined by the authors of a hypertext. In most systems, authors constrain the traversals users can make because links are defined in advance. They present the notion of transient hypergraphs as dynamic paths that the system creates "on the fly" as users traverse a database. Their system has been implemented and is illustrated with examples from a cocitation application. Their work blends the effectiveness of database management systems for managing data structures with hypertext's interface that supports browsing.

Krietzberg presents a vision of hypertext as a medium that expands information detail according to the needs of the user. He argues that such hypertext systems can help users manage information overload by providing details on demand. He suggests that many of the disorientation and cognitive-load problems are due to poor design of hypertexts rather than limitations inherent in the technology.

Lindeman, Bonneau, and Pocius present foundational work on organizational patterns that people actually use for information sources. The user's perspective they provide serves as a beginning for the development of virtual libraries and the creation of useful, large-scale hypertext systems.

9

Authoring Hyperdocuments: Designing for Interaction

Gary Marchionini, Peter Liebscher, and Xia Lin

Hypertext systems can be used to author original hyperdocuments or to edit and link fragments of existing text (post hoc authoring). This chapter presents examples of both types of authoring and characterizes the process of group authoring. Hyperdocuments using the Hyperties system were created by experts for use in a research project and by novices as part of formal course-work. Key problems for all authors include identifying proper node granularity for targeted topics and users and structuring a network of links that allows users to browse meaningful paths such as themes, chronology, or concept. Issues for original hyperdocuments that involve group efforts include creating discrete modules, integrating modules, assuring consistency of style, and controlling vocabulary. Issues for post hoc designs include copyright, importing text and graphics, identifying relationships in materials and implementing links, controlling vocabulary, and editing for style and length. Strategies used to support various authoring approaches are presented and discussed.

INTRODUCTION

Hypertext and hypermedia systems support both development and delivery functions for a variety of electronic information systems. Although the Memex and other visions of scholars' workstations have been with us for four decades, the recent availability of powerful microprocessors and advances in software engineering now provide the impetus for a variety of hypermedia implementations. A number of systems have been developed (Conklin, 1987), and hypermedia databases are emerging for information retrieval, software engineering, entertainment, and education. (See the *Proceedings of Hypertext '87*; the July 1988 issue of *Communications of the ACM*; the January 1988 issue of *IEEE Computer*; the November 1988 issue of *Educational Technology*; and the May 1989 issue of the *Journal of the American Society for Information Science* for diverse collections of hypermedia applications). Most of these applications have been completed by designers of specific systems or other computer specialists, but an increasing number of computer novices or casual computer users are beginning to use these systems to create their own hyperdocuments.

This chapter characterizes two distinct approaches to authoring in electronic environments and illustrates some of the problems inherent in the collaborative authoring of hyperdocuments. Illustrations are based upon ongoing work conducted by the authors and are limited to "static" documents (those that readers typically do not change) as opposed to "dynamic" documents that readers typically do change and supplement such as Xanadu (Nelson, 1988) and Intermedia (Yankelovich et al., 1988). Furthermore, this chapter focuses on authoring documents that are primarily textual rather than multimedia. The more specific term *hypertext* is used rather than the more generic term *hypermedia*, although the problems and issues of authoring apply as well to hypermedia systems.

THE AUTHORING PROCESS

Authoring is distinct from writing in that the results are meant to be presented and used primarily in electronic form. Authoring hyperdocuments is characterized by the representation of ideas as information units (nodes) and the linking of those ideas through explicit and implicit pointers. Card and Moran describe the NoteCards system as a promising way to structure and represent ideas during the authoring process. They state, "We use the term *authoring* to refer to the larger intellectual task of gathering information, extracting and discovering ideas, structuring them, and finally composing them into a readable product" (1986, 194). Conklin (1987) describes linking as the "essence" of hypertext and presents distinct types of links for different types of relationships (organizational, referential, and keyword). From an authoring perspective, linking includes the process of finding and explicating relationships between existing segments of text as well as expressing relationships between newly created text. It is important to note that representation and linking apply both to original text and existing text. To distinguish the process of creating new text for a hypermedia environment from the process of adapting existing text to such an environment, we use original authoring for the former and post hoc authoring for the latter. In actual practice, these distinctions are a matter of degree, with many designers using both types of authoring as appropriate for different parts of their hyperdocuments (e.g., the Perseus Project [Crane, 1988]).

POTENTIAL AND PROBLEMS OF AUTHORING

Writers have long used footnotes, citations, and parenthetical notes to customize or alter the strictly linear progression of their ideas. Several authors have used novel organizational strategies to give readers alternatives to the sequential, linear flow of text. For example, Donald Norman's *The Psychology of Everyday Things* uses italics for sections that are anecdotal or elaborative, and Marvin Minsky's *The Society of Mind* uses exactly a single page to present each unit of discussion. More radical examples include Ted Nelson's *Literary Machines*, where bold facing and alternative chapter sequences provide navigational cues to the reader, and Douglas Hergert's *Dbase III*, where icons and bold facing are used for rich cross-referencing.

Presenting text in electronic form offers unique potential for personalizing, augmenting, and activating one's ideas. Authors can personalize their work by providing alternative links among ideas and allowing the reader to select which links to follow at the time of reading. They can augment their ideas with optional elaborations or links to other external electronic resources such as dictionaries or encyclopedias, and they can activate their ideas by including animation or simulations.

Creating documents meant for electronic presentation also brings a series of problems. Problems for readers include slower reading rates, even for high-resolution workstation displays (Hansen and Haas, 1988), additional cognitive load due to the navigational requirements that accompany nonlinear organizations, and disorientation due to the absence of physical cues such as thickness or weight. In addition to minimizing these effects, a primary problem for all hypertext authors is organizing ideas to take advantage of the medium. In post hoc authoring, breaking linear text into fragments (nodes) that are conceptually meaningful is challenging and may be constrained by the idiosyncrasies of particular systems. Furthermore, linking nodes requires identifying key concepts to serve as links among nodes, managing vocabulary and distribution of links, and executing the mechanical tasks of implementing links. In addition, post hoc authors must deal with the technical and legal issues of importing and manipulating large sections of existing text (see Mylonas, 1987, for a description of content markup approaches to these problems). The original author is not constrained by shaving square pegs to fit into round holes, as is the post hoc author, but must deal with the organizational problem immediately. A framework of ideas and relationships must be built before text is actually written. Electronic outlining aids were early examples of tools for organizing text, but much more powerful organizational tools and techniques are needed. A thesaurus construction kit would be useful to manage nodes and would give some hierarchical link control, but more specific tools for managing the combinatorial explosion of cross-references that invariably arise would be a welcome addition to any hypertext author's toolbox.

All hypertext authors must struggle with the human-computer interface problem (Wright, 1989). There are few precedents for making choices about display characteristics such as colors, fonts, and windows, or about navigational tools such as selection devices, browsers, and tours or paths. In early systems, many of these choices were made by default since alternative interface features were not available. As systems continue to improve, these choices will increasingly be made by the author, who in turn will need an experience base from which to draw optimal decisions.

SETTING AND HYPERTEXT SYSTEM

For the immediate future, both post hoc and original authoring approaches will play an important role in building the experience and research base needed. The cases below are meant to illustrate some of the potential and problems of hypertext authoring. The first case arose from a project that examines information-seeking strategies in various electronic encyclopedias. A hypertext database was created to complement existing electronic encyclopedias. The purpose for creation of this hyperdocument was to support a more general research effort, and it illustrates collaborative authoring by a small group of experts using post hoc strategies. The second case comes from class projects done in two sections of a graduate course in computer applications. The purpose for creation of these hyperdocuments was to explore group authoring while exposing students to hypertext as a computer application. This case illustrates collaborative authoring by a large group of novices using original authoring strategies.

Both cases used the Hyperties system to implement the hyperdocuments (Kreitzberg and Shneiderman, 1988; Marchionini and Shneiderman, 1988). Hyperties was used because authoring is much easier with it than with HyperCard and because it runs in 256K MS-DOS environments. It is particularly well suited to tasks that require fragments of text to be linked since it was originally designed as an electronic encyclopedia system. Words or phrases embedded in the text of an article are highlighted to indicate links to other articles. Selection of a highlighted term (by keystroke, mouse click, or touch) displays the target article. In addition, at any time the user can select a backwards link to the previous article, jump to a table of contents or index, or conduct a string search. Figure 9.1 shows a Hyperties screen from one of the hyperdocuments described below. Words or phrases that are underlined in the figure actually appear in color or reverse video on the screen, and indicate articles the reader may select.

CASE 1: POST HOC AUTHORING BACKGROUND

Examples of post hoc authoring include the Hyperties, HyperCard, and KMS versions of the special issue of *Communications of the ACM* and Harris and Cady's (1988) HyperCard rendition of *Masque of the Red Death*. Adaptation of existing printed documents to hypermedia forms and creation of implicit links among various existing electronic databases are new levels of "retrospective conversion" and will clearly play an important role in the information industry for many years to come.

As part of the work to examine mental models for print and electronic encyclopedias (NSF grant no. IRI–8718075), a small hyperdocument of 77 articles dealing with the topic "environmental pollution" was created so that user

Figure 9.1
Hyperties Screen Display

GLOBAL AIR POLLUTION

                                                        PAGE 1 OF 2

> Humans also pollute the <u>atmosphere</u> on a global scale, although
> until the early 1970s little attention was paid to the possible
> deleterious effects of such pollution. Measurements in Hawaii suggest
> that the concentration of carbon dioxide in the atmosphere is
> increasing at a rate of about 0.2% every year. The effect of this
> increase may be to alter the Earth's climate by increasing the average
> global temperature (<u>Greenhouse Effect</u>).
>
>   Certain pollutants decrease the concentration of ozone occurring
> --

NEXT PAGE   RETURN TO AIR POLLUTION   INDEX

Source: Cognetics Corporation.

Figure 9.2
Steps in Post Hoc Authoring

Selection and Rights

Concept Map

Importation
   "Chunking"

Edit
   Content, Style, Level

Link
   Vocabulary Control

Edit
   Add, Delete

Iterate

Source: Cognetics Corporation.

searches of a print encyclopedia, two CD-ROM encyclopedias, and a hyperdocument could be studied. Three researchers were involved in authoring this document. With the publisher's permission, a set of 55 articles was downloaded from a full-text CD-ROM encyclopedia (Grolier's *The Electronic Encyclopedia*). The authoring process used the steps outlined in figure 9.2.

There are important reasons for downloading existing text rather than creating an entirely new hyperdocument. A common constraint in authoring a hyperdocument is time—authoring hyperdocuments by downloading existing text can be considerably faster than writing new text. A further constraint is subject expertise. Sufficient expertise may be available for evaluating and editing existing text on a topic. However, creation of new text on the same topic usually requires a considerably higher order of expertise. This may not be available, as was the case in this project. While downloading existing text is attractive for some applications, difficulties may arise in finding appropriate text in suitable electronic form as well as obtaining permission from copyright holders for a new use of the material. Scanning printed text is an increasingly viable alternative for text not already in machine readable form; however, it requires time to operationalize ("train" and edit) optical character recognition techniques as well as obtaining copyright permissions.

A problem with collaborative authoring of a hyperdocument, whether original or post hoc, is the imposition of uniform standards. This is important if the hyperdocument is to read as a unified whole rather than as a collection of disjointed and fragmented pieces. In the case of post hoc collaborative authoring, the problem is compounded by differences in the downloaded text as well as differences of style and opinion among the authors of the hyperdocument. Our downloaded text was of fairly uniform style and quality due to the editorial standards imposed by the publisher of the encyclopedia. Furthermore, the downloaded text was written at the appropriate reading and technical levels of the audience, which our research was addressing. Selecting documents that match the appropriate user level is as important in post hoc authoring as in original authorship.

Procedure

Separate, comprehensive searches were performed independently in the Grolier encyclopedia by two of the researchers. All retrieved articles were downloaded as ASCII files and then printed and distributed among the three authors. The use of high-recall search strategies in a full-text environment made the retrieval of many nonrelevant articles inevitable, and a great deal of time was spent in discarding articles that were not relevant to environmental pollution. Articles that were retrieved by only one researcher were discussed in a group meeting, at which time their relevance to the topic of environmental pollution was determined. For all articles, inclusion in the database required the unanimous agreement of all three researchers.

Every article selected as relevant was then edited to eliminate unwanted text. This was necessary because the majority of articles retrieved dealt only partially with pollution. For example, the encyclopedia article on the earth's atmosphere contained several sections on atmospheric pollution. Determination of which text was unwanted was done jointly by the three researchers. The remaining text was then examined for important concepts. If an article contained several concepts and each concept was discussed at length, the article was divided into separate smaller articles.

Structuring articles for importation. Although the authoring process to this point was very time consuming, it was fairly straightforward. However, the task of organizing the many separate articles into a hyperdocument was far from easy or straightforward since a hyperdocument must have a conceptual structure that makes sense to the user and must provide the user with paths appropriate for the task. For example, a hyperdocument meant for background reading on a topic will probably require a different organization than one designed for retrieval of specific items of information. Structuring and editing the articles was managed using the original ASCII files and a standard word-processing package.

An introductory article provides entry for the user to the hyperdocument. This article is the first one the reader sees, and authors can use it to provide links to the several most important top-level concepts (articles). The user selects a link to one of these articles and the selected article appears on the screen. Each of these articles in turn has links to other important concepts. The organization of a Hyperties document tends to have a hierarchical structure near the top, but much more of a network structure for the remainder of the document. Two different approaches to organization are therefore desirable—a hierarchical organization for broad concepts and a semantic network organization for narrow concepts.

A rather broad hierarchical conceptual scheme for environmental pollution was devised by the authors to provide the initial hierarchical structure. A concordance of terms from all articles was created using a popular style/grammar checker, and the most important terms (most numerous after common words were eliminated) were selected as potential links between articles. An online subject thesaurus, if available, could serve as a useful tool for the development of conceptual scheme.

Once the conceptual scheme was developed, linkages between many of the articles were made. It was not unusual, at this point, to discover gaps in the coverage of a database. Not all concepts identified by the scheme had corresponding articles. It was necessary to write new articles or append fragments to existing articles to fill these gaps. For example, the scheme contained the concepts air pollution, water pollution, and land pollution, and there were corresponding general articles that covered the first two topics but not land pollution. An article was then written to serve as a link between the general topic environmental pollution and articles on specific aspects of land pollution.

Important terms obtained from the concordance provided help in selecting links between articles not suggested by the hierarchical scheme. In general, if a term appears in two articles then a relationship can be inferred and the two articles are candidates for linkage. However, use of terms in this manner only provides candidates for article linkage. In this project, many of the suggested links did not make sense and were not included in the final hyperdocument.

Vocabulary control is a considerable problem for post hoc authors in the context of linking. While original authors will embed appropriate link terms in their text as they create it, the post hoc author must deal with text as found. Sensible link terms for some concepts may simply not exist in the article. Where they do exist, different articles (by different original authors) may use a variety of terms for the same concept. Systems such as Hyperties make it possible to link several synonyms to the same destination article, but users may believe that each variation gives access to a different article. This can cause considerable frustration and confusion.

A thesaurus, if available, can be used to introduce controlled vocabulary terms as links. As such it can be a source of link terms where these do not exist and a source for preferred terms that can replace original terms. If a suitable thesaurus is not available, the concordance of ''important'' terms can be used to create a minithesaurus. However, a simple concordance of words will not be useful for controlling multiword terms. A suggested solution for controlling multiword terms is to place all such terms into the minithesaurus as they are encountered. The first instance of a multiword term becomes the preferred term (this can be adjusted later), and subsequent variations are replaced by this term in the hyperdocument. Creating even a minithesaurus is a considerable undertaking, but can be made to serve a dual purpose. Once completed, the thesaurus can itself become an index to the hyperdocument and provide an additional and valuable conceptual access point.

Importing to Hyperties. When the articles had been structured and vocabulary identified for linking, ASCII files were imported into the Hyperties system from the word-processing package. It should be noted that the technical process of forming links in Hyperties is relatively easy. In Hyperties, links are created by placing tildes around a word or phrase in an article that is to serve as a link to another article. The author then gives the system the name of the destination article and the link is automatically made. This is an easier process than in HyperCard, where forming links involves either creating a button to overlay a word or phrase and then manually linking that button to another card, or writing scripts to link objects. This is just one example of how a particular system can constrain the authoring process.

For this relatively small hyperdocument (77 articles) it was possible to graph the network of articles as it was constructed. Article titles were written on paper and tacked to a wall with the root (introductory) article at the top. Colored yarn was used to connect articles (one color for links leading out and one for links leading in). The selection of suitable hierarchical links between articles was not difficult without graphic aids. However, the appropriateness of other relations was much more difficult to determine, and the graph proved useful. Even quite careful selection of links resulted in circular paths and ''dead ends'' that may have confused and distracted users. The graphic representation of the hyperdocument made such circularity easy to spot and suggested further links that were not obvious through inspection of text only. This hyperdocument has been used for the ongoing research on information seeking and for other research related to incidental learning (Jones, 1989).

CASE 2: A PRIORI AUTHORING BACKGROUND

Examples of existing a priori authoring include Shneiderman and Kearsley's *Hypertext Hands-On!* (1989), the multitudes of HyperCard stacks available in commercial and public domain sectors, and the growing number of databases produced with Hyperties, Guide, and other personal-computer-based systems. Shneiderman and Kearsley (1989), Kearsley (1988), and Shneiderman (1989) provide useful general sets of guidelines for authoring hyperdocuments. They recommend (1) designing for specific user populations and tasks, (2) using small chunks of text for nodes, (3) using a root node to give an overview and entry point to the user, (4) carefully managing node and link names, and (5) giving attention to all aspects of the human-computer interface. Many technical issues remain to be resolved, such as how links should be represented (e.g., is a standard set of button icons needed?) and how feedback for linking should be provided (e.g., left/right screen wipes for forward/backward references, or screen zooms in/out for narrower/broader nodes). As authors gain more experience with documents created specifically for electronic media these guidelines can be tested and used as evolving principles for hypertext authoring.

Procedure

As electronic systems facilitate more collaboration among workers in all areas, it is likely that group authoring of hyperdocuments will become increasingly common. To explore some of the authoring guidelines above and introduce students to hypertext systems, a series of investigations of group authoring of hyperdocuments was conducted in the College of Library and Information Services at the University of Maryland in the 1988 spring and fall semesters. The first group-authored class project was designed to parallel the creation of the pollution database described above, and the second built on the experiences of the first.

Class Project 1. An organization for a pollution hyperdocument aimed at young adult readers was provided by the instructor. The organization was designed to focus on air and water pollution and use a number of general topics to act as linkages between air and water pollution. Parallel articles (effects, causes, and control) were required for each of the subcategories of pollution. Students were assigned to one of three teams, each of which was responsible for one of the major topics. ASCII files of 100 to 1,000 words were required for each article. Within each article, students were asked to place special characters around the words or phrases to be linked to other articles. Three weeks were allowed for students to turn in their work. In this activity, the intention was that student authors would simply identify links, and the instructor and graduate assistant would implement them using the Hyperties system. This approach brought a host of implementation problems. Simple importation to Hyperties was problematic due to students using different computer systems and disk formats, and the tedium of importing dozens of articles one at a time. Content was uneven due to the range of writing abilities and styles as well as to the diverse amounts of effort applied in finding, understanding, and reporting information. Linking was extremely difficult due to variations in wording, both within and across articles, and disjoint nodes (rather than overlap each other's topics, some students politely avoided mention of common or peripheral terms that should have served as links between articles).

Class Project 2. After the spring semester's experience, a more detailed approach based on the guidelines of Shneiderman and Kearsley (1989) was taken for the fall 1988 semester. Two different classes composed of students with no previous hypertext experience were involved. One class created an organization for the general topic "electronic documents," including lists of synonyms and possible questions the hyperdocument should address. Students in the second class were given 1 of 13 topics and specific guidelines for content, linking, and file management. For each topic, students were to write an overview article with predetermined file name and four subarticles such as applications, advantages, or history, each having a specific variation on the main article file name (a system constraint imposed by MS-DOS-based systems is the eight-character limit on file names). An introductory article was prepared as a root article containing links to each of the 13 overview articles. Guidelines for linking were established that imposed a semihierarchical organization on the database (figure 9.3).

Authors were asked to link their overview article to only the respective subarticles (children on level 3) and the root article (level 1). They were encouraged to link their subarticles as fully as they wished within sibling subarticles, but to link to other subarticles across topics (cousins on level 3) only through that cousin's parent (uncle on level 2). For example, to link the subarticle "History of E-mail" to an article "History of Electronic Journals," link to the main article "Electronic Journals" and let the reader select "History of Electronic Journals" from the main "Electronic Journals" article. Although this imposed additional hierarchical structure on the reader's ability to jump about the network of articles, it provided a level of authoring control in that authors did not have to know the details of subarticles authored by others. Students were also encouraged to use synonyms as long as they specifically noted them as such. One student was to edit the resulting articles for style, grammar, and spelling, to improve consistency of content and to identify which synonyms were to be included as links in the final document. The teaching assistant was responsible for assembling the final articles into a Hyperties database.

The importation of ASCII files to Hyperties went smoothly due to the careful file-naming rules, albeit slowly, since the Hyperties system required that files be imported one at a time. Although the linking of articles required substantial time and effort, the process was much more successful than the previous experience. For some of the articles that were dead ends (had no links except back

Figure 9.3
The Structure of a Hyperdocument

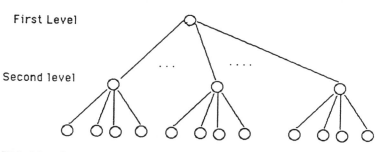

First Level

Second level

Third level

Links from the first level lead only to second level nodes.
Links from the second level lead only to third level children nodes and to
    the root node.
Links from the third level can lead to sibling nodes, any second level nodes
    or the root node, but not directly to cousin nodes.

Source: Cognetics Corporation.

to the article that led to it), links were added by providing additional text. The
resulting hyperdocument has a total of 81 articles and definitions displayed over
215 screens, and a total of 322 links. Of the 322 links, 83 are redundant within
articles, that is, the same term occurs as a selectable link more than once in the
same article.

Because efforts were made to control the authoring carefully, the resulting
hyperdocument is much more richly integrated than the previous hyperdocument.
However, the differing writing abilities and styles and the degree of knowledge
that authors brought to their topics are obvious. Moreover, although the amount
of time spent importing text and linking documents was less than the experience
with the first class, this still took substantial intellectual and technical effort.
Future collaborative authoring projects will include a peer review step where all
authors submit drafts to all other authors to give a sense of scope and style. This
should help diminish vocabulary control problems when forming links and provide more uniform node sizes and structures. Careful collaboration between the
editor responsible for grammar and style and the editor/compiler responsible for
importing and assembling the hyperdocument will also be encouraged.

DISCUSSION

Hypertext systems offer both opportunities and challenges for authors. This chapter illustrates some of the issues related to authoring in hypertext by describing efforts to import existing text into a hypertext system and the experiences of groups of novices authoring original hyperdocuments. Issues arising from these experiences are related to the concepts of nodes, links, system constraints, and group production of documents.

For post hoc authoring, node granularity, that is, dividing existing texts into appropriate fragments and standardizing on the length and level of technical detail, is a primary problem. Node granularity is also important for original authoring, but it can be controlled and optimized by careful planning that takes into account in advance the necessity of links and the fact that presentation will be strictly in electronic form.

Determining what relationships to illustrate with explicit links is a fundamental problem for all hyperdocument authors. Post hoc linking is similar to the problem of indexing since it requires finding concepts that identify relationships among units of information. For post hoc and original authoring strategies, attention to vocabulary control for both concepts (types) and terms (tokens) and consideration of the distribution of links by screen or node are important. Some systems such as Guide complicate while enriching the authoring process by allowing typed links that provide cues to readers about where (or to what) a link leads.

Systems constrain the authoring process. For example, by providing static user interfaces, defining what can be represented as a node or link, and limiting importation of text and graphics, systems limit the way nodes and links are defined and represented. Hyperties, for example, provides a simple encyclopedia metaphor for both authors and readers, allows nodes to be definitions, articles, or graphics, and limits links to words or phrases embedded in the text. HyperCard, on the other hand, provides an index card metaphor for nodes with a variety of field types as subnodes and a rich collection of button types for links between cards. Together with a programming language, these features offer HyperCard users great flexibility at the cost of more effort on the part of authors.

Group authoring offers the potential advantages of maximizing time and expertise as well as the problems of integrating various perspectives, skills, and styles. The experiences described in this chapter indicate that careful planning and communication among the participants can help minimize some of the problems, but much more remains to be learned about the authoring process itself.

Many claims have been made that hyperdocuments can reduce redundancy in text by allowing readers to select just the right units of information necessary for their needs. It is evident, however, that this requires readers to integrate the discrete units in an optimal fashion. The trade-off is between a reader's freedom and the cognitive load (responsibility) required to navigate and integrate nodes. In the hyperdocuments authored by students, we noted an excess of redundancy because authors tended to explain contextual details, claiming they were unsure what other articles readers would have visited before reading their articles. Especially for documents meant to be studied comprehensively, hypertext forms may not be appropriate unless accompanied by personalized tours or paths designed for readers. To what purposes hypertext should be applied and what level of redundancy is appropriate are related problems requiring considerable evaluation.

NOTE

The authors would like to acknowledge the assistance of Tricia Jones in implementing the Case 1 hyperdocument. This work was partially supported by National Science Foundation grant no. IRI–8718075.

REFERENCES

Card, S. K. and Moran, T. P. 1986. User technology: From pointing to pondering. In *Proceedings of ACM Conference on the History of Personal Workstations*, ed. A. Goldberg, 183–98. New York: Association for Computing Machinery.

Conklin, J. 1987. Hypertext: An introduction and survey. *Computer* 20(9):17–41.

Crane, G. 1988. Redefining the book: Some preliminary problems. *Academic Computing* 2(5):6–11, 36–41.

Hansen, W. and Haas, C. 1988. Reading and writing with computers: A framework for explaining differences in performance. *Communications of the ACM* 31(9):1080–89.

Harris, M. and Cady, M. 1988. The dynamic process of creating hypertext literature. *Educational Technology* 28(11):33–40.

Jones, T. 1989. Incidental learning during information retrieval: A hypertext experiment. Paper presented at the International Conference on Computer-Aided Learning, Austin, Texas, May 1989.

Kearsley, G. 1988. Authoring considerations for hypertext. *Educational Technology* 28(11):21–24.

Kreitzberg, C. and Shneiderman, B. 1988. Restructuring knowledge for an electronic encyclopedia. *Proceedings, 10th Congress of the International Ergonomics Association*.

Marchionini, G. and Shneiderman, B. 1988. Finding facts vs. browsing knowledge in hypertext systems. *Computer* 21(1):70–80.

Mylonas, E. 1987. Document and hypertext structure for Perseus: The advantages of content markup. Unpublished paper, Perseus Project, Harvard University.

Nelson, T. 1988. Managing immense storage. *Byte* 13(1):225–38.

Shneiderman, B. 1989. Reflections of authoring, editing, and managing hypertext. In *The Society of Text: Hypertext, Hypermedia, and the Social Contribution of Information*, ed. E. Barrett, 115–31. Cambridge, Mass.: MIT Press.

Shneiderman, B., and Kearsley, G. 1989. *Hypertext Hands-On!* Reading, Mass.: Addison-Wesley.

Wright, P. 1989. Interface alternatives for hypertexts. *Hypermedia* 1(2):146–66.

Yankelovich, N., Meyrowitz, N., Haan, B., and Drucker, S. 1988. Intermedia: The concept and the construction of a seamless information environment. *Computer* 21(1):81–96.

10

The User Interface: A Hypertext Model Linking Art Objects and Related Information

Judi Moline

This chapter presents a model combining the emerging technologies of hypertext and expert systems. Hypertext is relatively unexplored but promises an innovative approach to information retrieval. In contrast, expert systems have been used experimentally in many different application areas ranging from medical diagnosis to oil exploration. The information sources used in this model are limited to databases of images (object surrogates and maps), object descriptions, document surrogates (abstracts, references, excerpts), genealogical trees, and time lines of historical events. In addition to hypertext, the model uses an expert system shell to generate new information from data entered at a terminal or imported from a database. Sample uses of the prototype based on the model are studied to determine the range of activities that can be performed.

Apple's HyperCard and Cognition Technology's MacSMARTS are used with a knowledge base created by the author limited to Arab numismatics. Numismatists work with coins and coin surrogates. These objects contain information that is significant in isolation but that is even more important when aggregated. Further, a wealth of information related to each coin ranging from historical references to analyses by art historians needs to be linked to the specific objects. The prototype developed from the model is used to show how hypertext facilitated the resolution of some specific information needs.

INTRODUCTION

The hypertext model presented in this chapter was created to provide an environment in which the linking of art objects and related information could be explored.[1] In order to develop such an environment, a user community was identified and its needs were determined.

Recent research in information studies stresses the importance of considering the users' needs when designing information systems. Robert S. Taylor contends:

"The major, perhaps only, reason for the existence of an information system is to store and to provide information and knowledge in usable chunks to those who presently or in the future will live and work in certain environments, and who, as a result, have or will have certain problems which information may help in clarifying or even in solving" (Taylor, 1986, 24). Although information needs can be extremely personal, certain groups of individuals doing similar work or having similar training tend to need similar information systems. Thus, having an intimate knowledge of a particular user community facilitates the development of information resources for that particular group of information users.

The information system developed in this study is primarily for numismatists (coin collectors, dealers, and scholars). However, numismatic research contributes to a wide range of fields. Archaeology and ethnology, as well as historical studies in art, economics, linguistics, politics, and sociology, profit from numismatic documentation. As an information resource, numismatic literature and collections are widely distributed, difficult to access, and hard to integrate. Therefore, the development of this integrated, computerized information system designed for numismatists could serve a wider community.

Besides facilitating access of numismatic and related materials, the study of this particular user community has provided greater understanding of their needs. In working with traditional resources, each researcher juggles the information materials in an individual way. It is possible that by identifying the needs of this group, alternative ways of dealing with the resources might become apparent when using the new techniques. Further, it is expected that this model will provide input for similar studies.

NUMISMATISTS AND THEIR INFORMATION NEEDS

Collectors, dealers, and scholars often have large files itemizing their collections. Some of the files are records of coins held by the collector while others are records of coins pertinent to a particular research topic. In either case, the indexer sets up a cataloging system and creates the entries, which contain fields of information, usually in a prescribed order. Further, the vocabulary is often limited to a predetermined set of words. Thus, consistency in format or vocabulary is achieved only by rigid adherence to a scheme designed in advance of record entry. To date, uniformity and standardization among collections have not been a major concern.

In order to compile their coin catalogs, numismatists consult a variety of information sources. First of all, there is usually a standard reference for the particular type of coin against which coins are compared. This reference provides a number for each coin face. The reference for the obverse or front of the coin is not necessarily the same as for the reverse. The standard reference might be the catalog of a comprehensive collection or it might be a compilation of many collections with reference numbers unique to the publication. In addition to the standard reference, other coin catalogs are also necessary. The researcher dealing with unique or rare specimens wants to have as much information as possible about all of the extant coins of the type under study.

By matching details of the coins, a coin can be identified. Identification usually includes an identification number, physical information (the metal, weight, diameter, and die axis), descriptive information (images and inscriptions), historical reference information (dynasty, date, ruler, region, and mint), references (publication[s] including similar coin[s]), and information on where and when the coin was obtained. Further, depending upon the reason for the catalog, it may contain the cost of the item and its current value.[2]

Not all of this information is contained on the faces of the coin. Other resources are needed to relate named individuals to their period in history, to locate mints, to discuss minting customs and economic policy of the period, and to identify similar or identical objects.

Numismatists are using computers to help them with their research. Inventories are currently maintained on computers for museum as well as private collections. Further, a review of numismatic literature since the early 1980s points to increased interest in the use of computers. Twenty-two articles were found, and the topics include statistical methodology, classification, die link analysis and chronology, taxonomy, database, distribution, and estimating coinage and number of dies (*American Numismatic Society*, nos. 111–20).

THE MODEL

The model (figure 10.1) shows a variety of resources and tools surrounding hypertext. Hypertext serves to link the tools and resources. For example, the user can proceed from a record in one database directly to a record in another database. These records may be text, graphics, or both. The diagram takes into consideration the types of resources that might be needed by the users. The resources include a variety of databases. These databases replace the books or card files that a researcher would normally consult, for example, images, documents, and inventory. In addition to information resources, tools that would facilitate the researcher's work are included in the model (e.g., statistics, expert system).

The Collection Used in the Prototype of the Model

The collection of the British Museum (Walker, 1956, 5, 12–14, 32, 236–39) is used as the reference set for this model. It totals 28 coins, with 1 coin showing an emperor standing, 9 coins showing an emperor and his son standing, 2 coins showing a caliph standing, and 16 coins of the postreform type. The author has references for a total of 118 coins (1 of the emperor standing, 39 of the emperor and son, 7 of the caliph, and 71 postreform). The additional 90 coins were used as needed to simulate user input. All of these coins include the name of the mint

Figure 10.1
The Model

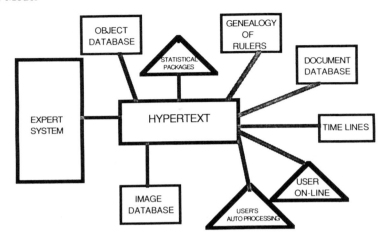

Note: Items in triangles have not yet been implemented.

because, to date, that is the only determining factor for a coin to have been minted in Baalbek.[3]

The objects used in this study are limited to Arab coins minted in Baalbek. Coins were minted at Baalbek under Byzantine rule, although there were no operational mints there at the time of its occupation by the Arabs. However, under the Arabs the minting of copper coins was reinstated. The copper coins that were minted there are similar in style and content to those of the neighboring cities.

The Tools Provided in the Prototype of the Model

Hypertext. Hypertext is ill-defined but includes the idea of nonlinear retrieval. When people read a journal article, they proceed in a linear fashion going from page one to page *n*. In contrast, when consulting a reference work, the user proceeds in a nonlinear manner. Topics are pursued as needed in a logical manner for that particular session, but that order may appear random at a later time. This latter method of nonlinear searching might be considered a basic model for hypertext. An initial interest or need for information results in accessing a particular database or information resource. Ideas, concepts, particular words, or illustrations spark interest in related ideas, and each user follows a particular interest or need. The materials with links built in allowing the user to jump from what appears to be one page to another, or one document to another, are referred to collectively as hypertext.

There are several hypertext software packages on the market.[4] What they all have in common is this facility of allowing the users to follow alternative paths through the contents of a database or databases. Some of the hypertext products provide complete functionality.[5] These products often have a prescribed default screen design, which allows input of material, particularly of text, without the user having to be concerned with layout design. They also usually have links that are associated with a particular word, phrase, or graphic. Other products facilitate the development of hypertext. These products do not provide a default layout but rather provide the tools that allow the creation of hypertext. HyperCard is of the latter type. In HyperCard the databases are called *stacks* and the primary type of link is called a *button*. Each record is called a *card*. Since HyperCard is an Apple product for the Macintosh, it uses the customary Apple menu interface. Clicking on a button results in an action, as does pulling down and pausing on an item in the menu bar. What is linked is dependent upon the individual or group setting up the particular implementation of hypertext.

Stacks are readily available as well as easily made. As stacks are developed, the author includes links that are appropriate to meet the objectives of the current work. Since links may be added at any time, the user could link stacks of diverse origin to make the information available in a way that is personally and immediately useful.

The model presented in this paper contains databases of text, graphics, and graphics integrated with text. The databases include records containing catalog entries (figure 10.2), genealogy (figure 10.3), maps (figure 10.4), passages from reference works concerning Baalbek (figure 10.5), minting as well as passages dealing with the analysis of Arab coins of the period under consideration (figure 10.6). Further, both scanned images (figure 10.2) and line drawings (figures 10.3 and 10.4) are included.

Expert Systems. Although not new, artificial intelligence, especially in the form of expert systems, is one of the newer tools to be provided for the researcher.[6] In its simplest form, an expert system has three components: a knowledge base, an inference engine, and a user interface. An expert system shell provides the inference engine and an interface to facilitate the construction of the knowledge base (Shafer, 1988, 132). The knowledge base depends on structured rules, called production rules, that may be written and entered as rules by the expert and/or may be generated by the software from a series of examples that are entered for this purpose or that are present in a database. The following are sample expert system rules:

Note: Early Umayyad Coin Types

Rule: 0

IF: coin obverse has emperor standing

AND: coin reverse has a large capital letter M in the field

AND: reverse has Greek letters on each side of the M in vertical rows

Figure 10.2
Object Database, Sample Card

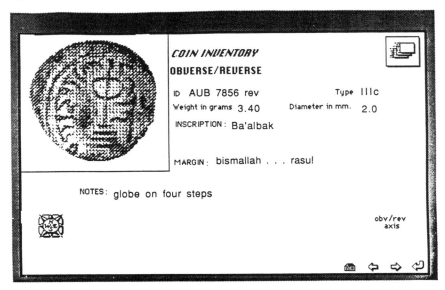

Source: Various HyperCard graphics and icons ©Apple Computer, Inc. Used with permission.

Figure 10.3
Genealogy of Rulers, Sample Card

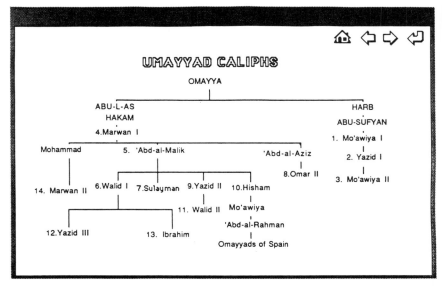

Source: Various HyperCard graphics and icons ©Apple Computer, Inc. Used with permission.

Figure 10.4
Image Database, Sample Card

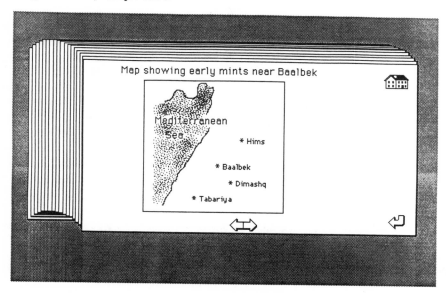

Source: Various HyperCard graphics and icons ©Apple Computer, Inc. Used with permission.

AND: reverse has Arabic inscription below the *M*

THEN: coin might be an early Umayyad fulus of Type IIb

Rule: 1

Show: COIN IIb

IF: coin might be an early Umayyad fulus of Type IIb

AND: coin diameter is approximately 2.16 mm

AND: coin weight is approximately 7.59 grams

AND: obverse has Greek inscription running downwards in right field

AND: vertical rows on reverse are POLE PLIO

AND: Arabic inscription below the *M* is Ba'labakk

CONCLUSION: coin was minted in Baalbek just before A.D. 692

Rule: 2

IF: coin obverse has two standing figures appearing to be Greek

ANDNOT: obverse has inscription

AND: coin reverse has a large capital letter *M* in the field

AND: reverse has Greek letters on each side of the *M* in vertical rows

AND: reverse has Arabic inscription below the *M*

THEN: coin might be an early Umayyad fulus of Type IIc

Figure 10.5
Document Database, History of Baalbek

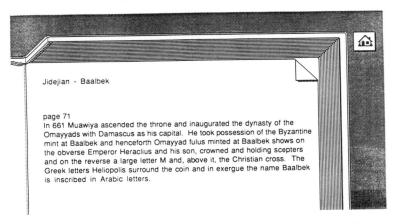

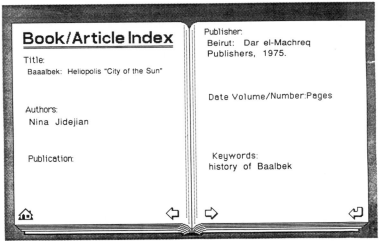

Source: Various HyperCard graphics and icons ©Apple Computer, Inc. Used with permission.

Rule: 3

IF: coin might be an early Umayyad fulus of Type IIc

SHOW: coin IIc

AND: Greek letters on reverse are (HE)LIO POLE

AND: Arabic inscription is Ba'labakk

CONCLUSION: Coin was minted in Baalbek about A.D. 692

Rule: 4

IF: coin obverse has bust of Greek emperor

Figure 10.6
Document Database, Minting of Coins

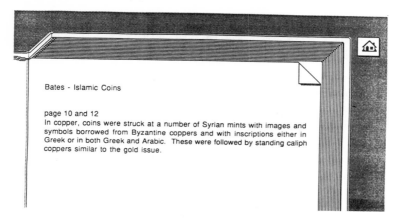

AND: obverse has Arabic letters on right side

AND: coin reverse has a large small letter *m* in the center

AND: reverse has Greek letters vertically placed on each side of *m*

AND: reverse has Arabic inscription below the *m*

THEN: coin might be an early Umayyad fulus of the Type IIe

Rule: 5

IF: coin might be an early Umayyad fulus of the Type IIe

AND: coin weight is approximately between 2 and 5 grams

AND: coin diameter is approximately between 1.5 and 2.5 mm

AND: obverse has Arabic inscription running down right side, b'Homs

AND: Greek letters on reverse are EMI CHC

AND: Arabic inscription on reverse below the line is tiyyib

CONCLUSION: coin was minted in Homs/Emesa about A.D. 692

Rule: 6

IF: coin obverse has an image of the caliph

AND: coin has Arabic inscription on both obverse and reverse

AND: coin has a cross on steps or a large letter *M* on reverse

AND: coin weighs approximately between 3.4 and 4.8 grams

AND: coin diameter is approximately between 19 and 21 mm

THEN: coin might be an early Umayyad fulus of the Type IIIc

Rule: 7

IF: coin might be of the Arab Type of early Umayyad coins

AND: coin obverse has caliph standing

AND: coin reverse has globe on steps

AND: reverse on right side of globe standard has mint, Ba'labakk

AND: obverse has marginal inscription

AND: obverse marginal inscription might begin with Bismallah

AND: reverse marginal legend begins, Bismallah

AND: reverse marginal legend contains, la ilah illa Allah wahadah

AND: reverse marginal legend ends with Muhammad

CONCLUSION: coin was minted in Baalbek between A.D. 694–696

When integrated into a hypertext system, the advice given to the user by the "expert" allows the generalist to benefit from the knowledge and experience of the real expert.

Generation of User Stacks and Reports

The user of the prototype system may decide to develop personalized stacks. These may consist of copies of any of the cards in the prototype or items added by the user. Allowing the user to manipulate the source materials and link them makes this resource appealing to many. If care is taken, the original stacks will remain as they were created so that the user can "seek, copy, and link" at will without spoiling the integrity of the materials for future users. Further, most of the products provide a print capability that allows particular cards to be printed as they appear on the screen or as part of a report.

In addition to the tools previously mentioned, a note-taking facility has been included in the prototype of the model. The button labeled *notes* takes the user to a file in which notes can be written for later access. When the user quits the word processor, the system returns to the screen at which the request for the word processor was made. Further, links to structured databases may be added.

Integration of an Expert System into Hypertext

It is possible to launch a knowledge base from some hypertext systems. For example, in HyperCard the button controlling the action is simply scripted to open a specific file or document with a particular application. When the user quits the knowledge base, the system returns to the same card that was being viewed when the interruption occurred. This is possible because the position in the file at the time of the interruption is noted. It is also possible to return the user to a place directly related to the result of the interaction with the knowledge base.

As an illustration of this, the following sample search is included. The user might have a coin to identify. The first step would be to flip through the stack of images to find the image most like the coin. The user would then select "Advice" on the screen and would be linked with the knowledge base that deals with similar coin faces. A series of questions would be asked (figures 10.7 and 10.8) by the "expert" to ascertain which of the coin records contained in the coin inventory would be most like the coin being described.

If the expert system is able to determine that the coin is like one in the coin inventory, the user would be advised that the coin is similar to British Museum coin X and would be advised to compare the coin detail by detail with the description contained on the inventory card for that coin. On the other hand, if the expert system is unable to reach a satisfactory conclusion, the user would be returned to the image stack for further matching.

Design of the Data in the Prototype of the Model

The data in the prototype of the model is limited to that which is directly related to the reference set of coins, those of the British Museum. The following

Figure 10.7
Expert System, Sample Question

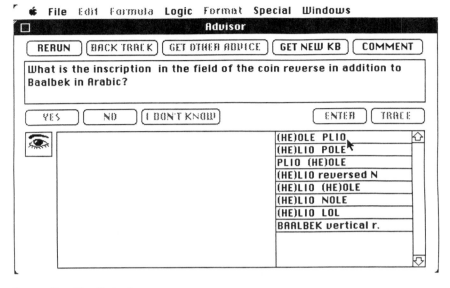

Source: Cognition Technology.

stacks or databases are included: table of contents, images, objects (inventory), genealogy, time line, documents (coin history and reforms, Baalbek history, and related use of computer in numismatics), maps, glossary, and Arabic-to-English term list. Various screen backgrounds are used to relate specific types of information with particular formats. However, the interface is consistent with regard to the ''buttons'' that are uniform in placement among the stacks, although not every button appears on each card. The visible buttons are uniform in type and placement among the stacks. However, not every button appears on each card.

Links in the data model. There are links in the prototype that connect the expert system and the related knowledge bases to the image stack, as well as the object stack. Further, the other stacks are all interlinked (figure 10.9). In addition, the word processor is accessible from each card in each stack for note taking or copying the contents of the card.

Status of implementation of the model. The amount of data contained in the prototype at this moment is limited. However, all aspects of the model presented as operational have been implemented.

DISCUSSION AND LIMITATIONS

The model facilitates the categorization of Arab coins. It is certainly easier to interact with the computer than it is to sort through catalogs trying to match

Figure 10.8
Expert System, Sample Log

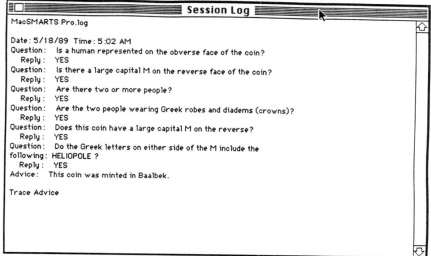

Source: Cognition Technology.

images or descriptions. The expert system environment of the prototype emulates working with an expert to identify a coin. An alternative to this, the hypertext environment, is also available. Hypertext allows "browsing" so that, for example, a user could identify a coin type and then browse the stack to look at other coins of the type. However, to be useful to the general collector of coins, there must be rules to cover a wider range of coins.

As regards the hypertext application, the linking of diverse materials is very effective. However, once the "stacks" become extensive, finding material that has not been properly linked is not easy. The importance of anticipating the uses is crucial. However, databases can be linked into the model and their search capabilities used.

Even better than linking a database search capability would be the development of an automatic linking capability. This would require an automatic indexing system. Another desired capability, which is not yet part of the implemented model, is the means for including statistical formulas. For example, the numismatist might be interested in discriminate analysis, probability, or covariance between coin production and remaining coins. If calculations and running totals could be kept on "marked" items as a separate file, aggregating information and doing cluster analysis to determine similarity of the items in a set would be facilitated.

Figure 10.9
Links Among Stacks and with the Expert System

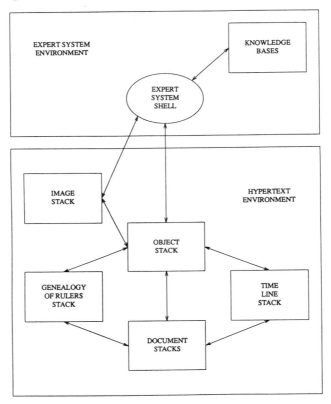

CONCLUSIONS

Hypertext provides a friendly user interface that facilitates access of material and information-processing resources that have been carefully structured and linked. The material may be included in a variety of types of databases and document or graphics files. Further, diverse applications might be available to the basic hypertext interface.

The needs of numismatists as information users may be facilitated by the use of computers and specifically hypertext and expert systems. However, the present study is on a small scale. More work is necessary to determine if the model could be scaled up and the scope of the materials could be increased to include all Arab coins or all ancient coins. Further, the issues of information retrieval and pre- versus postcoordinated links need to be analyzed based on case studies documenting uses of the prototype.

NOTES

1. The need for linking the objects and information is not discussed here. The Fall 1988 issue of *Library Trends* (Stam and Giral, 1988, 117–264) provides discussion of many of the issues.

2. To illustrate how extensive the fields for each coin entry might be, the following list is that contained in the *Islamic Manual* used by the American Numismatic Society (New York City) in 1983: analysis of coin's metal content, artist, die axis, first common era date, second common era date, color, counterstamp, department, decoration name, denomination, decoration guide, disposition (from ANS collection), date of object, dynasty or issuing government, edge marking, era by which coin is dated, estimated value, previous owner(s), where and when exhibited, date of valuation, place where found or acquired, other information, issuer, location (if abnormal), standard abbreviation of mint, maker, manufacture, material, dimension(s), mint where issued, object identification number, negative or slide number, obverse inscription, obverse type or image, person named on object, province (locality where issued), publication of *this* object, catalog reference, general area where issued, reverse inscription, reverse type or image, classification by subject, shape, classification by institution, series number, value of object, classification by person, classification by place, symbol, type (kind of object), undertype, and weight.

3. Baalbek is located in the Biqaa Valley of Lebanon. Since early times Baalbek was an important crossroads because it is on a major north-south corridor and near a mountain pass giving access to the city of Damascus. It was a major outpost of the Roman Empire and continued to be an important city with the Arab expansion by the Umayyads around A.D. 650.

4. "Hyper Activity" (*Byte*, 1988, 268) lists the following commercial hypertext products: Business File Vision (Marvelin Corp.), Document Examiner (Symbolics, Inc.), Graphic KRS/Text KRS/Hyper KRS (Knowledgeset Corp.), Guide (Owl International, Inc.), HyperCard (Apple Computer, Inc.), KMS (Scribe Systems, Inc.), Knowledge Pro (Knowledge Garden, Inc.), MacSMARTS (Cognition Technology Corp.), and Marcon (AIRS).

5. Certain commercial products are identified in this paper in order to specify adequately the procedures being described. In no case does such identification imply recommendation or endorsement by the National Institute of Standards and Technology, nor does it imply that the material identified is necessarily the best for the purpose.

6. Dan Shafer's article "Getting Smart," *Macworld* (October 1988), includes some expert systems that are available for the Macintosh computer. Those listed (p. 138) are Cognate (Peridom), Intelligent Developer/IntelliCard (Hyperpress Technology Group), Instant-Expert Plus (Human Intellect Systems), MacSMARTS (Cognition Technology Corp.), and Nexpert Object (Neuron Data).

REFERENCES

American Numismatic Society. n.d. "Islamic Manual." New York: The American Numismatic Society.

American Numismatic Society. 1984–1988. *Numismatic Literature*, nos. 111–20. New York: The American Numismatic Society.

Conklin, Jeff. 1987. "Hypertext: An Introduction and Survey." *Computer* 20 (September): 17–41.

"Hyper Activity." 1988. *Byte* 13(10): 268.

Marchionini, Gary, and Ben Shneiderman. 1988. "Finding Facts vs. Browsing Knowledge in Hypertext Systems." *Computer* 21(1):70–80.

Rada, Roy. 1989. "Writing and Reading Hypertext: An Overview." *Journal of the American Society for Information Science (JASIS)* 40(3):164–71.

Rada, Roy, and Lois F. Lunin. 1989. "Hypertext: Introduction and Overview." *JASIS* 40(3):159–63.

Saffo, Paul. 1987. "What You Need to Know About Hypertext." *Personal Computing* (December): 166–73.

Scacchi, Walt. 1989. "On the Power of Domain-Specific Hypertext Environments." *JASIS* 40(3):183–91.

Shafer, Dan. 1988. "Getting Smart." *Macworld* 5 (October): 132–39.

Shneiderman, Ben, Dorothy Brethauer, Catherine Plaisant, and Richard Potter. 1989. "Evaluating Three Museum Installations of a Hypertext System." *JASIS* 40(3):172–82.

Stam, Deirdre C. 1989. "The Quest for a Code, or a Brief History of the Computerized Cataloging of Art Objects." *Art Documentation* 8 (Spring): 7–15.

Stam, Deirdre C., and Angela Giral. 1988. "Linking Art Objects and Art Information." *Library Trends* 37(2):117–264.

Taylor, Robert S. 1986. *Value-Added Processes in Information Systems*. Norwood, N.J.: Ablex.

Walker, John. 1956. *A Catalogue of the Arab-Byzantine and Post-Reform Umaiyad Coins*. London: Trustees of the Bristish Museum.

Williams, Gregg. 1987. "HyperCard." *Byte* 12 (December): 109–17.

11

Information Chunking as an Interface Design Issue for Full-Text Databases

T. R. Girill

The division of text into chunks for retrieval and display affects how users perceive the interface of a full-text database. An online documentation system is a special case of a hypertext database, and its performance reveals strengths and weaknesses in alternative approaches to text chunking that could prove to have broad relevance.

One claim supported by our studies of online documentation is that large-scale text chunks (document-size composites of individual passages) help users focus searches, facilitate trend analysis in usage statistics, and support coordinated updates of related passages. A second claim for which our studies find strong counterevidence, however, is that the smallest text chunks in a hypertext database should be as fine-grained as possible. Careful comparison of the "threading" argument often given for this claim with the threading argument for multiprocessing programs actually demonstrates inefficiency and high overhead costs. Analysis of the rhetorical construction of documentation passages also reveals the extra explanatory, instructional, and search-support value that nonminimal text chunks usually exhibit.

INTRODUCTION

The way in which a full-text database, especially one with hypertext features, is divided into text nodes or chunks of prose appears to its readers as an important aspect of its user interface. This is because, even though text chunking is strictly speaking independent of the interface software, it nevertheless affects four aspects of database performance:

1. the efficiency with which users can search for and retrieve needed passages;

2. the precision and helpfulness of the text displayed in response to a query;

3. the convenience with which the database can be updated by those who maintain it;

Table 11.1
Comparison of Three Online Text-Delivery Systems

	Design Goals		
	NoteCards	Document Examiner	Document-Find-Theseus
	Organize working notes, file personal information	Deliver commercial documentation to customers	Respond to end-user reference queries on demand
	Features		
Structure			
Text	Little structure, small passages	Highly structured, long documents	Highly structured, long documents
Database (actual)	Directed acyclic graph (true trees)	Directed graph (pseudo tree)	Directed graph (pseudo tree)
Database (apparent)	Network of modules	Book-like structure	Book-like structure
Link Types	Reference only	Reference and inclusion	Reference and inclusion
Changes Expected			
Frequency	Few updates	Some updates	Many updates
Style	Most isolated	Most coordinated	Most coordinated
User Interface			
Passage Delivery	Simulates 3" x 5" cards and files boxes	Displays sections of online manuals	Displays sections of online manuals
Authoring	Same as delivery inerface	Specialized authoring tools	Specialized authoring tools
Navigation (access by position)	Primary access, maps available (browser cards)	Secondary access, maps available (overview of commands)	Never pure navigation, pseudo-maps available (index, menu)
Search Support (access by content)	Only full-text string searching on module text	Keyword searching with stemming and adjacency control	Keyword searching with stemming, "fuzzy matching" and aliasing

4. the extent to which the text can be easily reused for several purposes (reference, teaching, current awareness).

Online documentation, in which instructions for and examples of utility software, subroutine libraries, and other computational resources (such as file storage) are delivered to user terminals, resembles other full-text databases in many respects. But several distinctive features shape its behavior:

1. Document boundaries divide text into large, content-based clusters
2. Each document has its own within-book structure or rhetorical organization
3. Most passages are explanations or sets of instructions, built with characteristic layout and design techniques

These features make an online-documentation database most similar to a hypertext system. Indeed, hypertext software has been adapted to manage and deliver such documentation by some vendors.

Table 11.1 compares two hypertext systems widely noted in the literature (Halasz, Moran, and Trigg, 1987; Halasz, 1988; Walker, 1987; Walker, 1988) with the online-documentation system used at the National Magnetic Fusion Energy Computer Center (NMFECC), the one on which this chapter is based. This system now contains 210 online user manuals, comprising 23,000 pages (about 1 million lines) of explanatory text. Three software tools maintain the system. The DOCUMENT program updates the database and displays keyworded passages in response to user requests (Girill and Luk, 1983; Girill, Luk, and Norton, 1988). FIND locates passages by keyword or "synonym" (using an extended entry vocabulary) and incorporates truncation and fuzzy-matching algorithms (Girill, Luk, and Norton, 1987). And THESEUS manages and reports the structure of the extended entry vocabulary for planning and development purposes. For convenience here, I call this software combination the DFT system.

The three documentation features noted above (document boundaries, within-book structure, and explanatory text) make some decisions about text chunking (or node size) appropriate and others inept. Whether this influence on text-chunk appropriateness extends to other, general full-text databases (or at least to other hypertext systems) is a question of considerable interest. Studies show that 50% to 75% of those who use nonfiction books need and read only small excerpts of the whole text (Prabha and Rice, 1988). This fact makes the performance of online-documentation systems, which cater to such reading patterns, potentially relevant to the design of the user interface for a wide class of applications that deliver full-text passages at computer terminals.

This chapter focuses on two specific text-chunking ("granularity") issues prominent in constructing any online-documentation system. The first is the influence of the system's largest text nodes (i.e., whole documents) on user interactions with the software. The second is the more intricate influence of the system's smallest text nodes, and the related problem of choosing the right size for those smallest nodes.

THE "LARGEST-NODES" ISSUE

One of the design issues facing anyone constructing a full-text database is whether the system should support very large, document-size text chunks and whether such large, composite chunks are useful. After surveying several hypertext systems without these composite chunks, Halasz concluded that good hypertext really needs a way to represent easily "groups of nodes and links as unique entities separate from their components" (Halasz, 1988, 842). The behavior of the DFT online-documentation system confirms this conclusion. Documentation databases by their nature group passages into document-size chunks with permanent names and boundaries. This mechanical feature turns out to have three important intellectual benefits.

First, document boundaries play a heuristic role in focusing user searches for answers to their questions. Collecting all file-storage information in one online "manual," for example, and all job-control passages in another helps users narrow the scope of their search in a natural way. The DOCUMENT interface lets users specify a document they want to view, then select one or more passages using the keywords assigned within it. A study of 966 retrieval sessions (one month's activity on our CRAY X-MP) showed that 82% of the searches displayed text from some single document (rather than from a sequence of several), strongly suggesting the appropriateness of document boundaries as scope specifiers (Girill, Luk, and Norton, 1988, 239).

The FIND interface ignores document boundaries during a search. But those boundaries benefit users here too, because when FIND reports a list of hits it gives the passage size and names the containing document for each. Reporting document names in these global searches helps users easily disambiguate multiple hits (e.g., between file-transfer passages pertaining to different software, different paths, or different destinations).

Second, document boundaries promote effective usage monitoring. The DFT software counts the number of times each document and each individual passage is accessed (per month). Trends are much easier to spot in frequency reports at the document level, however, then at the passage level. A heavily used document may be hit 20 to 50 times in a single month, and the spread among document hit rates is pronounced. But even a "heavily" used passage is hit only 3 to 5 times in a month, and the spread among hit rates is flat. Thus we have found document-level monitoring to be the most helpful for prioritizing both editorial work and entry-vocabulary upgrades.

Third, revising or updating text by document instead of by isolated passage promotes the coordination of related passages and version control. It encourages editors to review critically other passages in the same document, for example, to check for changes needed as side effects of the original edit. Describing a new program feature might require updating comparison charts or summary tables elsewhere in the document (that mention or should mention the feature). Altering a limit might affect the accuracy of examples that embody or violate that limit. Document-based updating helps remind NMFECC's editorial staff to detect these textual side effects. It also promotes consistent presentation of intellectually parallel cases (execute lines, examples, error reports). Passages perceived as within-document neighbors are more likely to get parallel layout and explanatory treatments than if they seem to be isolated database nodes.

THE "SMALLEST-NODES" ISSUE

Another design issue for any full-text database is how small to make the smallest text chunks the system can retrieve and display. Some contend that a fine-grained approach is best: "Most theoreticians of hypertext feel that a node should consist of a single concept or idea" (Carlson, 1988, 96). In light of the performance of NMFECC's online-documentation system, I disagree. Two strong counterarguments exist that show that nonminimal text nodes are more cost-effective and often deliver information in chunks more beneficial to users.

Table 11.2
Comparison of Two Applications of the "Threading Argument"

	Multiprocessing Programs	Hypertext Documents
Threads	Tasks—sequences of instructions along a "thread of execution"	Views—virtual structures composed of linked text passages
Multiple threads	Programs with multiple tasks	Databases with multiple views
Number available	Depends on programmer	Depends on author or indexer
Number used at once	Depends on operating system	Depends on user
Threaded nodes		
Sharing	Subroutines on several threads	Passages in several views
Precautions	Must not modify themselves	Must use context-neutral wording
Granularity		
—Fine	Statement level	Sentence level
—Moderate	DO-loop level	Subsection level
—Coarse	Subroutine level	Section, chapter level

The Threading Argument

A threading or necklace analogy is often used to support the appropriateness of very small (fine-grained) text chunks. The smaller the beads on a necklace, the argument goes, the easier it is to rethread them in alternative ways. Likewise for text chunks, where a "fine-grained approach improves the potential to thread the same node into different paths" (Carlson, 1988, 96). When applied in a more thoroughgoing way, however, this very threading argument actually supports using text chunks larger than the smallest possible.

The threading analogy for hypertext nodes has also been applied to multiprocessing computer programs—codes, separate parts of which can execute on several separate central processing units (CPUs) at once. Table 11.2 spells out, feature by feature, the many direct parallels between these two threading arguments. Code developers, like full-text database developers, must decide how finely to divide their work to spread it among several CPUs.

Consider this (Fortran) code excerpt:

```
- - - - - DO 10 I=,N
        |
        |      . . .
        |
(b)  |   (a)  A = (B+C) + (D+E)
        |
        |      . . .
        |
- - - - - 10 A(I) = B(I) + C(I)
```

Attempting to multiprocess using minimal code chunks (here, statements) yields the greatest flexibility but also the highest overhead. For example, one CPU could add $(B + C)$ while another added $(D + E)$ in statement (a), but the computational cost of dividing these tiny operations, scheduling them, and then recombining their results far outweighs any speedup in code execution that would result.

Even at the multistatement level (b), where each iteration of this DO-loop could be independently calculated by a different CPU, the task-management overhead is almost always prohibitive. "Vectorizing" such loops using special hardware for simultaneous operations within one CPU is usually much more efficient. Indeed, a rule of thumb in multiprocessing is always to wring maximum performance from each CPU before paying the cost of bringing in another one. Thus, only with fairly coarse chunks of code is the use of multiple CPUs efficient. The burden of extreme threading flexibility is extreme resource commitment for overhead.

The Threading Argument for Text

Similar reasoning applies to text-node size. While the smallest nodes (individual sentences) do offer the greatest flexibility, they also are the most inefficient to manage. They require the same per node investment of overhead resources yet they return less payback in answering user questions than larger blocks of text.

A typical online manual contains 8 chapters, 60 topical sections, and 1,400 sentences. Subdividing only to the chapter level is almost always too coarse (it neglects important and revealing content distinctions). But delivering text in chunks at the smallest intellectual level (the sentence level) is too fine to justify the much higher (175-fold) resource investment to manage so many nodes. Multiple-sentence nodes—those that roughly correspond to sections in the text— deliver much more useful information per node than minimal ones. Hence they follow the multiprocessing rule mentioned above: Strive for the most efficient communication of facts and relationships within each node before paying the extra cost to manage and deliver more nodes. This analysis also leads us to look closely at how text chunks communicate facts and relationships well, which is central to the second argument against minimal nodes.

The Communication Argument

Documentation passages are always built rather than found. Their rhetorical construction (by an editorial staff) is vital to their problem-solving value. And often, building in worthwhile features calls for nonminimal text nodes.

Two decades of convergent psychological research show that certain design, layout, and exemplification techniques greatly improve the usefulness of non-fiction technical prose, such as computer documentation (Bernhardt, 1986; Jon-

Table 11.3

Techniques to Increase the Problem-Solving Value of Technical Prose

Technique	Explanation	Example
(1) Emphasize functional or explanative text features:		
Labeling	Assign each major cause, step, feature, or technique its own name to promote recal	Headings such as "labeling," "signaling," "organizing," and "indenting"
Signaling	Enumerate sequences; mark list items with bullets or asterisks	(1)..., (2)..., and (3)...
Organizing	Group text into overt sections by task or other features	Headings such as "technique," "explanation," and "example"
Indenting	Use headings and indented text block to indicated the grouping and relationships of ideas presented	
(2) Give concrete support for abstract rules and concepts:		
Modeling	Depict abstract relations concretely in diagrams, charts, or other models	See table 11.2
Exemplifying	Supply explicit examples, cases, or analogies for each general role or concept	See this table, column 3.
Visualizing	Choose terms andphrases that suggest vivid images for explanative features	"Flow of control," "virtual machine"
(3) Promote effective, active processing by the reader:		
Include study questions	Questions that stress functional relations and causes, not just rote memorization of facts	"How do disk directories support private batch jobs?" is better then "List three disk-directory utilities."
State problem-solving objectives	Use explicit statements and headings	"Problem-solving techniques" is better than "Some ideas form the literature"
Supply summaries	Note taking promotes problem solving; summaries let readers compare their notes with summaries	See summary preseented in table 11.1
Include a glossary	Missing prerequisite facts and inadequate definitions confuse readers and thwart problem-solving	List abbreviations; provide online glossary (e.g., via FIND command)

assen, 1982; Mayer, 1985; Wright, 1980). Table 11.3 summarizes the most thoroughly validated of these techniques. Evidence from many sources suggests that drafting text using these techniques not only increases reader recall of specific facts later, but, more important, also improves the success rate with which readers can apply what they have read to solve the problems that brought them to this reference material in the first place.

Effectively using these techniques requires documentation text chunks (1) large enough to accommodate the techniques, and (2) complex enough to deploy them consistently and reliably. Consider the labeling and signaling techniques (top of table 11.3), for example. They provide important comparative information to readers, but they require sufficient text to support such comparisons. We have found that 10-line isolated descriptions of intrinsic functions for a Fortran compiler, for instance, are much less helpful than 100-line analytic comparisons of several functions of the same type (arithmetic, Boolean, etc.). Similar remarks apply to concrete modeling of abstract concepts (middle of table 11.3). Overtly stating implicit relationships by installing scope and goal notes, or step-by-step annotations, on a JCL or programming example markedly increase its practical value but also increase its size. These larger examples prove more instructive than either the mere annotations or the annotationless cases alone.

Further Indirect Evidence

Separate studies of search strategies in general-interest full-text databases and the online tutorials provide further indirect evidence that nonminimal text chunks are often the most appropriate. Carol Tenopir searched for answers to the same fact-retrieval queries in the same database (Magazine ASAP, covering 100 popular magazines) using four search strategies that differed only in the range over which they linked terms: within 5 words (either order), within 10 words, within the same paragraph, and within the same document. She found that while small-zone searching missed many answers and whole-document searching produced many false hits, using (nonminimal) paragraphs optimized her success. "On the average, searching for concepts within the same paragraph offers the best balance of recall and precision for document retrieval. Recall is more than twice that when searching for concepts within 10 words of each other, and precision is slightly better" (Tenopir, 1988, 81).

Brenda Rubens studied the posttest learning performance of college students who worked through an online tutorial program in which she varied the step size between feedback exercises. Here, "a single step of information . . . provides the learner with a simple but adequate definition of [or practice with] a specific function, operation, or term" (Rubens, 1988, 164). One-step, 6-step, 12-step, and 24-step tutorial versions were compared. Student completion times and posttest scores showed that user performance peaked at either the 6-step or 12-step level, and that even "posttest scores for the 24-step version are not significantly lower than for the other versions, and, in fact, are higher than some smaller step levels" (Rubens, 1988, 179). While some users reported being uncomfortable with a 24-step delay before feedback, most agreed "that questions for step size 1 appeared too soon after the text" (Rubens, 1988, 178).

Neither of these other cases involved such elaborate or overt use of the text-design features (table 11.3) as computer documentation routinely does. Nevertheless, the communicative value of nonminimal text chunks emerged for both searching and learning, because of its perceived relevance to user goals and needs. Remember too that such larger nodes can still be exhaustively indexed by every "single concept or idea" they contain, without the delivery software actually managing text chunks at the micro level.

Online-documentation systems exist to deliver relevant text quickly that suffices to solve a user's technical problem. Passages meeting these criteria are just what good documentation drafters intentionally construct using the techniques listed in table 11.3. This rhetorical construction adds value to the text. Full-text databases should preserve, rather than pulverize, that added value by manipulating text nodes large enough to keep such features intact. Explanatory effectiveness is the goal of documentation drafting, so effectiveness should dictate node size instead of a well-intentioned atomism based on a superficially applied threading analogy.

CONCLUSIONS

This chapter has examined the impact on the performance of NMFECC's online-documentation system of the largest (whole-document) and smallest (single-sentence) possible text chunks. While-document divisions prove very helpful, but sentence-size nodes are less efficient to manage and less effective in delivering useful answers than are paragraphs or sections of text. Parallels between online documentation and other full-text databases (especially hypertext) suggest that these findings may be broadly applicable.

NOTE

This work was performed in part under the auspices of the U.S. Department of Energy by Lawrence Livermore National Laboratory under contract W–7405-ENG–48.

REFERENCES

Bernhardt, Stephen A. 1986. Seeing the text. *College Composition and Communication* 37: 66–78.

Carlson, Patricia. 1988. Hypertext: A way of incorporating user feedback into online documentation. In *Text, Context, and Hypertext*, ed. Edward Barrett, 93–110. Cambridge, Mass.: MIT Press.

Girill, T. R., and Luk, Clement H. 1983. DOCUMENT: An interactive, online solution to four documentation problems. *Communications of the Association for Computing Machinery* 26: 328–37.

Girill, T. R., Luk, Clement, and Norton, Sally. 1987. Towards automated consulting: Design feedback from the performance of online documentation. In *Proceedings of the 50th American Society for Information Science Annual Meeting*, 24: 85–90. Medford, N.J.: Learned Information.

————. 1988. The impact of usage monitoring on the evolution of an online-documentation system. *IEEE Transactions on System, Man, and Cybernetics* 18: 326–32.

Halasz, Frank G. 1988. Reflections on NoteCards: Seven issues for the next generation of hypermedia systems. *Communications of the ACM* 31: 836–52.

Halasz, Frank G., Moran, Thomas P., and Trigg, Randall H. 1987. NoteCards in a nutshell. In *Proceedings of SIGCHI 1987: Human Factors in Computing Systems*, 45–52. New York: Association for Computing Machinery.

Jonassen, David H., ed. 1985. *The technology of text: Principles for structuring, designing, and displaying text*. Englewood Cliffs, N.J.: Educational Technology.

Mayer, Richard E. 1982. Structural analysis of science prose: Can we increase problem-solving performance. In *Understanding Expository Text*, ed. B. K. Britton and J. B. Black, 65–87. Hillsdale, N.J.: Lawrence Erlbaum Associates.

Prabha, Chandra and Rice, Duane. 1988. Assumptions about information-seeking behavior in nonfiction books: Their importance to full-text systems. In *Proceedings of the 51st American Society for Information Science Annual Meeting*, 25: 147–51. Medford, N.J.: Learned Information.

Rubens, Brenda. 1988. Similarities and differences in developing effective online and hardcopy tutorials. In *Effective Documentation: What We Have Learned from Research*, ed. Stephen Doheny-Farina, 159–84. Cambridge, Mass.: MIT Press.

Tenopir, Carol. 1988. Search strategies for full text databases. In *Proceedings of the 51st American Society for Information Science Annual Meeting*, 25: 80–86. Medford, N.J.: Learned Information.

Walker, Janet H. 1987. Document Examiner: Delivery interface for hypertext documents. In *Proceedings of the Hypertext '87 Workshop*, 1: 307–23. Chapel Hill, N.C.

———. 1988. Supporting document development with Concordia. *Computer* 21: 48–59.

Wright, Patricia. 1980. Usability: The criterion for designing written information. In *Processing of Visible Language 2*, ed. Paul A. Kolers, M. Wrolstad, and H. Bouma, 183–205. New York: Plenum Press.

12

Hypertext: User-driven Interfaces

Michael A. Shepherd and Carolyn Watters

Hypertext provides an interface in which the user can browse text in a nonsequential manner. A problem for many hypertext systems is that the underlying hypergraph of nodes and links is static, thus restricting users to browsing the database along predefined paths. More flexible interfaces can be developed based on transient hypergraphs. A transient hypergraph is generated dynamically in response to a user query and exists only for the duration of a query or query session. Such a system dynamically generates nodes of sets of links by type and by type-value. The user selects elements from these sets and, in response, the system composes nodes and instantiates links to create transient hypergraphs.

A prototype system supporting transient hypergraphs has been developed using the relational database model as the platform. The system is implemented in INGRES on a SUN 4/280 using a SUN 3/50 workstation for the hypertext interface. The system provides hypertext access to a database of citations. The graphic nature of a citation network is well suited to browsing in hypertext.

INTRODUCTION

Most traditional forms of information have a physical organization that is linear, even though the logical organization of the information may be nonlinear. For instance, the logical organization of a text may be hierarchical, consisting of chapters, sections, subsections, paragraphs, subparagraphs, and so on, even though the text is presented in the linear physical organization of a book.

Hypertext is a methodology that provides the user with the capability of browsing information in a nonlinear manner. Hypertext is based on links between objects in a database where the objects in the database are associated with windows on the screen (Conklin, 1987; Fiderio, 1988; Halasz, 1988; Nelson, 1988). The database is then a hyperdocument consisting of both nodes and links.

A node is associated with a displayable atomic data object or "chunk," such as a paragraph of text or a single picture. A link is a labeled pointer from one node to another indicating some type of relationship between the objects associated with the nodes. Explicit links may be "next," "notes-on," "author," "earlier-version," and so on. There may be implicit links to external resources such as dictionaries and almanacs. These are implicit because they are always active from any node. The hyperdocument may be represented by a hypergraph— a labeled, directed graph of nodes and links between the nodes (Tompa, 1988).

Access to the data objects by the user can be described as a traversal of that hypergraph, such that arrival at each node in the graph results in the display of both the associated data object and the outward links from that node. The user controls or drives the traversal by employing one or more of the following techniques, following successive links from node to node, searching data objects by keyword, and direct access using the graphic display of the hyperdocument.

While hypertext does permit the user a great deal of browsing flexibility, the user is still restricted to the predefined structure of the information itself. The types of nodes and links in a particular hypergraph are defined, usually, by the database designed and are instantiated either by the system, as in the case of indices, or by the reader as in the case of notes-on, see-also, bookmarks, and so on. Such hypergraphs are static in that once the nodes and links are instantiated they are part of the database and define the hypergraph for that database (Halasz, 1988). Static hypergraphs may limit the ability of a user to query effectively a hypertext database as the user is unable to view the data objects from different perspectives and must query the database by traversing the set of previously defined (i.e., static) links.

The research project described in this chapter is the development of a hypertext system that supports transient hypergraphs: in other words, hypergraphs that are generated dynamically in response to a given query. The database is not stored as a graph, rather it is stored in a relational database system, and the transient hypergraphs are generated in response to user queries through the dynamic composition of nodes and the dynamic instantiation of the links connecting those nodes (Watters and Shepherd, 1989). This permits users to view the database from different perspectives and to superimpose their own access structure on the database during the course of a query session. In addition to the standard string search, users can superimpose an access structure based on attribute type(s) and browse these structures from one node to the next. The hypergraphs are transient in that they exist only for a single query or for a query session. A useful transient hypergraph could, of course, be saved as a static hypergraph.

The database used in this project is a citation network. Citations between documents have been used for some time to study the structure and development of a discipline, to determine the importance of an individual author or document, and as an aid to researchers in determining potentially relevant documents for their own work (de Solla Price, 1965; Garfield, 1979). A citation network was selected because it is a good example of a database that is difficult to browse effectively using traditional hypertext that supports only static hypergraphs.

Prior to the implementation of the transient hypergraph system, a prototype citation network was implemented using the Macintosh HyperCard software. This prototype identified a problem associated with browsing a citation network in a static hypergraph system; specifically, the restriction of not being able to superimpose user-defined access structures (views). This results in high cognitive overhead involved in developing such alternate access structures as cocitation structures. The static hypergraph, while an adequate structure for citation browsing, has no explicit structure for cocitation browsing. If one wishes to use a static hypergraph-based system to find the documents that cocite document A and document B, it is necessary to follow, in a linear manner, the list of citing documents associated with document A and the list associated with document B, write down or remember the elements of the lists, and manually find the intersection of the lists to determine the cociting documents. If one wishes to find the documents that cocite more than two documents, the cognitive overhead involved increases proportionately.

These problems can be overcome if the hypertext system supports transient hypergraphs. The platform selected in this project for the development of such a system is the relational database model (Date, 1982). The prototype system is implemented in INGRES on a Sun 4/280 using a Sun 3/50 workstation for the hypertext interface. The database consists of 507 entries of which 39 have full lists of references. The remaining entries consist of only the title, author, and source fields.

TRANSIENT HYPERGRAPHS FOR CITATION NETWORKS

The use of the relational model for the support of the transient hypergraphs permits the user to create, dynamically, transient hypergraphs that reflect a variety of browsing paths and cocitation structures of interest to the user. A transient hypergraph that was created in response to a query may be discarded at the end of the session; it can be recreated as required.

In order to implement a citation network in a hypertext system in a relational DBMS, it is only necessary to store the references to links. The references to links are stored as attribute values in the appropriate relation. The relational operators SELECT, PROJECT, and NATURAL JOIN are used to extract and manipulate this reference information from the relation to instantiate dynamically the transient cited-by and cocitation links and to compose the appropriate nodes, as required.

Two examples from the prototype system are given below in figures 12.1 through 12.4 and in figures 12.5 and 12.6. The figures were captured from the screen of the Sun 3/50, which is the hypertext interface to the system. Note

Figure 12.1
List of Documents Containing Keyword "CODER"

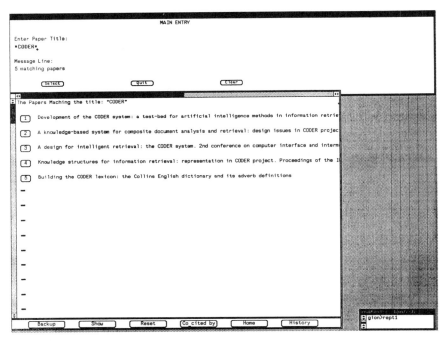

that the main window can be scrolled left-right and up-down. The only active window at any given time is the "top" window.

The first example is shown in figures 12.1 through 12.4. This example illustrates how to create a hypergraph based on a keyword, select nodes from this set for browsing, view the references associated with one of these documents, and select from the set of references. Figure 12.1 is a picture of the screen showing the list of documents in the database containing the keyword, CODER, in the title. The numbers (1–5) associated with the five documents containing the keyword, CODER, have no relevance other than to allow the user to differentiate among the documents.

The user does not have to view the entire set, but can select from the set. Figure 12.2 shows that the user has selected documents 1, 3, and 4 for viewing as a hypergraph. This is indicated by the X replacing the numbers associated with these documents. In order to select a document for the hypergraph, the user clicks the mouse button on the number associated with the document. The documents in the new hypergraph are connected by next links. The first node viewed by the user, document 1 in this instance, is displayed in the upper-right window, which is now the active window. It should be noted that the documents

Figure 12.2
Selecting Documents for a Hypergraph

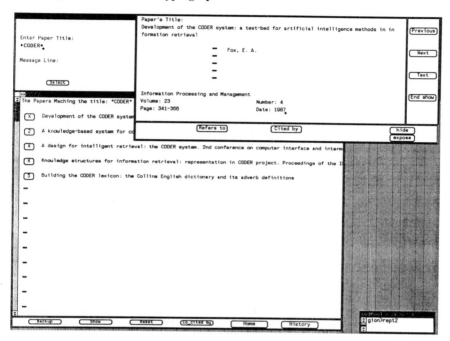

will be viewed in the order that the user selects the documents, not in the order of the numbers associated with the documents.

The list of references associated with a document can be viewed by clicking on the refers-to link button. Figure 12.3 shows the reference list associated with document 1. This window is now the active window. Again, the numbers assigned to the documents in this window are to help the user differentiate among the documents.

Figure 12.4 shows that the user has selected documents 9 and 16 from the reference list for viewing as a new hypergraph. The first node of this hypergraph is displayed in the upper-right window, which is now the active window.

The second example is shown in figures 12.5 and 12.6. In order to create a hypergraph of nodes that cocite a given set of documents, the user first selects the set of documents to be cocited. Figure 12.5 shows that the user has viewed a list of documents in the main window and wishes to find all documents that cite the five documents in the upper right window. These five documents were selected from the main window. Note that the order of the documents in the upper-right window is the order in which they were selected, not the order in which they were presented originally in the main window.

Figure 12.6 shows the hypergraph of nodes that cocite all five documents. In

Figure 12.3
List of References Associated with a Document

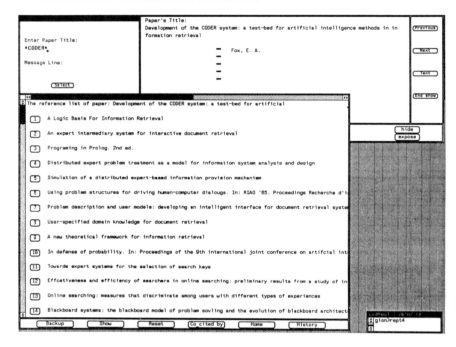

this example, the hypergraph consists of only one node. Note that hypergraphs using the cited-by links could have been generated at any time during the session, in the same manner as those using the refers-to links.

CONCLUSIONS

Transient hypergraphs increase the utility of hypertext by permitting the user different views of the database and expanded query types without requiring new permanent links to be defined and the database reloaded. This allows the user to ask questions that may not have been answerable, or only answerable with a high cognitive overhead cost to the user on hypertext systems with static hypergraphs.

The relational model supports the presentation of lists of values that describe sets of link, both by type and by type-value, from which the user can make a selection. This allows the dynamic composition of nodes and dynamic instantiation of links necessary for the generation of transient hypergraphs. Although the relational model is not generally the most effective model for text bases, the decomposition of the data into object-oriented ''chunks'' does appear to make it an appropriate platform for the development of a hypertext system with transient hypergraphs.

Figure 12.4
Generating a Hypergraph from References

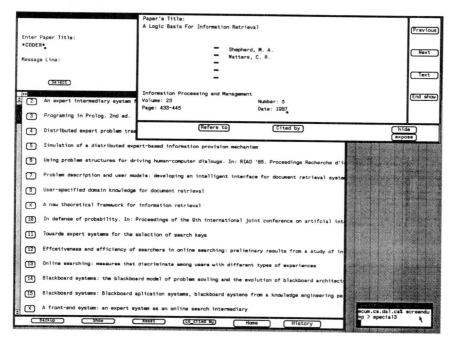

REFERENCES

Conklin, J. 1987. A Survey of Hypertext. Technical Report No. STP–356–86, rev. 2. Austin, Tex.: Microelectronics and Computer Technology Corporation.

Date, C. J. 1982. An Introduction to Database Systems. Vol. 1, 3d ed. Reading, Mass.: Addison-Wesley.

de Solla Price, D. J. 1965. Networks of Scientific Papers. *Science* 149(3683): 510–15.

Fiderio, J. 1988. A Grand Vision. *Byte* 13(10): 237–44.

Garfield, E. 1979. *Citation Indexing: Its Theory and Applications in Science, Technology and Humanities*. New York: John Wiley.

Halasz, F. G. 1988. Reflections on NoteCards: Seven Issues for the Next Generation of Hypermedia Systems. *Communications of the ACM* 31(7): 836–52.

Nelson, T. H. 1988. Managing Immense Storage. *Byte* 13(1): 225–38.

Tompa, F. W. 1988. A Data Model for Hypertext Database Systems. Technical Report. University of Waterloo, Canada.

Watters, C. R. and Shepherd, M. A. 1989. Transient Links in Hypertext. Presented at the 17th Annual Conference of the Canadian Association for Information Science, Toronto, May 31–June 2.

Figure 12.5
Selecting Documents That Must Be Cocited

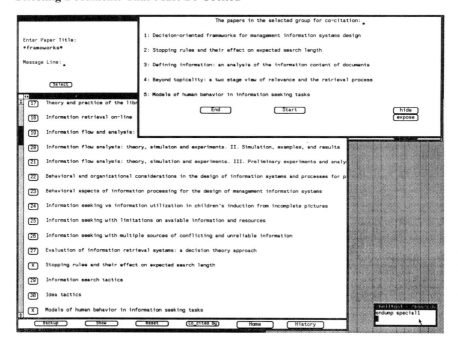

Figure 12.6
A Hypergraph of Nodes That Cocite Selected Documents

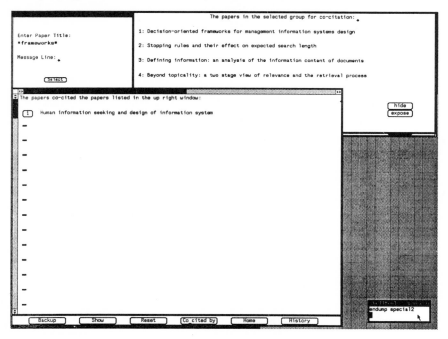

13

Details on Demand: Hypertext Models for Coping with Information Overload

Charles B. Kreitzberg

In this information age in which knowledge is power, information has become a commodity of great value. Corporations are beginning to realize that to maintain their competitive edge they must manage and disseminate information effectively. There is, however, a negative side to the information society in the problem of information overload. As the amount of information has increased, it is becoming increasingly difficult for individuals to keep up with it all. For example, in his book *Information Anxiety*, Richard Wurman notes that the 13 November 1987 issue of the *New York Times* was 1,612 pages long and contained over 12,000,000 words (Wurman, 1989). This chapter discusses one approach to managing information overload: "details on demand," a model based on hypertext, a software technology in which information is structured into logical networks of ideas (Kreitzberg and Shneiderman, 1988).

INFORMATION OVERLOAD

Information overload occurs when too much information is presented for an individual to process meaningfully. In everyday life, people are bombarded by vast amounts of sensory data. Normally this is not a problem because people have the capacity to evaluate the incoming stream of data, select relevant elements, and discard irrelevant ones. This process is called *selective attention*, and it protects the individual from an environment that otherwise would degenerate into raucous cacophony. It is selective attention, for example, that allows two people to carry on a conversation in a crowded train station.

Selective attention is a multistage process. First the individual must organize incoming data into information. Then the information is evaluated for relevance and selectively retained or discarded. Retained information is then passed on to deeper levels of cognitive processing. There is an interesting paradox inherent in selective attention in that information must be understood before the brain can determine whether it is worth paying attention to. The human mind seems able to perform this analysis rapidly and without a great deal of awareness or effort. It does this by rapidly (but superficially) looking at the patterns of incoming information and classifying it. The ability to identify meaningful patterns in the data is the foundation of selective attention.

The human cognitive apparatus is capable of dealing with an enormous amount of information and can perform great feats of selective attention. This is demonstrated by the well-studied "cocktail party phenomenon" in which people effortlessly tune out a number of conversations to focus on one. If, however, an individual's name is mentioned across the room, it is immediately separated from the din and becomes a focus of interest.

At the perceptual level (recognizing one's name at a cocktail party), selective attention is straightforward. As the cognitive demands of a situation become more complex, however, the amount of mental effort required to process information increases. For example, conversing about the weather at a cocktail party might be easy for most people. Negotiating a business deal would be far more difficult, because the cognitive load of processing the information and formulating a response would be greater. Under these circumstances the danger of information overload would increase.

Cognitive load also increases when an individual attempts to comprehend unfamiliar information. The perceptual mechanisms that organize and classify incoming data are not efficient when the material is unfamiliar. Deep cognitive processing is needed to analyze incoming information, relate it to existing cognitive structure, and incorporate the new information into existing learning.

Information overload is therefore not merely a problem of volume but also of cognitive load. The individual can process large amounts of familiar material efficiently but must work harder to process smaller amounts of less familiar material. Overload occurs when the processing demanded by information presented to the individual is greater than the individual's processing capacity. The factors which influence this are (1) the rate at which the information is presented, (2) the complexity of the information, and (3) how meaningful the new information is to the learner. Meaningfulness is important because the amount of effort that it takes for an individual to process information depends upon its meaningfulness. Information that is highly meaningful is easily accepted, organized, and filed for later use. Only information that is meaningfully stored can be used for problem solving.

Meaningfulness depends upon three elements: (1) the content of the information itself (for example, "The cat ate the mouse" is inherently meaningful while "The gru zat the glips" is not); (2) the coherence with which the information is presented (Is it logically structured, and can the learner see the relationship to existing knowledge easily?); and (3) whether the individual already has a knowledge base to provide a context for understanding (for example, "Je suis le roi" is meaningful only to a person who has knowledge of French).

Information overload may therefore be viewed as a problem of converting information into knowledge. One defense against information overload is to "shut down" and refuse to process incoming information. To reduce the discomfort of overload, individuals may decide that some data is irrelevant and will reject it. For example, computer technicians often need to train individuals in the operation of a particular computer program. An individual who understands the program acquires knowledge that can be put to good use, and that person becomes increasingly competent. But individuals who feel overwhelmed may defend against information overload by insisting that they don't want to understand the process but simply want to learn what buttons to push. In effect they reject cognitive understanding in favor of procedural or mechanical information.

By rejecting information that they perceive as entailing a high cognitive processing load and concentrating on the mechanics, these individuals reduce overload and the anxiety it engenders. This increased comfort comes at the price of lowered competence. Knowing what buttons to push without knowing why is rote, rather than meaningful, learning. Information learned by rote cannot be used for problem solving. If something goes wrong or the demands of the situation change, the button pusher is out of luck.

THE DETAILS-ON-DEMAND MODEL

At Cognetics Corporation, we have been developing hypertext-based models to address the information overload problem. Hypertext is a useful strategy for managing information load because it permits large amounts of information to be linked together and accessed at the reader's request.

Hyperties, our hypertext system, is a tool for creating electronic books. It permits text, graphics, and video sequences to be combined into a hypermedia database. Hyperties uses an embedded menu technique (Shneiderman, 1987) for representing links. Links are embedded in text and are *highlighted* to indicate that additional information is linked to them. Each node in Hyperties is called an article and may consist of multiple pages.

In Hyperties, links allow the reader to obtain further elaboration of text presented on the screen. The action of selecting a text link is analogous to the reader pointing to a piece of text and saying, "Tell me more about this." Our details-on-demand paradigm is that information overload occurs when the learner does not have adequate processing capacity to deal with the cognitive load imposed by incoming information. We seek to minimize the overload by organizing the information in a hierarchical fashion. In particular, we provide just enough information initially, and details on demand.

The details-on-demand paradigm is built around three assumptions. First is the assumption that information overload will not occur when the incoming information is meaningful to the learner. When incoming information is meaningful, a natural cognitive organizing process occurs. It is as if the new information "fits" existing templates in the receiving individual's cognitive structure. Therefore the individual can process a larger amount of information without a great deal of effort. If these templates do not exist (because the learner does not possess prerequisite information), or are not activated (because the learner has failed to recognize the relationship between existing knowledge and new information), the cognitive organizing mechanism does not function properly and overload results.

The second assumption is that information overload can be minimized if the amount of information presented is "just enough." Just enough means that the information is sufficiently complete to be coherent but is not excessively elaborated. There should be no gaps that impair understanding, nor should there be any unnecessary details to clutter the presentation. This initial presentation serves to establish the cognitive structure into which subsequent details (provided on demand) will be integrated.

The third assumption specifies that detail is most effectively provided "on demand." This means that the user can request elaboration of any points in the initial presentation but is never forced to confront them. Because the details are presented on demand, the control of the presentation is left to the learner.

The details-on-demand model is hierarchical. By organizing the material according to this model, the learner can approach it at various levels of depth. It can also be seen as a "spiral" model in which the learner can view the information in increasingly detailed perspective as learning progresses. The spiral results from the repeated application of the model to each level of detail. In effect, each level is designed so that just enough information for that level is presented.

We have developed the following rule for constructing the hypertext presentation:

1. Begin the presentation by establishing a context for the information to follow, because meaningfulness is highly dependent upon context (Bransford and Johnson, 1972). For example, the phrase "I want you to press a suit" has a very different meaning to a lawyer and a tailor

2. Identify any prerequisite knowledge that the individual needs for complete understanding. Make such knowledge available through appropriate hypertext links so the knowledgeable learner will not have to review such information while the less knowledgeable learner will have access to it

3. Present the information in a logical sequence so that the information that came before provides context for that which follows. This helps assure that the entire presentation forms a coherent whole

4. Identify the details to be made available at the next level of elaboration and provide links to them

A SIMPLE EXAMPLE

Figure 13.1 shows a Hyperties article that was constructed according to the four rules specified above. It discusses the question, "Should the XYZ corporation change its personnel policy on employee vacations?" The screen shown

Coping with Information Overload

Figure 13.1
Sample Hyperties Article

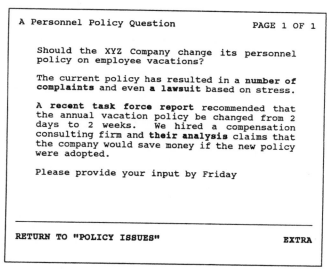

```
A Personnel Policy Question              PAGE 1 OF 1


     Should the XYZ Company change its personnel
     policy on employee vacations?

     The current policy has resulted in a number of
     complaints and even a lawsuit based on stress.

     A recent task force report recommended that
     the annual vacation policy be changed from 2
     days to 2 weeks.   We hired a compensation
     consulting firm and their analysis claims that
     the company would save money if the new policy
     were adopted.

     Please provide your input by Friday

     _____

     RETURN TO "POLICY ISSUES"                 EXTRA
```

Source: Cognetics Corporation.

in figure 13.1 is a complete, if brief, Hyperties article. The highlighted words in boldface are links. The link *RETURN TO* at the bottom of the screen assumes that the reader came from another article titled "Policy Issues." The link *EXTRA* is used to access various index and search functions that do not concern us here.

Note the heading in the upper left, "A Personal Policy Question." This serves to establish generally the context of the information that follows. The first sentence, "Should the XYZ Company . . ." establishes specific context. Imagine trying to understand the second sentence meaningfully in the absence of the heading and first sentence. The second sentence establishes prerequisite information. The reader is informed about the complaints and lawsuit that affect the current situation. If the reader wishes to learn more about them, the details are available on demand. The link "number of complaints" will take the reader to an article detailing the complaints, while the link "a lawsuit" will produce an article about the legal situation. Similarly, the reader can obtain details on the "recent task force report" and the compensation consulting firm and "their analysis."

Note that the findings of the task force report and the recommendations of the consulting firm are stated briefly. This results from the requirement for completeness in the "just enough" initial presentation. With this information, the decision as to whether to view the details is discretionary. Even if the reader chooses not to view the details, there will be no gap in overall understanding.

A CORPORATE POLICY MANUAL

One area of application in which the details-on-demand model is especially valuable is for organizing and managing corporate manuals. Almost every large corporation has a number of manuals that describe products, policies, and procedures. The ability of an employee to master the material in these manuals has a direct effect on the efficiency of the corporation. The sheer size of these manuals creates a serious information overload problem. Figure 13.2 shows a set of screens from an online safety manual that was developed for a chemical research facility. The hypertext version was developed from a printed manual that contained 84 full procedures dealing with various aspects of chemical handling and emergency procedures. The printed manual, which is about six inches thick and weighs 10 pounds, was an excellent candidate for the details-on-demand model because the amount of information contained in it was overwhelming. As a result, readers found it difficult to assimilate the material in the manual.

Each of the procedures in the manual was defined formally and consisted of a number of headings such as Purpose, Scope, Definitions, and Exemptions. This formality supported the maintenance of the manual but inhibited learning because it cluttered up the presentation with unneeded details. In developing a hypertext version of the manual, we decided to create a five-level presentation for each procedure. These levels were (1) job titles, (2) names of all procedures for each job title, (3) a one- or two-sentence summary of each procedure, (4) a brief text summary of each procedure, and (5) the full formal procedure. These levels are shown in figure 13.2.

A reader could approach the manual by identifying his or her job title. This immediately eliminated any procedures not relevant to the reader's job. Assume that a reader, viewing the job title menu, selected "First Level Supervisor." The second screen (level 2) shows the specific responsibilities of the first level supervisor. From this screen the reader can obtain an overview of scope of responsibility that the first level supervisor has. Assume that the reader wanted to learn more about the first level supervisor's responsibilities with regard to the emergency notification system. By selecting that link, the reader would be presented with the level 3 screen. This screen provides a one-sentence summary of the relevant procedures and a link to a more detailed explication of the procedure. The level 4 screen presents a more detailed summary of the procedure. From this screen the reader may select to go deeper to level 5, which presents the full formal procedure.

CONCLUSIONS

The hypertext-based details-on-demand model can reduce the problem of information overload by restructuring information so that just enough is presented up front and elaborations are hidden until requested by the reader. Such details can also be used to present background information that may be required by

Figure 13.2
Sample Details-on-Demand Sequence

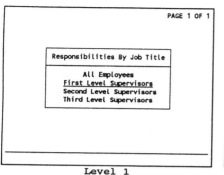

Level 1

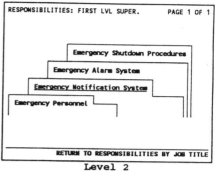

Level 2

```
                                    PAGE 1 OF 1

        ┌──────────────────────────────────────┐
        │      Emergency Notification System:   │
        └──────────────────────────────────────┘

        Each first level supervisor shall assure that all
          employees are familiar with and follow the
          Emergency Notification System.


        See Brief Procedure for Emergency Notification ...

        ───────────────────────────────────────────
             RETURN TO RESPONSIBILITIES: FIRST LVL ...
```

Level 3

```
BRIEF PROCEDURE: EMERGENCY NOTIFICATION   PAGE 1 OF 2

Report Accidents and Emergencies immediately, to the
  Manager of Safety, Francis Stamkes. He should be
  contacted at his office (extension 6635) or at
  home, (212)-555-1212.

Tell the Manager of Safety where you can be reached
  in case additional information is required.

If there is any doubt about whether or not an event
  should be reported, report it.

Note: Excerpted from full Procedure 1-01.

NEXT PAGE        RETURN TO EMERGENCY NOTIFICATION ...
```

Level 4

```
PROCEDURE 1-01: EMERGENCY NOTIFICATION    PAGE 1 OF 9

1.0 PURPOSE

The purpose of this procedure is to ensure that
  emergencies are reported properly to the Manager
  of Health, regardless of the hour or day, so that
  he may notify appropriate members of management
  and initiate needed respose activities.

2.0 SCOPE

The procedure applies to all employees and to all
  others who are following the Safety and Health
  Program.

NEXT PAGE                RETURN TO PROCEDURES ...
```

Level 5

Source: Cognetics Corporation.

some (but not all) readers. By implementing this model, two benefits are achieved: the amount of clutter and extraneous detail in the presentation is reduced, and the reader is in control of the level of detail presented.

The details-on-demand model can foster meaningful learning by increasing readers' comfort with the amount of information presented and their ability to process it.

REFERENCES

Bransford, J. D. and Johnson, M. K. 1972. Contextual prerequisites to understanding: Some investigations of comprehension and recall. *Journal of Verbal Learning and Verbal Behavior* 11: 717–26.

Kreitzberg, C. and Shneiderman, B. 1988. Restructuring knowledge for an electronic encyclopedia. In *Proceedings of the International Ergonomics Association's 10th Congress*, 18–25. Sydney, Australia.

Shneiderman, B. 1987. User interface design for the Hyperties electronic encyclopedia. Presented at Hypertext '87. University of North Carolina, Chapel Hill.

Wurman, R. S. 1989. *Information Anxiety*. New York: Doubleday.

14

A Task Analysis for a Hyperlibrary System

Martha J. Lindeman, John R. Bonneau, and
Kym E. Pocius

This chapter reports the process and results of a task analysis for the conceptual design (Foley, 1983) of a hyperlibrary system to be used by patrons in all types of libraries and scholars in their offices. A search for literature relevant to how people obtain information from printed documents yielded information at the document level (e.g., how people organize and classify documents; Kwasnik, 1989) and information about text organization and comprehension. The task analysis was designed to examine the factors involved in decisions made while reading and preparing to read paper documents.

This chapter discusses the process used to define a framework for describing users' goals, and the approach to defining (1) the actions involved in the task, and (2) the sample of potential users that could provide us with information about how the task was performed manually. The methods for data collection, the results, and the conclusions are discussed in separate sections.

ESTABLISHING A FRAMEWORK FOR DESCRIBING USERS

Norman (1986) stated that one of the critical requirements for good interface design is to bridge the gap between users' goals and the characteristics of the system. The characteristics and goals of library patrons vary greatly, particularly when the types of libraries range from public libraries to academic research libraries. Thus the first step was to identify the primary task for all users, which was obtaining information about a particular topic (domain) from published documents. Then the challenge was to define users' goals and intentions. Norman defined a user's goal as what the person wishes to achieve and an intention as the decision to act to achieve the goal. For example, Norman states that if a user has an overall goal to write a letter, one intention might be to improve the appearance of the first typed draft.

Figure 14.1
A Framework for Understanding Users' Goals

Complete coverage of the subject	Obtaining a list of courses offered by a college	Conducting a literature review for a dissertation	Writing a review paper for a professional journal
Synopsis or general overview	Researching a high school science project	Preparing an introductory lecture	Expanding into a newly relevant domain
Location of an isolated fact	Locating a "how - to" book	Finding details of a research methodology	Extracting a quotation

Breadth

of the

search

No Expertise   Some expertise   Practicing expert
                    (e.g. a graduate student)

Level of expertise in the domain

The two-dimensional matrix shown in figure 14.1 forms a framework for understanding users' goals. Users' expertise in the search domain could range from none to a practicing domain specialist (e.g., a research scientist at a university). As an example of how this could impact design, domain experts could use both general and very specific keywords to search a topic, whereas a nonspecialist may know only terms, such as *postpartum depression* or *baby blues*, that are relevant to the topic of psychological states of mothers following childbirth.

In figure 14.1, a two-dimensional framework is presented for understanding users' goals for use of a full-text retrieval system. Each of the nine cells contains a sample goal for a combination of (1) users' expertise in the database domain, and (2) desired breadth of domain coverage resulting from a search of the database.

The second dimension is the desired breadth of domain coverage for the information search. This dimension is descriptive of users' intentions as they approach the system. The search breadth could range from wanting just a single item (e.g., a particular book) to wanting an exhaustive search that retrieves all relevant information. This can impact design because search strategies range from searching for a particular document by a specific author to trying to retrieve everything relating to a specific topic.

The combination of these two dimensions, as shown in figure 14.1, provides a framework for describing concrete examples of system use that are extremes. Thus, identifying the level of domain expertise and desired breadth of search coverage helped identify the actions that a user might employ to achieve his or her goals. This strongly impacts design decisions; for example, the system being prototyped will include traditional library classification strategies as well as both controlled-vocabulary (keyword) and free-text searching. The situations identified in a matrix of this type can be used to check for adequacy of the first prototype design prior to implementation.

DEFINING A TASK TAXONOMY AND THE USER SAMPLE

The next stage in the analysis of users' tasks as proposed by Norman (1986) is the specification of action sequences necessary to accomplish users' goals. Meister refers to a task taxonomy, which is "a classification of behaviors involved in task performance" (Meister, 1976, 101). For a complete taxonomy, it would be necessary to determine the actions involved in (1) locating the desired documents, and (2) accessing the desired information within those documents. The first problem is a traditional information retrieval problem; the second problem is a new problem for information scientists, and it is particularly important for full-text and hypertext systems.

The issues involved in computerized searching for documents have been discussed in detail in the literature on bibliographic retrieval systems (e.g., research on computerized card catalogs). There is also literature on manually searching for documents in libraries. Thus, the task of locating documents was not considered in the task analysis. For that information, see Hildreth (1982) and Markey (1984).

Other studies have addressed the general issue of locating documents, with some of their effort directed toward the use of within-document information. These studies include, among others, Garvey (1979); Gates (1987); Prabha, Bunge, and Rice (1987); Prabha, Rice, and Cameron (1988); Raisag, Smith, Cuff, and Kilgour (1966); and Sabine and Sabine (1986). Although these studies were relevant, they did not provide a detailed description of how information is accessed within documents.

The literature on reading was then examined. Adler and Van Doren (1972) proposed that there are four levels of reading: elementary, inspectional, analytical, and syntopic. Elementary reading involves the rudimentary skills taught in beginning reading classes. There are two kinds of inspectional reading: (1) systematic prereading, in which the reader examines only portions of the documents; and (2) superficial skimming, in which the reader reads linearly through the document but does not stop to ponder things that are not understood. Analytical reading is when a reader attempts to understand the contents of a document. Syntopic reading is when the reader places a document in the context of other related documents and therefore may construct a frame of reference that is not contained in any one document. Syntopic reading includes all of the other levels. The four classes defined by Adler and Van Doren comprise the task taxonomy used for reading. Only one other task class, user-generated information such as bookmarks and annotations, was defined.

Because syntopic reading includes the other three types of reading, and based on the matrix discussed in the previous section, the team hypothesized that all of the actions needed to accomplish any user's goal would be included in the set of actions that might be used by domain experts, who were called "scholars." For example, scholars may search for a particular book by a particular author when tracing a reference citation; they may want complete coverage of a topic when writing a review paper for that topic; and they may be nonspecialists in a domain when obtaining information about a domain previously unrelated to their work.

DATA COLLECTION

A survey methodology was chosen because (1) there was inadequate information for a controlled procedure, and (2) scholars such as university faculty were accessible only in their offices. Face-to-face interviews were used, as these are optimal for asking and exploring the answers to open-ended questions.

The sample of domain experts was 15 full professors at a research university. Full professors were chosen on the hypothesis that (1) their data would be the most homogeneous, other than for across-domain differences, and (2) they could describe successful methods of manipulating documents that had evolved after many years of practice. One professor was included from each of the following disciplines: accounting, agronomy, architecture, botany, computer science (and electrical engineering), dance, engineering mechanics, English, history, law, mathematics, music, physics, psychology, and Romance languages. These domains were selected to form a heterogeneous population (Brunswik, 1947). The professor representing each discipline was selected by randomizing the names of all full professors within that department and then making one call to each professor in that order until an interview was arranged. Usually the first or second professor contacted agreed to be interviewed. The first author, assisted by the second author, did the interviewing. The audiotapes of the interviews were then transcribed and analyzed. Notes taken during the interviews were also studied.

Although scholars use many kinds of printed documents, the interviews were limited to journal articles (whether in a journal, as preprints, or as reprints) and two types of books (Bates, 1986): linear books, which are designed to be read sequentially, and reference books, which contain stand-alone units of information. A checklist was developed as a guide for the semistructured interviews. The first question, after doing the introductions and asking permission to record the interview, was, "Can you recall a recent time that you used a printed document?" Most of the scholars first mentioned one of the types of documents being considered. If the scholar mentioned a different type of document, the next question was, "Can you recall a recent time that you used any other type of printed document?" and that question usually elicited one of the desired three types of documents.

RESULTS

The interview yielded four types of information: (1) a major difference between two types of scholars, (2) descriptions of scholars' processes of document evaluation, (3) functionality necessary to support a scholar's normal use of the three types of documents, and (4) potential problems that may cause user resistance toward using a document retrieval system.

Two types of scholars. Although the departments were chosen to make a heterogeneous sample, the information provided by the scholars was extremely homogeneous, with the exception of one type of data. The scholars could be divided into two groups: (1) those scholars that concentrate on research and thus primarily use journals and journal articles in preprint and reprint form, and (2) those scholars that concentrate on undergraduate education and thus primarily use books. The essential difference is whether a scholar's focus is on information about current research issues or information about the fundamentals of the discipline, and does not seem related to whether a scholar was in the sciences or in the humanities. However, this may be a result of the sample size ($n = 15$).

Evaluation of documents. A scholar's normal reading process is a multistep one that winnows out irrelevant or unimportant documents or sections of documents. Regardless of the type of focus or the type of document, each document is first rapidly evaluated from the title (e.g., in a journal's table of contents) and from parts of the document such as the abstract, the conclusions section, the reference section, and so on. The document, or its relevant parts, is read in detail only if it successfully passes this series of evaluations. The interview data indicate that many scholars, even those that are heavy computer users, will primarily use a document retrieval system for locating information within documents and then require printed copies for detailed reading. Thus a scholar, after finding a section of a journal article that seemed interesting, would print out the article for reading rather than read it on the screen. A similar "reference use only" model is the accepted model of microform use; the model and its implications are discussed in more detail in the discussion of user resistance.

Direct access. The data indicate that a hyperlibrary should provide several types of direct access to portions of documents: (1) a table of contents that serves as a set of selectable options (e.g., a list of headings in a journal article); (2) an index that can be accessed by specifying one (or more) letters of the desired term, with each index entry being a selectable option that immediately displays the desired portions of the text; (3) other lists that allow selection and direct access (e.g., figure captions); (4) direct access to a user-specified page number (e.g., for quotations); and (5) browsing through the text by scrolling and/or paging. Both preprogrammed and user-definable links (hypertext links) should be available as direct access methods. Also, functionality that allows the user to retrace a path either sequentially or randomly back through previously viewed sections of the document would address the "Where was it that I saw . . . ?" question that is often asked by scholars while working with a document.

Search functionalities. The search functionalities needed or desired are fairly standard (e.g., a thesaurus), but there are some new ones. For example, scholars need free-text search for both bibliographic and the full text of documents. However, the sections of documents (e.g., reference sections) should be specifiable as target areas, as are the fields in bibliographic citations. Thus a scholar could specify an author's name and be provided with a list of citations of that author's works.

Personal database. It was also apparent that scholars need a personal database that allows them to make, store, and retrieve bookmarks, annotations, search results, links within and across documents, and so on. The scholar should be able to access, display, edit, search, sort, and print these items as can be done in some current hypertext systems. However, this is true even when the main database may have "read-only" status (e.g., when it contains published material residing on a library computer). The files in the personal database should be in a form that can be imported into word-processing programs, even if document-generating capabilities are integrated into the system.

Navigational aids and display control. User control and navigational aids were the major themes when the scholars described how they "got around" in a document. The ability to display sequential blocks of a document quickly (which may or may not include graphics) is needed to support rapid scanning of documents. Figures and graphs will require special attention in the design, as a user at different times may wish to view the same figure at different levels of detail (e.g., only to know it exists, to see the general details, or to view minute details by zooming and perhaps panning). Some scholars use multiple highlighting techniques, and more than one highlighting functionality should be provided in the hyperlibrary. These functionalities should include saving the highlighting so that it reappears whenever the document is displayed.

User resistance. The last topic (other than demographics) discussed in the interviews was access to electronic documents. The scholars expressed a lot of resistance to that type of access. For example, the scholars noted that reading is one of the few highly portable things done by a scholar, and this advantage would be lost by using a computer. Also, the scholars in the sample expect to have the same problems with electronic retrieval systems as are described in studies of the use of microforms such as microfiche and microfilm. Each problem discussed in the reviews of the literature on microform use (e.g., Saffady, 1985) was mentioned by at least one subject and often by several subjects.

The most common problems mentioned by the scholars were a subset of terminal users' complaints related to Video Operator's Distress Syndrome (VODS), which include backaches, eyestrain, burning or itchy eyes, headaches, neckaches, fatigue, moodiness, and nausea (Scalet, 1987). This was true even though these scholars are not novices to computer systems; three-fourths of the scholars either had a computer or word processor in their office for their own use or volunteered that they used a computer. Some were expert computer users and some were either hardware or software designers.

Scholars also mentioned other potential problems that were not related to VODS or contained in the microform model:

1. In some disciplines, there is a need for high-resolution graphics
2. Some documents, such as those by a scientist's peers in Poland and Russia, will not be available electronically and will require maintaining a manual system. Then a scholar would have to maintain two separate systems

3. A paper copy is needed for permanent storage in a scholar's current indexing system (e.g., file folders ordered by authors' last names)

4. A full page is normally not visible on the screen and thus the user must do a lot of scrolling, which is unpleasant

5. "Page flipping" on the computer is slower and requires more (perceived) effort than turning the pages in a book, which requires only "a flick of the wrist"

6. There is a psychological distance between the user and the text that does not occur with a paper document. This distance reduces the user's sense of control. (Although this concept has not been well defined, it is related to the success of direct-manipulation interfaces that inherently reduce the feeling of psychological distance from the task)

7. Writing is easier than using a keyboard

8. It takes time to learn how to use a computer system

9. There is a fear of "pushing the wrong button" and destroying something (e.g., the database). (This is true even for a scholar involved in computer design)

10. Sometimes it takes longer to do things with the computer than to do them manually

11. Scholars often need to look at several documents simultaneously

While some of these are included in discussions of reading on a computer (e.g., Hansen and Haas, 1988), others are not. In addition, user resistance can come from such general concerns as accessibility of the system (e.g., in the office versus in the library), irrelevance of the database contents (e.g., not from the user's discipline), and financial considerations.

CONCLUSIONS

The data indicate that a hyperlibrary that provides access to only one type of documents (either journals or books) might be appropriate for scholars that focus on either research or undergraduate education, respectively. This difference between types of scholars cuts across discipline boundaries and is a new factor that needs to be examined further before selecting documents to be included in a database.

A hyperlibrary should provide functionalities that allow scholars to evaluate documents quickly and easily at various levels. For example, the first paragraphs of each section of the document (such as methodology, conclusions, or reference section in a journal article) should be directly accessible, and then the user can scroll or page through the following paragraphs (without having to specify which links to follow). Other methods of document evaluation, such as scanning figures and tables, are used by scholars. These should be supported by direct access through a list (e.g., a list of figures) and also as a set of graphics (including captions or headers) that can be browsed without having to look first at a list. Much more research is needed to understand the various strategies that scholars use. For example, it has been suggested that linking the topic sentence of each paragraph would be one way of aiding this evaluation process. However, the proportion of documents that have strong topic sentences is unknown, and some scholars rely on both the first and last sentences of each paragraph to understand better how the paragraphs relate.

The data also strongly support the research team's original assumption that neither current approaches to hypertext/hypermedia systems nor current approaches to full-text retrieval systems are adequate for a hyperlibrary. Hypertext/ hypermedia systems emphasize a "browse" mode in which users follow links connecting related chunks of text (which may or may not be sections of documents). Traditional full-text retrieval emphasizes a "search" mode in which a text is retrieved in response to a specified query. The two approaches need to be integrated, and additional types of functionality, such as structures allowing easy nonlinear access to parts of documents, should be provided. This is true even when the published documents in the database are "read only."

While scholars were open to using a hyperlibrary to locate information, they were resistant to doing their detailed reading from a computer screen. The primary objection was portability, but many other reasons were also given. Any system providing computerized access to documents will have to provide enough advantages to overcome the problems that have plagued microfiche and microfilm in addition to numerous other obstacles. However, this may be much easier in a population that has not had years of manually doing the task. When a person has practiced a task repetitively for a long time, much of what is done becomes unconscious habit and thus does not require any conscious effort. This often makes new ways of doing things seem much more difficult for practiced individuals than for novices.

This task analysis identified many types of functionality that will be needed in a hyperlibrary system that will be acceptable to scholars. The examples used in this chapter are only a sample of those functionalities. The key is understanding users' current strategies, needs, and goals. The framework for understanding users' goals shown in figure 14.1 is just a beginning. The research team will continue to address the issue of what functionality is necessary for a hyperlibrary as the system is iteratively prototyped.

REFERENCES

Adler, M. J., and C. Van Doren. 1972. *How to read a book*. New York: Simon and Schuster.

Bates, M. J. 1986. What is a reference book? A theoretical and empirical analysis. *RQ* 26(1):37–57.

Brunswik, E. 1947. *Systematic and representative design of psychological experiments*. Berkeley: The University of California Press.

Foley, J. D. 1983. *Managing the design of user-computer interfaces*. Washington, D.C.: George Washington University, Institute for Information Science and Technology.

Garvey, W. D. 1979. *Communication: The essence of science*. New York: Pergamon Press.

Gates, M. Y. 1987. *A study of how books are used*. Dublin, Ohio: OCLC Online Computer Library Center.

Hansen, W. J., and C. Haas. 1988. Reading and writing with computers: A framework for explaining differences in performance. *Communication of the ACM* 31(9):1080–89.

Hildreth, C. R. 1982. *Online public access catalogs: The user interface*. Dublin, Ohio: OCLC Online Computer Library Center.

Kwasnik, B. H. 1989. The influence of context on classificatory behavior. Ph.d. diss., Rutgers, The State University of New Jersey.

Markey, K. 1984. *Subject searching in library catalogs*. Dublin, Ohio: OCLC Online Computer Library Center.

Meister, D. 1976. *Behavioral foundations of system development*. New York: John Wiley.

Norman, D. A. 1986. Cognitive engineering. In *User-centered system design: New perspectives on human-computer interaction*, ed. D. A. Norman and S. W. Draper, 31–61. Hillsdale, N.J.: Lawrence Erlbaum Associates.

Prabha, C., J. Bunge, and D. Rice. 1987. *How public library patrons use nonfiction books*. Report no. OCLC/OPR/RR–87/1. Dublin, Ohio: OCLC Online Computer Library Center.

Prabha, C., D. Rice, and D. Cameron. 1988. *Nonfiction book use by academic library users*. Report no. OCLC/OR/RR–88/1. Dublin, Ohio: OCLC Online Computer Library Center.

Raisag, L. M., M. Smith, R. Cuff, and F. G. Kilgour. 1966. How biomedical investigators use library books. *Bulletin of the American Medical Association* 54(2):104–7.

Sabine, G. A., and P. L. Sabine. 1986. How people use books and journals. *Library Quarterly* 56(4):399–408.

Saffady, W. 1985. *Micrographics*, 2d ed. Littleton, Colo.: Libraries Unlimited.

Scalet, E. A. 1987. *VDT health and safety*. Lawrence, Kans.: Ergosyst.

PART IV

Case Studies in Human-Computer Interaction

Thomas H. Martin

Much of the literature in human-computer interaction comes from design or evaluation activities. Often a new technology is being tackled (hypermedia, image databases, full-text help systems), and audiences are interested in learning what the designers or evaluators have discovered. For example, are zooming and panning—essential in filming—of use in navigating through large databases of text? The designers like to describe what they have been able to incorporate in the system, while the evaluators like to describe what users actually end up doing. There is an aspect of conjecture and refutation, with the designer striving for the ideal and the evaluator bearing bad tidings. For this reason, evaluators are encouraged to get involved early so that prototypes of the system can be refined through usage analysis to bring dream and reality closer together.

A classic article by John D. Gould and Clayton Lewis (*Communications of the ACM*, vol. 28, no. 3, 1985) describes three design principles: (1) focus on users and tasks, (2) measure prototype use empirically, and (3) revise based on feedback. The authors discovered that most designers do not mention these principles when asked. Designers say that users don't know what they want, that the designers can get it right the first time, and that testing would only slow things down and make systems more expensive. The reality is that testing exposes one to the risk of failure, but then so does building a system. Today, after years of experience with working and nonworking systems, the expectation should be that almost nobody gets it right the first time. Case studies should exhibit a log of learning derived from testing and revising, and authors should not be afraid to admit they learned through design and evaluation.

To maximize the value of case studies, what should they include? Typically, descriptions of three aspects of the system should be included: the goals for the system, the characteristics of the user population, and the nature of the tasks that the system will be used to accomplish.

1. Goals
   - Is the system a slight change or major departure from previous systems?
   - Is the system expected to show a profit or lead to some advantage?
   - Who has the most to gain (or lose) from successful implementation?
   - Are there special circumstances about the environment or user expectations that will impact on task accomplishment?

2. Users
   - What are the sizes of the various user populations?
   - Are they discretionary or captive users?
   - What level of experience do they have?
   - How frequently are they likely to use the system?

3. Tasks
   - What is the nature and range of tasks?
   - What level of intelligence and involvement do they require?
   - What is the time pressure and need for accuracy?

Once a clear picture of the goals, users and tasks is presented, it makes sense to describe the characteristics of the information system solution that is being proposed. This includes discussion of hardware (displays, interaction devices) and software (languages, databases) and user support (documentation, training, help facilities). A good case study provides examples of how users in their settings ideally use the system to perform representative tasks.

At this point the evaluator needs to step in and, through examples or aggregate data, indicate how things occur in practice. The following are among the particular questions to be addressed:

- How frequently are various system features used?
- How long do users take to become experienced at these tasks?
- What sorts of mistakes or errors do people make?
- How are they able to recover when they run into difficulty?
- What sorts of things would they like to do that they cannot?

Often there will be a surprising set of problems that people have, and the problems will lead the designers to rethink the system. In the field of information retrieval, the problem that continually arises is that people are not good at formulating queries in terms of Boolean operators.

The good case study indicates how user experience has led to revisions that bring the interface more in line with user behavior. Often the changes take the form of simplification of at least a portion of the interface, leading to levels of interface complexity. Other times, the system is revised to tolerate a diversity of user behaviors, shifting memory load from the user to the computer. The designer who has had to compromise with the vagaries of users has found that there are no perfect solutions, only a series of trade-offs that please some, but not all, of the users.

Finally, the well-done case study should make clear that far more is involved than just the user interface. There are concerns about economics, deadlines, marketability, and trends in the industry. Often, these larger concerns lead to low priority for interface design. However, the reader should ask if system design is carried out in such a way that, were resources available, redesign of the interface would be feasible.

We have come to expect that successful system implementers will come out with new versions of their systems. It would be nice to read in the literature sequels for the original case studies. A weakness in the case study literature is that the case studies almost always are near the beginning of the system's life cycle. There is a need for the mature system designers to look back and try to determine what the critical factors were that led to their victories. Maybe they will conclude that their concern with the user interface and the satisfaction of the users contributed to their success.

Turning to the chapters in this part of the book, the chapter by Pfuderer and Miller represents the learning that designers and systems analysts do as they refine design to fit the users. Pfuderer and Miller systematically allowed decision support personnel to participate in the analysis of military acquisitions information architecture. By aggregating data elements across projects, uniform standards could be set for screen interfaces and terminology. Prototype were developed that people could then react to and modify.

The Walker and Thoma chapter is different in that it involves the design of hardware rather than software. Walker and Thoma have helped design optical disc workstations for use in biomedical libraries. The optical discs will be used in conjunction with online biomedical searching to provide access to the contents of biomedical periodicals. Part of their design strategy involves experimentation in library settings to evaluate patrons' time searching, subjective satisfaction, learning, and errors.

Kaske is the lone evaluator of the authors. He measured types of searching over time by the entire population of users of a university online public access catalog (OPAC). He studied patterns in subject searching and found that usage of the Library of Congress subject headings increased as the semester passed, and increased at different hours of the day. In the early development of online public access catalogs, it was very hard to predict what types of searches users would carry out. Now that OPACs are becoming common, it is possible to show that users do in fact want to carry out subject searches, and that their preferences for different types of searching change over time. Kaske's chapter is descriptive and preliminary. A great deal of room has been left for research that clarifies the patterns and preferences of OPAC users.

15

The Variability of Subject Searching in an Online Public Access Catalog over an Academic Year

Neal K. Kaske

The percentage of subject searching in an online public access catalog (OPAC) at a university library was studied over a full academic year (1987/88) in this exploratory research effort. The full population of all searches was analyzed and reported; sample data were not used. The variability of subject searching over the year was measured by week, day, and hour. The level of subject searching varied over the weeks of the semester from a low of 35.64% (second week of the spring semester) to a high of 53.93% (16th week of the fall semester). The variability by days of the week ranged from a low of 37.8% (Fridays during spring semester) to a high of 50.26% (Sundays during the spring semester). The range by hours varied from a low of 36.54% (9:00 A.M.–10:00 A.M. during the spring semester) to a high of 55.17% (10:00 P.M.–11:00 P.M. during the spring semester). The OPAC studied was the Virginia Tech Library System (VTLS) in use at the University of Alabama. Management implications based on findings are offered.

INTRODUCTION

The goal of this research was to learn if the utilization of subject searching by patrons in an online public access catalog (OPAC) varied over an academic year. The first general null hypothesis tested was

H_o: The percentage of subject searching for a given time unit (hour of day, day of week, and week of term) will not differ more than 5 percentage points between the two semesters of the academic year studied.

The second general null hypothesis tested was

H_o: The percent of subject searching for a given time unit (hour of day, day of week, and week of term) will not differ more than 10 percentage points within each of the two semesters studied.

All the searches conducted at public terminals from 26 August 1987 to 18 December 1987 and from 7 January 1988 to 7 May 1988 were studied. These dates include the first day of classes through the last day of finals for both the fall and spring semesters for the 1987/88 academic year.

The data for this research were collected at the University of Alabama, which had an undergraduate enrollment of 14,041 (13,160 Full-Time Equivalents) during the 1987 fall semester and 13,106 (12,284 FTE) during the 1988 spring semester. Graduate students numbered 2,325 (1,748 FTE) in the fall and 2,338 (1,757 FTE) in the spring. The faculty was 954 strong (824 full-time and 130 part-time) during the fall of 1987, and staff numbered 2,421 (2,148 full-time and 273 part-time). The data on the number of faculty and staff are recorded only during October of each year. Student, faculty, and staff counts do not include the law school.[1]

The library system at the University of Alabama is composed of the main library and five branches (business, education, engineering, health science, and science). There is also a law library on campus, but it was not using VTLS (see below) at the time of this research and is therefore excluded from this analysis. The holdings in the main library and its branches are reported to exceed 1.5 million cataloged volumes. Microform units number 1.2 million. More than 90% of the collection was presented in the OPAC at the time of data collection.[2]

The OPAC in use at the time of this study was the Virginia Tech Library System (VTLS). The time units selected for analysis of variability between the semesters were time of day, day of week, and week of term. The data for this study were generated by patrons searching on any one of 28 public access terminals. Fifteen of the terminals are located in the main library, and there are two in each of five branch libraries. An additional three dial-in telecommunications ports provide a total of 28 public access points.

Patrons of these libraries were able to search by author, title, subject, and call number. Boolean searching is supported by the VTLS system but that function was not active at Alabama during this study.

Definition of Terms

Subject, author, title, and call number searches used the following commands: S/, A/, T/, and C/. The percentage of subject searching was calculated by dividing the number of subject searches by the sum of author, subject, and title searches. Call number searches were omitted from this study to provide a clearer picture of the percentage of subject searches. Call number searches could be for a subject or for a known item. The percentage of call number searching was found to be very low (5.42% for the fall semester and 3.27% for the spring semester).

RELATED RESEARCH

No research efforts into the use of subject searching by patrons in an OPAC that used a population of data for a full academic year have been reported. However, one study did report that the variability of subject searching (in an OPAC for a full university library system, branches, and the main library) ranged from 35% to 52% over the weeks of a semester. The same project reported a variability of subject searching over days to be between 44% and 64%; the variability over hours, 40% to 55%.[3] A second study investigated the variability of subject searching between branch libraries on campus for a semester and found that subject searching ranged from 12% to 70% over the weeks of a term, 17% to 64% across the days of the week, and 22% to 74% over the hours of the day.[4]

Karen Markey, in her work titled *Subject Searching in Library Catalogs*, has summarized research efforts that reported upon the percentage of subject searching via an OPAC. Markey details the findings of eight studies in her book; each study used sample data for a few days or one to two weeks. These studies were performed in the libraries of West Valley Community College, University of California, Dallas Public Library, Mankato State University, Syracuse University, Northwestern University, and the Ohio State University. The studies reviewed by Markey report a percentage for subject searching but not its variability over time. The values for subject searching ranged from a low of 34% to a high of 65%.[5]

METHODOLOGY

The source of data for this study comes from a VTLS statistical report titled *Alphabetic Searches*. This report in a machine-readable format was processed by programs that reformatted the values for the variables into a structure that was then used to analyze the data via Statistical Analysis System (SAS) programs on an IBM mainframe computer. The results of the SAS analysis were used directly or transformed, reformatted, and displayed on a microcomputer using Lotus programs. For a detailed description of how the data were extracted and reformatted, see Kaske (1988a, 1988b).

The independent variables for this research were the time units (hour of day, day of week, and week of term) and semesters. The dependent variables were the percentage of subject searches conducted per semester per time unit. The data were tabulated and graphed to learn if there were patterns in the use of subject searching over the selected time units and to explore the variations among and within the two semesters. Next, the two general null hypotheses and two alternative hypotheses were tested for each time unit studied. These four hypotheses are presented below.

The first general hypothesis is

Table 15.1
Searches for Fall Semester 1987 by Type

Time Unit	Type of Search					Subject (%)
	Author	Subject	Title	Call No.	Total	
Semester	49,585	89,654	60,884	11,477	211,600	44.8

H_o: The percentage of subject searching for a given time unit (hour of day, day of week, and week of term) will not differ more than five percentage points between the two semesters of the academic year studied.

The first general alternative hypothesis is

H_o: The percentage of subject searching for a given time unit (hour of day, day of week, and week of term) will differ more than five percentage points between the two semesters of the academic year studied.

The second general null hypothesis is

H_o: The percentage of subject searching for a given time unit (hour of day, day of week, and week of term) will not differ more than 10 percentage points within each of the two semesters studied.

And the second general alternative hypothesis is

H_o: The percentage of subject searching for a given time unit (hour of day, day of week, and week of term) will differ more than 10 percentage points within each of the two semesters studied.

RESULTS

The number of searches conducted via public terminals during the fall semester was 211,600, and 196,245 were made during the spring. That is a drop of 7.26% in the total number of searches from the fall to the spring. The student population (undergraduates and graduates) dropped from 14,908 (FTE) in the fall to 14,041 (FTE) in the spring for a loss of 5.8%. Some of the change in the volume of searching could be due to the smaller user base.

Totals for each type of search and the adjusted percentages of subject searches (call number searches omitted) for each semester are displayed in table 15.1 (fall) and table 15.2 (spring). Table 15.3 and table 15.4 report the searching activity over the weeks of the term. Each of the semesters has 17 weeks of classes. The 11th week of the spring semester was omitted because it was a

Table 15.2
Searches for Spring Semester 1988 by Type

Time Unit	Type of Search					
	Author	Subject	Title	Call No.	Total	Subject (%)
Semester	47,454	84,788	57,581	6,422	196,245	44.67

Table 15.3
Searches for Fall Semester 1987 per Week by Type

Week	Type of Search					
	Author	Subject	Title	Call No.	Total	Subject (%)
1	1,556	1,811	1,714	234	5,315	35.64
2	2,626	3,829	2,998	347	9,800	40.51
3	2,715	4,629	2,924	469	10,737	45.08
4	2,727	4,763	3,337	596	11,423	43.99
5	3,203	5,153	4,017	778	13,151	41.65
6	3,193	4,426	4,341	1,152	13,112	37.01
7	3,281	5,294	4,105	1,102	13,782	41.75
8	3,006	5,224	4,208	1,071	13,509	42.00
9	2,553	4,677	3,478	723	11,431	43.68
10	3,535	5,911	4,391	1,106	14,943	42.72
11	3,457	6,471	3,886	805	14,619	46.84
12	3,884	6,860	4,552	734	16,030	44.85
13	3,917	7,691	4,533	725	16,866	47.65
14	1,814	4,095	2,601	260	8,770	48.12
15	2,896	6,429	3,461	473	13,259	50.28
16	3,195	8,351	3,938	567	16,051	53.93
17	2,027	4,040	2,400	335	8,802	47.71
Total	49,585	89,654	60,884	11,477	211,600	44.80

break. Tables 15.5 and 15.6 report searching by day and week, and tables 15.7 and 15.8 show search types over the hours of the day.

The differences between the totals for the two semesters is very small (less than one-tenth of a percent). However, the differences between two semesters and within each of the time units (hour, day, and week) are considerable and worthy of exploration. This exploration will be done by testing the stated hypotheses.

Table 15.4
Searches for Spring Semester 1988 per Week by Type

Week	Type of Search					
	Author	Subject	Title	Call No.	Total	Subject (%)
1	295	346	348	33	1,022	34.98
2	2,934	3,089	3,187	279	9,489	33.54
3	2,846	4,902	3,396	422	11,566	43.99
4	3,022	4,706	3,176	388	11,292	43.16
5	3,381	5,474	3,850	524	13,229	43.09
6	3,309	5,654	4,052	560	13,575	43.44
7	3,241	6,125	4,023	460	13,849	45.75
8	2,868	5,683	3,561	364	12,476	46.92
9	2,806	5,470	3,700	423	12,399	45.67
10	2,448	4,616	3,737	321	11,122	42.74
12	2,681	4,738	3,569	307	11,295	43.12
13	3,042	6,018	4,055	443	13,558	45.89
14	2,841	6,053	3,940	362	13,196	47.16
15	2,680	5,638	3,321	475	12,114	48.44
16	3,421	5,704	3,503	478	13,106	45.17
17	2,874	6,385	3,541	355	13,155	49.88
18	2,765	4,187	2,622	228	9,802	43.73
Total	47,454	84,788	57,581	6,422	196,245	44.67

Looking first at the differences in the use of subject searching between the semesters by the weeks of the term, it is found that three of the weeks (2nd, 6th, and 15th) have differences greater than 5%. Therefore, the first null hypothesis is rejected, and the alternative hypothesis is accepted. The differences between the weeks are reported in table 15.9, which was created by subtracting the spring semester values from the fall semester values for the three time units. The differences between the weeks of the semesters are shown in figure 15.1. Note that the use of subject searching goes up over the course of the semester.

The differences between the days of the week are not as great as those for the weeks of the semester. There is only one day, Friday, that even comes close to the 5% difference. Its difference is 4.94%. The differences among the days of the week are listed in table 15.9, and the differences in the days of the week are shown in figure 15.2. The days of the week vary little from term to term except for Fridays, which differ by nearly 5%. The null hypothesis is not rejected in this case.

Table 15.5
Searches for Fall Semester 1987 per Day by Type

Day	Type of Search					
	Author	Subject	Title	Call No.	Total	Subject (%)
Monday	8,504	15,718	10,783	2,079	37,084	44.90
Tuesday	9,564	16,432	11,902	2,392	40,290	43.36
Wednesday	8,885	16,431	11,307	2,351	38,974	44.87
Thursday	8,322	14,348	10,139	1,813	34,622	43.73
Friday	5,592	9,118	6,624	1,038	22,372	42.74
Saturday	3,578	6,128	3,776	600	14,082	45.45
Sunday	5,140	11,479	6,353	1,204	24,176	49.97
Total	49,585	89,654	60,884	11,477	211,600	44.80

Table 15.6
Searches for Spring Semester 1988 per Day by Type

Day	Type of Search					
	Author	Subject	Title	Call No.	Total	Subject (%)
Monday	8,879	16,402	10,473	1,190	36,944	45.87
Tuesday	8,993	15,834	10,271	1,212	36,310	45.11
Wednesday	8,428	14,129	9,805	1,051	33,413	43.66
Thursday	7,529	13,859	9,957	1,061	32,406	44.21
Friday	5,311	7,704	7,364	757	21,136	37.80
Saturday	3,855	7,074	4,487	558	15,974	45.89
Sunday	4,459	9,786	5,224	593	20,062	50.26
Total	47,454	84,788	57,581	6,422	196,245	44.67

Turning now to the differences between the hours of the day, it is found that there are no times when the percentage is over 5% except during the first quarter hour (7:45 A.M.–8:00 A.M.) and after midnight. During these times the differences are large (from 7.02% to 17.56%), but the number of searches is very low. Because of the low use, these times are disregarded in this analysis. The differences between the hours are shown in table 15.9. Figure 15.3 shows the values from 8:00 A.M. through 10:00 P.M. for both semesters. The percentage of subject searching goes up most of the day from a low of 36.54% to a high of 55.17%.

The analysis of the differences within the semesters was pursued next. This was done by testing the second general null hypothesis. Looking first to the

Table 15.7
Searches for Fall Semester 1987 per Hour by Type

Hour	Type of Search					
	Author	Subject	Title	Call No.	Total	Subject (%)
7:45–8 a.m.	84	131	90	19	324	42.95
8	1,022	1,581	1,414	289	4,306	39.96
9	2,489	3,784	3,002	516	9,791	40.80
10	3,473	5,868	4,356	832	14,529	42.84
11	3,540	5,733	4,292	668	14,233	42.26
Noon	3,524	6,225	4,134	701	14,584	44.84
1 p.m.	4,785	7,443	5,777	1,170	19,175	41.34
2	4,922	8,201	6,432	1,175	20,730	41.94
3	4,601	8,572	5,919	1,135	20,227	44.90
4	4,158	7,364	5,284	977	17,783	43.82
5	3,233	5,885	4,110	743	13,971	44.49
6	3,342	6,223	3,668	759	13,992	47.03
7	3,494	7,160	4,059	968	15,681	48.66
8	3,282	7,249	3,883	749	15,163	50.29
9	2,482	5,278	2,998	540	11,298	49.06
10	1,081	2,710	1,391	225	5,407	52.30
Midnight	52	190	67	9	318	61.49
1 a.m.	21	57	8	2	88	66.28
Total (8 a.m.–11 p.m.)	49,428	89,276	60,719	11,447	210,870	44.77

Table 15.8
Searches for Spring Semester 1988 per Hour by Type

Hour	Author	Subject	Title	Call No.	Total	Subject (%)
				Type of Search		
7:45–8 a.m.	89	82	152	37	360	25.39
8	1,086	1,418	1,127	220	3,851	39.05
9	2,567	3,495	3,502	365	9,929	36.54
10	3,731	5,354	4,784	407	14,276	38.60
11	3,747	5,110	4,438	445	13,740	38.44
Noon	3,535	5,445	4,646	445	14,071	39.96
1 p.m.	4,151	6,912	5,746	628	17,437	41.12
2	4,707	7,866	6,136	650	19,359	42.04
3	4,644	7,922	5,587	659	18,812	43.64
4	3,615	6,747	4,253	463	15,078	46.16
5	3,000	6,198	3,523	434	13,155	48.72
6	2,531	5,397	2,807	351	11,086	50.27
7	3,236	7,090	3,204	443	13,973	52.40
8	3,263	7,305	3,687	386	14,641	51.25
9	2,324	5,331	2,663	309	10,627	51.67
10	1,117	2,901	1,240	173	5,431	55.17
Midnight	92	167	72	5	336	50.45
1 a.m.	19	48	14	2	83	59.26
Total (8a.m.–11 p.m.)	47,254	84,491	57,343	6,378	195,466	44.68

Table 15.9
Differences Between Semesters by Time Unit

Week	% + (−)	Day	% + (−)	Hour	% + (−)
1	0.66	Monday	(0.97)	7 a.m.	17.56
2	6.97	Tuesday	(1.76)	8	0.31
3	1.09	Wednesday	1.21	9	4.25
4	0.83	Thursday	(0.48)	10	4.24
5	(1.44)	Friday	4.94	11	3.83
6	(6.44)	Saturday	(0.43)	Noon	4.88
7	(4.00)	Sunday	(0.29)	1	0.22
8	(4.92)			2	(0.11)
9	(2.00)			3	1.26
10	(0.02)			4	(2.35)
11	3.72			5	(4.23)
12	(1.04)			6	(3.25)
13	0.49			7	(3.74)
14	(0.32)			8	(0.95)
15	5.11			9	(2.61)
16	4.05			10	(2.88)
17	3.98			Midnight	11.04
				1 a.m.	7.02

differences within the weeks of the semesters, it was found that the subject searching in the fall had a low of 35.64% during the first week of classes and a high of 53.93% during the 16th week. The difference is 18.29%, which is over 10%. The spring semester's low was 33.54% (second week) and the high was 49.88% (16th week) for a difference of 16.34%. Therefore, the second null hypothesis is rejected and the alternative hypothesis is accepted.

The analysis of the days of the week points out that during the fall semester the use of subject searching goes from a low on Fridays of 42.74% to a high on Sundays of 49.97%. This difference within the semester is less than 10%. As a result, the null hypothesis is not rejected for the fall semester. The spring semester does show greater variability. In the spring, subject searching moves from a low of 37.8% on Fridays to a high of 50.26% on Sundays. The difference of 12.46% for the spring semester causes the null hypothesis to be rejected in favor of the alternative hypothesis.

The final time unit studied is hour of the day. The hours studied are those between 8:00 A.M. to 11:00 P.M. The 15 minutes between 7:45 A.M. and 8:00

Figure 15.1
Percentage of Subject Searching (per week of the term)

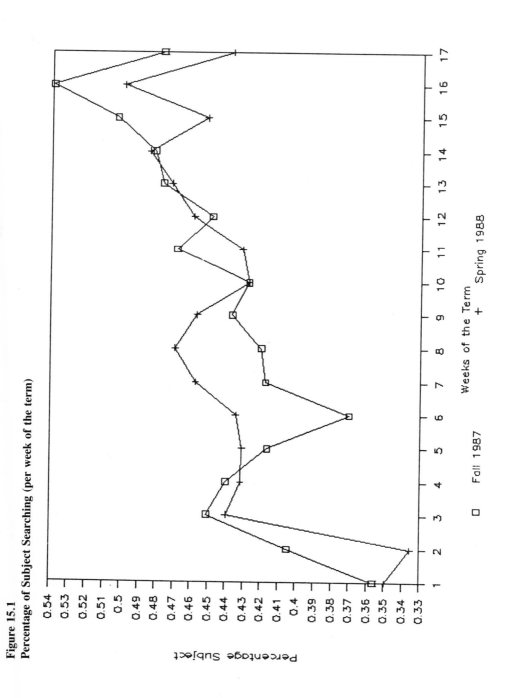

Figure 15.2
Percentage of Subject Searching (per days of the week)

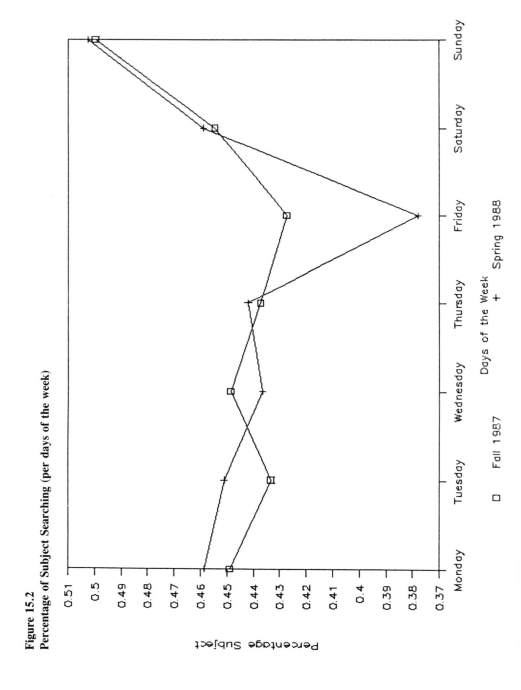

Figure 15.3
Percentage of Subject Searching (hour of the day)

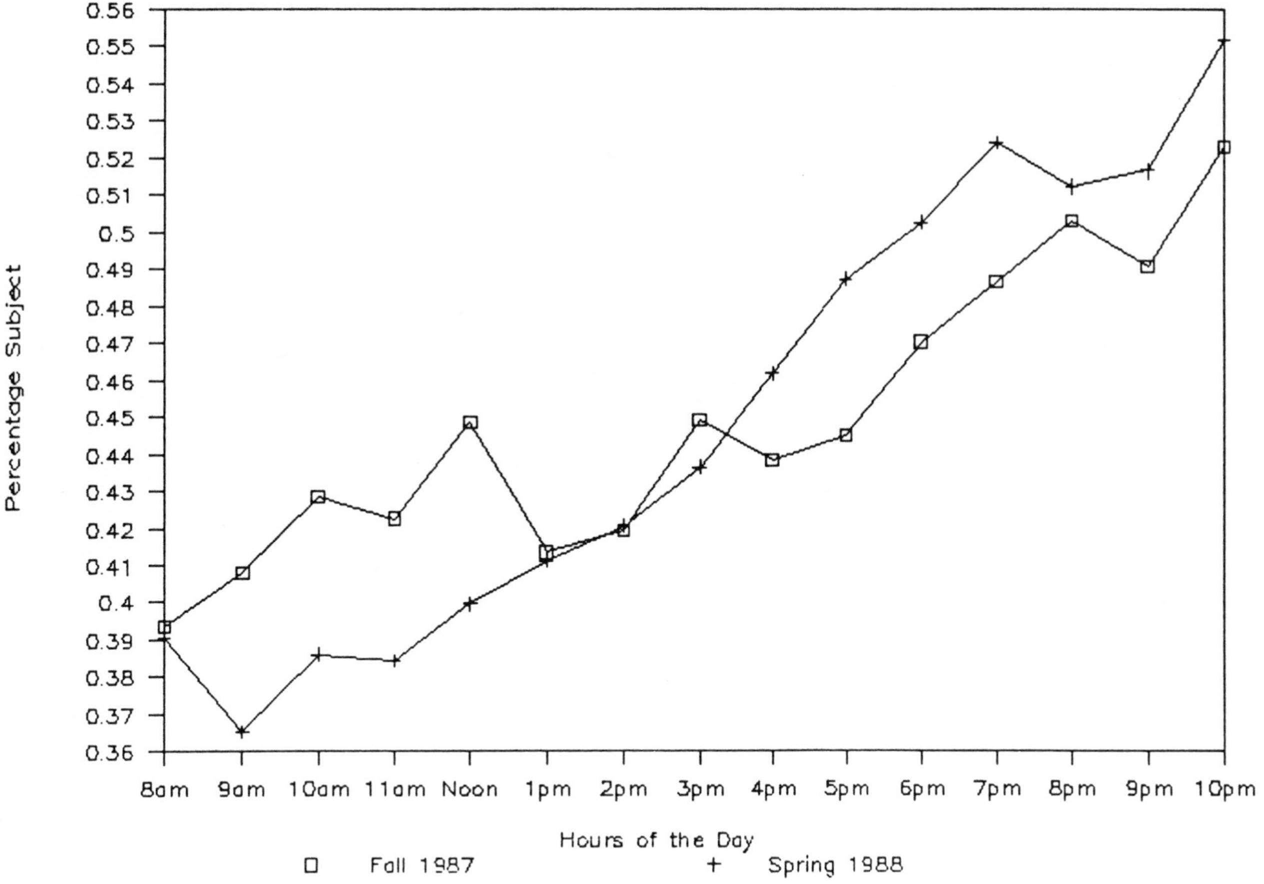

A.M. and the time during extended hours (11:00 P.M. to 2:00 A.M. only during finals week) are times of very light use. Therefore, these times are omitted from this analysis. In both the fall and spring semester the percentage of subject searching varies more than 10%. During the fall, the low comes during the first hour (8:00 A.M.–9:00 A.M.) and the high comes during the last hour (10:00 P.M.–11:00 P.M.). The difference is 12.94%. In the spring, the low comes an hour later (9:00 A.M.–10:00 A.M.), but the high again comes at the end of the day (10:00 P.M.–11:00 P.M.). These results show that the second null hypothesis must be rejected and an alternative hypothesis accepted.

DISCUSSION

Subject searching by patrons in the OPAC at the University of Alabama show a good deal of variability over the academic year (1987/88) studied. This variability is both within the time units analyzed (hour of day, day of week, and week of term) and between the two semesters (fall and spring) studied. The question of how best to use this information in the management of the library is now addressed.

First, bibliographic instruction programs and additional help for patrons who are searching the online system can be scheduled when patrons are in need of assistance. The knowledge that subject searching increases as the semester matures and that the percentage of subject searching increases during the day should influence programs and staffing patterns. The key for any service organization is to identify when services are needed and then supply the services at that point. Information on the demand for library services is not usually available. The information presented here should help the library staff harmonize its bibliographic instruction and terminal assistance programs with demonstrated subject-searching patterns. The patrons' needs show clear patterns upon which library management can capitalize as they fine-tune their services.

CONCLUSIONS

This research has shown us that there is a great deal of variability of subject searching in an OPAC over the course of an academic year. The time units investigated for variability were time of day, day of week, and week of term. The variability between the two semesters studied was also reported. The full population of patron searches for the entire academic year was used. Across the hours of the day, the percentage of subject searching ranged from a low of 35.64% (9:00 A.M.–10:00 A.M.) to a high of 55.17% (10:00 P.M.–11:00 P.M.). For the days of the week, Fridays were low at 37.8% and Sundays were high with 50.26%. The first and second weeks of the semester were low (33.54% for the second week of spring semester and 35.64% for the first week of fall semester). The next to the last week of the terms was high (53.93% for fall and 49.88% for spring).

Generalizations of the Findings

Generalizations of this exploratory research beyond the University of Alabama are not offered because this research, along with its sister projects (see notes 3 and 4), needs to be repeated for additional semesters at the University of Alabama and at other libraries before generalizations are made. However, this project has pointed out, as did the sister projects, that researchers should use population data when possible and should not rely on sample data because of the levels of variability in searching over time. There is little additional programming effort and computer time needed to provide complete information on the percentage and timing of patrons' use of subject and other types of searching. The size of the data files could be a problem for some libraries where the number of searches per day is large or where the transaction recording methods require excessive resources. It should be the goal of researchers and systems librarians to supply library administrators with complete systems utilization information.

Recommendations for Future Research

The next step is to investigate the patterns of subject searching across different academic libraries (and all types of libraries) using the same and/or different OPACs. It would be ideal to have data from OPAC use studies reported on an annual basis in some form. If other researchers and systems librarians were to conduct and report the results of similar research, the data could be tabulated and presented once a year.

NOTES

This research project would not have been possible without the help of John C. Johnson, Systems Programmer with the campus computing center, who provided the basic ''use'' data from the VTLS system. I would also like to thank the library staff members for permitting the study to be conducted.

1. The Office of Institutional Research at the University of Alabama provided the enrollment and staffing data.
2. Kate Ragsdale, Planning Officer for the University of Alabama Libraries, provided the information about the library.
3. Neal K. Kaske. 1988a. ''The Variability and Intensity over Time of Subject Searching in an Online Public Access Catalog.'' *Information Technology and Libraries* 7:3 (September):273–87.
4. Neal K. Kaske. 1988b. ''A Comparative Study of Subject Searching in an OPAC Among Branch Libraries of a University Library System.'' *Information Technology and Libraries* 7:4 (December):359–72.
5. Karen Markey. 1984. *Subject Searching in Library Catalogs: Before and After the Introduction of Online Catalogs* (Dublin, Ohio: OCLC Online Computer Library Center, Inc.).

16

A Prototype Workstation for Accessing and Using an Optical Disc-based Database of Biomedical Documents

Frank L. Walker and George R. Thoma

As part of a research program on the electronic conversion of biomedical documents for preservation, the Lister Hill National Center for Biomedical Communications, a research and development (R&D) division of the National Library of Medicine, is performing electronic imaging research spanning the entire gamut from scanning, digitizing, image processing, storage, and archiving to image retrieval, transmission, display, and manipulation. Once a database of biomedical electronic document images has been created on a set of optical discs, it is important, from a human-factors standpoint, to determine the best ways to access and use it, that is, the design of the user interface. The motivation for this design is not only to retain the ease and flexibility one expects in using paper documents, but also to provide features not possible with a paper-based collection.

Key factors in the design of the user interface to a database of electronic document images include: (1) access techniques (either by searching bibliographic databases or by browsing through a title list, in which the results are automatically linked to the document images for rapid retrieval); (2) error-minimizing menu design (where circumstances dictate allowable menu choices, thereby eliminating user-induced errors); (3) speed of access, retrieval, and display; (4) image manipulation functions such as zoom, pan, and scroll (for greater legibility); and (5) electronic bookmarks (to keep track of important pages in one or more documents, and to facilitate quick movement from one document to another). To investigate these issues, a prototype Advanced Image Workstation has been designed to permit user access to biomedical documents stored on a set of optical discs, either locally from an optical disc drive or remotely from an image server. This chapter outlines the workstation's hardware and software design, describes the design of the user interface, and suggests ways in which the interface may be evaluated. It also describes plans to incorporate imaging functions that permit a user to create a personal library from existing document images and annotations, and to create a function that will permit access to related documents.

INTRODUCTION

In line with the mission of the National Library of Medicine to preserve biomedical literature, inhouse research was conducted in the application of electronic imaging to document preservation. This involved the design and development of prototype systems to convert paper documents to bit-mapped image documents stored on optical discs and the use of these systems as experimental testbeds. Both centralized and distributed computer prototype systems were designed and implemented.[1] The systems were designed to scan fragile, bound paper documents at 200 dots per inch (dpi) resolution, produce bit-mapped images of about 4 million bits each, compress the images, then archive them on optical disc. To determine how the archived documents could best be accessed and used, a prototype document image retrieval workstation, called the Standalone Display Workstation, was designed, built, and demonstrated.[2] Recently, a refined version of this retrieval workstation, the Advanced Image Workstation (AIW), has been developed with additional capabilities. As shown in figure 16.1, the AIW is controlled by an IBM AT-class personal computer, and it is equipped with a high-resolution softcopy image display device for viewing document images and an alphanumeric display for the user interface. It has a laser printer for obtaining hard copies of the document images and a mouse for manipulating images on the soft copy display. Finally, it has a telecommunications link to NLM's mainframe resident database, MEDLINE and CATLINE.

While MEDLINE is a database containing citations to articles from approximately 3,000 biomedical journals, CATLINE is a database of citations to over 700,000 monographs and other materials in the NLM collection. The AIW permits a user to access, retrieve, and use document images archived on optical disc drives, which may be local, that is, connected to the AIW (figure 16.2), or remotely located on a Local Area Network connected to an image server (figure 16.3). For the first option, the AIW may have one or more local optical disc drives. For the second option, there may be one or more image servers and several retrieval workstations. Each retrieval workstation has an Ethernet connection to a baseband Ethernet network in place of the local optical disc drive. In addition, each AIW has a telecommunications link to NLM's databases.

If the AIW has a local optical disc drive, it is possible for the user to maintain a collection of optical discs and to use one disc at a time in the drive. The networked case is intended for the user of the AIW to gain access to those disc drivers and media connected to the server. The advantage of a local optical disc drive is that it is suitable for an environment where there is a small number of users, none of whom would need to share simultaneously the same archived collection. The advantage of having a network of one or more image servers and several retrieval workstations is that a large number of users can simultaneously access a single archived document collection.

A third case is also possible: where the AIW is both networked and equipped with a local optical disc. This is the most flexible option since it offers the

Figure 16.1
Advanced Image Workstation Hardware Configuration

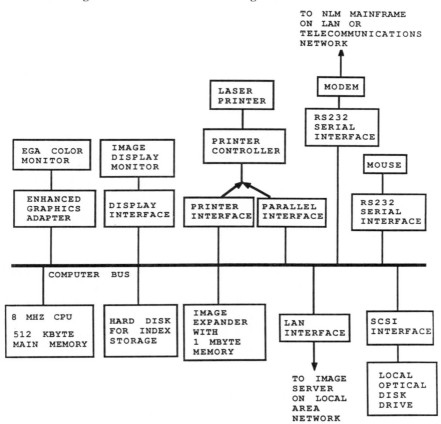

Figure 16.2
Retrieval from a Local Disk

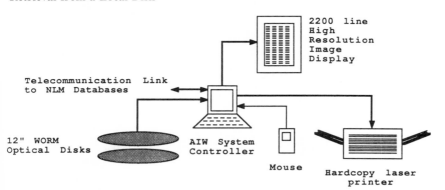

Figure 16.3
Retrieval from an Image Server

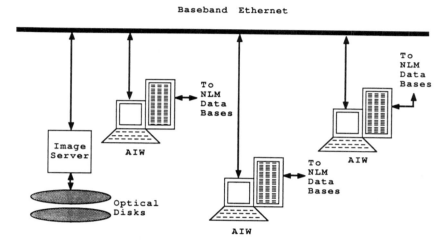

advantages of having a permanent, centrally located collection of archived documents while also offering a user the choice of using discs from a local collection.
This case is most useful if the document collection can be classified by different
degrees of demand, so that those documents that are frequently accessed by the
group might be located at the server; those that are infrequently accessed, at
each user's AIW.

The AIW has the following basic functions:

1. A *database search* function that allows a user to perform a bibliographic search in
   MEDLINE or CATLINE using GRATEFUL MED, a user interface to NLM's databases. Once the database search is complete, the user has the ability to view the results
   of the search, that is, the retrieved citations, following which the system links each
   citation to the corresponding document images on optical disc

2. A *browse* function that presents a user with a list of titles of books or journal articles
   archived on the optical disc collection. A user selection of an item from the title list
   activates the AIW to provide an automatic link to the archived document images

3. A *display* function that permits the document images obtained from the linkup in (1)
   or (2) to be retrieved and displayed in soft-copy form on the high-resolution (200 dpi)
   image display device or in hard-copy form on a laser printer. The user may move
   forward or backward through the document, or go directly to any arbitrary page in
   the document

4. An *image manipulation* function that permits an image displayed on the soft-copy
   display device to be zoomed, shrunk, rotated, panned, or scrolled

5. An *electronic bookmark* function that permits a user to place bookmarks (visual icons
   marking the displayed page) on up to 10 pages in each document, without any limit
   on the number of marked documents. The AIW permits a user to move from the

marked section in one document to the marked section in another document, and also to retrieve the most recently marked document

6. A *list* function that displays a list of all optical discs that have been indexed and from which the AIW may access the archived documents

The remainder of this chapter discusses various aspects of the user interface design, plans for testing it, and future directions in development of the AIW.

ROBUSTNESS IN SYSTEM AND MENU DESIGN

As emphasized in the literature,[3] a computer system should be designed for robustness, that is, it should tolerate errors and protect both itself and the user. This design philosophy has been applied to the AIW in two ways. First, the system hardware was tested to determine reliability. In the Standalone Display Workstation, the predecessor to the AIW, the only component that showed some potential reliability problems was the optical disc drive. Tests revealed that an occasional read error occurred upon retrieving images from the optical disc. This usually caused severe problems, since the images were stored on the discs in compressed form. Any incorrect bits in a compressed image will not permit the image to be expanded properly to its original size. The result was that the image either would not be displayed properly, or was lost altogether, requiring the user to try again to retrieve the image. This problem was compounded by the fact that the software displayed ''unfriendly'' messages, which listed the contents of all the registers in the disc drive's controller.

To solve this problem for the AIW, the software driver for the optical disc drive was redesigned so that an image would be read up to three times if there was an error detected by the error-detection logic during the first attempt. From a user's perspective the problem went away, since these read problems turned out to be ''soft'' errors, which could be corrected by rereading the image data. In addition, the error messages displayed by the AIW were significantly reduced in number and simplified so that they were more understandable to a casual user. Instead of dumping all the registers in hex on the screen and stating that a ''Fatal Hardware Error'' had occurred, a simple, less-threatening message such as ''Check the Optical Disc Drive'' was substituted. So, from a hardware sense, the system became more robust and from a user interface viewpoint the system became more friendly.

Another technique used to make the AIW more robust than the Standalone Display Workstation was to reduce significantly user-induced errors. This was accomplished by borrowing a menu design technique used in the Macintosh family of personal computers and some software programs for the PC such as Xerox Ventura Publisher. This technique permits the user to select only currently valid choices. While a menu may have six choices, only four may be valid at any given time. Valid choices appear in dark type on a light screen, while invalid choices appear in gray. The AIW does not permit the user to choose one of the invalid menu items; the cursor skips over them to the next valid item. This eliminates user-induced errors and subsequent error messages. In addition, the menus change dynamically, depending on the current situation, making invalid choices valid, and vice versa. This method of menu design improves the robustness of the system because the user is protected from making mistakes, and by eliminating potential error messages, tends to increase the subjective satisfaction of the user.

ACCESS TECHNIQUES

The main method of document access used in the Standalone Display Workstation, also incorporated in the AIW, is by searching either MEDLINE or CATLINE. The citations from the search are linked to the archived document images, and the user is permitted to retrieve the images and display them. It was felt that this method of access, while quite useful to some information seekers, was not suitable for others. For the type of user who wants to come into a reading room and pick a journal from a shelf to read, requiring a database search could be an unnecessary imposition. To serve this type of user, a document-browsing method was incorporated into the design of the AIW. The browsing technique is similar to one described by Anderson, which is used for a group of library materials that are maintained separately from the general collection.[4] A collection of images on optical disc, for instance, is separate from the general collection and can best be accessed if it has a self-contained indexed database that permits fast retrieval by a few simple strategies, such as by title or author.

The AIW's browse function permits document access without a database search. It is intended for the casual user who wants to browse through the collection of archived documents. By listing all document titles, the browse function provides a one-to-one correspondence between document titles and archived documents; the user is guaranteed that the document images corresponding to the listed titles are available. This is not the case for the database function, which does not provide such a one-to-on correspondence. The database function, intended for more serious researchers, lists all citations relevant to a user's search strategy, whether or not they correspond to archived documents. While intended for different purposes, the database and browse functions are both useful and complement each other well.

The browse function permits a user to access each archived document either through a list of book titles or a list of journal article titles. If the user is interested in books, the browse function will alphabetically list all available book titles on the color monitor screen. The user may start a search on book titles by entering a single character, which finds the first title beginning with that character. It is also possible to search on a string of characters appearing within a title. An example would be to find the next title that contains the word *doctor*. Once the search has been completed, an arrow appears on the screen at the title of interest.

The user can move the arrow about the screen to select any other title, if desired. Once a title of interest has been selected, the system retrieves the document and displays it.

If, instead of books, the user is interested in journals, the browse function will list all journal titles of archived journal articles. Once the user selects a journal title, the issues available for that title are listed. After the user picks a journal issue, the browse function lists all articles available for that issue. At this point the user may search on article titles in the same manner available for searching on book titles: either by the first letter of the title, or through a strong search of the contents of all titles. Once an article is selected the system retrieves and displays the images.

By providing two methods of accessing electronic documents, the document image access and retrieval system is designed to accommodate two types of information seekers interested in the documents preserved electronically: the "serious researcher" and the "casual patron." The serious researcher is assumed to be searching for all biomedical documents related to an area of interest. The casual user, on the other hand, is assumed to be less interested in doing database searches than in browsing through a book or journal issue. The paradigm for this kind of use might be to take a volume off a shelf, skim through the table of contents, and read any chapter or article of interest.

There are trade-offs in choosing between the database search function or the browsing method to retrieve archived documents. On the one hand, the database search provides all citations that might be relevant to a user's field of interest, but for every citation an archived document may not actually exist on optical disc. Because the database search function also takes time, the user must also be prepared to spend this time waiting for the citation query to complete. On the other hand, the browsing function guarantees that an archived document is immediately accessible for every listed book or journal title. This function therefore best serves the casual user who simply wants to browse through a book or journal without the time and effort involved in searching a database.

SPEED OF ACCESS

The response time of a computer system is critical in designing a good user interface. It has been stated in the literature that a good rule is to get system response time to within a two- to four-second range.[5] After about two to four seconds, a computer user begins to wonder whether the system is still functioning properly. The Standalone Display Workstation clearly did not meet this goal, since it took about 11 seconds to retrieve an image from optical disc and display it. To reduce the retrieval time in designing the AIW, image compression was employed. A study of off-the-shelf compression technology revealed that CCITT group 4 two-dimensional compression delivered a compression ratio of about 14 for biomedical documents.[6] While the primary goal of image compression is to achieve a greater storage density of images on the archival medium, another goal is to increase throughput. By achieving a compression ratio of 14, an uncompressed image of 465 kB is reduced to about 33 kB. Reduction in the size of the image file results in a significantly reduced retrieval time from optical disc. Through an analysis of the component processes involved in retrieving images from an optical disc, it was shown that an average NLM document image could be retrieved, expanded, and displayed in about three seconds.[7] Testing of the AIW shows that it meets this response time for images stored on a local optical disc.

Occasionally an image retrieved from the image server may take longer than the three-second retrieval time available from a local optical disc. This is due to the possibility that several users may be simultaneously requesting images from the server. It has been suggested that for delays longer than four seconds, these delays by announced.[8] This feature has been incorporated into the design of the AIW and image server. The server can notify the AIW whether it can expect a potentially long delay due to a long queue of image requests. The AIW, in turn, displays a message on the screen, notifying the user of the delay. Simulations of the multiple AIW workstations using the image server show that if two AIW workstations simultaneously request an image from the image server, the longest retrieval/expansion/display time for one of the users will be about 3.8 seconds.[9] This includes 1.4 seconds for retrieval over the network, 1.9 seconds for expansion, and .5 seconds for display. In discussing infrequent long response times, Shneiderman reports the result of a study showing that a user will wait approximately seven to nine times the customary response time before taking action.[10] Nine times the normal retrieval time, or 27 seconds, corresponds to 34 users requesting images at exactly the same time. Since this situation is likely to be infrequent, the network has a capacity for at least this number of users before this second criterion would be applied.

IMAGE MANIPULATION

To allow a degree of flexibility in viewing and using an electronic document image, image manipulation functions have been designed for the AIW. By using a combination of menu item selection and direct manipulation, the user can manipulate the image displayed. The image manipulation functions permit the image on the soft-copy image display monitor to be zoomed, shrunk, panned, scrolled, and rotated. A menu permits the choice of zoom/shrink, rotate right 90 degrees, and rotate left 90 degrees. If the zoom/shrink option is chosen and if the existing image is a normal size, the image is zoomed 2:1. If the zoom/shrink option is chosen and if the existing image has previously been zoomed, the image is then shrunk to normal size. A mouse controls the panning and scrolling functions. Here, panning refers to moving the image right and left on the screen. Scrolling refers to moving the image up and down on the screen. The image is panned or scrolled in proportion to the mouse movement and is most effective for images that have been zoomed or rotated.

ELECTRONIC BOOKMARKS

The AIW also provides an electronic bookmark function that provides the user of the AIW a degree of flexible control over the electronic document in a manner similar to the control a reader has over a paper document. Analogous to the case of paper documents, where bookmarks keep track of important sections, the electronic bookmark does the same thing for electronic documents. Up to 10 pages in every document can be marked with an icon representing the bookmark, with no limit on the number of marked documents. Even when the AIW is turned off, the bookmark information is not lost, since it is kept in a file. The bookmark function permits the most recently marked document to be retrieved directly without going through the database search or browse function. It also permits the user to jump to other marked pages in the document or to jump to other marked documents. In the world of paper documents, this last feature is analogous to the situation where a researcher may have a number of books spread out on a desk, each opened to an important section, to allow moving from the section of interest in one book to that in another book.

Bookmarks also solve another problem that occurs when storing a printed volume in electronic form: page-number sequencing. It is quite common for the table of contents of a volume to begin with roman numerals (e.g., i, ii, iii), and the first chapter to start with arabic numerals (e.g., 1, 2, 3). While the workstation permits a direct jump to any page in the document, the page number in the electronic document may not correspond to the real arabic number in the printed volume. This problem is solved through a feature of the workstation termed *relative jumping*. If a bookmark is placed at the page immediately preceding page 1 (arabic) of the document, then by jumping relative to that marked page, the user is able to move directly to the correct page.

TEST STRATEGIES

There are several goals to be sought for testing the AIW's user interface:

1. Determine the benefits in terms of increase in both user productivity and library staff productivity in having an optical disc-based subcollection
2. Determine the degree of difficulty in using electronic documents. For example, is it faster or easier to use electronic documents than paper documents?
3. Determine whether electronic documents are as well accepted as their paper-based originals

The first item is best measured through experiments in a library reading room, measuring such things as time spent by patrons in the reading room, and by determining whether the rate of requests for paper-based materials decreases as a result of having them on optical disc. The second and third items can be determined by measuring factors listed by Shneiderman:[11]

1. time to learn;
2. speed of performance;
3. rate of errors by users;
4. subjective satisfaction;
5. retention over time.

By monitoring keystrokes and times at which major system functions occur, it is possible to measure the speed of performance, the time to learn the system, and the retention over time of how to use the system. These techniques can also be used to measure the times to access documents either through the database search or browse functions. This time is of interest to help determine whether documents archived on optical disc can be accessed faster than paper documents stored on bookshelves.

The rate of errors is designed to be low, due to the error-minimizing menu design technique. The subjective satisfaction of the user may be measured reliably by a user satisfaction questionnaire such as that outlined by Chin.[12] A questionnaire may be given a user either in paper form or in an online electronic form on the AIW.

FUTURE DIRECTIONS

A facet of user interface design is that it is an evolving process that can always be improved. Future plans for the AIW include incorporating imaging functions that permit a user to create a personal library from existing document images and annotations, and a function that will permit access to related documents. The personal library function will be implemented using direct manipulation of the image information. Shneiderman describes direct manipulation as a user interface that "represents objects that users act upon directly."[13] The objects in this case are the pages of the electronic document. By using a mouse, cursor, and keyboard, a user will be able to create a personal document by annotating images, cutting and copying archived images and pasting them into a new document, erasing portions of images, rearranging image pages, and inserting and deleting images. The new document may be either printed on the local laser printer or removed from the system on one or more floppy disks. An example of a system that permits new documents to be created from archived ones is the Grolier Encyclopedia on CD-ROM. Because the entire text is on a CD-ROM disc, parts of the text may be downloaded to a magnetic disk file for further editing by a word-processing package.[14]

The second planned improvement is to create a function that permits access to related documents. This will be done by creating an image database that contains searchable text, in addition to graphics, for any page containing line art or photographs. At the time a document is scanned, the scanning system will segment each image into its textual and graphic regions. The text is then converted into ASCII codes using an omnifont character recognition process. The ASCII text, graphic regions, and information for linking the two together are then archived on optical disc. The text will then be indexed by creating an inverted database of words in all archived documents. The documents can then be accessed either by searching the full text or by searching the text index; then each image is reconstructed from the textual and graphic components to form a composite image for display. Related documents may be found by searching the bibliographic database, the full text, or the text index. The literature suggests another method that could be used to supplement these techniques: to search through a cross-reference index.[15] A reference index of cross-references between related documents could be embedded within each document. The index could be created for each archived document by searching MEDLINE or CATLINE, the full text, or the text index for related documents, then storing pointers to them within each document. Then, to retrieve a related document, the AIW would check the cross-reference information in the current document without going back to the original search. This technique would increase the speed of finding related documents.

SUMMARY

A prototype workstation has been implemented that permits access to an archive of biomedical document images stored either on a local optical disc drive or on a remote image server. A number of features were built into the design of the user interface to make it easy to use electronic documents, including methods for accessing documents by two types of users, minimizing errors, using image compression to speed document access, image manipulation, and electronic bookmarks. Methods for testing the workstation's user interface have been described, as well as directions toward future expansion of the workstation's capabilities.

NOTES

1. George R. Thoma, S. Suthasinekul, F. L. Walker, J. Cookson, and M. Rashidian. "A Prototype System for the Electronic Storage and Retrieval of Document Images," *ACM Transactions on Office Information Systems* 3: 3 (July 1985): 279–91. See also Frank L. Walker, et al. "A Distributed Approach to Optical Disk-Based Storage and Retrieval," *Proceedings of the 26th Annual Technical Symposium of the Washington, D.C. Chapter of the ACM*, Gaithersburg, Md., June 11, 1987, 44–52.

2. F. Walker, et al. "A Hybrid System for Retrieval of Online Biomedical Citations and Optical Disk-Based Documents," *Proceedings of Optical Publishing and Storage '87 Conference*, November 11–13, 1987, 179–91.

3. R. Rubinstein, et al. *The Human Factor* ([Burlington, Mass.]: Digital Press, 1984).

4. M. R. Anderson, "Molli: Micro Online Library Information," *Library Software Review* (March-April 1987): 100–103.

5. Rubinstein, *The Human Factor*, 147.

6. F. Walker, et al. "Issues in Archiving the Medical Literature with Electronic Imaging Techniques," *Proceedings of Electronic Imaging '88 East*, October 3–6, 1988, Boston, Mass., vol. 1, 590–95.

7. F. Walker, "Compression Study," Unpublished Inhouse Technical Report, Lister Hill National Center for Biomedical Communications, National Library of Medicine, August 1987.

8. Rubinstein, *The Human Factor*, 148.

9. S. E. Hauser, M. I. Felsen, M. J. Gill, G. R. Thoma. "Networking AT-Class Computers for Image Distribution," *IEEE Journal on Selected Areas in Communications* 7: 2 (February 1989): 268–75.

10. B. Shneiderman, *Designing the User Interface: Strategies for Effective Human-Computer Interaction* (Reading, Mass.: Addison-Wesley, 1987), 287.

11. Ibid., 14–15.

12. J. P. Chin, V. A. Diehl, and K. Norman. 1987. "Development of an Instrument Measuring User Satisfaction of the Human-Computer Interface," Research Report no. TR–1926. Dept. of Psychology and Human-Computer Interaction Laboratory, University of Maryland, College Park.

13. B. Shneiderman, "The Future of Interactive Systems and the Emergence of Direct Manipulation," *Behavior and Information Technology* 1: 3 (1982): 237–56.

14. P. Van Brakel, "The Electronic Encyclopedia: Facts on CD-ROM," *Electronic and Optical Publishing Review* 7: 4 (December 1987): 186–91.

15. L. Helgerson, et al. "In Search of CD-ROM Data," *PC Tech Journal* 6 (October 1988): 67–75.

17

Designing a User-System Interface

Helen A. Pfuderer and K. C. Miller

A team at the Oak Ridge National Laboratory (ORNL) has been successful in guiding managers of government organizations in planning and implementing successful strategic information systems. The essence of the ORNL methodology is to provide users at all levels in the organization with many opportunities to participate in systems development. This user involvement included incorporating their own critical success factors into the planning process; defining the business objectives, processes, and needed systems implementation in a team approach; and providing down-to-earth usability feedback in prototyping the most strategic systems.

INTRODUCTION

A recent project to design and implement an information architecture for the Support Equipment Division of the Naval Air Systems Command serves as an example of a successful approach to designing a user-system interface. With an annual acquisition budget of $800 million, Support Equipment Division staff purchase equipment for navy aircraft and for aircraft sold to foreign governments. The engineers in Support Equipment Division plan for maintenance of the avionics, airframe, and propulsion systems of aircraft and airborne weapons being developed in current use. The division is a matrix organization with some managers responsible for the support equipment for a particular airframe and others responsible for specific commodity areas (e.g., electro-optics), thus there is some overlap in job responsibilities.

As the Support Equipment Division engineers gain experience in major procurements, they are in demand for high-paying jobs with industry, and many leave the division with less than 10 years on the job. This factor and the navy policy of two-year rotations result in high turnover of staff in the division. As with many government organizations, clerical time is at a premium in the division and, consequently, is nonexistent for time-critical input to a computer system.

Most of the approximately 30 Support Equipment Division engineers are experienced with personal computing. Several have designed their own systems to assist in the many computations required for procurements. However, obtaining and inputting the data for these user-designed systems is a very large effort, and often the time requirements mean using ballpark data taken from associates rather than the more traceable computerized data. In another example, engineers had been requested to use a system provided by their field organizations. The system contained data of potential value but the interface was hard to use, and they found obtaining the data was not worth their time. Consequently, they did not use the system. Thus, when procurement requests or budgets for several years in the future were completed, the data and computations were not stored for future reference.

INFORMATION ARCHITECTURE STUDY

The first step in designing a successful system interface was to ensure that the system fulfilled the needs of the users. One objective was to implement a series of system modules designed to provide accurate and timely data to fulfill the mission of the Support Equipment Division and its staff. Other objectives were to prioritize systems development to fund the projects most important to the mission of the division, to provide traceability in case of changing budgets, and to provide historical data for teaching new staff. The first step in addressing these objectives was a top-down planning study that included: (1) interviewing the managers and staff of the Support Equipment Division to find out what their jobs entailed and the factors that determined their success, and (2) conducting a workshop with division managers to analyze and define organization-wide business processes and data requirements for each of these processes.

The product of the top-down planning study was an information architecture for the Support Equipment Division (figure 17.1). The business processes are given on the left axis, and the data needed to support the business processes are given across the top. Acquisition was defined to be the priority subject module and was thus put in the middle of the information architecture design. The FMS module stands for Foreign Military Sales, a separate but related staff group within the Support Equipment Division. The acquisitions module is further defined here to provide an example of some of the Support Equipment Division business processes and data classes. There were four business processes defined for the acquisition module, as follows: (1) plan procurements to meet site requirements (administrative lead time), (2) ensure support equipment contract award (procurement lead time), (3) track support equipment design and delivery schedule (manufacturing lead time), and (4) process support equipment engineering change proposals. There were eight data classes for the acquisition module, as follows: (1) milestones to support equipment contract award, (2) procurement price estimate, (3) procurement strategy, (4) support equipment quantity and inventory objectives, (5) support equipment contract deliverables,

Figure 17.1
Support Equipment Division Information Architecture

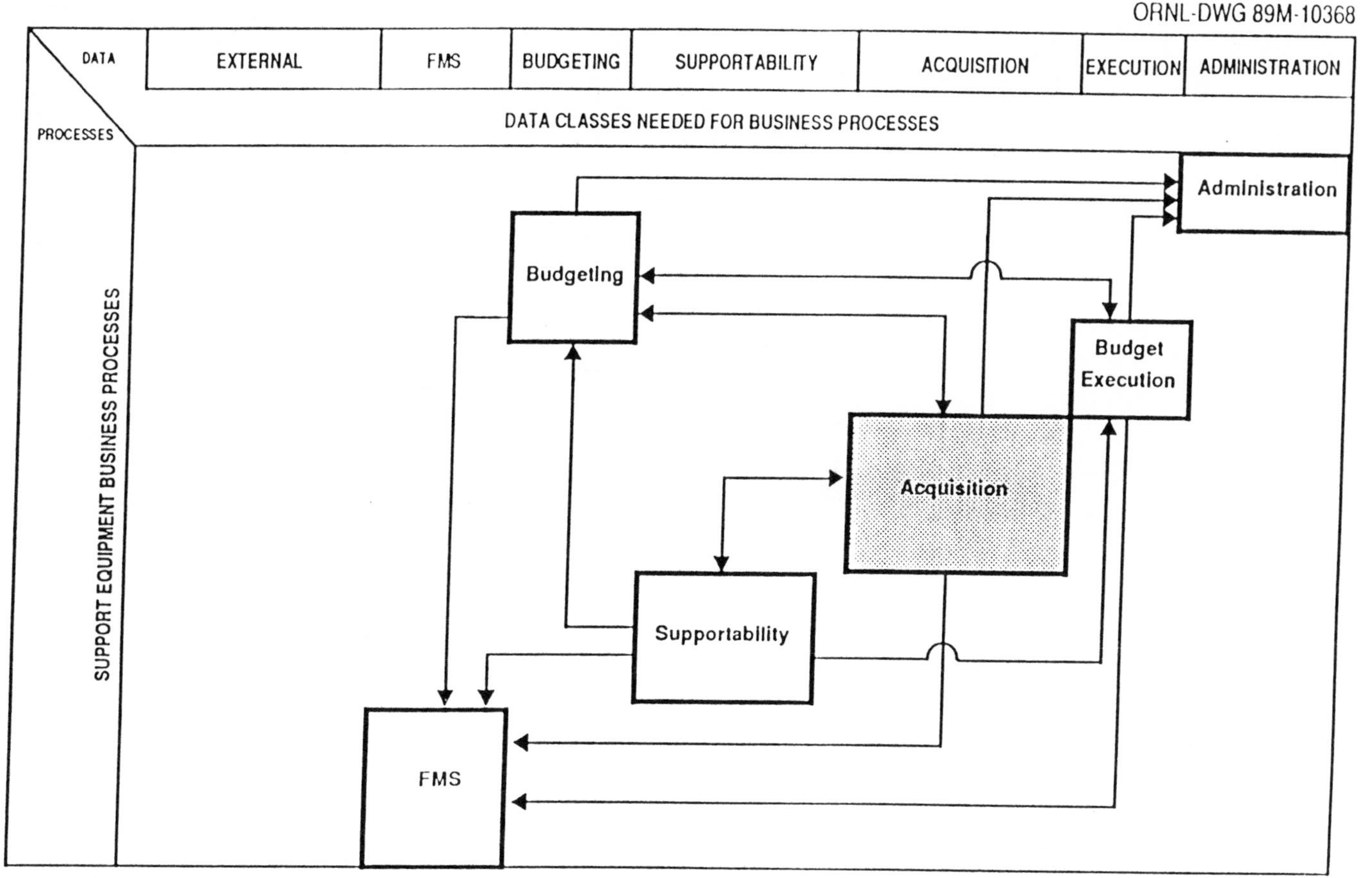

ORNL-DWG 89M-10368

(6) contract award status, (7) approved support equipment design and specifications, and (8) support equipment engineering change proposals. The information architecture represented a plan for information systems development that showed the priority of business process modules, and thus the priority for incorporating the associated data in systems used by the division staff.

The study of current systems, which was part of the information architecture study, revealed that data from 30 systems had been used on occasion by Support Equipment Division staff. Often data were output from one system to be manually reinput into another system. Many forms of essentially the same data were represented in the systems, for example, costs for each of the separate parts, for the subassemblies, and for the entire aircraft. The data contained in the systems currently used by the division were examined to determine if the data were the same as the data requirements defined in the information architecture. When there was a match between the data in the current systems and the data requirements, the data in the current systems were to be integrated into the appropriate module in the information architecture. New applications were to be developed to capture and use data that were missing in the current systems. An example of missing data was the data on obligated dollars (dollars in contract award status, a data class in the acquisition module). Each staff member and the division staff were evaluated on the total obligated dollars, but no system captured that data for the division staff.

Policies were defined to ensure the accuracy, integrity, and timeliness of the data. A position was defined for a data administrator, who would oversee the system development and ensure the quality of the data. Each data element was assigned an entry point into the system (generally the source of the data element or when it was first used), and a person was made responsible for the continuing quality of that data element. A common data dictionary was created for the Support Equipment Division and was used for all the modules and systems in the information architecture.

INTERFACE DESIGN

The second step to a successful user interface was to provide a well-designed and documented interface with common command procedures for entrance to and exit from all the systems. Prior to the common interface project, each staff member would need to learn as many as 10 to 15 different interfaces to be able to access the data they needed from the current systems. As part of the common interface project, guidelines and standards were defined for screens, menus, function keys, help files, error messages, and keywords. The guidelines and standards were defined bearing in mind the many database management systems and hardware systems already in use by the division staff and their respective field activities. The discussions with division staff pointed out that to fulfill their needs, the interface need not be an easy-to-use system, such as a series of menus, but instead needed to select efficiently the specific data needed by frequent and knowledgeable users. Since both the established and new staff were familiar with personal computing packages such as Lotus 1–2–3, dBase, and Word-Perfect, the interfaces were made to mimic these packages, whenever possible. A continuing oversight board was created to make decisions on introduction of changes and enhancements to the user-system interface. After a decision was final on some aspect of the user-system interface, but prior to introduction of the change into the operation of the systems, the change was documented in users manuals and online help files.

The design of the screens is especially important because it represents the system to the user. What the user can put into and select from the system and the degree of difficulty of these tasks depends upon the design of the screens. The screens for the acquisition module were designed to show the data in that module that came from other systems and to display, if needed, how that data was combined to give the data requested by the user (e.g., the parts that were combined to make a subassembly). A provision was made to allow the users to perform "what if" type computations. Thus, if Congress provided less money than requested, the division could respond with an updated budget based on the needs of the navy fleet, rather than cutting all the procurements by the same percentage, as had been previously done.

Help screens provided succinct documentation on use of the system. Since the Support Equipment Division engineers were generally familiar with personal computing, the help screens were designed to assist new staff members to the division with the special characteristics of the system and software queries. They were designed to provide instructions on navigating the system and an index of commands. Error messages and how to correct errors were explained.

SYSTEMS DESIGN

The system for the Support Equipment Division was developed using the prototyping approach. The users and programmers worked together to design the system and the user-system interface. The programmers built the screens and screen navigation protocols and entered data into the new system to enable the users to test and evaluate the new system. This building of prototyped systems can be done in a few days using a fourth-generation language. In fourth-generation languages, many of the basic instructions to the computer, which would require coding in languages such as COBOL or Fortran, are hidden in the natural languagelike commands. Shortcuts are generally available for screen design and report formats. Different report formats could be fairly easily generated by the users using the fourth-generation interface to the acquisition module. These prototypes could also be easily changed. Such changes were often necessary for the Support Equipment Division, as Congress frequently changed the funding and the reporting requirements of their organization.

Prototyping proved to be very effective for user and programmer communication and planning; however, structured analysis methods were also necessary for the integrated system development for Support Equipment Division. The conventional, structured analysis methods require specification of the essential checkpoints from the user requirements to implemented systems (functional requirements) and specification of run-time performance, security, and data integrity (operational requirements). The structured analysis methods gave review points to enable the data administrator to monitor the contract for the systems development and, if necessary, to provide an audit trail. The structured analysis approach would avoid the problems of an earlier, aborted effort in prototyping systems for the Support Equipment Division. This earlier, unsuccessful effort had promised myriad capabilities, none of which fully met the needs of the division staff. The problems with this effort were: (1) no prioritization and focus on developing critical capabilities; (2) partial development of any capabilities; (3) little interaction with the division staff, who would not devote time to developing a system or agree on selection of development options; and (4) lack of clear deadlines and deliverables. The best ideas in the aborted system were used in the development of the acquisition module and subsequent modules.

The design of common interfaces among systems was also part of the structured design. These written specifications allowed the many users in the Support Equipment Division to ensure that the integrated systems design included their needs. The users could check for their user-system interface requirements at several scheduled reviews of specifications and prior to acceptance of the system.

USER ACCEPTANCE TESTING

Formal acceptance testing was instituted throughout the system development cycle. Written specifications allowed the users and programmers to be certain that their communications, as understood during the prototyping of the design, were accurate and complete. The acceptance testing included an evaluation to ensure that the system followed all of the defined specifications and that any innovations were reviewing by a board for systemwide compatibility, prior to being implemented in the system. Requirements for documentation of the system and training, including providing manuals and appropriate classes, were milestones to be completed prior to implementation. The user acceptance procedures during the system development cycle are outlined in figure 17.2.

CONCLUSIONS

The Support Equipment Division is prototyping development of the acquisition module, which is the priority subject module as defined by the information architecture study. The individual screens are reviewed weekly by several of the Support Equipment Division engineers to ensure the system will meet their needs. Because these users have discovered many sources of valuable data in systems defined in the information architecture study, they have demanded that the data specific to acquisition be available from these systems in an automated format

Figure 17.2
User Acceptance Procedures During the System Development Cycle

System Definition	System Design	System Implementation	System Maintenance and Review
User needs information	Guidelines for designers and implementors	Objectives and characteristics	Utilization of the system
Acceptable system characteristics	Documentation and/or training requirements	Verify system design	Assess necessary changes
User's perception of system quality	Evaluation of software design prototypes	Verify system interfaces	Online suggestion box
		Increase user acceptance	
		Assess additional training needs	

to use in this module. This large amount of additional data has necessitated studies of the current hardware configuration, future hardware and needs, and telecommunications options to ensure the module will run effectively. The relational database management system used for the module would probably not give reasonable response times when the hundreds of thousands of data items from other systems were combined.

While the acquisition module is still in the development stages, the information architecture study was evaluated as being successful even without consideration of systems implementation. The study made the division staff aware of the commonality of job functions across the organization and fostered a team approach to problem solving. There was enthusiastic agreement on which systems to fund first, and the staff actively discussed interface options and made team decisions on guidelines and standards. Interface being developed as part of systems development by field organizations were brought into compliance with Support Equipment Division guidelines and standards, and the field systems developers became full participants in the user-systems interface guidelines and standards decision-making process.

NOTE

Oak Ridge National Laboratory is operated by Martin Marietta Energy Systems, Inc., for the U.S. Department of Energy under Contract No. DE-AC05–84OR21400.

Exploring Discretionary Users' Interaction with Word-Processing Technology

Susan Wiedenbeck and Radhika Santhanam

Today, many non–computer professionals have integrated word-processing technology into their work. Termed *discretionary users*, such people as lawyers, professors, administrators, students, and business persons are experienced but intermittent users of word-processing software. The goal of our research was to examine the activities and cognitive processes that occur when discretionary users interact with word-processing software. Using verbal protocol analysis, we investigated discretionary users' interaction with two commercial word-processing software packages. Our results indicate that discretionary users are expertlike when using a small set of basic commands. However, they are much more novicelike in being slow, prone to errors, and nonoptimal when they go beyond the basic commands.

INTRODUCTION

The phenomenal growth in availability of personal computers in recent years has spurred the use of word-processing technology by non–computer professionals, called discretionary users. With more than 300 different word-processing software packages available, word processing has become some of the most widely used software on personal computers (Software Catalog, 1988). It is important to study the requirements and needs of discretionary users because they make up a large proportion of people using word-processing technology. By understanding the characteristics of discretionary users, design guidelines that enhance these users' interactions with computers can be developed.

Existing research on learning and using word-processing technology has been confined mostly to secretarial personnel (Mack, Lewis, and Carroll, 1983; Carroll, Mack, and Lewis, 1985) and to technical expert users of text editors, such as computer programmers (Card, Moran, and Newell, 1983). The results of these studies cannot be applied to discretionary users because their needs and patterns of using word processing are markedly different. Unlike secretaries, discretionary users do not utilize word processing every day, nor is their choice of software dictated by their job. Unlike technical expert users, discretionary users have less motivation to be conversant with all the functions and capabilities of the system. Many of the assumptions made regarding the behavior and knowledge of these groups of users are not applicable to the discretionary user. Therefore, discretionary users form a distinct group of users of word processing that is worthy of investigation.

Results of an earlier study (Santhanam and Wiedenbeck, 1988) indicate that discretionary users often forget commands, fail to use optimal commands, have gaps in their knowledge, and commit errors. All of these characteristics could be termed novicelike. On the other hand, it was also found that discretionary users know a set of basic commands, are seldom confused by system behavior, and in almost all cases, are able to figure out a method to carry out editing tasks. All of these characteristics suggest expertlike behavior. The interesting question that arises is, how should the discretionary user by characterized? Does the discretionary user possess only a superficial knowledge of the system or a deeper understanding of the functionality of the system? What are the common patterns of behavior of discretionary users when they edit documents? One helpful way to answer these questions is to observe the behavior of discretionary users as they perform word-processing tasks in order to understand their mental organization and cognitive processes. Cognitive processes have been studied to differentiate expert and novice behavior in complex tasks, such as computer programming (Adelson, 1981; Wiedenbeck, 1985), solving physics problems (Chi, Feltovich, and Glaser, 1981), and preparing accounting statements (Bouwman, 1984). Our research was designed to understand the cognitive behavior and processing of discretionary users of word processing.

In addition to increasing our understanding of the behavior of discretionary users of word processing, we are also interested in studying interface design issues. Shneiderman (1987) discusses underlying principles of design that are applicable to most interactive systems. The principles include consistency in commands, action sequences, and terminology, informative feedback, simple error handling, easy reversal of actions, reduction of short-term memory load, shortcuts for frequent users, dialogue designs that yield closure, and support for internal locus of control. Another objective of our study was to determine how important these design guidelines are to discretionary users and what observable effect, if any, their violation has.

METHODOLOGY

The study was conducted using techniques of verbal protocol analysis (Ericsson and Simon, 1984). Discretionary users performed word-processing tasks and were asked to think aloud as they accomplished these tasks. A continuous image of the screen and the subjects' verbalization were captured on videotape. In addition, another camera was trained on the keyboard to record subjects' hand movements.

While the primary purpose of this experiment was to investigate discretionary users' editing behavior, we were also interested in determining whether their behavior was similar across different word-processing software. Hence, we used two commercially available word-processing software packages, one command-driven and the other menu-driven. In the command-driven software, users specified actions by typing a command code consisting of several characters. A few common commands could be performed by using function keys. In the menu-driven software, users normally specified actions by selecting commands from one of several menus using a mouse. The use of two different software packages with different modes of interaction increased our opportunity to observe the effects of design decisions on discretionary users.

Fourteen volunteers who fit the profile of discretionary users served as subjects. Each subject had edited a minimum of 30 documents on the test system and used the primary word processor. Care was taken to ensure that subjects had good verbal skills. Prior to the actual experiment, subjects were asked to perform five or six easy editing tasks. This familiarized them with our setup and trained them to think aloud. During the actual experiment, subjects were prompted to speak up if they remained silent for more than 30 seconds. The records of verbal protocols were transcribed and annotated before analysis.

In the experiment the subjects were asked to perform 15 editing tasks (shown in the appendix) in a document six pages long. Subjects in the command-driven system had to perform one extra task, namely, reformat text in the document, a function automatically done in the menu-drive system. They could perform the edits by any method they chose. The instruction sheet contained the tasks and the location of the tasks in the document. The editing tasks were chosen so that about half of them were routine editing tasks. The rest were chosen to be new to most of the subjects and to be complex enough that they would require some learning by the subjects. The subjects were free to refer to manuals and guidebooks or to use the help options provided by the system.

ANALYSIS OF THE PROTOCOL DATA

We analyzed four protocols in detail, trying to identify behavior, problems, and cognitive processes of discretionary users of word-processing technology. Two of the protocols were from users of the command-driven system and the other two were from users of the menu-driven system. As explained above, the benchmark our subjects performed included some routine tasks (e.g., delete a word, insert a sentence) and also some less routine tasks (e.g., insert a superscript, set a top margin). Our objective was to observe subjects' behavior in some straightforward cases and some that would call on their problem-solving resources. The following sections describe the important behavioral characteristics and problems that we observed.

Smooth Accomplishment of Tasks

In analyzing our subjects' behavior on the first six tasks, which were quite basic, we discovered that discretionary users develop smooth procedures to accomplish routine tasks. Subjects simply moved to the location in the document, issued a command, and verified its effect in one unbroken sequence of action. There was never any indication of hesitation or thinking time in the actions of the subjects. Moreover, there were no errors other than a few slips in typing, which were noticed and corrected immediately. Clearly this group of tasks was in the everyday repertoire of the subjects, and in this context they had developed expertlike performance skills. Performance on the other less routine tasks was markedly different, lacking this smooth appearance. However, even there one still observed the smooth, automatized quality of behavior in parts of the task that were well known to the subject (e.g., highlighting text).

Strong Habits

We observed that discretionary users have developed strong, individual habits, which they follow consistently in word-processing tasks. The habits differ from person to person and may not always be optimum, but they are executed quickly and without hesitation. They appear to be a kind of mental set that speeds word-processing choices. A good example of such habits is choices for movement and positioning within a document. In the command-driven system, one subject moved almost exclusively by using arrow keys even when that involved many successive keystrokes to cover a relatively long distance. The other subject in the command-driven system used the page down function key to get to the right general location of a task, then adjusted with the arrow keys, a pattern that he followed quite consistently. The subjects in the menu-driven system were similar. They had a choice of moving the mouse by single lines or by larger units, and each usually preferred a single method for most movements in the document.

The role of fixed habits could be seen in other areas besides movement. One subject in the command-driven system always deleted a character by typing the control-*g* command rather than by using the delete key. In later discussions with him it became quite clear that he was aware of the delete key, but simply was not in the habit of using it. Likewise, on the menu-driven system one subject almost always called up the menu and selected the cut command to delete units of text rather than highlighting the desired text and backspacing to achieve the same thing.

Avoidance of Having to Remember

The fixed habits of discretionary users described above might be attributed in part to an inability or unwillingness to remember multiple commands and procedures for achieving the same goal. Much evidence was seen not just of failure to remember commands and procedures but also of conscious decisions not to know them. Discretionary users often did not use the most direct method to carry out even frequently performed tasks. For example, it was common to see subjects on the command-driven system delete a paragraph by issuing a series of delete-sentence commands rather than using a block command to delete the whole paragraph at once. Subjects were aware of the block operations and could use them when there was no alternative (e.g., moving a paragraph to a new location), but they did not choose them spontaneously over less efficient but more frequently used commands. Many times subjects, not knowing a powerful command to achieve a task, would do the task in a series of smaller steps with a well-known command. For instance, in reformatting the whole document, subjects on the command-driven system used control-*b* to reformat each paragraph individually. Even though they commented that there must be a more efficient way, they did not take the trouble to look in the documentation to find it.

The same phenomenon was observed among subjects on the menu-driven system. The menu-driven system actually allowed the use of many command equivalents to menu items. However, we seldom observed them being used in place of the menu, even when achieving a task using the menu was fairly complex and involved a lot of moving and pointing with the mouse. Our observations show that discretionary users avoid remembering a large repertoire of commands. On the one hand, this may reflect an inability to remember a large number of commands given intermittent use of a system. On the other hand, it may also reflect a judgment by users that looking for a command in the documentation will take too much time. Based on our data, it appears that designs that provide many shortcuts and alternatives may be of limited use to discretionary users, given their intermittent pattern of use.

Subjects made up for not knowing many more powerful commands and procedures by making approximations and carrying out tasks manually. In centering a heading, command-driven subjects who did not know the center command were observed to approximate the center of the line and then insert blank spaces to move the heading over. Likewise, to create a page break they would manually insert blank lines at the appropriate point in the document until the end-of-page marker was seen. To leave a three-line header at the top of each page they would go to the top of each page and insert blank lines with the carriage return. On the menu-driven system the manual approach was used too. One subject who could not figure out how to use the menu to triple-space the document even suggested going through the whole document inserting extra blank lines between every line. Fortunately, he rejected this approach as being too time consuming and eventually found another way to do it, but only after much search of the menus and documentation. The subjects' frequent choice to make approximations and carry out tasks manually was probably influenced by the moderate length of the document and the lack of a specified recipient. (They might have been more careful if the recipient were their company vice-president.) Nevertheless, it shows a clear tendency to avoid learning and using a large number of commands, unless pressed to do so.

Organization of Knowledge

Discretionary users had a lot of difficulty using the systems because their mental organization of knowledge about the system did not match that of the system designer. This problem was observed repeatedly in the use of the menus and system documentation. Subjects on the menu-driven system had great difficulty locating the correct menu containing commands that were new to them or infrequently used. We saw a great deal of apparently random menu scanning in these cases, followed by reference to the index of a system guidebook. Subjects later commented that they often had difficulty anticipating where new commands would be in the menus and preferred to use a guidebook immediately rather than scanning menus. Command-driven subjects had similar problems trying to use the table of contents of a system guidebook to locate information. The command-driven system also had online help screens, which were seldom referred to. The reason most often given for not using them was that items were difficult to locate. For instance, the subscript and superscript commands are on the print helpscreen because they have to do with how characters will look when printed. However, discretionary users did not typically perceive the logic of this connection. Thus, even when the design does follow the principle of consistency, discretionary users may not be able to take advantage of that consistency because they do not understand it.

Aside from not understanding system organization in the same way as the system designers, discretionary users had some difficulties matching their terminology to system terminology. This occurred on infrequently performed tasks and especially on ones where the way of accomplishing a task in the system was indirect. For example, in the menu-driven system triple-spacing is difficult because it requires changing point size in the menu. Subjects spent a long time looking for line spacing and various synonyms in the menus and finally had to resort to the index of the system guidebook. This underlines the importance in design not just of consistent terminology, but of terminology adapted to the user.

Concentration on the Task

Subjects showed a strong drive toward completing the task at hand. This had several ramifications. Clearly, one reason why subjects failed to look up efficient commands or procedures was that they felt they could accomplish the task more quickly using what they already knew, including methods that were essentially manual. Another indication of their concentration on the task was that, when they did look up information in the documentation, they never read the whole description carefully. Instead, they scanned quickly to pull out the key points, then resumed their attempts to do the task. This partial reading of the documentation usually was sufficient but occasionally led to further problems, for instance when one subject reading quickly picked out the subscript command instead of the superscript command that he actually wanted.

When subjects concentrated strongly on a difficult task they had a tendency to forget elementary facts about the system, which they clearly knew and used correctly under normal conditions. This came out clearly in the menu-driven system when subjects tried to triple-space the document. As mentioned above, the method is indirect and not obvious. Subjects searched a good deal and finally had to resort to documentation. However, having discovered which menu option to use, they incorrectly tried to execute the task without first selecting the whole document as the object. Selecting objects of text with the mouse is routinely required in almost all editing operations, but in this and similar cases the focus on the problem itself interfered with carrying out a well-known subprocedure correctly. This problem shows how easily a user's short-term memory becomes overloaded, especially when engaged in problem-solving tasks. It underlines the importance of designs that reduce memory load.

Need to Verify Results

Our subjects verified the success of an edit before moving on to the next task. This verification was especially important to them in tasks that were less familiar. In general, the verification itself presented no difficulties. However, problems arose when the word-processing system violated its general rule of what you see is what you get. In the command-driven system, certain features (e.g., superscripts and subscripts) are seen only when the document is printed. After executing these commands and not seeing an immediate effect, subjects at least briefly believed that the command had failed. Only after some thought did they make an analogy to other more familiar features like boldface where the same thing happens. Similar verification problems were observed in the menu-driven system. Although most results appear on the screen, some, such as line spacing, can only be seen by calling up a page preview. Subjects knew about the page preview, used it often, and liked it. However, in the heat of figuring out how to do the task, they sometimes did not think of it. One subject correctly inserted a three-line header at the top of the page, but failing to see it, thought it had not been done. He repeated the same action several times and, by the time he remembered the page preview, had made his page header fully half a page long. In both of the cases just mentioned, the design violated the principle of consistency, since it failed to show results of actions on the screen as is usually done. This lack of consistency led users into tangles where they attributed the lack of visible results to spurious causes. Even though the principle of consistency was violated, the interaction might still have been smoother if some other kind of informative feedback on success of the command had been given. However, lacking that, they concluded that their commands had failed.

Other verification problems occurred when a task was unfamiliar and the verification was given in a window outside the text. For example, after doing a global search and change, menu-driven subjects who were new to the task questioned whether all instances had been located and changed. A small window at the bottom of the screen actually tells how many changes were made, but subjects failed to notice it. Instead they resorted to repeating the search and, after that, got a reassuring message (in a more familiar location) that the object was not found. Thus, informative feedback is only useful when the users expect it and know where to find it.

CONCLUSIONS

The preliminary results of our study indicate that discretionary users of word processing cannot be characterized either as novices or experts. Even though they exhibit many expertlike characteristics in accomplishing routine editing tasks, their knowledge of system behavior and functionality is far different from that of an expert. Their goal-oriented behavior and unwillingness to learn efficient commands suggest that discretionary users probably will never attain the breadth of knowledge of an expert or achieve the same relatively error-free and optimum performance. We believe that discretionary users reach a steady state of performance where they are satisfied that they are able to get their job done. They seek an "easy way out," using inefficient procedures rather than being curious to learn a new efficient procedure.

We did not find striking differences in editing behavior across the two word-processing systems. However, considering that the command repertoire of discretionary users is very limited, a well-designed menu-driven system may be useful as a memory and problem-solving aid. Menu scanning did in some cases allow our subjects to figure out how to accomplish a task. The help option on the command-driven system was seldom used, suggesting that rudimentary help options consisting of online lists of commands may at best serve as memory aids for recalling commands but not as a guided approach to learn to achieve new tasks.

In terms of design principles, we observed many problems for discretionary users because of inconsistencies in design, lack of informative feedback, and apparent short-term memory overload. These problems occur when discretionary users are forced to go beyond their normal repertoire of commands. Inconsistencies cause problems because users try to make sense of new tasks in terms of what they already know about the system. If that knowledge is not applicable in the new situation, they become confused. When informative feedback is lacking, discretionary users have difficulty judging whether new tasks have been successfully completed. This uncertainty may lead them to repeat actions or try other actions that actually put them further from the goal. Short-term memory overload may take place during tasks that involve problem solving and result in users forgetting elementary facts and procedures of the system. This may lead to a complex tangle of problems.

In summary, we feel that our analysis reiterates our hypothesis that discretionary users form a distinct group of people whose requirements and needs have to be studied to design more useful systems. This is a preliminary report of our investigation. We are conducting more research and are attempting to develop a model that will describe and predict discretionary users' interaction with word processing. We intend to extend our study to other kinds of information technology important to discretionary users, such as spreadsheets, databases, and graphics packages.

APPENDIX

Editing Tasks

1. Delete a word
2. Delete a paragraph
3. Insert a word
4. Insert a sentence
5. Change a character
6. Change a word
7. Change a word in all occurrences in the text
8. Change to superscript notation
9. Change to subscript notation
10. Move a paragraph
11. Center the heading
12. Underline the heading
13. Insert a page break
14. Set the left margin
15. Set a top margin

Note: Subjects using the command-driven software had to do one extra task, namely, reformat text in the document.

REFERENCES

Adelson, B. 1981. Problem solving and the development of abstract categories in programming languages. *Memory and Cognition* 9: 422–33.

Bouwman, M. 1984. Expert vs. novice decision making in accounting: A summary. *Accounting Organizations and Society* 9: 325–27.

Card, S. K., Moran, T. P., and Newell, A. 1983. *The psychology of human computer interaction*. Hillsdale, N.J.: Lawrence Erlbaum Associates.

Carroll, J. M., Mack, R. L., Lewis, C. H., Grischkowsky, N. L., and Robertson, S. R. 1985. Exploring exploring a word processor. *Human Computer Interaction* 1: 283–307.

Chi, M. T., Feltovich, P. J., and Glaser, R. 1981. Categorization and representation of physics problems by experts and novices. *Cognitive Science* 5: 121–52.

Ericsson, K. A., and Simon, H. 1984. *Protocol analysis: Verbal reports as data.* Cambridge, Mass.: MIT Press.

Mack, R. L., Lewis, C. H., and Carroll, J. M. 1983. Learning to use word processors: Problems and prospects. *ACM Transactions on Office Information Systems* 1: 193–210.

Santhanam, R. and Wiedenbeck, S. 1988. Assessment of word processing technology needs of the discretionary user. In *Proceedings of the 51st Annual Conference of the American Society for Information Science*, vol 25, 107–10. White Plains, N.Y.: Knowledge Industry.

Shneiderman, B. 1987. *Designing the user interface: Strategies for effective human-computer interaction.* Reading, Mass.: Addison-Wesley.

The software catalog: Microcomputers. 1988. New York: Elsevier.

Wiedenbeck, S. 1985. Novice/expert differences in programming skills. *International Journal of Man-Machine Studies* 23: 383–90.

PART V _____

EVALUATION

Martin Dillon

No one starts out trying to design a system that is user friendly, or a system that is difficult to use. Typically, the aim is to design a system that even beginners can approach and begin to use with a minimum of difficulty. Why then is the shoreline crowded with the wrecks of systems that have failed to find safe haven with the user community?

Systems fail for many reasons, of course; user unfriendliness is only the most immediately noticeable. The foremost responsibility of a system is to do what it is supposed to do, and systems most frequently fail by not accomplishing their defined tasks: database management systems that under obscure conditions destroy the files they are supposed to protect; statistical packages that deliver the wrong answers. We see few of these; the competition in software production usually keeps them from the marketplace. They are never released, or if they are, they fade quickly from sight. Shortcomings in the range or degree of functionality are probably the next most frequent cause of failure. Competitors do more, or do the same things far more quickly. Increasingly, however, especially in applications with a broad market and a relatively long history—the word processor is a good example—where one may study exhaustively what functions are required, or what is already offered in the market, the interface becomes a dominant ingredient in success or failure.

Of course, it is not a simple matter to say where the interface ends and the rest of the system begins. The functionality of a system and the detailed design of individual functions so constrain the range of what is possible in the interface that functionality is hard to separate from the interface. Retrieval systems that depend on Boolean queries, for example, cannot hide that fact from the user through an artful interface design without altering retrieval functionality.

This part of the book is about evaluation. How does one evaluate a system? There is nature's way, of course, a Darwinian struggle with the marketplace substituting for the jungle, where the best survive and the others fade from the scene. This is a crude form of evaluation, and often the method selected by default, despite its inefficiency both for society and for software developers.

It helps to understand what we are trying to evaluate. According to Ben Shneiderman (1987), the principal human factors of an interface design are

- time to learn;
- speed of performance (human and system);
- rate of errors by users;
- subjective satisfaction; and
- retention over time.

Measuring these factors is central to the evaluation process.

In a study by Anderson and Olson (1985), these evaluative methodologies are listed as follows:

1. gathering reports and evaluations from real users;
2. observations of real users;
3. field tests on users;
4. prototyping; and
5. controlled experiments.

The first three methods apply to systems that already exist. The first two methods imply that a system is already being used in the field, while the third comes into play when a system is nearing release. Two chapters included in this part belong to the first category, and it is possible through them to see the strengths and weaknesses of this approach. One, "Generic Approach to CD-ROM Systems," presents an analysis of the search capabilities and ease of use of 20 different CD-ROM systems. The approach is to use a feature analysis of the 20 systems, noting the presence or absence of each of 17 features for search capabilities and 26 features for ease of use. The other chapter, "The User Interface for CD-ROM Systems and Online Catalogs," is similar, carrying out an analysis that compares three public access catalogs with five CD-ROM systems.

All three of these approaches are necessary in the evolution of any system. A comparison with methods 4 and 5 reveals a paradox. On the one hand, it is probably true that a system can only be evaluated through serious use by real users. On the other hand, it is also true that deficiencies in design discovered after a system is built are far more difficult to remedy than at any previous stage in a system's development. Consider an analogy from a more familiar arena: What if an architect were to overlook the need for closets in a house until after the owners moved in?

Methods 4 and 5 are ideally used to guide the design of a system. Method 4 incorporates any approach that employs some form of prototyping, surely the single most important method for evaluating system concepts prior to their incorporation in a real system. The general idea in prototyping is to build a system that is capable of behaving like the system one is trying to design, but is unlike the real thing in that it is far less expensive to build. At its lowest level, a prototype is somewhat of a sham, with the look and some of the feel of the real system, but with little or none of its behavior. At its best, the prototype will behave like the real system in key respects, to the point where a prospective user can actually use the system to do real work. In this latter form, a prototype can do the work of the real system and, from an evaluative point of view, provide results that rival the insight provided by field tests using operational systems.

The other chapter included in this part, "User Interface Modeling," describes a prototyping effort and enables us to gain some insight into the benefits and drawbacks of this method of evaluating interface ideas. The chapter describes the Rapid Prototyping System, which, as its name implies, enables a designer to build a prototype of a system rapidly and therefore inexpensively. Using such a tool it is possible to explore alternative designs quickly and easily. This is far preferable to building the system without seeing it first.

Method 5, the controlled experiment, is much lauded in theory but rarely used in practice. An excellent example of the approach at its best is presented in Card, Moran, and Newell's (1980) seminal article, "The Keystroke-Level Model for User Performance Time with Interactive Systems." The paucity of material in this category, only slowly being remedied by experimentalists, explains much of the poor design we see in today's systems. In defense of the designer, such research is difficult, time consuming, and expensive; few systems could await definitive results of this sort in order to proceed. There are literally hundreds of decision points in the design of an interface, most of which could require one or more experiments to gain trustworthy insight into the proper direction to take. No wonder so many designers depend on their own intuition or the intuition of those around them.

A final word. The scientific evaluation of software systems and particularly interfaces to systems is, like the software industry itself, a relatively recent invention. We are likely to see dramatic advances both in our understanding of how to evaluate them and in the techniques used for evaluation. Efforts invested here should be encouraged: they can protect the investment of consumers by alerting them to faulty products, and they enable the designer to avoid mistakes in the evolution of new systems. Although arduous and expensive, proper evaluation is far less costly than purchasing the wrong system or building one that does not meet its purpose.

REFERENCES

Anderson, Nancy S., and Judith Reitman Olson, eds. 1985. *Methods for Designing Software to Fit Human Needs and Capabilities: Proceedings of the Workshop on Software Human Factors.* Washington, D.C.: National Research Council.

Card, S. K., T. P. Moran, and A. Newell. 1980. The keystroke-level model for user performance time with interactive systems. *Communications of the ACM* 23(7): 396–410.

Shneiderman, Ben. 1987. *Designing the User Interface: Strategies for Effective Human-Computer Interaction*. Reading, Mass.: Addison-Wesley.

19

User Interface Modeling

Carla L. Burns

Requirements specifications should be precise statements of need intended to convey an understanding of a desired result, in this case, a user interface of a system. Yet user interface requirements are typically large, natural-language specifications that are incomplete, inconsistent, ambiguous, and imprecise. Consequently, when the system is developed, the user interface does not live up to the end user's expectations.

Rapid Prototyping is a technique that can be applied during the requirements phase of the software life cycle to improve, validate, and verify the requirements specifications. The errors caught up front in the requirements phase are much less costly to fix than errors detected further on in the design and coding phases of the life cycle. Using the Rapid Prototyping System significantly reduced the time to develop a demonstration user interface, and the functionality of the prototype was judged superior when compared with other development methods.

INTRODUCTION

The intent of rapidly prototyping a user interface, also known as user interface modeling, is to generate quickly a demonstration consisting of a set of displays representing the user interface requirements. These displays illustrate what the end user will see on the screen when the system is developed. Once these displays have been developed, the end user of the system is brought in to confirm the requirements. The implementor uses the displays to walk through a scenario or set of events with the end user, who provides comments along the way. Typical comments might include: objects are a different color, objects should be located in a different area on the display, or additional capabilities are required.

Changes are likely to be made to the prototype as a result of running the demonstration for the end user. These changes can be incorporated into the demonstration at a relatively low cost. Once the changes have been incorporated,

Figure 19.1
User Interface Modeling

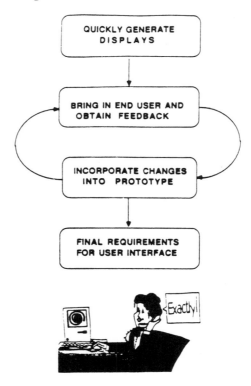

the end user can be brought back again for another assessment. This is an iterative cycle and is typically how the final user interface requirements for the system can be identified and verified. This approach should also result in a more satisfied end user. The user interface methodology described is illustrated in figure 19.1.

GOALS OF THE RAPID PROTOTYPING SYSTEM

Rome Air Development Center (RADC) recently developed a set of prototyping tools known as the Rapid Prototyping System. In addition to providing a set of tools that allows prototypes to be created rapidly, an additional objective in developing the tools was to make them easy to use. The user of the Rapid Prototyping System does not need to be a computer scientist or a programmer. Prototypes are generated quickly through the use of high-level graphics editors and templates. It is even envisioned that the end user of the system could use the Rapid Prototyping System and develop displays.

The Rapid Prototyping System

The Rapid Prototyping System (RPS) contains a collection of tools to prototype the user interfaces of Command, Control, Communications, and Intelligence (C3I) systems. Some of the key capabilities of the RPS that facilitate the impressive and "rapid" generation of displays are the following: (1) the RPS provides a world database from which to extract areas of the world, (2) the RPS supports color, (3) no programming is involved in generating demonstrations (the RPS automatically generates the code while the demonstration is being created through high-level user interfaces), and (4) the RPS is able to trigger various types of functionality during the demonstration such as placing additional objects on the display, removing objects from the display, and accessing a database. Collectively, these capabilities provide a powerful tool.

The RPS user interface modeling tools are hosted on Apollo workstations. Input to the tools is communicated through a keyboard and a mouse. The set of RPS user interface modeling tools includes: (1) a map builder, which generates maps to be incorporated into the prototype; (2) a graphics editor, which is used to draw all of the other graphical objects associated with the prototype; (3) a switch table builder, which defines the functionality for the prototype; (4) a tray editor, which stores all of the files to be associated with the prototype; (5) a demonstration builder, which automatically generates the executable demonstration; and (6), a run interface prototype facility, which executes the prototype demonstration. All of these tools are easy to use and consequently allow non-programmers to develop user interface prototypes.

REQUIREMENTS DEFINITION

Before the RPS can be used to implement the user interface prototype, the requirements for the prototype itself must be developed. This is the first and most crucial stage in the prototype's development. It consists of the following sequence of events: (1) acquiring baseline requirement specifications for the user interface, (2) defining a scenario or set of events that would suit the baseline specifications, (3) defining the types of graphical objects that are required for the scenario, and (4) determining how the user is going to interact with the system.

Prototype Example

In order to allow the reader to obtain a firm understanding of the RPS tools, a small, hypothetical prototype will be built. As each of the RPS tools is described in more detail, the example prototype will be updated, reflecting the actions taken in each tool. This example assumes that baseline requirements for the user interface have been acquired.

Scenario Definition

The following represents a scenario for the prototype example. An operator is in charge of monitoring the Alaskan region. Initially, display simply consists of a map of Alaska. Assume that the user will be notified if any problems arise by a message alarm, and that objects such as microwave sensors, radar coverage, and tracks (potential enemies) that are located in the region can be viewed.

First, the operator decides to place microwave sensors on the display; next, to observe the radar coverage; finally, to place any tracks on the screen. Upon doing so, the radar coverage changes from green to red.

Graphical Object Definition

Since a scenario has been provided, the next step is to identify the graphical objects needed for the scenario. They are a map of Alaska, microwave sensors, radar coverage, tracks, and user options.

USER OPTION DEFINITION

The last step in the requirements definition phase for the prototype is to determine how the user options are to be captured on the display. User options represent all of the functions the user can access from a given display. Typical ways to depict user options are listed below. The dashed lines indicate that the user can select the area enclosed within the dashed lines with the mouse and have some action occur.

For the prototype example, a table could be used to represent the operator placing the sensors, radar coverage, and tracks on the display as illustrated in figure 19.2. Quit would exit the demonstration. The user would simply position

Figure 19.2
A Table of User Options

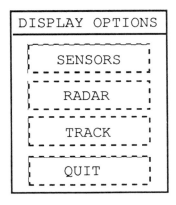

Figure 19.3
Graphical Objects Such as a Plane

the mouse over the appropriate region and select it with the mouse. Instead of the user positioning the mouse over a table and selecting an action to be performed, the user could move the mouse over a graphical object, such as a plane, select it, and have it result in some action being performed. This is illustrated in figure 19.3. An appropriate action might be to select a specific plane to view relevant database information.

PROTOTYPE IMPLEMENTATION

Once all of the requirements have been developed the prototype implementation can begin.

Map Builder

The map-builder tool would be used first to generate the map of the world area required. For the prototype example, this would be Alaska. Upon invocation of the tool, a map of the world would be displayed, as depicted in figure 19.4. The implementor would graphically select the area of the world to map by drawing a rectangle around the desired area. The map's projection and features (such as rivers, coastlines, and state boundaries) are also graphically chosen from a table of options. The colors for the map and each of its associated features are also specified. The result is a map that may be viewed or edited in the graphics editor. The graphics editor is the next tool discussed. Figure 19.5 shows the map that was generated for the example.

Graphics Editor

The graphics editor, called GED, contains the facilities for the creation of displays that contain multiple graphical objects arranged to depict the user interface requirements. These graphical objects will represent the real-world objects as they would be seen on the C3I display.

GED has three categories of objects: graphical objects, database objects, and objects representing selectable regions. Graphical objects include polygons, circles, ovals, polylines, arcs, and text. Database objects represent object attributes of graphical objects, that is, a plane, and are used in the demonstration to convey textual information. The location of the database information on the display is

Figure 19.4
Map Builder

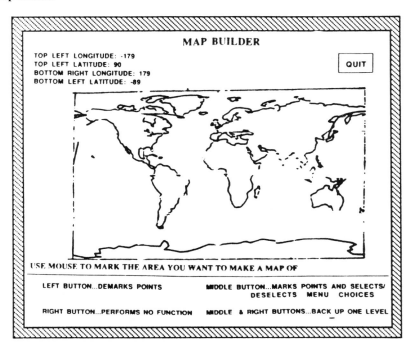

specified using GED, which also allows for the creation of graphical objects called selectable regions. Selectable regions are mechanisms for defining functionality; that is, during a demonstration the user will be able to move the mouse over a selectable region on the display, select it, and have it result in some action being performed. Thus, the selectable regions are used to activate the user options on the display. GED allows for the identification and location of these selectable regions.

Figure 19.6 gives a picture of the graphics editor. It resembles the Apple Macintosh tool, MacDraw, for those readers familiar with Macintosh tools. For the example, all of the remaining graphical objects (microwave sensors, radar coverage, track, and user options) would need to be drawn using the graphics editor. The objects would initially be drawn on the map of Alaska to position them where they are to appear during the demonstration. Recall that the table depicted in figure 19.2 will capture the user options. Figure 19.7 shows all of the graphical objects required for the example drawn on the map of Alaska.

Since the scenario does not require any objects other than the map and user options to be on the display initially, the remaining objects (microwave sensors, radar coverage, and tracks) are to be stored in separate file structures and are not to be saved or associated with the file containing the map of Alaska. Figures

Figure 19.5
Map Selection

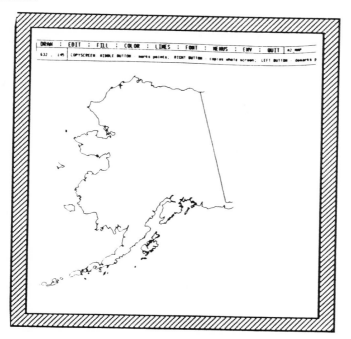

19.8 to 19.12 illustrate all of the graphical files required for the example. Each file name is specified in the lower right-hand corner of the file. Each file has been named its appropriate graphical object. Notice that two files have been created for the radar. One file contains the radar colored red while the other one depicts it in green. This is required since in the example scenario the radar color changes from green to red. Once all of the objects have been stored in their appropriate files, the objects that are not to be associated with the map of Alaska would be deleted from the file containing the map, as depicted in Figure 19.8.

Switch Table Builder (STEDI)

The switch table builder, called STEDI, is used to define the functionality for the selectable regions or user options identified in GED. The types of functions that can be associated with selectable regions include displaying new objects, removing objects, performing database operations, and executing programs. More than one function can be defined for a single selectable region. The definition of the functionality for a selectable region of a display is stored in a file structure called a switch table. There is exactly one switch table for each file containing selectable regions. The name of the switch table file is automatically

Figure 19.6
Graphics Editor

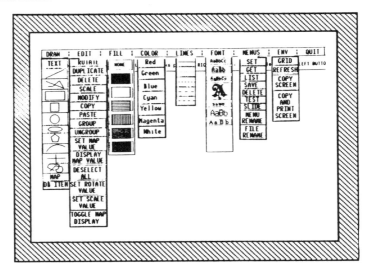

Figure 19.7
Alaska: Graphical Objects

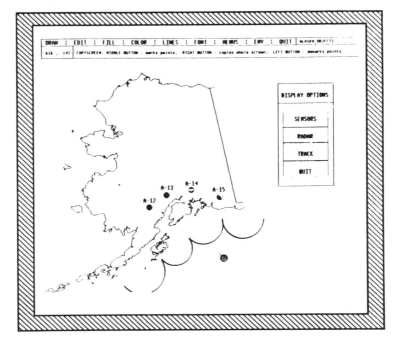

Figure 19.8
Graphical Files: Alaska Options

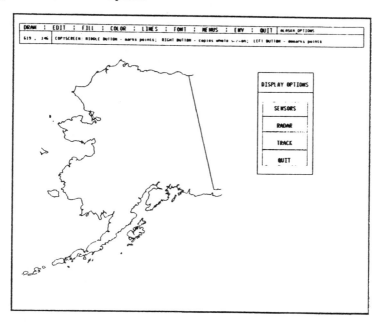

generated from the name of this file containing the selectable regions. An ".st" extension is appended to the name of the graphical object file. This provides a consistent naming convention.

Upon invocation of the tool, the implementor specifies the name of the file for which functionality is being defined. Only files containing selectable regions will have switch tables. Continuing with the example, the only file that requires a switch table is the one containing the map and user options, "Alaska Options." The other files simply contain graphical objects and have no selectable regions associated with them. After specifying the name of the file, the tools would bring the file up on the display. The sensors' selectable region would be highlighted, signifying that the implementor is currently defining functionality for this region. When the definition of functionality for the sensors' selectable region was complete, the next selectable region would be highlighted. This is represented in figure 19.13.

Recall from the example scenario that when the operator selects the sensors option from the table, the sensors are placed on the display. To accomplish this task, the overlay file containing the sensors object is placed on top of the display. When the operator chooses the radar option, the radar is placed on the display. Again, an overlay consisting of the radar is placed on the display. If the operator selects the track option, the track comes up on the display, and the radar changes

Figure 19.9
Sensors

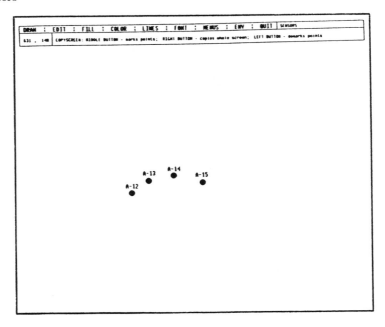

from green to red. For this option, the track overlay is placed on the display, the green radar overlay is removed, and the red overlay is placed on the display. Finally, the operator chooses the quit option to exit from the demonstration. Figure 19.14 provides a listing of events defined for the switch table associated with the map of Alaska and its user options.

Tray Editor (TREDI)

The tray editor, called TREDI, allows the implementor to identify all of the graphical files and switch table files that are to be associated with the demonstration. The resulting structure that is created is called a tray. It simply contains a listing of all of the graphical files and switch tables that are to be used to generate the executable program. The tray for the example is illustrated in figure 19.15.

Demonstration Builder and Demonstration Execution Tools

The demonstration builder generates a program written in the C programming language, which is based upon the tray, switch tables, and graphical files. The C program is compiled and linked into an executable program. The final step is to execute the program using the demonstration execution facilities. The example demonstration generated 189 lines of code. It was executed to verify that it performed as expected. It took 15 minutes to create this small prototype.

Figure 19.10
Radar: Green

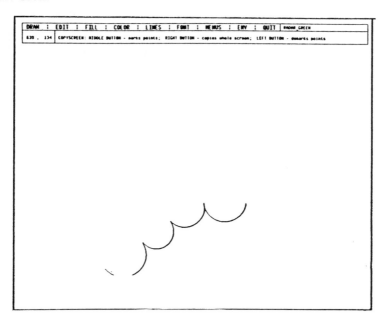

GRANITE SENTRY PROTOTYPE DEMONSTRATION

To determine the usefulness and overall quality of the RPS tools, the development of a user interface prototype for a large C3I system was performed. The Granite Sentry Program Office was in the process of developing the requirements for updating the Air Defense Operations Center computer system, which is located at the Cheyenne Mountain Complex in Colorado Springs. This effort was chosen to be prototyped.

A set of 14 baseline slides representing the user interface requirements for the system upgrade was received from the Granite Sentry Program Office. The slides sent were black and white and difficult to read. One of the baseline slides is illustrated in figure 19.16.

There were several problems with the set of baseline slides that RADC received. First of all, there was no apparent scenario or set of events that the displays seemed to follow. In addition, it was not clear how the user options were to be captured on the display. Furthermore, since the slides were black and white, a color scheme had to be derived. The convention signifying red as a trouble situation, yellow as a warning situation, and green as a normal situation was adopted.

RADC developed a scenario for the set of 14 slides. The display that RADC

Figure 19.11
Radar: Red

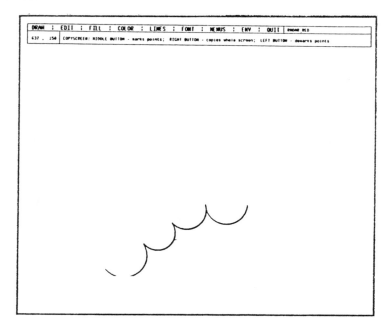

generated from the baseline slide depicted in figure 19.16 is captured in figure 19.17. Additional graphical objects, not in the baseline slides, had to be added to the displays to complement the scenario and capture the user options on the screen. Notice, for instance, that the altitude matrix in the bottom right corner of the display is not in the set of baseline slides that RADC received.

While RADC was implementing the demonstration, it was brought out that the Granite Sentry Program Office was already in the process of prototyping the requirements. They did not have a prototyping tool to use and were programming. It took them one year to prototype the user interface requirements. It took RADC six person-weeks to complete the task. The demonstration that RADC generated consists of 53 unique displays. The prototype was demonstrated to individuals from the Granite Sentry Program Office. Members were impressed with what RADC had accomplished in such a short amount of time.

ADVANTAGES OF RPS

There are many advantages to using the RPS user interface modeling tools. One advantage is that a great amount of time is saved by having the source code automatically generated. As was mentioned, the Granite Sentry user interface prototype took six person-weeks to develop. Approximately 10,000 lines of code

Figure 19.12
Track

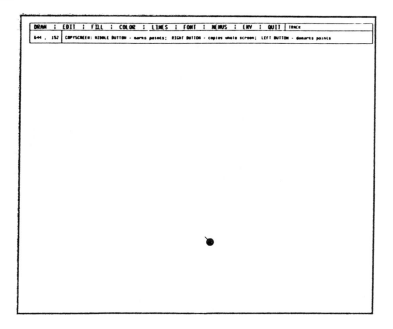

were generated. Typically, a programmer generates 10 lines of fully documented code per day. The RPS is not production code and consequently is not documented. Therefore, even if the programmer's average number of lines of code per day were raised to 50 lines to compensate for the RPS not producing documented code, it still would take 40 weeks for a programmer to generate the Granite Sentry prototype. The average amount of code generated for the Granite Sentry prototype per day using the RPS tools was 333. Using the RPS resulted in a productivity factor of six.

Figure 19.18 compares the productivity of the RPS tools for the Granite Sentry demonstration versus a programmer. Another advantage is that the RPS allows a programmer to add any additional capabilities to the prototype by writing C code and compiling and linking it into the automatically generated source code. This was done in the Granite Sentry prototype to trigger alarms. The RPS does not support this capability. In addition, the flashing of graphical objects had to be programmed into the automatically generated source code. The flashing of graphical objects can be implemented easily by removing and displaying the object to be flashed several times on the display. However, when the prototype was run, this simulation did not accurately depict the rate at which the flashing would occur on the real system; that is, the flashing was occurring too rapidly.

Figure 19.13
Switch Table Builder

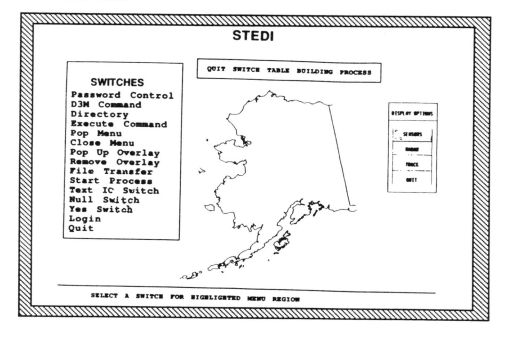

Figure 19.14
Switch Table Events

	STEDI
SELECTABLE REGION FOR:	**ACTION**
• SENSORS	1. POP UP OVERLAY NAME OF OVERLAY: SENSORS
• RADAR	1. POP UP OVERLAY NAME OF OVERLAY: RADAR_GREEN

• TRACK	1. POP UP OVERLAY
	    NAME OF OVERLAY: TRACK
	2. REMOVE OVERLAY
	    NAME OF OVERLAY: RADAR_GREEN
	3. POP UP OVERLAY
	    NAME OF OVERLAY: RADAR_RED

• QUIT	1. QUIT

Figure 19.15
Tray Builder

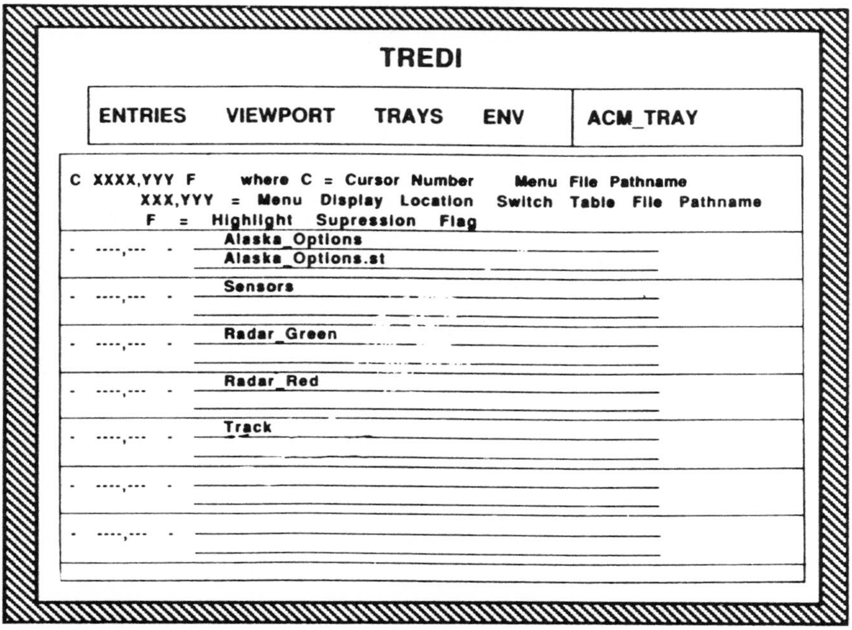

Therefore, code to make the simulation appear more realistic was compiled and linked into the Granite Sentry automatically generated code.

RPS TOOL ENHANCEMENTS

As one can see, the RPS provides a powerful set of tools for quickly implementing a user interface prototype. This section of the chapter describes some of the various enhancements that could be made to the RPS tools to provide additional functionality and to make the tools even more efficient.

The tool methodology discussed in this chapter should be incorporated into the tools themselves; that is, GED, STEDI, TREDI, the demonstration builder, and the demonstration execution facility should be combined into a single tool. This would allow the prototype to be generated in a single tool.

The RPS tools should have various levels of user interfaces for the implementor. The current set of tools is straightforward to use. The tools can be thought of as the "learning" level user interface. However, once the implementor has developed a few prototypes, this learning-level user interface becomes cumbersome to use. The second-level user interface might be more object oriented and template-driven. For example, while defining switches, the implementor could simply select the type of switch that was to be used. Associated with this

Figure 19.16
Baseline Slide Sample

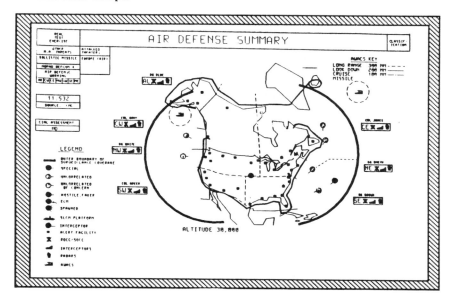

Figure 19.17
RADC Display

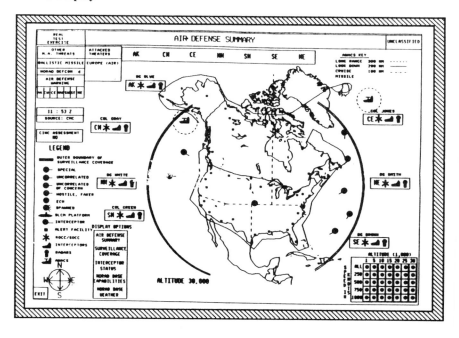

Figure 19.18
RPS Tool Productivity Chart

	GOAL	NUMBER OF LINES OF CODE PER DAY	AMOUNT OF TIME TO COMPLETE JOB
PROGRAMMER	10,000 LINES	50	40 WEEKS
RPS TOOLS	10,000 LINES	333	6 WEEKS

type of switch would be a template consisting of the automatically generated C code required for this type of switch, which the implementor would be unable to edit. This template would also require information such as the file names that could be associated with the switch that the implementor could fill in and edit.

The functionality for the GED selectable regions includes displaying overlays and viewing database information. As a result of implementing a few Air Defense–oriented prototype applications, some additional capabilities or new switches were identified. They are an alarm, the flashing of graphical object(s), and a real-time clock.

CONCLUSIONS

The RPS was used to prototype the user interface of a large, real-world C3I system. As a result, some of the ambiguities, inconsistencies, and incompleteness in the baseline requirements were identified. The RPS provides a very powerful set of tools for quickly implementing a user interface prototype demonstration. The increased productivity of the RPS over conventional programming is significant. Prototyping the user interface in the requirements phase of the life cycle is well worth the time and effort spent.

REFERENCES

Burns, Carla L., and Elizabeth S. Kean. "User Interface Modeling Using the Rapid Prototyping System." RADC-TM–88–10 In-house Report, May 1988.
Rzepka, William E., and Philip C. Daley. 1986. "A Prototyping Tool to Assist in Requirements Engineering." In *Proceedings of the Nineteenth Hawaii Interna-*

tional Conference on System Sciences, 1986, vol. 2, ed. Bruce D. Shriver, 608–18. North Hollywood, Calif.: Western Periodicals.

Generic Approach to CD-ROM Systems: A Formal Analysis of Search Capabilities and Ease of Use

Tian-Zhu Li

Difficulties that many end users encounter in searching for information from large databases on CD-ROM are caused in part by the diversity of system interfaces. Search capabilities and ease of use of 20 CD-ROM systems in academic libraries are identified and analyzed with two lists of established criteria. These criteria are selected from those developed by information professionals. Boolean search, using truncation, downloading, and a dozen other search capabilities are common among the majority of existing systems. But the systems vary greatly regarding ease of use. Only systems of the DIALOG family meet almost all the criteria. An examination of the use of Boolean operators, truncation symbols, and the way to limit a search in a defined field failed to find features that all systems share. There is also no agreement in using the function keys. It is suggested that standardization in interface design and cognitive approach in user training can help multisystem users. Another study using an approach grounded in the "mental models" literature is planned to investigate the user behavior on these systems so that effective training can be designed for multisystem users.

BACKGROUND AND PROBLEMS

CD-ROM has brought a revolution (or evolution?) to our information society today. Because of its huge capacity for storing information, many large electronic databases, once only accessible from online information retrieval utilities such as DIALOG or BRS through telecommunications, are now available to end users in many libraries and information centers using microcomputers. Users no longer rely on reference librarians as intermediaries to do searches for them. CD-ROM not only makes powerful databases directly accessible to the end users, but it also saves on the cost to pay for online searches.

However, problems arise as more and more CD-ROM systems and products get into the library. The most crucial problem that many users encounter, especially those with no online search experience, is the difficulty in using some of these systems. Some of us have realized that it is not always easy to search the ERIC database on CD-ROM, even when one is in the so-called Easy Mode. Experienced reference librarians indicate that users not only have problems in formulating searches, but also in the displaying and printing steps. Even in the Easy Mode, which is menu-driven and is considered much easier than the Command Mode, some users still get confused or feel lost somewhere. Although some help can be obtained from the screen, and there is a manual and an instruction sheet nearby, few users seem to consult them.

The purpose of the study reported here was to identify and analyze the search capabilities and ease-of-use aspects of existing CD-ROM systems in libraries, so that useful hints can be generated to help both designers and multidatabase users.

At present, all CD-ROM systems are still at the development stage. Most important, there is no standard among the existing systems and products (Befeler and Einberger, 1988). Every system is different. This problem is especially a hindrance when one needs to search several databases to do an exhaustive literature review that requires using several systems—a headache to both the librarians and the multidatabase users. If delivering information on CD-ROM offers the opportunity to change the model of what the end user of large databases must know, how do the systems empower the user to explore the information contained in the databases? What search capabilities does each system provide? And how easy are they for users (user-friendliness)? Is there anything generic among the existing CD-ROM systems? What are the differences? These questions must be answered first if we want to identify and solve the problems that users face in working with these systems.

A CD-ROM system usually has five components: (1) a computer such as an IBM PC, (2) software to access the data, (3) an interface card, (4) disc player (reader, driver), and (5) compact discs. At the moment, most of the hardware and software are not compatible among existing systems. For example, a recent survey shows that over 30 different retrieval packages are used to manage and access the information contained on over 120 database products (Nicholls, 1988). This means there are over 50 different command languages to master.

Due to many factors, almost all libraries have to buy different systems in order to provide users access to different databases, and users must learn how to use different systems if they need information from more than one database. It would be a little easier if a library had CD-ROM products provided by the same vendor so that the user need only know one interface (the way a system communicates with a human). Unfortunately, this is rarely the case because of problems in hardware compatibility, software compatibility, space requirements, training needs, scheduling and security concerns, hidden costs, and licensing restrictions, which are characterized as "the seven deadly sins of CD-ROM" (Reese and Steffey, 1988).

A wealth of useful materials on CD-ROM already exists. It is now the responsibility of educational technologists and information professionals to determine how best to make the technology most accessible to users. Since most users' problems with CD-ROM occur during their interaction with the system, a brief review of human-computer interaction studies is in order.

USER INTERFACE AND MENTAL MODELS

Human-Computer Interaction (HCI)

Research on human-computer interaction (HCI) spans the literature of computer science, engineering, information science, psychology, artificial intelligence, and several other disciplines. However, the principal goal of research on human-computer interaction, according to Carroll (1987), "is to provide an understanding of how human motivation, action, and experience place constraints on the usability of computer equipment." One central issue of HCI is the interface, which is described as "computers as experienced and manipulated by human users" (Carroll). In broad terms, we can say the user interface is the medium through which the user and the information come together.

Norman (1986) suggests that there are two sides of the interface: the system side and the human side. The system side of the interface is changed through proper design, and the interface at the human side is changed through training and experience. Norman's idea of solving the interface problem of a system is based on some recent research in cognitive science, which indicates that the difficulty humans face in dealing with any system may be due to the forming of an incorrect mental model of that system. Once people have the right mental model (or the incorrect model is corrected), they will know how to deal with the system.

The phrase "mental model" is not new, and a large body of literature exists on the topic. For example, in their review of research in this area, Rouse and Morris define mental models as "the mechanisms whereby humans are able to generate descriptions of system purpose and form, explanations of system functioning and observed system states, and predictions of the future" (Rouse and Morris, 1985). Tweney (1987) characterizes scientific thinking in light of a mental model approach and outlines its attributes.

Using the concept of mental models, Norman (1986, 46) further suggests that the system can be manipulated easily if the "user model" (the mental model of the system held by the user) is brought close to the "design model" (the mental model of the system held by the designer) through the "system image" (a physical image of the structure of the system including on-screen displays, documentation, and instruction). "The problem is to design the system so that, first, it follows a consistent, coherent conceptualization—a design model—and, second, so that the user can develop a mental model of that system—a user model—consistent with the design model." Norman thinks that the user model is not formed from the design model: it results from the way the user interprets the system image. Thus in many ways, the primary task of the designer is to construct an appropriate system image, realizing that everything with which the user interacts helps to form that image: the physical knobs, dials, keyboards, and displays; and the documentation, including instruction manuals, help facilities, text input and output, and error messages.

Further, the designer should want the user model to be compatible with the underlying conceptual model—the design model. This only happens through interaction with the system image. Therefore, as Norman points out, for the user to understand a system, to use it properly, and to enjoy using it, the designer must make the system image explicit, intelligible, and consistent.

Kerr (1987) actually explored aspects of system image, which he calls "wayfinding." His study of strategies to cue users to their location in a database (using text, graphic, and color) showed that the presence or absence of physical cues was less important to successful searching than the user's ability to represent the structure of the information internally (forming mental models). The "metastructure" of a book—cover, title page, verso page, preface, table of contents, chapters, references, indexes, appendices, and so on—helps readers to find what they want. This is the result of a heritage of hundreds of years dealing with print. The metastructure provided us with a consistent system image of a book, which in turn helped us in forming a consistent user model of a book. Compared with printed material, organizing information in electronic databases is very new. Whether totally proper or not, we have transferred some of our technical and psychological heritage of print into electronic texts (Hartley, 1987), but the metastructure of organizing information in electronic databases, particularly on CD-ROM, has not been formed yet. Most databases on CD-ROM today are just duplications of the online databases, or even conversions of their printed counterparts.

CD-ROM and User Interfaces

Since the existing CD-ROM systems are not standardized, there is no "metastructure" of CD-ROM systems. But are there features in common among the existing systems concerning the interface that might lead us to constructing such a metastructure? What are the differences among systems? The study described here set out to answer these questions. More specifically, using the theory of mental models, the study focused on the question: Can a generic model be derived from similar groups of systems, if not all the existing systems?

An answer to this question is of great importance. If such a model can be found, it might be possible to find the generic user model and compare the user model with the system model. Once differences are found, we can narrow the gap between the two sides of the interface by bringing the user model of the systems close to the design model of the systems through user training, or by changing the design model to fit the user model more closely. To accomplish all these, we must first know the existing systems better, because our knowledge of the design model of a system comes from the system image, and our knowledge of the generic design model of existing systems can only be obtained by comparing the interfaces of various systems.

Many articles have evaluated or reviewed CD-ROM systems (e.g., Peters, 1987; Reese and Steffey, 1988; Herther, 1988; Graves, L. G. Harper, B. F. King, 1988). Most articles, however, are guidelines or offer experiences in selecting CD-ROM products. Only a few articles compared the interfaces of some databases on CD-ROM (e.g., Brunell, 1988; Kittle, 1988; Kahn, 1987; Bills and Helgerson, 1987; Stewart, 1987), but each author used a distinct set of criteria for the comparison. For example, Kahn reviews the user interface feature in six CD-ROM systems with five criteria: browsing, using menus, referring a search, accessing an online version, printing and saving results. In contrast, Bill and Helgerson set 15 criteria to evaluate the user interfaces for CD-ROM public access catalog systems, while Stewart established five categories of evaluation criteria for libraries to consider when they acquire databases on CD-ROM: collection development, administrative considerations, vendor considerations, search capabilities, and ease of use.

The study described here focused on the design model of CD-ROM system and concentrated, therefore, on the type of searches a CD-ROM system can perform. This type is defined by the indexing strategy and retrieval software, and by the way the user communicates with the system through the interface software. Therefore, for the purpose of this study, only criteria of search capabilities and ease of use were selected to compare the various systems.

METHOD

The study examined 20 databases on CD-ROM that are available to the public in the University of Washington libraries (table 20.1). They cover almost all subject areas from social sciences and humanities to science and technology. The 20 databases studied for the analyses are from 11 families. A family here means a line of products from the same producer, or from the same vendor, that share the same interfacing software. The interfaces of databases from the same family are the same or very similar. Twenty databases of 11 families means that if a user wants to try all these databases, this user must encounter at least 11 different interfaces. All the systems tested use IBM PCs or compatibles (Zenith or Delph) and Philip CM100 disc drivers. The versions of the interface software of these systems are the latest ones used, in October 1988.

After receiving permission to examine the CD-ROM systems, the investigator selected the criteria for the comparison. The majority of the criteria used in this study are adaptations of guidelines developed at Cornell University to help library staff determine which compact-disc databases are more suitable for public use in their libraries (Stewart, 1987). The criteria selected are presented in the appendix.

With these criteria and a list of the selected databases, data were collected

Table 20.1
List of CD-ROM Systems in the Study

Title	Family
BOOKS IN PRINT PLUS (BIP+)	Bowker
ULRICH'S PERIODICAL DIRECTORY+ (ULRI)	Bowker
BRS/COLLEAGUE MEDLINE (COLG)	BRS
MEDLINE	Cambridge
AQUATIC SCIENCES & FISHERIES ABSTRACTS (ASFA)	Cambridge
LIFE SCIENCES COLLECTION (LSC)	Cambridge
NTIS	Dialog
ERIC	Dialog
COMPACT DISCLOSURE	(Dialog)*
AGRICOLA	OCLC
INFOTRAC	OTHER
NEWSBANK ELECTRONIC INDEX	OTHER
BUSINESS INDICATORS	SHIP
CENSUS OF AGRICULTURE	SHIP
POPULATION STATISTICS	SHIP
COUNTY STATISTICS	SHIP
PSYCLIT	SLVPLT
ABI/INFORM	UMI
MLA BIBLIOGRAPHY	Wilson
APPLIED SCIENCE & TECHNOLOGY INDEX (AST)	Wilson

* COMPACT DISCLOSURE is, in fact, not a DIALOG product, but its interface is similar to that of DIALOG. For the purpose of this study, it is grouped in DIALOG family.

about search capabilities and ease of use, as well as on the use of Boolean operators (AND, OR, NOT . . .), truncation symbols, examples of field limit search, and the use of function keys in each family of databases.

About two hours were spent with each database depending on how familiar the investigator was with the database. Online introduction and help screens were read and printed if a ''Print screen'' function was available. Every criterion in each category was checked and recorded. System summary sheets/cards, manuals, and printed thesauri were used if necessary. Reference librarians responsible for the use of the systems were also consulted when confusion or problems arose. Printouts of sample searches and records were also collected for verification and comparison. To prevent missing features that exist but were not found by the investigator, the two-part checklists were given to the reference librarians to verify. Features were double-checked if disagreement appeared.

After all the data were collected and recorded, each database and family were examined across all criteria, and each criterion was examined across all the databases and families. Databases were compared against the criteria to detect common patterns, and a comparison among features was also carried out.

RESULTS

The information provided by the selected databases and the primary sources they cover varied. Of 11 families, BOWKER, WILSON, and OTHER (including two families) are indexes to printed literature and do not include abstracts, and SHIP (Slater Hall Information Products) contains only statistical information. All the other systems contain abstracts. The following are the findings of the analysis and comparisons.

Search Capabilities

The data illustrating the search capabilities of various systems are displayed in table 20.2. As this table shows, systems in the DIALOG family are the only ones to possess all 17 search capabilities, except Compact Disclosure, which has only 13 capabilities. These are followed by SilverPlatter's Psyclit and BRS's Colleague with 15 capabilities each, and by systems in Wilson, Cambridge, and OCLC families, which provide 14 capabilities each. Next are the two systems in the Bowker family and UMI's ABI/INFO, with 13 capabilities each. The four statistical databases from the SHIP family each have only 5 search capabilities according to the valuation criteria used. InfoTrac and Newsbank only offer subject search. They possess the fewest search capabilities (3) among all systems.

Capabilities in common. In comparison to online searching, all CD-ROM systems are slower. Nevertheless, all systems studied, except UMI's ABI/INFO, can perform a search in less than twice the time it takes online. Almost all the systems can be interrupted when they are processing a search. Boolean searches can be performed on all the systems except those from SHIP and OTHER. Except systems in the SHIP family and the OTHER family, all other systems possess most of the search capabilities, such as phrase search, using truncations, nesting, save search set for later use, limit search in certain fields, limit the search by language or year, and global search. They also offer printing and formatting options. Except systems from Wilson and OTHER, all other systems allow users to download (copy or transfer) the records searched to their own floppy disks for word processing or other applications.

Uncommon features are PURGE, SORT (in DIALOG), and change the search from disc to ONLINE (in DIALOG and Wilson) for the recent information. Although systems in the Bowker family lack the capability of going online for the latest information, they possess the capability of connecting to the systems of large book dealers such as Baker and Taylor, and Blackwell for ordering items for libraries. With the sort function, customized format option, and the download capability, ERIC and NTIS are the only systems that enable a user to compile a bibliography in the style that a user prefers and combine it directly with the user's database on a floppy disk with minimum editing.

Table 20.2
Search Capabilities*

FAMILY	DIALOG	BOWKER	WILSON	CAMBRIDGE	UMI	SLVPLT	SHIP	OCLC	BRS	OTHER
DATA-BASE	ENC RTO IIM CSP	BU IL PR +I+	MA LS A& BT	LMA IES FDF ELA	ABI/	PSY C	BCPC UAON SGPT IRUY	AGRI	COLG	INNE FWOS
1 TIME	xxx	xx	xx	xxx		x	xxxx	x	x	xx
2 STOP	xxx	xx	xx	xxx	x	x	xxxx	x	x	
3 BOOIEN	xxx	xx	xx	xxx	x	x		x	x	
4 PHRASE	xxx	xx	xx	xxx	x	x		x	x	xx
5 TRUNCA	xxx	xx	xx	xxx	x	x		x	x	
6 NESTIN	xxx	xx	xx	xxx	x	x		x	x	
7 SETSAV	xxx	xx	xx	xxx	x	x		x	x	
8 PURGE	xx					x			x	
9 LIMIT	xxx	xx	xx	xxx	x	x		x	x	
10 LA/YR	xx	xx	xx	xxx	x	x		x	x	
11 GLOBE	xxx		xx	xxx	x	x		x	x	
12 SORT	xxx									
13 PRTMO	xx	xx	xx	xxx	x	x	xxxx	x	x	
14 PRTSL	xxx	xx	xx	xxx	x	x	xxxx	x	x	xx
15 FMTCS	xxx	xx	xx	xxx	x	x		x	x	
16 DWNLD	xxx	xx		xxx	x	x	xxxx	x	x	
17 ONLIN	xx		xx							
Total	17 (13)	13	14	14	13	15	5	14	15	3

*All tested with the latest version of interface software being used in October 1988.

EASE OF USE (USER-FRIENDLINESS)

The data collected for the category of ease of use are presented in table 20.3. This table shows that systems vary greatly in this aspect. Except Compact Disclosure, DIALOG and Wilson are the only families that seem more user-friendly, if we define user-friendliness according to the criteria selected in this study. Although most of the systems are not strong in this aspect of the interface, some features are still common to almost all of them. For example, every system has an introduction screen and a printed summary sheet for easy consultation; 19 of 20 systems allow index browsing, have logically organized, easy-to-read documents, and provide sample searches in their documents. Fifteen of the 20 systems tell the user how to back up the menu screen and exit individual functions, and allow users to select searching terms from their indexes without retyping these words or phrases.

Half of the systems have a menu mode to help novice users and a command mode to accommodate the experienced user. In most cases, the search in command mode is separated from the search in menu mode. For most systems, however, changing the mode will lose the search set already created. Although most systems with command search capability use some mnemonics to help the user to remember the command, they fail to provide examples of command search on-screen when searching is in that mode. They also overlook telling the user where to look for prompts and menus, and they do not show the user clearly how to select menu items or respond to prompts. Some of this information might be available from online help, but a novice user may not be aware that such help is available, or know how to get it. The limited prompts, which usually appear at the bottom or top of the screen, may not be understood by novice users because the meanings of those abbreviations or acronyms are not explicit.

It is a little surprising that over half of the systems do not have tutorials. Even for those that do, the quality varies greatly. Some systems call their help screens tutorials. Systems in SilverPlatter and DIALOG provide better tutorials, compared to that offered in the other systems. Providing context-specific help and cross-references to suggest better vocabulary would be very helpful to novice users; unfortunately, none of them offers such help.

Comparing the systems against all the criteria shows that ERIC and NTIS from the DIALOG family meet almost all the criteria for ease of use. Agricola, Psyclit, the Wilson family, and BRS/Colleague possess over 80% of the criteria. Examination of the documentation reveals that all the systems, except NewsBank and ABI, came with manuals or summary sheets. Some are well designed; others are poorly arranged and printed.

BOOLEAN SEARCH, TRUNCATION SYMBOLS, AND SEARCH LIMIT EXAMPLES

Differences among systems are many. For multidatabase users, understanding how the databases are organized and what the systems can do is essential.

Table 20.3
Ease of Use (User-friendliness)

FAMILY DATA-BASE	DIALOG ENC RTO IIM CSP	BOWKER BU IL PR +I+	WILSON MA LS A& BT	CAMBRIDGE LMA IES FDF ELA	UMI AB I/	SLVPLT PS YC	SHIP BCPC UAON SGPT IRUY	OCLC AG RI IG	BRS CO LG	OTHER IN NE FW OS
1 INTROD	xxx	xx	xx	xxx	x	x	xxxx	x x	x	xx
2 TUTORI	xx	xx	xx			x	xxxx	x x	x	xx
3 PROMPT	xx		xx	xxx	x			x	x	
4 MENUSL	xxx		xx	xxx	x			x	x	
5 CMDXPL	xxx		xx	xxx	x			x	x	
6 BACKUP	xxx		xx	xxx	x		xxxx	x	x	
7 EXITDB	xxx		xx	xxx				x	x	
8 FCTNHP	xxx	xx	xx	xxx	x	x		x	x	
9 CTXTHP										
10 EROMS	xx		xx			x		x	x	
11 EXCMD	xx	xx	xx	xxx				x	x	
12 EXSCH	xx	xx	xx					x	x	
13 IDXBZ	xxx	xx	xx	xxx	x	x	xxxx	x	x	xx
14 SLIDX	xxx	xx	xx		x	x	xxxx	x		xx
15 SMIDX	xxx	xx			x	x	xxxx	x		
16 SGVOC										
17 OPDSP	xxx		xx	xxx			xxxx	x	x	
18 OPPRT	xxx		xx	xxx				x	x	
19 SHTCT	xxx	xx	xx	xxx	x	x		x	x	
20 SMSHT	xx	xx	xx	xxx	x	x	xxxx	x	x	xx
21 DCMEZ	xxx	xx	xx	xxx	x	x	xxxx	x	x	x
22 DCLGC	xxx	xx	xx	xxx	x	x	xxxx	x	x	x
23 DCIDX	xx	xx	xx		x			x	x	x
24 SMPSC	xxx	xx	xx	xxx	x	x	xxxx	x	x	x
25 NUMNX	xxx	xx	xx	xxx	x	x		x	x	x
26 FCTNK	xxx	xx	xx		x	x		x		xx
Total	24 17	14	23	17	13	14	10	17	21	10 6

Table 20.4
Boolean Search in CD-ROM Systems

System Family	Set Combine* (AND,OR,NOT ...)	Truncation Symbol	Limit (Field Define) Examples
Dialog	?C S1 AND S2	?	word/TI word/AU word/AB
Bowker	CS=1 AND 2	$	TI=word AU=word YR>1986
Cambridge	.S /1 AND /2	*	word [AU] word [TI]
Wilson	F 1 AND 2	:	word (AU) word (TI)
SilverPlatter	#1 AND #2	*	word IN TI word IN AU
OCLC	1! AND 2!	*	word:AU word:TI word:AB
UMI	[1] AND [2]	?	TI (word) AU (word)
BRS	1 AND 2	$	word .TI. word .AU.

Note: SHIP and OTHER systems do not have Boolean search capability in the tested version.

Knowing the differences between systems is also important. An examination of the use of Boolean operators, truncation symbols, and the way to limit a search in a certain field failed to find common features that all systems share. When combining two search sets, every family has its own protocol except the position of the Boolean operator in the search string. Families of systems also use their own truncation symbols, although three of the eight families use an asterisk (*). For limiting a search in a certain field, no two systems work the same way. The only thing we can observe from the comparison is that most of the families put the limit parameter after the search word or words (table 20.4).

Use of Function Keys

There is no agreement in using function keys among all the systems studied except for the F1 key, which is dedicated to help (table 20.5). Almost all the systems prefer using the Esc key to back up to the main menu or exit. In most systems, function keys work only in easy mode (menu-driven mode). InfoTrac and NewsBank, the only two systems restricted to search by subject headings, labeled all the F keys with specific functions. If a computer is dedicated to one database only, this approach will be very helpful to novice users because the function of these keys is obvious. InfoTrac and NewsBank are the only two systems that use the F1 key for START/END, and the F2 key for HELP.

Table 20.5
Function Keys Used in CD-ROM Systems

FUNCTION	DIALOG	WILSON	BOWKER	SLV-PLT	UMI	OCLC	SHIP
HELP	F1	F1	F1	F1	F1	F1	F1
START/END	F9	F2		F7	F10	F10	
BACK/ESC	Esc	Esc	Esc	Esc	Esc	Esc	
PRINT	F8	F4/F6	F5	F6	F4	F7	
DOWNLOAD	F8		F4			CTRL+F7	
FORMAT	F4					F9	
DISPLAY	F8		F10	F4		CTRL+F5/F6	
INTRODUCTION				F3		CTRL+F1	
SEARCH/FIND				F2	F3		
INDEX				F5		F2	
SORT	F5						
CHANGE DISK		F3					

Note: All F Keys in InfoTrac and NewsBank are labeled. All Cambridge systems use no F Keys.

DISCUSSION

This formal analysis of the existing CD-ROM systems in the University of Washington libraries is an attempt to find something generic among these systems. The results of the study do show some agreement or consistency, at least within databases from the same family. Regardless of how they are used, Boolean search, nesting, truncations, limiting, and so on are common among these systems. Once users understand how these things work in one system, they can transfer this knowledge when using other systems. The only differences users need to remember are the specific symbols and the positions that are used within a search string in a specific system. A sample sheet with examples of these differences might help some multidatabase users to work with different databases more easily.

The study also reveals what most systems provide to make the databases easy to use and what they lack in this respect. A comparison of table 20.2 and table 20.3 shows that the majority of the systems possess most of the search capabilities in table 20.2, but they fail to provide sufficient help to make the systems easy to use. For example, half of the systems do not have tutorials. All systems lack content-specific help and suggested vocabulary. Most of the systems do not provide sample commands or searches. If we compare all the CD-ROM systems with the online catalog (Geac) used in the University of Washington libraries, we will notice the online catalog, also menu-driven, is much easier to use than any CD-ROM systems in this study. One important factor might be that the online catalog provides explicit explanations and different search examples. These findings, if also true among other systems not tested, could be very helpful to system designers and multidatabase searchers.

What this study cannot answer is the question: Which system is the easiest, or most difficult to use? There are many "it depends." The criteria compared in this study are only some components of the design model and part of the system image. Two questions remain unanswered: How do users think about the system through their interaction with it and what are their mental models of the system—the "user model"? For example, all the data show that ERIC and NTIS have all the search capabilities and almost all the features for easy use. Do they suggest that ERIC and NTIS are the easiest systems to use among all the systems studied? No.

Although it was not the intention of this study, it did in some ways evaluate the CD-ROM systems purchased by the University of Washington library, at least in the aspects discussed above. The results of the study show that most of these systems are usable, although all the criteria selected might not have been used by the library. The fact that SHIP and a few other products failed to meet most of the criteria may be due to the fact that they are the only systems of their kind available on the market at the moment, or different criteria are needed for some of these databases (e.g., numeric databases).

SUGGESTIONS FOR INTERFACE DESIGN

Those of us who are familiar with the interfaces of the current online information retrieval services might have noticed that features of the interface of most CD-ROM systems are similar to those of the online systems. This is understandable since the CD-ROM industry is very young, and many information workers and information customers are familiar with some of the online interfaces. In fact, some CD-ROM database vendors, such as DIALOG and Wilson, are themselves online information providers. But the interfaces of the online services have their limitations due to the limitations of hardware, software, and telecommunications in the development of the online industry. Technically speaking, there is no reason to duplicate the limitations of the current online industry when delivering a large database or groups of databases using CD-ROM on personal computers, especially when the majority of the end users are not previously trained online users.

To avoid duplicating the limitations of the online industry, designers should be creative in designing interfaces for CD-ROM systems. But in order to build a "metastructure" of CD-ROM systems to help users in forming the right user model, designers should also acknowledge the conventions that have already proved helpful in the interfaces of existing systems, such as those common features found in this study. Guidelines and standards for the user-system interface are more than necessary if CD-ROM continues to be one of the major devices for information storage in the future. Otherwise, the system images of CD-ROM systems will lack consistency, and the user will have problems forming the user model of the system. Consequently, the metastructure of CD-ROM systems will never be built.

SUGGESTIONS FOR END-USER TRAINING

It is obvious that there is a need to teach or train users how to operate the systems—not only which key to push and what to consult, but how to formulate or organize searches so that recall (number of related items retrieved vs. the number of related items in the database) and precision (number of related items retrieved vs. the total number of items retrieved) can be improved.

Knowing what the system can do and what help they can provide will enable us to decide what to teach and how to train multisystem users. Users should understand how most databases are organized and why some search strategies are better than others. With the theory of mental models, we can assume that if a user understands how information is organized or how documents are indexed in the database, he knows how to formulate a search and how to adjust a search strategy if a search is not successful. The approach to a system using mental models is a kind of cognitive, or a conceptual approach. Research on online searching shows that the cognitive approach using mental models helps users perform better, and the performance differences suggested that conceptual training is superior to procedural training, given that the user will need to do more than the simplest tasks (Borgman, 1986). A case study of professional online searches also shows that searchers using a conceptual approach perform better than those using a procedural approach (Fidel, 1984).

The discussion above will lead to the next stage of research: a CD-ROM system user study. This research will help us to know how users think about these systems and the exact nature of their problems in using these systems. Are they aware of, or have they taken advantage of, the search capabilities of the systems? Do users find the ease-of-use features helpful to them? Do they have any mental models (user models) when they use the systems? If they do, what are those models and what are their origins (use of traditional library systems, experience with PCs, etc.)? What is there in common among mental models of similar systems? The answers to these questions will help us to design efficient and effective training programs for multisystem users. They can also help designers to design better systems—systems with more search capabilities that are more user-friendly.

APPENDIX

Evaluation Criteria (Short Version)

Part I: Search Capabilities

1. Is response time (accessing time) reasonable?
2. Can the processing be interrupted?
3. Are Boolean operators AND, OR, and NOT or their equivalents available?
4. Can multiword phrases be searched?
5. Are truncation, wild-card, or stem-searching features available?
6. May several operators be used in the same search statement, with the user specifying which operators will be performed first?
7. Can previously created sets of search statements be saved and reused?
8. May previously created sets of search statements be purged?
9. Are field-defined searches possible?
10. Can searches be limited by language and by date of publication?
11. Can all indexed fields be searched at the same time? (global search)
12. Can sets be sorted before display or printing?
13. Can user print more than one record at a time?
14. Can user select specific records for display or printing?
15. Can user customize display/print formats or choose from a variety of formats?
16. Can records be saved to the user's floppy disk for use with file managers or word-processing software?
17. Can searcher transfer the search online for more current information?

Part II: Ease of Use (User-friendliness)

1. Is there an introductory screen that identifies the database and time span covered?
2. Is an on-screen tutorial included?
3. Is the user told where to look for prompts and menus?
4. Is the user shown how to select menu items or respond to prompts?
5. Is the meaning of commands and menu items explained on-screen?
6. Is the user told how to back up through menu screen and exit individual functions?
7. Is the user instructed in exiting the database and leaving the system ready for the next person?
8. Is function-specific online help provided?
9. Is context-specific online help provided?
10. Are useful error messages provided?
11. Are examples of commands displayed?
12. Are examples of logical search operations displayed?
13. Can the index be browsed for selection of search terms?
14. Can users select an item from the index without retyping?
15. Can users select several items from the index without retyping?
16. Does the system provide suggestions on improving searching vocabulary?

17. Is explanation of display options thorough and clear?
18. Is explanation of print options thorough and clear?
19. Does the system offer shortcuts for experienced searchers?
20. Can explanations not available on-screen be summarized on a one-page printed crib sheet?
21. Is the documentation (user's manual) easy to understand?
22. Is the documentation arranged in a logical manner?
23. Is the documentation well indexed?
24. Does the documentation include samples of searches?
25. Does the search language use mnemonics and few keystrokes?
26. Is there efficient use of function keys?

REFERENCES

Befeler, M., and Einberger, J. 1988. "CD-ROM standardization." *Laserdisk Professional* 1(2): 70–72.

Bills, L. G. and Helgerson, L. W. 1987. "User Interfaces for CD-ROM PACs." *Library Hi Tech* 6: 73–115.

Borgman, C. L. 1986. "The user's mental model of an information retrieval system: An experiment on a prototype online catalog." *International Journal of Man-Machine Studies* 24(1): 47–64.

Brunell, D. H. 1988. "Comparing CD-ROM products." *CD-ROM Librarian* 3(3): 14–18.

Carroll, J. M., ed. 1987. *Interfacing thought: Cognitive aspects of human-computer interaction.* Cambridge, Mass.: MIT Press.

Fidel, R. 1984. "Online searching styles: A case-study-based model of searching behavior." *Journal of the American Society for Information Science* 35(4): 211–21.

Graves, G. T., L. G. Harper, and B. F. King. 1987. "Planning for CD-ROM in the reference department." *College and Research Libraries News* 48(7): 393–400.

Hartley, J. 1987. "Designing electronic text: The role of print-based research." *Educational Communication and Technology Journal* 35(1): 3–17.

Herther, N. K. 1988. "How to evaluate reference materials on CD-ROM." *Online* 12(2): 106–8.

Kahn, P. 1987. "Making a difference: A review of the user interface features in six CD-ROM database products." *Optical Information Systems* 8(4): 169–83.

Kerr, S. T. 1987. "Finding one's way in electronic space: The relative importance of navigational cues and mental models." Paper presented at the Annual Convention of the Association for Educational Communications and Technology, Atlanta, Ga., February 26-March 1.

Kittle, P. 1988. "Medline on CD-ROM: A review of six products." *Laserdisk Professional* 1(3): 18–28.

Newhard, R. A. 1987. "Shopper's guide to CD-ROM." *Public Libraries* 26(4): 149–50.

Nicholls, P. T. 1988. "Statistical profile of currently available CD-ROM database products." *Laserdisk Professional* 1(4): 38–45.

Norman, D. A. 1986. "Cognitive engineering." In *User centered system design*, ed. Donald A. Norman and S. W. Draper, 31–61. Hillsdale, N.J.: Lawrence Erlbaum Associates.

———. 1987. "Cognitive engineering—cognitive science." In *Interfacing Thought*, ed. John M. Carrol, 325–36. Cambridge, Mass.: MIT Press.

"Optical products review guidelines." 1987. *Optical Information Systems Update* 12(3): 16–18.

Peters, C. 1987. "Databases on CD-ROM: Comparative factors for purchase." *Electronic Library* 5(3): 154–60.

Reese, J. and Steffey, R. 1988. "The seven deadly sins of CD-ROM." *Laserdisk Professional* 1(2): 19–24.

Rouse, W. B. and Morris, N. M. 1985. "On looking into the black box: Prospects and limits in the search for mental models." Technical Report no. GIT-TR–85–2 (NTIS no. AD-A159 080/1/HDO). Atlanta: Georgia Institute of Technology.

Stewart, L. 1987. "Picking CD-ROMs for public use." *American Libraries* 18(9): 738–40.

Tweney, R. D. 1987. "What is scientific thinking?" Paper presented at the Annual Meeting of the American Educational Research Association, Washington, D.C., April 23–25.

21

The User Interface for CD-ROM Systems and Online Catalogs

Steven D. Atkinson, Judith Hudson, and Geraldene Walker

The most important goal for online public access catalogs (OPACS) and for database provided on CD-ROM is the facilitation of independent end-user access. In developing these systems, some vendors have begun to design database interfaces intended to simplify access to bibliographic information for users with minimal training. Others have merely transferred their databases available from information utilities to CD formats, utilizing similar software features. This chapter uses a matrix format to compare the interfaces of selected CD-ROM and OPAC systems, in an attempt to identify those features that are most helpful for users. Such an analysis will help to identify features that can contribute to the development of an improved user interface for the next generation of search systems.

INTRODUCTION

The increasing recognition of information as a vital national resource in recent years has been mirrored by the rapid evolution of the online industry itself. This development is reflected not only in the number of online systems and databases available and the number of searches being performed, but also in the variety of formats in which the same information is now available. We have seen a move from the original online bibliographic search service, which required considerable expertise for effective use by trained professionals, to simplified access for direct searching by untrained end-users. In addition, the online industry has broadened its offerings to encompass a range of access formats, from direct online connection to interface access (such as BRS After Dark or Knowledge Index), gateway front ends (such as EasyNet or Western Union's InfoMaster), and inhouse databases on CD-ROM. Each of these moves represents an attempt to expand the market for online information services.

While use of these systems has not increased as quickly as expected, many new users have been exposed to the basic features of online searching through the spread of online public access catalogs in libraries. Many of these OPACs incorporate features such as Boolean operators, truncation, menus, function keys, and online help messages, so that user sophistication is gradually increasing. At the same time, developments by the online vendors have been largely technology-driven, changing from their early concentration on maximizing the number of databases and increasing processing capacity to the introduction of simplified systems and their marketing to a wider spectrum of potential users. The eventual goals of these developments are independent user workstations with access to a range of different information resources, built-in assistance available through expert system interfaces, and some means for integrating new information into personal files using hypertext.

The method would be similar to the "Memex" suggested by Vannevar Bush over forty years ago (Bush, 1945). Despite these developments, a considerable gulf still exists between such possibilities and currently available systems. Many of the CD-ROM systems merely replicate the traditional online search systems, using protocols initially developed for expert intermediaries, but eliminating the telecommunication and online connect charges. The technology continues to evolve, and considerable information is available regarding effective search techniques. The design of a new user interface that will contribute most effectively to the system interactions of untrained users is a critical requirement. Information regarding the online search behavior of these users is gradually becoming available as more direct access systems are implemented. This information can indicate features that have proved most useful for incorporation into the user-system interface. This chapter reports an analysis of desirable system features in light of information regarding the search behavior of different types of users.

SEARCH BEHAVIOR

Although a number of empirical studies have suggested that end users are indeed able to perform simple searches using the newer search systems (Janke, 1983; Trzebiatowski, 1984) and are happy with their results, research indicates that their search effectiveness is poor in terms of time per relevant citation retrieved (Penhale and Taylor, 1986; Walker, 1988a). Their search behavior has been shown to be disorganized and unsophisticated, and they are easily distracted and discouraged. They make little use of documentation, Boolean logic, or advanced system features (Janke, 1984; Sewell and Teitelbaum, 1986), they generally use more search terms, and they are slower and less efficient than intermediaries (Hawkins and Levy, 1987). They commit more errors and often find it very difficult to identify and correct them. Their major area of difficulty appears to be the selection of effective search terminology and the appropriate combination of terms in a logical strategy (Walker, 1988b).

Information professionals who provide assistance for end users at the online catalog or at CD-ROM workstations are aware of the kinds of "moves" or "tactics" that they use to prompt the naive searcher. They range from the

Table 21.1
Types of Searchers

	Level of Subject Knowledge	
Level of IR Knowledge	High	Low
High	Elite	Intermediary
Low	End-user	Layman

definition and clarification of the topic to how to print and download relevant information identified in the search process. Other types of assistance may include term selection and Boolean combinations, assistance with displays, and reformulation of strategy based on relevance feedback. It may also be necessary to suggest limits of language, publication format, or time frame. The type of assistance required is related to end users' level of subject expertise and their knowledge of IR techniques and system features.

The design of CD-ROM and OPAC interfaces needs to reflect the knowledge structure of the user with regard to these two aspects—subject knowledge and techniques of information retrieval. Using this framework, Ingwersen (1984) has identified four types of searchers (see table 21.1).

Many of the search techniques and heuristics that contribute to the expertise of the trained information retrieval (IR) professional have been identified by Bates and others (Bates, 1987; Bates, 1979a; Bates, 1979b; Bates, 1981; Harter and Peters, 1985; Vigil, 1983), while Fidel has formalized a number of effective strategies using a decision tree (Fidel, 1986). A good *elite* and *intermediary* searcher develops these techniques based on logical and intuitive skills that stem from years of experience and professional training. It is unrealistic to expect untrained searchers, who use a system on an occasional basis, to be aware of more than a minimal subset of these techniques. In order to maximize end-user performance, elite searcher skills and techniques should be incorporated into the interface itself. The problem is to enable users to move from natural-language descriptions of their information needs to effective search formulations without knowing much about search strategy development. What should be added to Bates's ''tactics'' are artificial rubrics that the system could apply transparently to the initial search input and modification strategies based on user feedback elicited by the system as the search progresses. Such an ''expert'' interface would ideally perform like a good friend—transparent, but always there when needed.

Belkin and Croft (1987) have suggested that a variety of additional system features such as partial matching, document ranking, relevance feedback, automatic thesaural relationships to expand queries, clustering, and natural-language processing would also contribute to the enhancement of user performance. They conclude that ''multiple retrieval techniques'' will be needed to facilitate optimal performance. Hawkins (1988) has pointed out that online search processes fall into two broad categories: mechanical operations and intellectual operations. Although progress has been made in automating many of the mechanical aspects of searching (Fenichel, 1981), an analysis of some operating systems will help to identify features that contribute to ease of use. The more difficult aspects of assisting with vocabulary selection and the development of an effective search strategy are still in the development stages. This investigation concentrates on the effectiveness of system features currently available.

FEATURE ANALYSIS

Selected OPACs and CD-ROM systems have been analyzed to isolate the interface characteristics that appear most likely to simplify the search process for end-users. A number of writers have investigated some of the visual aspects of the user-system interface—the use of color (Christie, 1985) or the layout or density of text (Crawford, 1987), for example. This study is concerned not with visual aspects but with the way in which the user-system interaction is organized—the presentation of information, the content of individual messages, the linking information that is required at different stages of the search process, as well as the search protocols. An attempt is made to identify optimal features currently available on the systems and to relate them to knowledge of end-user information-seeking behavior and to the search techniques utilized by expert search intermediaries.

OPACs and CD-ROM systems for searching bibliographic databases have two important characteristics in common. First, both types of databases contain bibliographic information. OPAC databases are made up of cataloging records, which are usually in the Library of Congress MARC (Machine-Readable Cataloging) format; CD-ROM systems usually contain bibliographic citations for journal articles, books, and, occasionally, other library materials. Second, the audience for both OPACs and CD-ROM systems is the end user.

On the other hand, OPACs and CD-ROM systems differ. While OPACs provide information about the books, serials, and other library materials owned by the library, they rarely analyze the contents of the materials. CD-ROM systems normally provide bibliographic information about the contents of individual periodical articles and other types of material, such as specialized reports, which are not catalogued individually by most libraries. In addition, the CD-ROM systems often provide abstracts and, in some cases, full text of the articles or documents listed. Since OPACs are usually made up of cataloging records for the materials owned by the library, the circulation status of any given item is often included in the record. CD-ROM systems (including OPACs) in this format are unlikely to provide information about the location and/or availability of the materials listed. The two types of systems also differ in the currency of their listings. Online catalogs tend to be more current than CD-ROM systems, since records can be added to their databases in-house, while CD-ROM systems must be updated by producing new compact discs incorporating the latest records.

In spite of these differences, the goal of OPACs and CD-ROM systems is the same: to allow a user who is unfamiliar with the system to use it successfully with little help or assistance. As a result, the requirements for user interface features of both are similar.

In investigating the features of the user interface on OPACs and CD-ROM systems, three public access catalogs were examined—one developed by Geac and implemented at the State University of New York at Albany, one developed and installed at the New York State Library, and a CD-ROM public access catalog developed by Marchive and installed at the Gelman Library of the George Washington University. In addition, five varied CD-ROM systems—ERIC and PsycLit as presented by Silver Platter, Auto-Graphics' Government Documents Catalog Service, OCLC's Search CD450 systems, the Wilsondisc system, and Grolier's American Academic Encyclopedia were also examined.

Tables are presented that compare various aspects of the user interface on the systems examined: Tutorials and Help Features (table 21.2), Modes of Operation (table 21.3), Searching Protocols (table 21.4), and Display and Output of Results (table 21.5).

HELP SCREENS AND TUTORIALS

Tutorials, which take the user through the procedures required to operate the system, are a desirable feature, although they may not be necessary if the system is a simple one. They should give the basics of operation, but not in too much detail, and users should be referred to the system manual for more sophisticated features. Only one of the systems examined, that produced by Silver Platter, has such a tutorial, which is very thorough but takes about 20 minutes to complete. Fortunately, the introductory screen includes a directory of "help" screens, which allow the user who wishes to do a quick search to get started without completing the tutorial.

All of the systems examined supply help screens, though some of them only provide definitions of the functions they illustrate, failing to inform the user about the procedures that must be followed in order to make the functions work. This obvious disadvantage could be minimized by directing the user to the appropriate section of the guide. None of the systems investigated here provided this type of help.

At times, help screens may give confusing or misleading information. For example, OCLC has a standard set of help screens that send the user to the library's card catalog to determine whether an item is available at the library. Such a direction is inappropriate when searching ERIC, since most libraries do not catalog ERIC documents. Another example of confusing help screens is found in Wilsearch, where the screens describing the search template include "Earliest Date" and "Latest Date," two fields that do not appear on the template.

Table 21.2
Tutorials and Help Features

System	Tutorial	"Get Started" Screens	Help Screens	On-Screen Command Line
Geac	None	Gives basic information	Gives definitional and procedural information	At bottom of screen
Marchive	None	Gives brief introductory information and menu	Gives definitional and procedural information	At bottom of screen
NYSL	None	Gives basic information	Yes, only basic mode	At top of screen
Silver Platter	Yes, takes 20+ mins.	Lists Help screen	Gives so many that finding the ones needed may be a problem	Bottom two lines of screen
Auto-Graphics	None	Yes	Yes	Display of relevant function keys at side of screen
OCLC Search CD450	None	Gives brief information	Some screens are misleading	At bottom of query window and at bottom of screen
Wilsondisc	None	Only a menu listing available modes	In Wilsearch, useful; in Wilsonline, HELP and EXPLAIN give assistance	At bottom of screen
Grolier	None	Rudimentary	Tend to define rather than give instructions	Windows at top of screen come down to list commands

Another help function, which all of these systems supply, is an on-screen list of commands that are operable at any specific time. The list of possible "next moves" changes as the user moves through the various stages of a search. For example, the Auto-Graphics Government Documents Catalog Service has an on-screen display of function keys. Those that are operable at a particular point in a search are labeled, while those that are not operable at that point are omitted. Grolier also has a series of windows with options appearing at different stages of the search.

It appears that most systems of both types fail to offer anything more than very basic start-up features. Perhaps such help can be expected to be covered by bibliographic instruction programs for the OPAC systems, but the growing variety of CD-ROM software makes it necessary for most libraries to provide full-time staff to assist in the initial process of getting started. It is also clear that in most cases online help is not as useful as it could be. Providing too much information before it is needed is overwhelming. The ideal is to provide search assistance in an instructional mode rather than a definitional mode, and make it specific to the current stage of the search.

MODES OF OPERATION

Mode of operation refers to the way in which the user interacts with the system, using either a menu or command mode and the ability to use function keys to abbreviate in selection of either mode. Geac, Marchive, Auto-Graphics, and Grolier offer only the menu mode, while Silver Platter and OCLC offer only the command mode. Although Geac offers only the menu mode, it is possible to combine commands by stacking or chaining, which allows the experienced user to shorten the search process. For example, the command CAT/TIL/CAN-NERY ROW/FUL combines four commands: (1) initiate a search, (2) search the title index, (3) search the string "Cannery Row," and (4) display the record in the full format.

Two of the systems examined, Wilsondisc and NYSL, offer both the menu and command mode. In fact, Wilsondisc offers three modes of search: a browse mode, which allows the user to search and retrieve words from a dictionary index; a menu-driven search (Wilsearch), which provides a template into which the user enters the desired search string; and a command driven search (Wilsonline), which requires that the user know the command language of the system. The command mode in NYSL is limited to searches on subject and title words and subject numbers. Rather than indexing subject headings as phrases, NYSL assigns a unique number to each subject heading and indexes the number. This is somewhat clumsy, because the user must consult a printed list to identify the appropriate number for the desired subject heading.

It seems clear that function keys are the most efficient means for interacting with a system. They should, ideally, be linked to menu-type help screens in order to prompt the novice searcher and eliminate the need for the duplication of access modes.

SEARCH PROTOCOLS

The searching protocols of a system determine how it can be searched. All but one of the systems allow for searching by word or phrase. The exception is the NYSL online catalog, which, in its basic searching mode, requires the use of search keys, similar to those used by OCLC for searching authors and titles. All OPACs limit their searching to author, title, subject headings, and, usually, keywords and call number fields. Most of the CD-ROM systems allow for searching in many more fields of the record. Geac allows for browsing of all the indexes, while Marchive allows for browsing only in the call number index.

Table 21.3
Modes of Operation

System	Menu Mode	Command Mode
Geac	Yes	No, but command stacking allows experienced user to search more efficiently
Marchive	Yes	No
NYSL	F1 key puts user into basic search mode; uses OCLC-type search keys for author, title, and author/title searches; F3 key puts user into basic search mode with template for subject/title word search	F2 key puts user into advanced mode, but can only search subject and title words and subject numbers
Silver Platter	No	Function keys used for many commands
Auto-Graphics	Yes	No
OCLC Search CD450	No	Function keys used for many commands
Wilsondisc	Wilsearch and Browse mode provide templates for user to complete	Wilsonline and Expert Wilsonline have command searching only
Grolier	Yes, template is supplied for user to complete	No

Three CD-ROM systems, Silver Platter, OCLC, and Wilsondisc, allow for browsing of a dictionary index. Auto-Graphics allows for browsing of all indexes, while Grolier restricts browsing to two indexes: keyword and title word.

Features that assist the user in limiting a search help to improve specificity. The most common features are the use of the Boolean AND and NOT operators, which link search terms in such a way that they either must (in the case of the AND) or must not (in the case of the NOT) appear together in the specified field or document. Other useful limit features are year of publication, language of publication, and publication format. The use of such qualifiers specifies that the results of a search must meet the qualification and also contain the subject term or terms searched. Proximity features require that search terms must be found in the text near each other: adjacent to one another, within a specified number of words of each other, or in the same field or paragraph of the record. Other limit features include the ability to limit a search to specified fields and the ability to limit retrieval to records that have not been previously retrieved in a given session. The CD-ROM systems tend to have more of these limit features than the OPACs.

All of the systems have some sort of Boolean capacity, although that of Geac is very cumbersome and slows response time tremendously. As a result, many libraries have chosen not to implement this feature. Marchive and Wilsearch automatically AND words in a phrase together. Automatic combination creates a problem when the words are common ones, but many records are retrieved. In such cases, the ability to specify adjacency and to indicate only single-word titles are desired and important adjunct search features.

Common broadening features include the Boolean OR operator and the ability to truncate at the end of a word. The NYSL online catalog and Wilsondisc also allow for the use of a "wild card" character that, when used within a word, retrieves all words that match the search term regardless of what letter is in the position of the wild-card character. Embedded truncation allows the user to retrieve names when the exact spelling is unknown: for example, the search term "Anders#n" would retrieve both Andersen and Anderson. It is particularly useful to cover differences between British and American spellings.

Silver Platter provides an interesting feature called "lateral searching," which allows the user to search words found in a record by highlighting the desired word through a function key command. Linking avoids the necessity of having to rekey search terms discovered in reviewing documents and thus provides for more efficient searching. It also enables the integration of broader, narrower, or synonymous terms into the search strategy, but it does require an understanding of Boolean logic. New documents added by this strategy can be isolated by using NOT to eliminate sets previously reviewed. Grolier has a similar capability, which allows the user to move between related articles and save selections to a notepad for future reference.

The search features available on any system are the most important means for assisting search efficiency and effectiveness, and search fields are most easily

Table 21.4
Searching Protocols

System	Mode	Index Browsing	Limiting Features	Broadening Features
Geac	Word or phrase; 3 keyword indexes: author, title, subject	Can browse all indexes	Bolean AND and NOT, but slow and clumsy; adjacency	Boolean OR, but slow and clumsy, automatic right truncation
Marchive	Words; all words in a phrase are automatically ANDed; free-text searching in author, title, subject, and number searches	Can browse call number index only	Boolean AND and NOT	Boolean OR, right truncations
NYSL	Basic mode uses OCLC-style search keys for author, title, and author/title search; title word or subject number in subject search; advanced search allows search by word or phrase	None	In advanced mode only; Boolean AND and NOT; adjacency	Boolean OR in advanced mode; right truncation in both modes; wild-card character for one letter within a word in advanced mode

Silver Platter	Word or phrases; free-text searching in all but limit fields	Can browse dictionary index of words from all but limit fields; can highlight terms from index; system ORs them together	Boolean AND and NOT; adjacency	Boolean OR; right truncation; "lateral" searching allows users to link to dictionary index
Auto-Graphics	Word or phrase; SUDOCS or report number	Can browse all indexes	None	None
OCLC Search CD450	Word or phrase; hyphenated phrases search only descriptor indexes; for unhyphenated phrases, adjacency is assumed; free-text searching in other fields	Can browse dictionary files of terms from all indexes	Boolean AND and NOT; field limiting; adjacency	Boolean OR; right truncation
Wilcondisc	Browse search for word only; other modes include word or phrases	Can browse dictionary index, but online linked to records in browse mode	Boolean AND and NOT (in Wilsearch, the AND is automatic); field limiting	Boolean OR; right truncation; wild-card character for one letter within a word
Grolier	Word or phrases; free-text searching in all fields	Can browse word and title word in indexes	Boolean AND and NOT; field limiting	Boolean OR; right truncation; LINK command to related articles

accessed using function keys. The browse feature provides limited assistance with search term selection, while Boolean and proximity operators enable the searcher to focus or broaden the search strategy based on feedback regarding the number of postings or sample of documents retrieved. It is clear that the flexibility in search strategy development needs to be transparent. The ability to link to related terms via an online authority file is particularly useful for the novice searcher. This is a feature available on online bibliographic search systems (DIALOG EXPAND command, for example). It is worth pointing out that it should have made the transfer to CD-ROM. In addition, many of today's OPAC systems do not include access to the *see* reference structure.

DISPLAY AND OUTPUT OF RESULTS

Most systems allow the user options regarding the format in which search results will be displayed, since all the information found in a full record is not necessarily required. The ability to shorten the record for display purposes allows for more efficient review of search results and saves time and paper when printing. All but two of the systems examined provide a number of different formats for display. Silver Platter, Grolier, and NYSL's advanced mode allow the user to select which fields are to be displayed, while the other systems have a choice of two or three predefined formats.

In databases that use controlled vocabularies (such as the Library of Congress Subject Headings or the ERIC Thesaurus), the ability to display cross-references, which lead the user to preferred or related terms (*see* and *see also* references), is of particular assistance to searchers. Only half of the systems examined display cross-references. In the case of Geac, users are automatically shifted to the preferred form of a term when the authorized form is entered. A comment at the top of the screen indicates that the retrieved record was retrieved using a preferred term, rather than the term the requester keyed. Other systems display the preferred terms, but the user is expected to key the preferred form in a new search to retrieve records.

All of the systems allow for the printing of research results, and two of them also permit downloading to disk. The procedures that must be followed to save and print or download, however, are not always obvious. They should be explained by online help screens, which are frequently not as helpful as they might be.

EVALUATION OF FEATURES

On the basis of the analysis of these eight systems, it is clear that basic features can be implemented in a variety of different ways. A study of this kind can help to identify techniques to be incorporated into transparent systems for end-user searching in the future. The following are believed to be optimal features identified from these ''user-friendly'' systems:

Table 21.5
Display and Output of Results

System	Choice of Formats	Display Cross-References	Sorting, Saving, & Downloading
Geac	Brief, full, or MARC format; print output is screen dump which takes up a lot of room	Yes; shifts user to established heading when "see" form is entered; "see also" references are displayed	Can save records and print or download to disk; Help screens give instructions
Marchive	Displays in a labeled format; gives catalog card information; prints only in citation form	Yes, but user must renter correct form	Can mark records for bibliography; stores only 25 titles at once; online instructions available for this procedure
NYSL	Labeled catalog card format only; 14 displayable fields in advanced mode; no online instructions for printing	Not available	Not available
Silver Platter	Several formats; user can select fields for display and printing	Not available	Can save records and search strategy; Help screens give instructions for saving and downloading
Auto-Graphics	Labeled catalog card format only	Displays cross-references for names and subjects	Not available
OCLC Search CD450	Brief, full, and labeled record	Not available	Can save records or search strategy; sort by sending to specific save field; print or download to disk
Wilsondisc	One format only in Browse and Wilsearch; 3 defaults (S, M, L) or user can select in Wilsonline	Displays cross-references for subjects; in Wilsonline, EXPAND displays related subject headings	Can save and download records and search strategy
Grolier	User can select	Not available	Can mark, save, and download all or parts of records; if saved to notepad, cannot be downloaded

Table 21.6
Evaluation of Features

System	Desireable Features	Undesireable Features
Geac	Basic functions easy; "see also" references displayed; user automatically switched to established form of heading when "see" form is entered; provides circulation status; Help screens clear and easy to understand	Boolean operation is unusable; keyword search is often a problem without Boolean search; no limit features; cannot search notes field; screen dump of records takes up a lot of room, wastes paper, and slows printing process
Marchive	Boolean operation fast and easy; producing bibliographies easy; planned qualifiers will assist in limiting searches	Some Help screens tend to define procedure rather than give instructions; automatic ANDing in searches causes problems when retrieving titles with common words; lacks currency; no circulation status
NYSL	Subject/title word search is easy to use; Help screens in basic mode are clear; advanced mode, though limited to subject headings and title words, is flexible and not too confusing	In basic mode must use search keys for authors and titles; to search subjects, must use assigned numbers; no online Help for advanced mode; cannot qualify searches by language or format; lacks circulation status; no search by call number; cannot browse indexes
Silver Platter	Lateral searching; tutorial is informative but time consuming; provides dictionary index	System offers many options but is complex to use

Auto-Graphics	Screen display of operable function keys; system easy to use but not flexible; displays cross-references for names and subjects	Browse mode linked directly to records without title browse to assist selection; no truncation; cannot broaden or narrow searches except by using Boolean operators on keywords
OCLC Search CD450	In history window user can highlight a previous search and combine it with a new search; when in index, can move desired term and search it by pressing Tab key; selection of display format by menu; window design of screen easy to read, doesn't obstruct record on display	Some Help screens give misinformation; sorting capability is rudimentary
Wilsondisc	"See" and "see also" references are displayed; offers different levels of sophistication; Browse mode eay to use; Wilsearch template easy to use; Wilsonline NBR search allows user to look at terms alphabetically near the term entered	In Wilsearch, use of "any" instead of OR is unique and confusing; EXPAND command is complicated
Grolier	Search words highlighted in text; can stack and save related concepts; windows at top of screen for various functions effective; can "bookmark" articles to review later in search session	LINK concept is confusing; information saved to Notepad cannot be downloaded to disk; printing is cumbersome

- help screens that give procedural as well as definitional information (Marchive) and are specific to current search status (Grolier);
- tutorials for complex systems (Silver Platter);
- both menu and command modes; use of templates in most basic mode (Wilsondisc, Grolier);
- command selection by function keys (Auto-Graphics, Marchive);
- linking to related subjects or documents (Grolier, Silver Platter);
- display of *see also* cross-references (Geac, Marchive, Auto-Graphics, Wilsondisc);
- automatic shift to preferred term when *see* reference is input (Geac);
- choice of display fields for browsing or printing (Silver Platter, Wilsondisc, OCLC); and
- ability to download to disk (Wilsondisc, Silver Platter, OCLC, Grolier, Marchive).

Although these features are only a minimal subset of the desirable features that need to be available for a truly user-friendly system, none of the systems surveyed incorporated all of them. An individual evaluation of the eight systems follows (table 21.6)

THE FRIENDLY INTERFACE

The term *user-friendly* does not refer to objective characteristics that can be systematically identified and operationalized (Wallace, 1985), but it should at least mean that a naive user can use the system without a great deal of prior training and instruction. The goal for the ideal front-end interface is to make the system transparent so that users can see through ''the complexity of the sequence and retrieval activities'' (Williams, 1986). Most current systems attempt to achieve these ends through the use of menus. It is possible to use menus to guide the user through the construction of complex Boolean statements, though the transparent building of concept blocks (as provided by Wilsearch) is probably less confusing.

The most ''friendly'' features can be identified as the use of

- natural language input, with suggestions for the selection of related terminology;
- consistency in ways of moving backwards and forwards by offering a list of options activated by function keys; and
- error messages, which are relevant to the current situation and nonaccusatory and forward moving (Brenner, 1980).

Stibic (1980) provides the following summary of the requirements of the novice user:

A system that is simple, transparent, explicit and of maximum help. He is not willing to learn and remember complicated rules, he will not use many commands, codes, tips or parameters, but also dislikes being helped, corrected and reprimanded by the system again and again. He prefers conversation in natural language, clear advice as to what to do at every step, explicit messages without unknown terms, abbreviations or codes, and a direct path from the beginning to the end without too many crossings and decision points. He often appreciates it if his decisions are limited to plain YES/NO answers. He prefers a standard, though less efficient routine.

Menus that provide too many options or that have complicated hierarchies are too difficult to understand. Each one should be limited to between four to eight options, and submenus should not be more than three or four levels deep (Shneiderman, 1987). These interface requirements suggest that any system that is "friendly" will need to be relatively simple, and they are a far cry from the preferences of experienced users, who favor the speed of complex, stackable commands. This approach to the design of a naive user system is based on adapting the standard intermediary search strategies (building blocks, pearl growing, etc.), developing multilevel menus, and combining expert system techniques in order to maximize user performance. Basic requirements include the ability to

- move upward hierarchically to a broader term(s),
- move downward hierarchically to a more specific term(s), and
- move sideways hierarchically to a coordinate term(s).

A variety of these search tactics could be incorporated into the design of the interface through the use of prompts. Bates (1979a, 1979b, 1981, 1987) has suggested a series of tactics to help address the problems of set size, which could be implemented as subroutines to assist in broadening or narrowing the search in a transparent fashion.

FUTURE SYSTEM ENHANCEMENTS

It is widely believed among the advocates of computer systems that more people would use them if they were easier to use. This assumption ignores the fact that most users do not want to expend large amounts of effort to do things with a machine that they believe they are doing effectively by manual methods. The current technology expects the users to adapt their behavior to the requirements of the machine, and also to change their information-seeking style to that adopted by a professional searcher. "Scholars employ less [sic] structured methods, such as browsing, consulting with colleagues, or taking footnotes and bibliographies" (Stoan, 1984). Research, however, is believed to be a process of discovery and reconceptualization, which is largely intuitive and cyclical.

It should be possible for online technology to be used for just this type of exploratory, serendipitous research, if the searcher were able to take full advantage of the interactive features of the system. It would seem that in the future, systems designed for end users will eventually need to do more than formalize the structure of a search by suggesting appropriate term combinations for the construction of a strategy after the style of the intermediary's building blocks. Menus may in fact not be as effective an approach as the use of a mouse-activated, "object-oriented" command interface. This type of interface is not only faster, but can accommodate greater levels of complexity in a way that is easier for the user to understand. Such a high-level system interface is coming nearer to reality with the development of the new hypertext systems on the Apple Macintosh and the incorporation of graphic images into the software for some CD-ROM and online search systems.

Librarians and information professionals have traditionally made the "links" between end users and the multiple types of information sources needed to satisfy their information needs—a function we call "hyperwork." In the future, full-text hypermedia library packages containing materials in a variety of publication types, which are already available in separate bibliographic files, will be linked by pointers to related materials in other files. Ideally, links to other full-text hypermedia libraries would simplify interdisciplinary research and assist under selection of materials in an idiosyncratic fashion tailored to individual information needs and reminiscent of manual, serendipitous browsing.

CONCLUSIONS

All of the current systems discussed here permit naive users to perform relatively simple searches, which may well be satisfactory for limited purposes, but none of them provides all of the optimal features that would allow them to take full advantage of online access. They give no answer to a query such as, "I have found 3,000 postings, what do I do now?" To provide such an answer would require the incorporation of artificial intelligence (AI) techniques into the search software. AI implies the design of a system that exhibits characteristics normally associated with intelligence in human behavior, such as the abilities to understand natural language, to perform reasoning on facts and heuristics, and to solve problems. Such an "expert system" for bibliographic searching would not require the user to know about controlled vocabulary, understand Boolean logic, or make decisions on the basis of error messages. In fact, it would mimic the expertise of the human intermediary in almost every respect. It would be able to translate natural language requests into a properly constructed search strategy using an online thesaurus and assist with the modification of that strategy based on relevance decisions after some retrieved citations or documents had been inspected. The major limitation at present is the representation of intermediary knowledge, since much of it appears to be based on experience and "rules of thumb" (Walker and Janes, 1984). Experimental systems have been developed in limited subject fields (Pollitt, 1987), and more generalized systems are in the developmental stages (Vickery and Brooks, 1987), but it seems unlikely that they will be able to automate more than a fraction of the skills and capabilities of the trained online intermediary within the foreseeable future (Paice, 1986).

The technology is available today for friendlier systems, but a truly "expert" search system is much farther away. The kinds of technological developments suggested here will require a whole new range of social, cultural, and economic infrastructures, as well as more sophisticated computer-based retrieval systems. Such a design is no longer adaptation—it is a brave new world of information access.

REFERENCES

Bates, Marcia. 1979a. "Idea Tactics." *Journal of the American Society for Information Science* 30 (September): 280–89.

———. 1979b. "Information Search Tactics." *Journal of the American Society for Information Science* 30 (July): 205–14.

———. 1981. "Search Techniques." In *Annual Review of Information Science and Technology*, 139–69. White Plains, N.Y.: Knowledge Industry.

———. 1987. "How to Use Information Search Tactics Online." *Online* 11 (May): 47–54.

Belkin, Nicholas J. and Croft, W. Bruce. 1987. "Retrieval Techniques." In *Annual Review of Information and Science Technology*, 109–45. Amsterdam: Elsevier.

Brenner, Lisa P., Huston-Miyamoto, M., Self, David A., Self, Phylis C., and Smith, Linda C. 1980. "User-Computer Interface Designs for Information Systems: A Review." *Library Research* 2 (Spring): 63–73.

Bush, V. 1945. "As We May Think." *Atlantic Monthly* 176 (July): 101–8.

Christie, Bruce. 1985. *Human Factors of the User-System Interface: A Report on an ESTRIT Preparatory Study*. Amsterdam: North-Holland.

Crawford, Walt. 1987. "Testing Bibliographic Displays for Online Catalogs." *Information Technology and Libraries* 6 (March): 20–33.

Fenichel, Carol H. 1981. "Online Searching: Measures Which Discriminate Among Users with Different Types of Experiences." *Journal of the American Society for Information Science* 32 (January): 23–32.

Fidel, Raya. 1986. "Towards Expert Systems for the Selection of Search Keys." *Journal of the American Society of Information Science* 37 (January): 37–44.

Harter, Stephen P. and Peters, Anne Rogers. 1985. "Heuristics for Online Information Retrieval: A Typology and Preliminary Listing." *Online Review* 9 (October): 407–24.

Hawkins, Donald T. 1988. "Applications of Artificial Intelligence (AI) and Expert Systems for Online Searching." *Online* 12 (January): 31–43.

Hawkins, Donald T. and Levy, Louise R. 1987. "A Year's Experience with End-user Searching." In *Eighth National Online Meeting Proceedings*, 155–59. Medford, N.J.: Learned Information.

Ingwersen, Peter. 1984. "A Cognitive View of Three Selected Online Search Facilities." *Online Review* 8 (October): 465–92.

Janke, Richard V. 1983. "BRS/After Dark: The Birth of Online Self-Service." *Online* 7 (September): 12–29.

————. 1984. "Online After Six: End-User Searching Comes of Age." *Online* 8 (November): 15–29.

Paice, Chris. 1986. "Expert Systems for Information Retrieval?" *ASLIB Proceedings* 38 (October): 343–53.

Penhale, Sara J. and Taylor, Nancy. 1986. "Integrating End-User Searching into a Bibliographic Instruction Program." *RQ* 26 (Winter): 212–20.

Pollitt, Steven. 1987. "CANSEARCH: An Expert Systems Approach to Document Retrieval." *Information Processing and Management* 23: 119–38.

Sewell, Winifred and Teitelbaum, Sandra. 1986. "Observations on End-user Online Searching Behavior over Eleven Years." *Journal of the American Society for Information Science* 37 (July): 234–45.

Shneiderman, Ben. 1987. *Designing the User Interface: Strategies for Effective Human-Computer Interaction*. Reading, Mass.: Addison-Wesley.

Stibic, V. 1980. "A Few Practical Remarks on the User-Friendliness of Online Systems." *Journal of Information Science* 45 (December): 277–83.

Stoan, Stephen K. 1984. "Research and Library Skills: An Analysis and Interpretation." *College & Research Libraries* 45 (March): 99–109.

Trzebiatowski, Elaine. 1984. "End User Study on BRS/After Dark." *RQ* 23 (Summer): 446–50.

Vickery, Alina and Brooks, Helen. 1987. "Expert Systems and Their Application in LIS." *Online Review* 11 (June): 149–65.

Vigil, Peter. 1983. "The Psychology of Online Searching." *Journal of the American Society for Information Science* 34 (July): 281–87.

Walker, Geraldene 1988a. *A Comparative Evaluation and Analysis of End-user Search Performance in an Academic Environment*. Ph.D. diss., Syracuse University.

————. 1988b. "The Search Performance of End-Users." In *Ninth National Online Meeting Proceedings*, 403–10. Medford, N.J.: Learned Information.

Walker, Geraldene, and Janes, Joseph W. 1984. "Expert Systems as Search Intermediaries." In *Proceedings of the 47th ASIS Annual Meeting*, 103–5. White Plains, N.Y.: Knowledge Industry.

Wallace, Danny. 1985. "A Preliminary Examination of the Meaning of User Friendliness." In *Proceedings of the 48th ASIS Annual Meeting*, 337–41. White Plains, N.Y.: Knowledge Industry.

Williams, Martha E. 1986. "Transparent Information Systems through Gateways, Front Ends, Intermediaries and Interfaces." *Journal of the American Society for Information Science* 37 (July): 204–14.

PART VI

TRENDS IN TECHNOLOGICAL STANDARDS

M.E.L. Jacob

User interfaces are affected by standards and the standard development process. Standards affect and are affected by trends influencing all information service provision. To understand the relationship of standards development to user interfaces, it may be helpful to look first at some of the trends affecting all standards development activities and then to look more specifically at the activities of the National Information Standards Organization (NISO) Z39. Among the significant trends affecting standards are technology, intellectual property rights, integration of services, media, functions, globalization, European unification, and electronic information services.

From a user's perspective, standard interfaces make it easier to move from one system to another, and for systems designers it can significantly narrow the choices. The latter is both a blessing and a curse. While ideally standards should be designed that are independent of a particular implementation or technology, that seldom happens. New technology can make new functions and new applications practical. Old methods forced into a new technological base can be cumbersome and restrictive. The trick in standards development is to determine when enough experimentation has occurred to make standardization practical versus standardizing too soon and stifling potential innovation.

Most users favor standardization as early as possible, while systems designers vary depending on their perception of technological developments. Both groups need to remember that standards are not fixed and immutable, but subject, at least in the United States, to periodic review. All American National Standards must be reviewed every five years and reaffirmed, revised, or withdrawn. Increasingly, standards efforts are focused on developing useful consensus standards and getting them into the field for use, rather than continuing to refine the standards indefinitely.

Technology continues to offer new means to design systems. We have seen massive changes brought about by miniaturization and the advent of low-cost, compact microcomputers. The variety and capability of software continues to expand. Spreadsheets, word processing, desktop publishing, and now hypertext programs expand our capabilities and our awareness. We have yet to see the full impact of these and of CD-ROM, interactive CD-ROM, and fiber optics.

We have seen a rapidly changing definition of what is a desirable user interface and what is a satisfactory level and rate of response. Some users prefer icon and menu-driven systems, while more experienced users prefer command-driven systems. System designers are pushed to find the right balance for their particular application and for the differing needs and preferences of users.

The issue of intellectual property rights has caused further confusion, particularly those related to the "look and feel" of screen displays.

Arguments are under way as to whether the icon interface developed by Xerox and popularized by Apple is proprietary or available as an industry standard. The results of pending court suits could have a significant effect on user interfaces and on user interface standards.

A third major trend presenting both opportunities and challenges is the move toward integration. Users want one-stop information services. They want to acquire all relevant information to an inquiry with one search and not be forced to repeat a search because of arbitrary policies of information providers or database developers. They are focused more on the content and less on the niceties of differing thesauri or vocabulary.

Publishers are recognizing this need within their own processing, but still have not dealt with the need for integration of information among publishers. Elsevier has tried to consider the multipublisher aspects of this in its Adonis service, but is focusing primarily on journal literature. CD-ROM applications probably come closest at present to integrating various information sources into one.

More diverse bodies are involved in standards development, and it is difficult to draw firm boundaries, particularly as more and more applications groups become participants. It is unclear at present how the office automation, computer processing groups, and publishing communities will apportion responsibilities for desktop publishing standards. Electronic interchange standards being developed by the financial and banking communities are moving into the computer protocol areas already covered by NISO's ANS Z39.50 and the American National Standards Institute (ANSI), Subcommittee X3. At present, ANSI's Board of Standards Review is responsible for resolving such conflicts, but this only works for those standards developed under the ANSI umbrella. As systems and media integration proceed, more participants will arise and more jurisdictional disputes will follow. One hopes common interest and the need to communicate with others outside the primary application area will promote cooperation.

With the trend to globalization in business, we also see a similar trend in standards activities. As companies compete across national boundaries, they prefer to develop goods and services that can be widely used and will meet international standards. By citing International Standards Organization (ISO) standards, they hope to gain better acceptance for their products. They also hope that adhering to one set of standards will minimize their development, production, and servicing costs.

With the proposed unification of Europe, one of the major issues that will face ISO in the near future is whether the European countries that now have separate membership and voting rights will, once European initiatives to move to a united Europe are complete, remain separate or become one. If they were to remain separate, but vote as one on standards, this could put other ISO countries in a less favorable position on standards development. However, European countries are also substantial financial contributors to ISO, and it is unclear whether others will or can assume a greater share of ISO costs. Questions both of influence and finance must be settled. As in any new sphere, economic conditions and competition have much to do with the ultimate solutions.

Electronic information services are creating new applications, attracting new users, and are the impetus to new demands. Electronic services have been available since the early 1970s, but have only recently been employed by large numbers of users. Specialists will always find ways to acquire the information and the services they need whether directly or through others. Financial analysts, business planners, chemists, some health professionals, and lawyers are direct users of electronic services. Other areas are less well served, but as new information services and better user interfaces are developed this will change. Some applications in the humanities are being developed, fueled by Apple's Hypercard and other hypertext software. Simulations such as Simcity will push the frontiers further.

These same factors are also affecting the work of the National Information Standards Organization Z39, which celebrated its 50th anniversary in 1989. Over the years, its focus has changed and moved to an increased emphasis on electronic services and user interfaces. At its Futures Conference in April 1985, these were among the top three issues. NISO's current work program includes a number of projects in these areas with the Common Command Language, format standards for the exchange of circulation data, CD-ROM extensions, and computer protocol standards.

The Common Command Language activities have been ably described by Peggy Morrison, chair of NISO's Subcommittee G (1989). NISO has completed balloting on its standard and is resolving the comments and the negative ballots. Internationally, the International Standards Organization has agreed to move forward the ISO work in this area as an ISO standard. This will have a significant impact on information providers operating in Europe and may require at least an interface using the ISO standard.

Every effort has been made to harmonize the NISO and ISO standards, but some differences still remain. The Europeans have been strongly influenced by their practice of almost exclusive use of intermediaries for searching, while the growing participation of users directly searching is more fully recognized in the United States.

The computer protocols, of which Z39.50 is only the first, will also influence user interfaces. At present, systems must translate from their native representation into the metarepresentation required by the protocol. In the future, as new systems are designed and existing ones modified, more will incorporate Z39.50 as a primary representation or at least as a standard option. OCLC and NYSERNET are already implementing a terminal-based version, and OCLC's EPIC information retrieval system was designed with Z39.50 as one of its interfaces.

Clifford Lynch is active in standards development, both as chair of the ASIS Standards Committee and as a member of NISO's Subcommittee D and its Standards Development Committee. Subcommittee D was responsible for drafting Z39.50, and Clifford has taken an active role in the committee work. He speaks from a base of extended professional computer experience and out of a long association with library and information retrieval applications. He is one of those rare people who is a computer expert, but also has sympathy with, understanding of, and acceptance of user needs. His article relates Z39.50 to database inquiry systems such as SQL (Standard Query Language). He also challenges us to concern ourselves with the underlying information retrieval problems and not to expect standards to provide solutions to problems they were never asked to address.

REFERENCE

Morrison, Peggy. 1989. Common Command Language. *LITA Newsletter* 10, no. 1 (Winter), 30–31.

22

The Client-Server Model in Information Retrieval

Clifford A. Lynch

The American National Standard Z39.50 for computer-to-computer access to information retrieval (IR) applications is clearly a milestone in the process of interconnecting systems, and thus in the opening of a far wider range of information services to the end user through a common user interface. The Z39.50 protocol offers the tantalizing prospect of being able to divorce a user interface from a database management/information retrieval system, and to allow use of the same user interface with multiple back-end systems functioning as servers. The user interface can potentially be hosted on a PC or workstation or provided to terminals by a time-sharing system.

The goals of Z39.50 are far more ambitious than those of lower-level protocols intended to support distributed file systems or remote access to relational databases. This chapter discusses the differences between database servers and the information servers that can be built through Z39.50. There are practical limitations to the degree of separation between front-end and back-end systems in IR applications. This chapter explores the following specific issues: (1) the exchange of outside-of-protocol information that enables two systems to communicate meaningfully, including the prospects for standardizing this exchange and the ways in which this information shapes a user interface; (2) the use and importance of optional features of Z39.50, such as resource management, in the development of a high-quality user interface, as well as design implications of these features in development of database servers necessary to support such sophisticated interfaces; (3) current or proposed features of sophisticated user interfaces, which are difficult or impossible to support within the current framework of Z39.50 client-server interactions; and (4) problems in the varying semantics that different server systems may impose on searches communicated through Z39.50.

INTRODUCTION

NISO Standard Z39.50[1] provides the protocol specifications for implementing a basic client-server model of information retrieval. With the proliferation of databases, this is a key technology for accessing a wide range of resources through a common user interface across computer networks.[2] Under the client-server model, one host (called the client, or the "origin" in the terminology of the Z39.50 standard) runs a user interface that communicates with an end user (a human being).[3] This user interface translates the user's requests into Z39.50 protocol and passes them across a network to a remote machine (a server, or a "target" system in Z39.50 language). Software on the server then translates the Z39.50 protocol back into server database queries, executes these queries, and optionally passes interim status reports back to the client during execution. When the query is completed, the server uses Z39.50 to inform the client of the final status and size of the query results. The client can then employ the protocol to request transfer of part or all of the query results across the network from the server; the server employs the protocol to respond to these requests.

In evaluating the practicality of Z39.50 as it currently stands and identifying the need for possible extensions to the existing standard, the benchmark for comparison must be the best of existing user interfaces for databases. There are clearly benefits to using a common, familiar user interface to access many databases. But if the capabilities of such a generalized interface appear impoverished compared to existing user interfaces that are tightly coupled to specific databases, the impact of Z39.50 will be relatively limited and general-purpose Z39.50 client interfaces will be used only for casual, superficial access to remote databases, while serious users of databases will still have to learn the specialized user interface for each database. The purpose of this chapter is to begin an evaluation of Z39.50 by examining key user interface areas (with emphasis on public access information retrieval systems such as online catalogs) that may present difficulties within the protocol framework of Z39.50, and by analyzing the common knowledge that must exist in both the server and the client for Z39.50 to provide effective communication.

DATABASE SERVERS AND INFORMATION SERVERS

The term *database* has several definitions, and the varying use of the term is at the root of many misunderstandings about Z39.50. The information retrieval community uses database to refer to an organized, interrelated complex of information (such as an online catalog). The mainstream computer science community, including database management systems researchers, uses the term *database* simply to name a collection or relationship of the information contained in those files. In an information retrieval environment, a database is a collection of information that is organized and searchable (and perhaps also updatable) in the context of one or more specific applications. One speaks of queries that have meaning at an application level, such as finding books by a given author. At the level of traditional databases, such an application query may translate into a series of complex database queries that are highly dependent on the way the logical applications data has been mapped into the structures provided by the underlying database management systems (for example, into a set of relations); an example of this is given below.

The Z39.50 protocol is primarily designed to support application-level queries in a distributed environment. The client need not know about how an information resource has been organized into a database on a particular server, as long as it understands the logical content of the information resource. Thus, it is confusing and misleading to speak of a Z39.50-based server as a database server in the same sense as, say, a SQL database server. Rather, we might speak of information servers and information bases as the appropriate constructs in a Z39.50 context. Z39.50 queries deal with the semantics of data stored in the server—and thus cross over the gap between data and information.

AN OVERVIEW OF THE Z39.50 PROTOCOL

There are really two parts to Z39.50. One part is a general mechanism for moving any type of query from the client to the server through a SEARCH request, allowing the server to report on the progress and result of the query through RESOURCE CONTROL requests and responses and a SEARCH response, and for managing the transfer of results from the server back to the client through the PRESENT service. This apparatus could be used with many query languages, including the native query language of the server, the query language that is part of Z39.50 (described below), SQL,[4] and FIND commands as defined by the proposed common command language for online catalogs.[5] There are some mild restrictions imposed by the protocol discussed below.

It is assumed that the query passed to the server produces a single result set which is identified (named) as part of the query transmission apparatus in the text of the query. Thus, any server that automatically creates multiple result sets as part of query evaluation will not fit neatly within the Z39.50 framework. Similarly, the use of query languages such as SQL, which explicitly specify what is to be done with a query result, will cause complications. Even this restriction is somewhat deceptive since a PRESENT request that asks for transmission of part of a result set can specify a result set name that is not created as part of a SEARCH request while remaining legitimate under the protocol. However, there is no way within the protocol for the client to determine the cardinality of a result set that has been created through some mechanism other than a SEARCH request that specifies that result set name, except by issuing a PRESENT request against this result set.

The result set created by a query must be finite. Search methods that rank an entire database are not readily incorporated in Z39.50 except by the crude expedient of making the whole database a result to each search, using a transfer format that includes a relevance value, transferring it in decreasing order of relevance, and letting the client halt the transfer when the relevance value gets too low. Numerous practical problems arise when using Z39.50 in a context in which the server responds to a query by ordering a large set of records. For example, there is the issue of how the server should scale assigned relevance values so that the client can understand them. How does the client know that a given result record is judged highly relevant to a query by the server, other than relative to other records in the result set with lower relevance values? In addition, the client may want to know something about the distribution of relevance values. Often, there are a small number of result records judged highly relevant to a query, and then the relevance value drops off sharply. Some tightly integrated user interface/database systems now offer the user a relevance distribution graph. There is no way to pass this information reasonably within Z39.50, so that a client could produce such a graph without first moving the entire result set from the server, other than to use a transfer format that includes only the relevance value for each record in the result set—and even this will only be useful if the server provides the result set in sorted order by relevance value.

Both SEARCH and PRESENT include optional element set names that tell the server which data elements the client wants returned from objects in the database being searched. The element set name is passed on SEARCH because it may be useful in allowing the server to choose a query evaluation strategy. If only a restricted set of data elements will be required, a query optimizer may be able to exploit this knowledge with certain database designs. If a query language such as SQL is being used, the element set name will likely be ignored in favor of specification of column names in a SQL SELECT statement passed as a query.

Aside from these rather mild restrictions, which can be "bent" to accommodate a wide range of uses, the mechanics of Z39.50 do not make any assumptions about the semantics of the database being searched. The database does not need to have any special characteristics; it does not have to be an online catalog or any other particular type of database; and the mechanical part of Z39.50 does not know anything about the data or what it means.

The other part of Z39.50 is the definition of a specific, Boolean search-oriented query language (type 1 queries, in the language of the standard) that can be passed across the mechanical part of the protocol. This is still very general; basically, it allows a series of predicates consisting of attribute lists and values that are linked together by the Boolean operators AND, OR, or ANDNOT. For example, a predicate might amount to a requirement that a title contain a specific word. However, the query language as defined in the protocol standard does not include the specification of any actual attributes that a database is required to support, or even a specification of the different classes of attributes to be supported by a server that conforms to the standard. Again, the protocol is operating at a nonsemantic level and does not care about the nature of the data in the database, but only that queries against it can be expressed in the given syntax.

The nature of the syntax is less restrictive than it may appear. Some IR systems have been proposed that simply allow the user to enter a series of search terms (words or phrases) in ranked order of importance and attempt to find records in the database that match these search specifications in some sense. Such a search specification could be cast into a complex attribute/term structure. Since ANDs and ORs are not appropriate to such a searching paradigm (which is intended to compute something more restrictive than ORing all the terms and less restrictive than ANDing all the terms), the whole search would be encoded into a single predicate. The protocol provides sufficient flexibility to do this.

Appendix C of Z39.50 (which is not part of the actual standard and does not specify a requirement that must be met by a conforming implementation of the standard) lists a sample set of attributes that might be appropriate for a bibliographic database. Appendix C is important because it illuminates the intent of Z39.50. The basic concept of the protocol design is to allow the client to pass queries to the server that express a fairly high level of applications semantics. For example, it should be reasonable to request books where the personal author has a last name of X and whose name contains Y as other than a last name (i.e., X is in the first word in the field and Y appears in the field in other than the first position, where the field is of the form "lastname, othernames"). The ability to formulate such a query means that a client can transparently take advantage of a name authority system implemented on a server, for example, without knowing anything about the implementation details of such an authority control system.

Contrast this procedure to SQL, which does not allow the expression of much applications-oriented semantics (without the use of nonstandard SQL extensions for user-defined operators). A relational database implementation of author names with authority control can be structured in any number of ways, and the client has to understand how the server has actually structured the relations comprising the database being searched in order to submit a query by author name. To illustrate the complexity of searching a relational implementation of personal author names with authority control at the SQL level, consider the following example in which one might use five separate relations:

BOOKS, which would contain full bibliographic data and a BOOK-ID field for each book

AUTHORS, which would contain an AUTHOR-ID and BOOK-ID field in each row, attaching author names to books as an access path

AUTHOR-ANAMES, which would contain a full authoritative name (AANAME) and an AUTHOR-ID column

AUTHOR-ACCESS, which would contain rows holding a last name (ALNAME), a non-last name (AONAME), and an AUTHOR-ID for each authoritative or nonauthoritative form of the name

AUTHOR-NANAMES, which would contain a full nonauthoritative name (ANNAME) and an AUTHOR-ID column for each nonauthoritative form of the name.

Suppose that we have a book by Mark Twain and the authority control system knows Twain by the authoritative name of Samuel Clemens and the additional nonauthoritative name of Quintius Curtius Snodgrass. Then the relations would look like this:

BOOKS:

BOOK-ID	other information
1	(citation for the book by Twain)

AUTHORS:

AUTHOR-ID	BOOK-ID
1	1

AUTHOR-ANAMES:

AUTHOR-ID	AANAME
1	Clemens, Samuel

AUTHOR-ACCESS:

ALNAME	AONAME	AUTHOR-ID
Clemens	Samuel	1
Twain	Mark	1
Snodgrass	Curtius	

AUTHOR-NANAMES:

AUTHOR-ID	AANAME
1	Twain, Mark
1	Snodgrass, Quintius Curtius

To perform the analog of the Z39.50 query (with appropriate attribute definitions for a bibliographic file) of ''books with a personal author with TWAIN as the last name and MARK as other than the last name'' in SQL in this context, we would have to do something like the following:

SELECT * FROM BOOKS WHERE BOOKS.BOOK-ID = AUTHORS.BOOK-ID AND AUTHORS.AUTHOR-ID = AUTHOR-ACCESS.AUTHOR-ID AND AUTHOR-ACCESS.ALNAME = ''TWAIN'' AND AUTHOR-ACCESS.AONAME = ''MARK''

Obviously, for the client to generate such an SQL query, it must have a full understanding of how the server has mapped the semantics of the application into a specific relational database structure. This examples underscores the difference between database servers, as they are traditionally viewed, and the information servers envisioned by the design objective of the Z39.50 protocol.

COMMON AGREEMENTS REQUIRED BETWEEN Z39.50
CLIENT AND SERVER

Since Z39.50 is so general and says so little about the semantics of the data being searched and transferred, there must be a considerable base of common knowledge between the client and the server.

Within the protocol as defined there is no provision for the client to learn the relevant information dynamically. It would be necessary to define a method for a server to describe a database and to refer to appropriate standards for such things as record transfer formats and search attributes. This is not simply a protocol issue; it is also a registry issue. There is a need for global names for record transfer formats, search attributes, and similar types of data. However, as we will see below, even this is not fully adequate to allow the client to obtain all the information needed for meaningful server/client interaction. Somehow the client must either know in advance or be able to learn the information about the server discussed in the rest of this section.

The format of the data objects ("records") that are being transferred from server to client. For bibliographic applications, this would presumably be one of the MARC formats. For other applications, such as access to journal abstracting and indexing databases, no commonly accepted standard record transfer format exists, which creates a serious problem.[6] Even with the use of common record transfer formats, local extensions and locally interpreted fields provide ample opportunity for problems and misunderstandings between client and server.

The search attributes available for an information base and their meaning. There are several different types of search attributes, logically speaking, although the Z39.50 protocol does not separate them into groups and register them. (ISO TC 46 SC 4, in its work on the international analogs of Z39.50 and ISO DPs 10162 and 10163, is making an effort to split attributes and register them in an orderly way.) One group—perhaps most easily standardized into a common attribute set and registered—deals with relational predicates: equality, field contains keyterm, field contains a value less than, field contains words subject to proximity constraints, and so forth.

More problematic attributes are those that define fields—for example, author, title, subject, and place of publication. In a bibliographic database setting, these fields typically map to large numbers of fields or fields/subfields in MARC records, possibly with the interposition of authority control operations. The mapping is not uniform from system to system: some systems index added entry names as authors; others do not. It is unlikely that anyone will reindex a massive existing bibliographic database just to conform to some standard mapping if one was defined, particularly given that the database was probably constructed initially to best meet the needs of the organization hosting the database.

Thus, as long as one sticks with high-level constructs such as author, systems will exercise a considerable amount of local license in interpreting these constructs against the logical record data elements in each local information base.

The other alternative—equally unrealistic—is to tie field attribute names directly to the field names in the transfer format (such as MARC) that are commonly understood by the client and server for meaningful communication to occur in the first place. While this greatly reduces the ambiguity of a field name like author, it is unrealistic for two reasons. First, the indexing that is done on existing information servers will not support retrieval by MARC field name and subfield name, and the amount of indexing required to support such queries is impractical. Second, even if such indexing existed, the queries that would have to be run against a database so indexed would be verbose and inefficient. For example, rather than just specifying AUTHOR = value, it would be necessary to provide an extensive list of MARC field name = value predicates ORed together.

The entire problem of standardized interpretation of attribute descriptions will create endless subtle problems to confuse users, even if we can agree on which fields in a data structure like a MARC record correspond to which attribute field names in the protocol. Consider the apparently well-defined query requesting those records where the title contains a given word. As well as the question of what fields in the MARC record are indexed by a given system as part of the title, there is the problem of keyword extraction. Most systems stoplist; some normalize spelling. (They might change *colour* to *color*, or generate two indexing keyterms, *colour* and *color*, for a title containing the world *color*. A hyphenated term such as *data-base* in a title might give rise to *data* and *base*, *database*, or all three terms. Words might even be stoplisted contextually, with the title *a salty dog* suppressing the term *a* because it is used as an article, but the title *vitamin a* or *symphony in a* retaining the term *a*.) The only way to resolve this problem would be to standardize indexing practice completely, which is not feasible. In the absence of such standardization, different systems will interpret predicate operators such as "field contains keyterm" differently.

Matters become even worse as one considers various approximate match operations that appear to be quite useful in public access systems, such as linguistic stemming, term conflation, and phonetic matching schemes (e.g., SOUNDEX).[7] It is unlikely that a user will obtain even roughly consistent results from database to database when employing these types of matching options.

The names of the information bases that are available on a given server. Presumably, one would also want some human-readable descriptive text along with these names to help the end user understand what is in each database. It may be unreasonable to expect the client, at the current state of the art, to actually select appropriate databases on servers without some guidance from the human end user or some other program using a directory of databases to select specific servers and databases to be searched.

Data element set names (display formats) for records from the databases. Definition of these data element sets is the prerogative of each server system. As long as the elements are selected from a standard record transfer format, and as long as there is a default, this does not affect successful communication since the client can request the default or most comprehensive data element set (if it knows the name of this element set) and filter data elements according to local needs of the client. The standard requires only a single default element set name. If you ask for an element set name unknown to the server, you get the default element set, with no error indication. A practical operating convention would have all servers use as their default the most complete set of data elements available. A client, in approaching an unfamiliar server, would then use the default data element set. Any actual selecting of elements would be done by the client. This is not the most efficient implementation, of course, since it may require the transfer of unneeded data from server to client, but it does simplify the client-server interaction, which is likely to be the higher priority in constructing general-purpose client implementations. Special rules can always be added to the client for specific servers that are heavily used, where efficiency is a real consideration and the server offers a range of data element set names.

In a sense, data element set names are just shorthand. If client and server understand a common record transfer format, then a server can unambiguously "explain" the definition of each of its element set names to a client, although the protocol does not provide any way for the server to pass this information to a client.

Error messages and diagnostic record formats. One of the major faults in the standard, in my opinion, is its failure to include any type of search error report as part of the standard. (A sample set is provided in Appendix D of the NISO standard, which is not part of the formal standard.) It appears that the ISO standard will provide a registry for error message sets. While it is true that some error messages are likely to be tied to specific attribute sets and specific implementations on servers, it is possible, as Appendix D suggests, to define a fairly comprehensive "core" set of error reports. Beyond this core set, a registry might be established to which server implementors could add unique messages, and each registered standard attribute set could be accompanied by a series of supplementary core error reports for that attribute set. In this scenario, when dealing with a server, a client would have to handle three types of error messages: standard universal error messages, standard attribute set-specific error messages, and (hopefully very few) server-specific error messages. The lack of standard error reports is likely to be a major problem since, while display of records received in different transfer formats could be handled to a great extent by relatively straightforward tables and format parsers in a client implementation, processing of error returns is likely to become much more intimately linked to the actual processing done by a client in presenting the user interface functions.

Resource control formats. The protocol allows the server to notify the client, at the server's discretion, about resource utilization for active searches and to request confirmation that search processing should continue. The format of the resource utilization report is not part of the standard; it is defined externally (with an example given in Appendix E of the standard, which is not part of the formal standard). For the client to process a resource utilization report usefully, it must understand the format being used by the server. Since there does not seem to be much variation in the possibilities here, the best way to resolve this issue might be to standardize some generalization of the example given in Appendix E of the standard.

Authentication. The protocol allows the server to issue authentication challenges to the client. The client must respond to them. Although it seems reasonable that these challenges be server-specific, an ancillary standard covering the most common challenges issued by current systems (e.g., userid/account number/password) would greatly improve interoperability prospects and eliminate another requirement for extensive per-server specialized code in generalized Z39.50 client implementations.

THE STRUCTURE OF THE SEARCH PROCESS

Quality implementations of information retrieval systems—particularly public access information retrieval systems—differ greatly from more traditional database management systems in that they do not simply accept and execute searches, but make searching a somewhat interactive process, particularly when there are problems with the search. (For example: The search does not match any records in the database, or it matches a very large number of records.) This section examines several of these cases and the extent to which they can be supported in a Z39.50 environment.

Long searches. Here a traditional system usually asks users if they want to proceed (sometimes after giving an estimate of search cost or expected result set size) before expending a huge amount of resource in evaluating the search. This type of interaction can be fully supported by Z39.50, subject to a couple of caveats: (1) the server must generate resource control messages (the equivalent of recognizing long or large searches), and (2) the client must understand the format of the resource control message sent by the server, which is not standardized (see above).

Reason for long searches. Some advanced user interfaces will tell the user why a search is long. For example, if the user entered the query

FIND TITLE CONTAINING AMERICAN OR AUTHOR SNODGRASS

the system might say that titles containing the word *american* are very common and will cause a long search and/or produce a large result. There is no provision for the server to pass such information to the client in a structured way. The best the server could do is place a textual message for display to the end user of the client in the text field of a resource control report, although this limits the client's ability to integrate it with the overall user interface presented by the client. The client then could display only a note to the user such as

FURTHER INFORMATION ON YOUR QUERY PROVIDED BY THE DATABASE BEING SEARCHED: TITLES CONTAINING THE WORD "AMERICAN" ARE VERY COMMON.

In this situation the quality of the client interface as perceived by the user is likely to be heavily influenced by the quality of the text messages generated by specific servers, which are no fault of the client and which the client can only display. This also effectively rules out multilingual support by a client (unless client and server agree on a language in advance, for which there is no protocol mechanism, and which has the added disadvantage of forcing servers to be highly multilingual), or translation of errors by client to graphical forms.

Zero result situations. Usage statistics for online catalogs suggest that zero results (no records in the database matching the user's search criteria) are a major problem.[8] The situation occurs often (because users have trouble typing, spelling, or understanding subject classification), and can be frustrating unless the system offers some guidance on how to recover from the situation. While the server easily reports back to the client that a search produces a zero result, it cannot return any supplementary information to the client. (For example, ''The following search terms did not match any terms in the database index; check your spelling.'') It would not be overwhelmingly difficult to extend the protocol to allow a text message to be passed from server to client in the zero result case, but this is only a poor start on really solving the problem, much like the case of explaining why a search is long, discussed above.

Partial results as a search proceeds. Some systems, particularly PC-based systems, display to the user a series of intermediate set cardinalities as part of search processing to help the user understand what the search is doing and recognize the source of unexpected search results. For example, a search such as

FIND AUTHOR WILLIAM SHAKESPEARE AND TITLE THE TEMPEST

might produce the following display from the system:

2222 BOOKS WITH AUTHOR = WILLIAM SHAKESPEARE
181 BOOKS WITH TITLE = THE TEMPEST
49 BOOKS WITH AUTHOR = WILLIAM SHAKESPEARE AND TITLE =
THE TEMPEST

Again, there is no facility within the protocol for the system to transmit this kind of information back to the client, though some form of resource control report might carry it in a text field for display to the user of the client. Coming up with a means of transmitting such information in a structured form suitable for processing by the client (rather than just display) seems to be a very difficult problem.[9]

It should be noted, incidentally, that standard database management systems, such as SQL-based relational systems, do not support any interaction during the search process. Z39.50 is far superior to lower-level approaches such as remote database access (RDA) specialized to SQL in this regard.[10] Further, it is unlikely,

if Z39.50 were used to support SQL interactions with a relational DBMS, that
such a database server would make use of functions such as resource control in
the protocol.

OTHER USER INTERFACE FUNCTIONS

We have seen that a great deal of common information needs to be established
between server and client for effective communication to take place. Even within
the simple structure of searching and results display there are significant limits
to the ability of a Z39.50 protocol interface to replicate some of the features of
traditional tightly coupled user interfaces that are helpful to users of public access
information retrieval systems. However, typical public access systems have a
much larger repertoire of functions than simply issuing queries and displaying
results. This section examines the prospects for supporting some of these functions across a Z39.50 client-server protocol interface.

Browsing. Browsing is a term actually used to describe several different functions. One function is the examination of a sample of the records that meet a
set of search criteria, possibly without the performance of the entire search.
Z39.50 supports complete random access to the records in a search result once
the search is completed and contains provisions for terminating a long search
with a partial result. It does not allow a search to be suspended while records
from the result computed to that point are browsed by the user. Another simple
form of browsing is just perusing random database records, which is also un-
supported by Z39.50.

A third type of browsing is the examination of the terms in an index that are
proximate in some ordering (i.e., alphabetic) to a given search term. Z39.50
does not support this function directly, but it can be simulated by treating the
index as a database in its own right and defining query attributes for proximity
to a given term (i.e., the n terms in sequence immediately preceding or following
the search term). This process would allow retrieval of a group of terms on both
sides (alphabetically) of a given search term. There are some problems, such as
establishing a record transfer format for the index entries that will be familiar
to most clients. In addition, the more general function of scanning through a list
of alphabetized index terms for an arbitrary distance is tricky. The client would
have to perform repeated searches against the index as a database, using the
proximity operator just discussed; to get the next set of terms in alphabetical
order, it would search the last term from the previous search result. (There are
also grotesque solutions: server returns entire index as result. Client does binary
search to find part of the result it wants to display to user as part of the browse.)

Finally, browsing sometimes refers to the keyterm searching of a set of headings (such as name or subject headings), which are then displayed to the user,
who selects one or more of these displayed headings as search criteria. The
BROWSE command in the MELVYL catalog does this, for example. There is
no problem implementing this function in the existing Z39.50 protocol as long

as the heading file can be treated as a separate database for searching and appropriate record transfer formats and search attribute sets are defined.

Result set ranking and sorting. There is no provision to cause sorting of a result set at the server based on client-supplied criteria. The server is free to provide the result set in any order. This does not present a major functionality problem, but it may have performance implications. Some user interfaces want to display records to a user in orderings such as reverse chronological order (most recent first) under the assumption that the user will typically stop looking at the records after a few screens. To do this, the client would have to move the entire result set across the network, sort it into reverse chronological order in the client system, and then display it to the user, which may be a fairly slow process. Obviously, if a given server uses a specific sort sequence for result sets, and the client knows what this sequence is, it is possible to program the client to exploit existing sort order where advantageous. There is no way for a server to tell clients how it sorts result sets within the existing protocol.

Result set ranking is a much more subtle issue, and presents functionality problems as well as the efficiency problems that it shares with more routine sorting of result sets. Some ranking algorithms can be implemented by moving the entire result set to the client and ranking it there. However, the efficiency issues are more acute since the result set that has some relevance, however minimal, may be huge, and the user may only want the few most relevant results. Other, more complex, ranking algorithms (for example, maximum entropy approaches,[11] assign weights to retrieved records based not only on the user's query but also on statistical information about the frequency with which the user's search terms actually occur in the database being searched. In these cases, unless the client is programmed to execute a potentially complex (and possibly costly) set of additional queries to determine these frequency statistics (which may be impossible to determine in any reasonable way), only the server can perform the ranking; the client does not have enough information to do so. This is true of many of the probabilistic retrieval techniques that have been proposed in the IR community.[12]

Certainly, under the current protocol definition, the server is free to rank results in any way it pleases. Additional protocol development to make result set sorting and ranking a cooperative process between server and client will be necessary to support advanced IR techniques.

A closely related topic is automatic query formulation or modification based on criteria such as term frequency, which is used to assign or modify weights for query terms under some proposals. The server is free to apply such algorithms to searches that it receives, but has no way of explaining what is done. The client may not have the requisite statistical information about term frequency (although browsing, if the results of the browse include term frequency, will help) to perform such query interpretation. Yet ideally, the client should have the option of interactive consultation with the user about such query modification and knowledge of how the query modification has been applied so that he or she can algorithmically further modify and retry the search. Moving the feedback query modification methods into a client-server framework promises to be a valuable, if difficult, research area.

Help and tutorial functions. Clearly, the client must be able to explain to the user how to formulate searches and needs to be able to assist the user in recovering from zero result searches or in reducing a large result set to a more manageable size. At the very least, for each database it needs to be able to tell the user about the available search attributes and their meanings. It must be able to display error messages to the user in a comprehensible form and to suggest actions for recovering from errors. We have already seen that little of this is addressed by the current protocol specification, and that the protocol contains little provision to aid in these areas except for the ability of the server to transmit a test message to the client for display to the client's end user (under some circumstances). Presumably, if we can establish standard search attribute sets, these can be tabled in the client along with explanatory text. If the client can determine which attributes are supported by a given server, it can tailor its help displays for that attribute set. Sample search term values might be obtained through the use of the browse function by the client system where necessary. Functions providing explanatory text on demand (for example, a description of each information base available on a server) were explicitly excluded from the design of the current version of Z39.50. They are being considered for inclusion in the international computer-to-computer information retrieval protocol, however. Retrieval of explanatory text from the server upon demand does not present any great conceptual difficulty—such a body of text might be set up as a database on the server, indexed by explanation name, by language, and by length of explanation (short or full), for example, and then be retrieved using Z39.50 with an appropriate search attribute set. Dealing with this issue is mostly a problem of grinding through all the details of standardizing the attribute set and the transfer format.

Other areas where current nondistributed systems offer help to the user are likely to create conceptual problems because a tightly coupled interface uses knowledge about the database being searched to help the user formulate and refine searches. A discussion of these problems follows.

Contextual help when recovering from problems. The problem of explaining why a search produced a zero result has already been discussed. Another example is large results. In an online union catalog, a tightly coupled interface might suggest that the user limit a result to English-language material published in the last 10 years and held by libraries that are geographically close to the user. In a general-purpose client interface it is unlikely that the client can come up with appropriate database- and search-specific suggestions for the user. The best we might hope for is a rule system (perhaps a series of embedded expert systems)[13] that is associated with some popular databases that the client supports, which can generate such suggestions when the particular databases are being used. The point of using small embedded expert systems is that they are fairly easy to define and modify. More complex approaches can be imagined. For example, an advanced information retrieval server might include some additional services that return suggested new searches when passed a search and told to recommend one more or less specific than the input search. It is difficult to envision how the client interface would explain the function of such a service to the end user.[14]

Heuristic search techniques. In some tightly coupled user interfaces logic has been added to help the user find material using heuristic techniques that have been identified by experience. In an online catalog, for example, when a subject search produces a zero result, the same search terms are often sought in a title keyterm search, and then the user is offered the subject headings of retrieved material in the hope that relevant subject headings for further searching will be identified. Such techniques are highly database-dependent; or, more accurately, they work with certain types of databases. Again, it is hard to believe that they can be offended by a general-purpose client interface except as specialized functions that are associated with specific databases, or, at best, classes of databases like online catalogs. To what extent will all this lead to the development of *general* heuristics? One does wonder, particularly with clients running in a workstation environment with ample computational capacity, to what extent more general techniques can be developed. For example: download a result, correlate values for a wide variety of data elements in the result set transferred to the client, and then use the results of this general statistical analysis to formulate additional searches. There is simply no experience on which to base an analysis of such techniques.

CONCLUSIONS

It should be clear from this analysis that the success of Z39.50 as a means of constructing general-purpose user interface clients for server systems depends critically on further de facto or formal standards in various areas. In relation to Z39.50 we need to standardize error reports, resource control reporting messages, and basic sets of query attributes through a registry process. As a more general issue, Z39.50 depends on commonly understood record transfer formats. These are in relatively good shape for bibliographic data (the MARC formats), but do not exist in other areas that are prime candidates for the use of Z39.50, such as access to article abstracting and indexing databases. There is also a strong case to be made for extensions to Z39.50 to provide better support for result set ranking, sorting, and browsing. The issues of transmitting information to explain long searches and zero results are still research problems, and they need to be solved.

Yet it is important as well to maintain a perspective on the progress that has been made to date. Terming a Z39.50 server a "database server" does not do it justice. We are really trying to develop a whole new technology of information retrieval servers and clients. The distributed database community has been working for a decade to produce SQL and remote database access; these are now at a state of considerable maturity achieved by almost entirely ignoring applications semantics. The design goals of Z39.50 specifically allow queries to incorporate user-oriented semantics, and this is unquestionably a difficult problem. As we have seen, application semantics is not a clear issue. Implementors of different systems do not agree on what it really means to do a search for personal names meeting specific criteria, or even for titles that contain specific keywords. Technologies such as Z39.50 only add clarity to these problems; they cannot resolve them. Resolution of these issues must await a deeper understanding and greater consensus about a number of basic issues in information retrieval.

NOTES

An earlier version of this paper was the basis of a talk given at ASIS Mid-year, San Diego, May 1989 ("Applications and Limitations of the Z39.50 Information Retrieval Protocol Standard: Can the User Interface and Database Backend Be Separated in Information Retrieval Applications?"). I would like to thank Nancy Gusack for her editorial assistance.

   1. *American National Standard Z39.50–188, Information Retrieval Service Definition and Protocol Specifications for Library Applications*, developed by The National Information Standards Organization (New Brunswick, N.J.: Transaction, 1988).

   2. Michael Buckland and Clifford A. Lynch, "The Linked Systems Protocol and the Future of Bibliographic Networks and Systems," *Information and Technology Libraries* 6:2 (June 1987), pp. 83–88. See also idem., "National and International Implications of the Linked Systems Protocol for Online Bibliographical Systems," *Cataloguing and Classification Quarterly* 8:3/4 (Spring 1988), pp. 15–33.

   3. Note that a program could also talk to a server through a Z39.50 client interface without involving an end user. This gives rise to a number of additional considerations that are outside the scope of this chapter, but certainly it is worth keeping in mind that if a human being has trouble understanding what a server is doing, then a program is certainly going to have difficulty dealing with the same situation.

   4. C. J. Date, *A Guide to the SQL Standard: A User's Guide to the Standard Relational Language SQL* (Reading, Mass.: Addison-Wesley, 1987).

   5. *Z39.50, American National Standard for Information Sciences—Common Command Language for Online Interactive Information Retrieval* (draft), developed by NISO Committee G, 1989.

   The Z39.50 standard makes explicit provision for use of native query languages (type 0 queries) and its own query language (type 1 queries). The draft ISO analog to Z39.50 also defines a type for the command language once it is adopted. Both the ANSI/NISO and draft ISO standards are extensible. Additional query languages can be defined as query types in the protocol.

   6. Actually there are subtle issues concerning the use of MARC formats and the presentation layer. When the protocol was being designed, some saw the role of the presentation layer in transferring records from server to client as that of simply passing a string of data, which both the client and server would know should be interpreted in a specific MARC format (for example, USMARC or UK MARC). The other, more sophisticated school of thought, viewed a "generic" MARC record as a logical data object that was transferred by the presentation layer, permitting the client application layer to receive MARC records in whatever national format it desired, with translation to the

specific national format occurring in the presentation layer mapping. If the latter view is taken, where the presentation layer understands a record format as a logical structure, additional barriers arise if Z39.50 is used to transfer records not in MARC formats. Not only must the applications have a common understanding of the logical data elements of the format being used, but the presentation layers in the server and client must also get involved in the communication. For other applications some other relevant standard (if one existed) would be used.

7. Martin Lennon, David S. Pierce, Brian D. Tarry, and Peter Willett, "An Evaluation of Some Conflation Algorithms for Information Retrieval," *Journal of Information Science* 3:4 (September 1981), pp. 177–83.

8. Clifford A. Lynch, "Large Database and Multiple Database Problems in Online Catalogs," *OPACs and Beyond, Proceedings of a Joint Meeting of the British Library, DBMIST, and OCLC* (Dublin, Ohio: OCLC Online Computer Library Center, 1988), pp. 51–55.

9. In fact, passing this information from a commercial DBMS to a calling program is an extraordinarily difficult problem. The information that will be available without additional computation by the DBMS to obtain information about the selectivity of each component predicate in a query will depend critically on the query evaluation plan selected by the query optimizer for each query.

For discussion of some aspects of this problem, see Francisco Corella, S. J. Kaplan, G. Wiederhold, and L. Yesil, "Cooperative Responses to Boolean Queries," *IEEE Computer Society, Computer Data Engineering Conference, April 1984*, pp. 77–93. See also Clifford A. Lynch, *Extending Relational Database Management Systems for Information Retrieval Applications*, Ph.D. diss., University of California, Berkeley, 1987, and "Nonmaterialized Relations and the Support of Information Retrieval by Relational Database Systems," *Journal of the American Society for Information Science* 42:6 (1991), 389–96.

Extending the availability of this information into a distributed environment compounds the problem. The DBMS may or may not provide some information to the Z39.50 application running on the server. The server application will then have to decide how much, if any, additional information to obtain from the DBMS by running additional queries. Finally, whatever information the application on the server ultimately collects— which may vary radically from query to query—must be expressed in some as-yet-undefined, flexible format that can be interpreted by the client and linked by the client to component parts of the query *as the client transmitted it to the server, not as the server application translated it for the DBMS on the server* and sent through the protocol to the client. This is a major unexplored research area.

10. For a fuller comparison between RDA and Z39.50, see Clifford A. Lynch, "Intersystem Linking and Distributed Database Technology: A Comparison of Two Approaches to the Construction of Network-Based Information Utilities," *Proceedings of the Fourth Integrated Online Library Systems Meeting, New York, NY, May 10–11, 1989* (Medford, N.J.: Learned Information, 1989), pp. 107–12.

11. William S. Cooper, "Exploiting the Maximum Entropy Principle to Increase Retrieval Effectiveness," *Journal of the American Society for Information Science* 34:1 (1983), pp. 31–39.

12. Gerard Salton and Michael J. McGill, *Introduction to Modern Information Retrieval* (New York: McGraw-Hill, 1983).

13. Clifford A. Lynch, "Applications of Artificial Intelligence Techniques to Public

Access Information Retrieval Systems,'' *Artificial Intelligence: Expert Systems and Other Applications (Selected Papers)* (forthcoming, Greenwood Press).

14. Geo Wiederhold, ''The Architecture of Future Information Systems: A Mediator Architecture for Abstract Data Access,'' Report no. STAN-CS–90–1303 (Stanford, Calif.: Department of Computer Science, Stanford University, 1990).

Selected Bibliography

Bates, Marcia J. 1981. "Search Techniques." In *Annual Review of Information Science and Technology*, ed. Martha E. Williams, 139–69. White Plains, N.Y.: Knowledge Industry.

———. 1986. "Subject Access in Online Catalogs: A Design Model." *Journal of the American Society for Information Science* 37(6): 357–76.

Belew, R. K. 1989. "Adaptive Information Retrieval: Using a Connectionist Representative to Retrieve and Learn About Documents." In *SIGIR '89: Proceedings of the Twelfth Annual International Conference on Research and Development in Information Retrieval, Cambridge, MA, June 25–28, 1989*, ed. N. J. Belkin and C. J. van Rijsbergen, 11–20. New York: Association for Computing Machinery.

Belkin, Nicholas J., R. N. Oddy, and H. M. Brooks. 1982. "ASK for Information Retrieval: Part I, Background and Theory." *Journal of Documentation* 38(2): 61–71.

———. 1982. "ASK for Information Retrieval: Part II, Results of a Design Study." *Journal of Documentation* 38(2): 145–64.

Belkin, Nicholas J., and W. Bruce Croft. 1987. "Retrieval Techniques." In *Annual Review of Information Science and Technology*, ed. Martha E. Williams, 109–45. Amsterdam: Elsevier.

Bewley, William L., Teresa L. Roberts, David S. Schroit, and William L. Verplank. 1983. "Human Factors Testing in the Design of Xerox's 8010 'Star' Office Workstation." In *Human Factors in Computing Systems: Proceedings of the CHI '83 Conference, Boston, MA, 12–15 December 1983*, ed. Ann Janda, 72–77. New York: Association for Computing Machinery.

Borgman, Christine L. 1985. "Designing an Information Retrieval Interface." In *Research and Development in Information Retrieval: Eighth Annual International ACM SIGIR Conference, Montreal, Quebec, Canada, June 5–7, 1985*, 139–46. New York: Association for Computing Machinery.

———. 1986. "The User's Mental Model of an Information Retrieval System: An Experiment on a Prototype Online Catalog." *International Journal of Man-Machine Studies* 24(1): 47–64.

————. 1986. "Why Are Online Catalogs Hard to Use? Lessons Learned from Information-Retrieval Studies." *Journal of the American Society for Information Science* 37(6): 387–400.

Brajnik, Giorgio, Giovanni Guida, and Carlo Tasso. 1987. "User Modeling in Intelligent Information Retrieval." *Information Processing & Management* 23(4): 305–20.

Brenner, Lisa P., Mary Huston-Miyamoto, David A. Self, Phyllis C. Self, and Linda C. Smith. 1980. "User-Computer Interface Designs for Information Systems: A Review." *Library Research* 2(1): 63–73.

Buckland, Michael, and Clifford A. Lynch. 1987. "The Linked Systems Protocol and the Future of Bibliographic Networks and Systems." *Information Technology and Libraries* 6(2): 83–88.

Bush, Vannevar. 1945. "As We May Think." *Atlantic Monthly* 176(1): 101–8.

Card, S. K., and T. P. Moran. 1986. "User Technology: From Pointing to Pondering." In *Proceedings of ACM Conference on the History of Personal Workstations*, ed. A. Goldberg, 183–98. New York: Association for Computing Machinery.

Carroll, John M., ed. 1987. *Interfacing Thought: Cognitive Aspects of Human-Computer Interaction*. Cambridge, Mass.: MIT Press.

Conklin, Jeff. 1987. "Hypertext: An Introduction and Survey." *Computer* 20(9): 17–41.

Crane, Gregory. 1988. "Redefining the Book: Some Preliminary Problems." *Academic Computing* 2(5): 6–11, 36–41.

Crawford, Walt. 1987. "Testing Bibliographic Displays for Online Catalogs." *Information Technology and Libraries* 6(1): 20–33.

Croft, W. Bruce. 1987. "Approaches to Intelligent Information Retrieval." *Information Processing & Management* 23(4): 249–54.

Croft, W. Bruce, and R. H. Thompson. 1987. "I³R: A New Approach to the Design of Document Retrieval Systems." *Journal of the American Society for Information Science* 38(6): 389–404.

Daniels, P. J. 1986. "Cognitive Models in Information Retrieval—An Evaluative Review." *Journal of Documentation* 42(4): 272–304.

Dickson, Jean. 1984. "An Analysis of User Errors in Searching an Online Catalog." *Cataloging & Classification Quarterly* 4(3): 19–38.

Ellis, David. 1984. "Theory and Explanation in Information Retrieval Research." *Journal of Information Science* 8: 25–38.

————. 1989. "A Behavioural Approach to Information Retrieval System Design." *Journal of Documentation* 45(3): 171–212.

Ericsson, K. A., and H. Simon. 1984. *Protocol Analysis: Verbal Reports as Data*. Cambridge, Mass.: MIT Press.

Fidel, Raya. 1984. "Online Searching Styles: A Case-Study-Based Model of Searching Behavior." *Journal of the American Society for Information Science* 35(4): 211–21.

Foley, James D. 1983. *Managing the Design of User-Computer Interfaces*. Washington, D.C.: George Washington University, Institute for Information Science and Technology.

Gittins, D. T., R. L. Winder, and H. E. Bez. 1984. "An Icon-Driven End-User Interface to UNIX." *International Journal of Man-Machine Studies* 21(5): 451–61.

Goodwin, Nancy C. 1987. "Functionality and Usability." *Communications of the ACM* 30(3): 229–33.

Harter, Stephen P., and Anne Rogers Peters. 1985. "Heuristics for Online Information Retrieval: A Typology and Preliminary Listing." *Online Review* 9(5): 407–23.

Hildreth, Charles R. 1982. *Online Public Access Catalogs: The User Interface.* Dublin, Ohio: OCLC, Online Computer Library Center.

———. 1987. "Beyond Boolean: Designing the Next Generation of Online Catalogs." *Library Trends* 35: 647–67.

Hjerppe, Roland. 1986. "Project HYPERCATalog: Visions and Preliminary Conceptions of an Extended and Enhanced Catalog." In *Intelligent Information Systems for the Information Society. Proceedings of the Sixth International Research Forum in Information Science (IRFIS 6), Frascati, Italy, September 15–18, 1985,* ed. B. C. Brookes, 211–32. New York: Elsevier.

Hollands, J. G., and Philip M. Merikle. 1987. "Menu Organization and User Expertise in Information Search Task." *Human Factors* 29(5): 577–86.

Hutchins, Edwin, James D. Hollan, and Donald A. Norman. 1986. "Direct Manipulation Interfaces." In *User Centered System Design: New Perspectives on Human-Computer Interaction,* ed. Donald A. Norman and Stephen W. Draper, 87–124. Hillsdale, N.J.: Lawrence Erlbaum Associates.

Jervell, Herman Ruge and Kai A. Olsen. 1985. "Icons in man-machine Communications." *Behaviour and Information Technology* 4(3): 249–54.

Jonassen, David H., ed. 1982. *The Technology of Text: Principles for Structuring, Designing, and Displaying Text.* Englewood Cliffs, N.J.: Educational Technology.

Kaske, Neal K. 1988. "The Variability and Intensity over Time of Subject Searching in an Online Public Access Catalog." *Information Technology and Libraries* 7(3): 273–87.

Lansdale, M. W. 1988. "On the Memorability of Icons in an Information Retrieval Task." *Behaviour and Information Technology* 7(2): 131–51.

Luqi. 1989. "Software Evolution Through Rapid Prototyping." *Computer* 22(5): 13–25.

Marchionini, Gary, and Ben Shneiderman. 1988. "Finding Facts vs. Browsing Knowledge in Hypertext Systems." *Computer* 21(1): 70–80.

Marcus, Ridrend S. 1983. "An Experimental Comparison of the Effectiveness of Computers and Humans as Search Intermediaries." *Journal of the American Society for Information Science* 34(6): 381–404.

Mark, William. 1986. "Knowledge-Based Interface Design." In *User Centered System Design: New Perspectives on Human-Computer Interaction,* ed. Donald A. Norman and S. W. Draper, 219–38. Hillsdale, N.J.: Lawrence Erlbaum Associates.

Markey, Karen. 1984. "Barriers to Effective Use of Online Catalogs." In *Online Catalogs, Online Reference: Converging Trends,* ed. Brian Aveney and Brett Butler, 57–73. Chicago, Ill.: American Library Association.

———. 1984. *Subject Searching in Library Catalogs: Before and After the Introduction of Online Catalogs.* Dublin, Ohio: OCLC Online Computer Library Center.

Mischo, William H., and Jounghyoun Lee. 1987. "End-User Searching of Bibliographic Databases." In *Annual Review of Information Science and Technology,* vol. 22, ed. Martha E. Williams, 227–63. Amsterdam: Elsevier.

Nielsen, Brian. 1986. "What They Say They Do and What They Do: Assessing Online Catalog Use Instruction Through Transaction Monitoring." *Information Technology and Libraries* 5(1): 28–34.

Norman, Donald A. 1986. "Cognitive Engineering." In *User Centered System Design: New Perspectives on Human-Computer Interaction,* ed. Donald A. Norman and S. W. Draper, 31–61. Hillsdale, N.J.: Lawrence Erlbaum Associates.

Norman, Donald A., and S. W. Draper, eds. 1986. *User Centered System Design: New Perspectives on Human-Computer Interaction*. Hillsdale, N.J.: Lawrence Erlbaum Associates.

Prabha, Chandra, and Duane Rice. 1988. "Assumptions about Information-Seeking Behavior in Nonfiction Books: Their Importance to Full-Text Systems." In *Proceedings of the 51st American Society for Information Science Annual Meeting*, vol. 25, ed. Christine C. Borgman and Edward Y. H. Pai, 147–51. Medford, N.J.: Learned Information.

Rada, Roy. 1989. "Writing and Reading Hypertext: An Overview." *Journal of the American Society for Information Science* 40(3): 164–71.

Rada, Roy, and Lois F. Lunin. 1989. "Hypertext: Introduction and Overview." *Journal of the American Society for Information Science* 40(3): 159–63.

Salton, Gerard, and Michael J. McGill. 1983. *Introduction to Modern Information Retrieval*. New York: McGraw-Hill.

Saracevic, Tefko. 1975. "RELEVANCE: A Review of and a Framework for the Thinking on the Notion in Information Science." *Journal of the American Society for Information Science* 26: 321–43.

Shneiderman, Ben. 1982. "The Future of Interactive Systems and the Emergence of Direct Manipulation." *Behaviour and Information Technology* 1(3): 237–56.

———. 1987. *Designing the User Interface: Strategies for Effective Human-Computer Interaction*. Reading, Mass.: Addison-Wesley.

Shneiderman, Ben, Dorothy Brethauer, Catherine Plaisant, and Richard Potter. 1989. "Evaluating Three Museum Installations of a Hypertext System." *Journal of the American Society for Information Science* 40(3): 172–82.

Smith, David Canfield, Charles Irby, and Ralph Kimball. 1982. "The Star User Interface: An Overview." In *AFIPS Conference Proceedings: 1982 National Computer Conference*, vol. 51, ed. Howard Lee Morgan, 515–28. Arlington, Va.: AFIPS Press.

Smith, L. C. 1987. "Artificial Intelligence and Information Retrieval." In *Annual Review of Information Science and Technology*, vol. 22, ed. Martha E. Williams, 41–77. Amsterdam: Elsevier.

Index

Adelson, B., 228
Adler, M. J., 179
Adonis service, 298
Advanced Image Workstation (AWI), design of: access techniques, 212–13; background of, 208–11; browsing, 212–13; electronic bookmarks, 215; functions of, 210–11; future of, 216–17; image manipulation, 214; robustness and menu design, 211–12; speed of access, 213–14; Standalone Display Workstation, 208, 211, 213; testing goals, 215–16
AIR, 41–45, 50, 51–52
American National Standards Institute (ANSI), 298
Amiga: Intuition system for, 23; UICAD, 26, 28, 32–33, 34–35
Anderson, J., 108
Anderson, Nancy S., 238
Andrew system, 23
Apple Computer, Inc.: HyperCard, xxii, 26, 27–30, 34, 122, 130, 133, 137; icon interface of, 298; Lisa system, 25; MacDraw, 246; Macintosh interface, 12; metaphors and, 24; Presentation Manager, 22; SonicFinder, xix; Toolbox, 23
Arend, U., 14
Argumentation, 108; authoritative, 111;

classification approaches, 110–11; methodology used, 111–12; motivational, 111; substantive, 110–11; Toulmin's construct, 109; results, 112–13
Artificial intelligence: approaches to, 71; description of, 70; domain knowledge and, 72–74; domain knowledge/natural-language for bibliographic information retrieval, 83–104; expert processing and, 63, 64, 65; interface design and, 71–72; modalities and, 78–81; natural-language processing and, 63–64, 65; narrowing of subject or task domain, 64–65
Atkinson, Bill, 28
Authoring. *See* Hypertext, group authoring of
Authoritative arguments, 111
Auto-Graphics Government Documents Catalog Service, 281, 282, 283, 285, 292

Barnett, Jim, xx, 85
Bates, Marcia J., 14, 55, 59, 60, 180, 279, 293
Befeler, M., 260
Belew, Richard K., 43, 44, 45, 47, 51
Belkin, Nicholas J., 55, 68, 107, 279
Bernhardt, Stephen A., 154
Berry-picking model: browsing and, 59;

About the Editor and Contributors

STEVEN D. ATKINSON is assistant coordinator of Computer Search Services at the State University of New York at Albany. He has been active in providing online searches as an intermediary and working with end users of online catalogs, CD-ROM, and database systems. He has recently coedited a collection of essays, *Women Online: Research in Women's Studies Using Online Databases* and coproduced *Hypertext/Hypermedia: An Annotated Bibliography*. He received a joint Faculty/Librarian grant from the Council on Library Resources in 1987/ 1988 to study "Online Access in the Humanities: Implications for Scholars in the Humanities."

MARCIA J. BATES is associate professor in the Graduate School of Library and Information Science at the University of California, Los Angeles. Her principal research interests are in the areas of subject access and interface design in information retrieval systems, information search strategy, and information-seeking behavior. Recent publications include "Subject Access in Online Catalogs: A Design Model" and "Where Should the Person Stop and the Information Search Interface Start?" She is a coauthor of the forthcoming *For Information Specialists: Interpretations of Reference and Bibliographic Work*.

RICHARD K. BELEW is an assistant professor of computer science and engineering at the University of California, San Diego. His primary area of research is the development of knowledge representations for learning systems. He is currently involved with the investigation of connectionist networks, Genetic Algorithms, and hybrids of these. His primary area of application is in the area of free-text information retrieval, where machine learning techniques are used to automatically develop indices based on the browsing behavior of users.

JOHN R. BONNEAU, currently an engineer with CTA Incorporated, was a programmer/analyst at OCLC Online Computer Library Center, Inc. He graduated from Kearney State College in computer science and human factors and worked on design issues for OCLC's DIADEM project, including the X-MEMEX prototypes.

CARLA L. BURNS is a computer scientist for Rome Air Development Center (RADC), which is located at Griffiss Air Force Base, New York. She works in software engineering and served as the principal evaluator for the C3I Rapid Prototype Development effort that developed a set of user interface modeling tools. She worked on several projects that used these tools to prototype various C3I user interfaces. Based on her work, she identified enhancements to the tools, currently being implemented in a new effort. Ms. Burns has published several papers on this topic.

ROBERT CHAFETZ is associate director, Artificial Intelligence Research, at Quatro R&D Partnership in Saint-Laurent, Quebec, where he is researching building design automation expert systems. He designed and prototyped expert system applications in previous positions at Philips Electronics, the Gould Research Center, and Texas Instruments Central Research Labs. He received his master's degree in computer and information science from the University of Pennsylvania in 1983. His research interests include the acquisition, communication, and representation of knowledge in expert systems.

DUDEE CHIANG is information specialist at the Norris Medical Library of the University of Southern California. She received her master's degree in library and information science from University of Illinois at Urbana-Champaign. Her research interests include human-computer interaction and end-user searching.

MARTIN DILLON is director, Office of Research, OCLC Online Computer Library Center, Inc. He previously taught at the University of North Carolina at Chapel Hill, both in the School of Library and Information Science and in the Department of Computer Science. He has designed and directed the development of numerous automated systems, particularly in the area of library applications and information retrieval. These include a bibliographic processing system for special libraries, and experimental indexing system based on partial syntactic analysis, and a microcomputer-based retrieval system for Harris survey data.

DORIS FLORIAN is head of the Information Management Department, Forschungsgesellschaft Joanneum Ges.m.b.H in Graz, Austria. She received her master's degree in computer science from Graz University of Technology. Her research interests include information management, library automation, international standards for bibliographic data formats, networks, and the application of artificial intelligence to information retrieval.

HANNAH FRANCIS is a doctoral student in the School of Information Studies, Syracuse University, New York. Her current research interests focus on the process of information interpretation in organizations. She holds on M.L.S. form McGill University and a C.A.S. from Syracuse University.

T. R. GIRILL manages the Documentation Group at the National Energy Research Supercomputer Center and teaches continuing education courses at the University of California, Santa Cruz. His primary concerns are the design of effective online documentation, the refinement of user interfaces to deliver it, and the analysis of their performance with usage monitoring. A frequent contributor to professional journals and conferences, he has also consulted for IBM and Cray Research Inc.

JUDITH HUDSON is head of the Cataloging Department, University Libraries, State University of New York at Albany. She has written a number of articles concerning the automation of cataloging and local online systems and is coeditor of the book *Women Online: Perspectives on Women's Studies in Online Databases.*

M. E. L. JACOB, consultant and author, has written extensively in the field of library automation and library standards. She is past chair of the National Information Standards Organization and has served on committees of most professional library and information science organizations.

NEAL K. KASKE is a senior associate in the U.S. Department of Education, Office of Library Programs. He has worked in library education at the University of Alabama and at Case Western Reserve University, and in research and research management at OCLC and in research libraries at the University of California, Berkeley. His research efforts center around the utilization of online public access catalogs and the measuring of the effectiveness of libraries.

CHARLES B. KREITZBERG, Ph.D., is president of Cognetics Corporation in Princeton Junction, New Jersey. His specialty is designing interactive systems that require synthesis of computer technology with human cognition. He is the designer of several successful software products, coauthor of four textbooks, and has lectured at corporations and universities nationwide.

RAY R. LARSON is assistant professor in the School of Library and Information Studies of the University of California, Berkeley. His research and publications concentrate on the design and evaluation of information systems.

TIAN-ZHU LI is a doctoral candidate in educational technology at College of Education, University of Washington, in Seattle. He has a master's degree in library and information science from University of Washington and was a librarian in a university library in Xian, China, for three years. His primary research interest is user interface with mental models. He has presented several papers about his research on CD-ROM systems, training methods, and other topics at professional conferences at home and abroad.

ELIZABETH D. LIDDY is assistant professor in the School of Information Studies at Syracuse University. Her research focus is the application of linguistic theories and techniques to the problems of representing and retrieving information. She is interested in the use of machine-readable dictionaries and general-purpose thesauri to facilitate information-related tasks. Her work has been published in *Information Processing and Management* and *Journal of the American Society for Information Studies.*

PETER LIEBSCHER is a doctoral student at the College of Library and Information Services, University of Maryland, College Park. His research interests focus on the human-computer interface and on the use of hypertext for information retrieval systems. His dissertation research blends quantitative and qualitative research methods to examine the use of multiple access methods for information retrieval from a full-text hypermedia database.

XIA LIN is a doctoral student in the College of Library and Information Services, University of Maryland, College Park. His primary research interest is information retrieval in hypertext and neural networks. He is a coauthor of the *Annual Review of Information Science and Technology* chapter, "Connectionist Models and Information Retrieval" (vol. 25, 1990).

MARTHA J. LINDEMAN, Ph.D., is a research scientist at OCLC Online Computer Library Center, Inc. Her research focuses on how people process information, particularly as it relates to the design of user interfaces. Her current major project is designing and building an electronic library that provides integrated access to both electronic books and scholarly journals.

CLIFFORD A. LYNCH, Ph.D., is director of the University of California Office of the President Division of Library Automation. He is responsible for the UC MELVYL online catalog, which also offers access to the National Library of Medicine MEDLINE database, and is currently putting ISI's Current Contents into production. (MELVYL is a registered trademark of The Regents of the University of California.)

GARY MARCHIONINI is an associate professor in the College of Library and Information Services at the University of Maryland, College Park, where he teaches courses in computer applications and research methods. He received his doctorate in mathematics education from Wayne State University and conducts research related to information seeking in electronic environments. He has published numerous articles related to hypertext and serves as the general editor of Hypertext Publications for the Association of Computing Machinery.

THOMAS H. MARTIN is associate professor of information studies and coordinator of the Information Resources Management program at Syracuse University, New York. His major areas of research involve human interaction with computers and information networking. He recently published a chapter on office automation in the *Annual Review of Information Science and Technology.*

ZBIGNIEW MIKOLAJUK, Ph.D., is principal designer at Gandalf Data Ltd. He is concerned primarily with transfer of artificial intelligence technology from research institutions to industry and leads the expert system project for computer network management. Previously he held academic appointments at Warsaw

Technical University and Central School of Planning and Statistics in Warsaw, Poland. He worked as consultant at Shell Co. in Nigeria. At Philips Electronics Ltd. in Montreal he conducted research and development activities in the area of artificial intelligence application in office automation and information retrieval. He is author and coauthor of 17 publications.

K. C. MILLER is manager of the Computing Applications Development Section, Central Training and Development, at Martin Marietta Energy Systems in Oak Ridge, Tennessee. She has twenty years' experience in information technology research areas. She is now concentrating on how to develop expert or knowledge-based system advisers for use in developing electronic field performance support systems.

JUDI MOLINE is a computer scientist for the National Institute of Standards and Technology working in the Office Systems Engineering Group of the National Computer Systems Laboratory. She has previously served as an adjunct faculty member in the School of Information Studies of Syracuse University and as a lecturer in English and art history at several universities in the Middle East. Her current research focuses on providing computing power to arts and humanities scholars. She has published on Islamic art and is currently publishing on hypertext for the arts and humanities.

HELEN A. PFUDERER is an information specialist at the Oak Ridge National Laboratory. She is presently the project leader for the development of a series of personal computer-based expert systems. Previous positions include director of Environmental Information Systems at the Oak Ridge National Laboratory and technical assistant to the associate laboratory director. She recently headed an information architecture study including systems planning, analysis, and implementation for the Naval Air Systems Command, and her earlier studies have been on improving the usefulness and accessibility of computing systems.

KYM E. POCIUS is pursuing a doctorate in psychology at Ohio State University and is currently a part-time programmer and interface designer for the Cataloger's Workstation project at the OCLC Online Computer Library Center, Inc. Her research primarily is in the field of personality theory. Research efforts have been directed toward identifying personality factors in human-computer interaction and the relationships between Jung's theory of personality and vocational interests.

DANIEL E. ROSE is a doctoral candidate in cognitive science and computer science at the University of California, San Diego. His research focuses on combining connectionist techniques with traditional artificial intelligence, particularly for the problem of computer-assisted legal research. He is also interested in natural language processing and human-computer interaction issues for information retrieval systems.

RADHIKA SANTHANAM received her doctorate from the University of Nebraska, Lincoln in 1989 and is now an assistant professor in the College of

Business at Florida International University, Miami. In addition to the design and evaluation of interfaces she is interested in the application of artificial intelligence techniques to decision support systems in business.

MICHAEL A. SHEPHERD is associate professor of computing science at Dalhousie University and previously held appointments at the Technical University of Nova Scotia. He has been concerned with the integration of user profiles into the search process and with the development of front ends for searching of bibliographic databases. His current interests include the development of a formal hypergraph-based model of data access.

GEORGE R. THOMA is chief of the Communications Engineering Branch, Lister Hill National Center for Biomedical Communications at the National Library of Medicine. His principal research interests are image processing and communications engineering, and he is a regular contributor to the literature in the field. He has a Ph.D. in electrical engineering from the University of Pennsylvania.

FRANK L. WALKER is an electronics engineer at the National Institutes of Health in Bethesda, Maryland. As a staff member of the Lister Hill National Center for Biomedical Communications, a research and development division of the National Library of Medicine, he has designed, developed, performed research, and published a number of papers on complex computer systems utilizing electronic imaging, primarily for the purpose of electronic document storage, retrieval, and transmission.

GERALDENE WALKER is professor of information science at the State University of New York at Albany. She previously taught at Syracuse University, the College of Librarianship in Wales, and at universities in Egypt, Nigeria, and the Philippines. Her research interests center around the problems of information retrieval, search vocabulary, and the user interface to computerized retrieval systems.

AMY J. WARNER is assistant professor in the School of Information and Library Studies at the University of Michigan, where she teaches in the areas of information retrieval and subject access. She was previously on the faculty at the University of Wisconsin-Madison and is currently engaged in research projects concerning the application of linguistics to the design of information retrieval systems.

CAROLYN WATTERS is an adjunct assistant professor of computing science at Dalhousie University, Nova Scotia. For 1989/90, she was a visiting assistant professor of computer science at the University of Waterloo, Ontario, she pursued her research interest in interfaces with the Centre for the New Oxford English Dictionary. She is interested in retrieval systems for text-dominated databases, from the database design aspects to the user interface. She is currently writing a handbook for information science and technology and is also pursuing research on the history of computing in Canada.

SUSAN WIEDENBECK is an assistant professor of computer science and engineering at the University of Nebraska, Lincoln. Her research interests include the cognition of programming, interface design, and intelligent tutoring systems. She is currently working on an intelligent tutoring system to aid programmers in transferring to new programming languages.

DIANA D. WOODWARD, deceased, was an assistant professor in the College of Information Studies, Drexel University, Philadelphia. Her research interests included information issues in the philosophy of science, applications of formal logic systems, natural language processing, and the theoretical basis of studies in artificial intelligence. In 1989 she published "Teaching Ethics for Information Professionals" in the *Journal of Education for Library and Information Science*.